Y. Doğan Çetinkaya is Assistant Professor in the Faculty of Political Sciences at Istanbul University, Turkey.

THE YOUNG TURKS AND THE BOYCOTT MOVEMENT

Nationalism, Protest and the Working Classes in the Formation of Modern Turkey

Y. DOĞAN ÇETİNKAYA

I.B.TAURIS
LONDON • NEW YORK • OXFORD • NEW DELHI • SYDNEY

I.B. TAURIS
Bloomsbury Publishing Plc
50 Bedford Square, London, WC1B 3DP, UK
1385 Broadway, New York, NY 10018, USA

BLOOMSBURY, I.B. TAURIS and the I.B. Tauris logo
are trademarks of Bloomsbury Publishing Plc

First published in Great Britain 2014
Paperback edition first published 2021

Copyright © Doğan Çetinkaya, 2015

Doğan Çetinkaya has asserted his right under the Copyright,
Designs and Patents Act, 1988, to be identified as Author of this work.

For legal purposes the Acknowledgements on p. ix constitute
an extension of this copyright page.

All rights reserved. No part of this publication may be reproduced or
transmitted in any form or by any means, electronic or mechanical,
including photocopying, recording, or any information storage or retrieval
system, without prior permission in writing from the publishers.

Bloomsbury Publishing Plc does not have any control over, or responsibility for,
any third-party websites referred to or in this book. All internet addresses given
in this book were correct at the time of going to press. The author and publisher
regret any inconvenience caused if addresses have changed or sites have
ceased to exist, but can accept no responsibility for any such changes.

A catalogue record for this book is available from the British Library.

Library of Congress Cataloging-in-Publication Data

ISBN: HB: 978-1-7807-6472-6
PB: 978-0-7556-4299-1
ePDF: 978-1-7867-3516-4
eBook: 978-1-7867-2516-5

Series: Library of Ottoman Studies, volume 41

Typeset by Newgen Publishers, Chennai

To find out more about our authors and books visit
www.bloomsbury.com and sign up for our newsletters.

To Bilge Seçkin

CONTENTS

Acknowledgements	ix
Introduction	1
1 Class and the Problem of Agency in the Ottoman Empire	12
Non-Muslim Bourgeoisie and the State	13
Muslim Merchants	20
The Muslim Working Class	30
Culture, Class-Consciousness and Islam	35
2 The Emergence of the Economic Boycott as a Political Weapon, 1908	39
People Take Action: Mass Actions and Public Demonstrations	42
The Organization	55
The Workers' Boycott: Oscillating between Strike and Boycott	58
Merchants during the Boycott: The Weakest Link	71
The Popularization of the National Economy	79
3 The Shift from Foreign to "Internal" Enemies, 1910–11	89
The Cretan Question	90
Meetings, Direct Actions and the Mobilization of Society	91

	The Boycott Society	111
	Muslims versus non-Muslims: "Our Greek Citizens are Exempt from the Boycott!"	119
	The National Economy, Muslim Merchants and the Working Class	135
	The State and the Boycott Movement	145
4	**The Muslim Protest: the Economic Boycott as a Weapon in Peacetime, 1913–14**	**160**
	The Political Milieu	161
	Pamphleting the Muslim Public	163
	"Henceforth Goods to be Purchased from Muslim Merchants"	176
	Banditry and Agency in the Boycott Movement	190
Epilogue	The Boycott Movement and Mass Politics in the Second Constitutional Period	204
	The Popularization of Politics and the Shift in Mass Politics	204
	Mass Politics, the National Economy and the Boycott Movement	215
	Popular Ideology, Islam and the Mobilization of the Masses	226

Notes   231
Bibliography   272
Index   287

ACKNOWLEDGEMENTS

I owe many thanks to many people without whose help this study would never have been completed. It is more than a pleasure for me to acknowledge my indebtedness to them. First and foremost is my former advisor Eric Jan Zürcher, whose guidance enabled me finally to finish this study. His neverending support, inspiration and comments made it easier to clarify my arguments throughout the book. I also received valuable comments both from my *promotiecommissie* and committee of defense at Leiden University, which included Touraj Atabaki, Marcel van der Linden, Yavuz Selim Karakışla, Jan Lucassen, Leo Lucassen, H.P.A. Theunissen and Jan Schmidt.

I also would like to express my gratitude to Mehmet Ö. Alkan whose advice and encouragement was more than valuable for me. Yavuz Selim Karakışla was always ready to lend a hand whenever I needed support during the writing process. I am indebted to many of my professors for supporting me. I learned a great deal from my advisors Nadia al-Bagdadi and Aziz al-Azmeh during my stay in Budapest at Central European University. I owe thanks to Edhem Eldem and Zafer Toprak, who supported me throughout my graduate years. I am also grateful to Prof. Sia Anagnostopoulou who admitted me to her program in Panteion University in Athens and facilitated my travel to Greece.

The Greek lessons that I received from Yorgo Benlisoy for many years helped me a lot in finding my way in the archives and libraries of

Athens. I am still grateful for his patience during our lessons. Without the help of Foti Benlisoy I would never have completed my research on the sources in Greek. I have learned a lot from our collaboration both in the academic and political field. His twin Stefo Benlisoy was always ready to lend a hand when needed.

I am also grateful to Vangelis Kechriotis and Anastasia Ileana Moroni who showed their solidarity whenever I needed. Our collaboration was very fruitful. Ileana passed on what she found in the French archives, which fitted well with the material that I found in other archives and libraries. Vangelis handed me the articles that he found in the Greek journal *Amaltheia*, and provided me with the opportunity for an exchange of thoughts on late Ottoman history.

I owe particular thanks to Sinan Birdal who, as always, spared his precious time to read and comment on some parts of the manuscript. Our discussions on the broader subject of this study greatly helped to improve my argument. Nina Ergin and Joe Nankivell edited the English of the whole text and helped prospective readers a lot; I am sure all who read this text will be grateful to them.

I should also like to thank American Research Institute in Turkey (ARIT) and Boğaziçi Vakfı, which supported me materially with their PhD research grants. They helped me in particular with my journeys to the Netherlands, Britain and Greece.

The staff of the archives and libraries in various towns and countries were really very helpful, and saved my time with their assistance in finding necessary documents in the right place and at the right time. These are the people in the Ottoman Archive in Istanbul, the National Archives in Kew, London, the Greek Foreign Ministry Archives in Syntagma, Athens, the Center for Asia Minor Studies in Athens, the National Library in Ankara, the National Library in Izmir, the Atatürk University Library, Erzurum, and the Atatürk and Beyazıt Libraries in Istanbul.

In the course of my graduate years I received assistance from many individuals in different times and places. I would like to thank Seda Altuğ, Sarah McArthur, Konstantina Adrianopoulou, Barış Çatal, Başak Özçarıkçı, Erkan Doğan, Henrik Lindolm, who hosted me in their flats during my visits to Amsterdam, Leiden, London, Athens,

Acknowledgements

Smyrna and Ankara. İlkay Yılmaz helped me a lot in Leiden while I was running between different bureaucratic desks at Leiden University. I have profited greatly from discussions with my colleagues Erhan Keleşoğlu, Görkem Doğan, Ahmet Bekmen, Emre Taylan, Erol Ülker, Eylem Özdemir, Sevgi Uçan, Zeynep Kıvılcım, Hakan Güneş, Sinan Yıldırmaz, C. Burcu Kartal, Kerem Ünüvar, Barış Alp Özden, Marko Zubak and Ferenc Laczo.

My family, İsmail, Hamdiye and Alper Çetinkaya, have gone beyond the limits of ordinary family support. Although they question my continuing to spend time on books in my thirties, they never step back in supporting me economically.

Bilge Seçkin, to whom this book is dedicated, has simply made life more beautiful and always generously offered her insights and enthusiasm, not only to my academic studies, but also to our common adventure.

INTRODUCTION

The boycott as an economic weapon appeared in the Ottoman Empire after the 1908 Revolution. The revolution gave rise to a chaotic social and political atmosphere in which the order of things changed drastically. The new era brought with it new social phenomena: elections, worker strikes, and public demonstrations at the grassroots level had a deep impact on the different segments of Ottoman Society. State authority broke down, and amidst the post-revolutionary political and social turmoil, a diplomatic crisis emerged between the Ottoman Empire and Austria-Hungary, the Principality of Bulgaria, and Greece. This diplomatic crisis made the new regime's situation even more precarious, and was an unexpected development such a short period of time after the revolution. Austria-Hungary proclaimed its annexation of Bosnia-Herzegovina, which had been under its rule in practical terms for more than 30 years. The Bulgarian Principality declared its independence and cut off its last ties with the Ottoman Empire. Meanwhile, the Cretans, with whom the Ottoman state had had many problems in the nineteenth century, reformulated their wish to form an *enosis* (union) with Greece. Bulgaria and Greece worried that the 1908 Revolution and the promulgation of the constitution might trigger a regeneration of Ottoman power, and therefore quickly moved to realize their political aspirations. The parliamentary elections and the deputies elected from these domains might have reinforced the Ottoman Empire's relationship with these regions.

The young constitutional regime responded to its first diplomatic crisis in its own way. The nature of this particular reply was also an indication of the transformation that the revolution had brought to the empire. This study will trace how the politics of the new era and the boycott movement influenced each other. Thousands publicly demonstrated on the streets all over the empire. Neither the Ottoman Empire nor Ottoman society were in favor of a war, and the mass actions paved the way for a boycott against the economic and commercial assets of these countries.[1] These two weapons—the boycott and public meetings—would be the most typical tools in the repertoire of the early Muslim/Turkish nationalism. Subsequently, whenever a diplomatic or national problem appeared, the Muslim/Turkish nationalist movement convened protest meetings and organized economic boycotts against the empire's enemies. This work will depict how these two crucial instruments of mass politics emerged and functioned at the beginning of the twentieth century.

Bosnia–Herzegovina and Bulgaria were lost in 1909. Yet, the boycott movement and the political and social environment that the revolution precipitated left their imprint on the political life of the Ottoman Empire. Boycotts were a crucial part of the mass politics that experienced a fundamental transformation after the revolution. This study searches for answers to the following questions: how did boycotts provide an opportunity for the ruling elite to manipulate the population and control its reactions? How did the different segments of society express their interest within this mobilization process and represent themselves in the expanding political and public spheres? How did different issues—such as the diplomatic crisis, economic problems, the tragedy of the Muslims in the newly lost territories, and municipal affairs—turn into national and public issues? And how did ordinary people begin to think of themselves as part of these public issues, and find various ways to participate in and influence politics through this mobilization process?

In this context, one specific point should be highlighted. Throughout the book, I will use concepts such as class, public sphere, civil society, mass politics and mobilization. Without these borrowings from the social sciences, it is not possible to analyze a boycott, which has economic, social and political aspects. Historiography in Turkey does not look favorably upon concepts, categories and theories derived from the social sciences. Nationalist and conservative historiography is overwhelmingly based on descriptive narratives, and consistently underlines the uniqueness of the Turkish case. History as a profession provides a favorable ground for this vision, since studies are generally based on research on unique and peculiar cases. However, an over-emphasis on the uniqueness of a particular country or case may lead scholars to get mired in exceptionalism. On the other hand, theories, concepts and categories afford us an opportunity for comparison. Comparison is one of the most crucial methods of evaluating or even confirming the uniqueness of a particular case. At the same time, a debate on the meaning of a concept is only possible when it is applied to a particular context. Therefore, the profession of history and philosophical and sociological debates should nourish each other. Furthermore, the refusal to make use of theoretical concepts also paves the way for explaining causes and effects based on cultural essences; exceptionalism may entail essentialism. Therefore, this book starts and ends with debates on the relevant historiography, and the place of the Ottoman boycott movement within these discussions and theoretical problems. Without them, it is virtually impossible to make sense of many aspects of the movement.

The boycott movement was not peculiar to the Ottoman Empire, and neither was the constitutional revolution. The 1908 Revolution was a crucial link in the wave of constitutional revolutions that took place at the beginning of the twentieth century, in Russia (1905), Iran (1906–09), Mexico (1910) and China (1911). Their causes and effects show significant similarities and discrepancies, which might be instructive to students of this particular era. In a similar vein, the boycott emerged as an influential political and social weapon in the era. Interestingly, the term boycott although it was coined in Ireland during the land struggles, was internationalized and passed into different languages—such as Dutch, French, German and Russian—without any linguistic alteration.[2]

The use of the boycott weapon was so widespread across different empires that one may call this era the "Age of Boycotts." A mere mention of the eight boycotts in China between 1905 and 1932 may indicate its prevalence. The boycotts in Ireland, Iran, the Ottoman Empire and China took place in the initial stages of rising nationalism, and helped to popularize nationalist thought and issues in general. Different social and professional classes collaborated in these movements. The tobacco protest in Iran, the anti-Japan and anti-American boycotts in China, and boycotts against non-Muslims in the Ottoman Empire managed to mobilize the masses throughout the respective countries, using the press, telegraph services and civil organization in the process. These mobilizations also coincided with the rise of national political organizations, such as the Guomintang in China and the Committee of Union and Progress (CUP) in the Ottoman Empire. These social movements and political organizations nurtured each other. The boycott movements in different empires gave rise to organizations such as the Economic Warfare Society in the Ottoman Empire, and the National Humiliation Society and the Society to Propagate the Use of National Goods in China. The public demonstrations and direct actions employed various means, such as placards, letters, handbills, pamphlets and visual materials. Moreover, similar symbolic acts appeared in different empires. For instance, one of the spectacular acts of merchants proclaiming their adherence to the boycott was the burning of boycotted merchandise, which was used to provoke an emotional reaction in Iran, China and the Ottoman Empire. Inspection teams appeared in order to control the loyalty of the people, and people believed to buy or use boycotted goods were assaulted. In these three empires, the boycott movements labeled the boycotted items under a common terminology, such as "inferior," "unclean" and "rotten," while the national merchandise was called "sacred." National products became a symbol of these movements.[3]

The boycott movement in the Ottoman Empire comprised different social classes and segments of society, which had diverse agendas during its long time-span. The variety of goals within the movement made it a complex social phenomenon. This diversity was not only based on social class, but also on the geographical scope of the movement. The boycott was executed in almost all urban centers, particularly the port cities of the Ottoman Empire. Understandably, the boycott in Salonica, Beirut, Smyrna, Konya, Giresun and Erzurum had significant dissimilarities. This study will depict how the boycott network and different civil organizations and initiatives succeeded in imposing the boycott on an empire-wide scale, and how heterogeneous social groups—such as port workers, merchants, urban notables, low-ranking officers and the professional classes—played a part in the last decade of the Ottoman Empire.

This is significant because the historiography on Turkey generally depicts Turkish nationalism as an exclusively intellectual current. Studies on nationalism concentrate on the thinking of several political and intellectual figures, or the design of political and civil organizations. However, nationalism is also a social phenomenon. Nationalist movements are also social movements that mobilize a wide range of social groups and deeply influence the daily life of the population. Therefore, one should not be content with research on intellectual history, but also focus both on the official nationalist policies from above and the mobilization of society from below. The boycott movement in the Ottoman Empire contributed to the rise of Muslim/Turkish nationalism and turned particular ethnic or religious problems into a social problem or national question. The movement constituted the social and economic aspect of Muslim/Turkish nationalism. This study tries to indicate how political figures, civil organizations and different social classes played a role in the rising nationalism and in the elimination of non-Muslims. Yet, although this particular period is considered an era of rising Turkish nationalism, the era's discourse was predominantly based on Muslim identity. The main frame of reference of the nationalist movement was Islam as a distinct marker of a communal identity. This is why the nationalism of this particular era is defined as Muslim/Turkish nationalism throughout this book.

The boycott movement also reveals a different side of the CUP, which is generally ignored. The underground activities of the Committee members both before and after the revolution have led to the creation of a literature on *komitadjis*, but secret gangs were in fact only a part of the history of the Committee: the CUP also had a broader social base. This study tries to show how the network of the Committee and their inclinations changed over time and from one place to another during the boycott movements. Therefore, one should refrain from depicting an overall monolithic picture of the CUP. Social movements, such as boycott actions, may provide insights for understanding the different aspects and tendencies of the nationalist movement in the Ottoman Empire.

The historiography on Turkey and the Ottoman Empire attributes agency only to "Great Men." The state elite and the intervention of the Great Powers are the main forces that changed the Ottoman Empire in these narratives. Therefore, the large majority of studies are based on the activities of Great Men, the transformation of state structure, or the activities of intellectuals and political figures. These studies are restricted to the political or intellectual history of the empire. Even studies on the state, high politics and nationalism that treat these as socially constructed phenomena are still marginal. Sociological approaches, on the other hand, focus mainly on social and economic structures.

Human agency, the role of social class and the world of ordinary people is generally excluded from the literature. Even rarer are history-from-above studies that look at the impacts of the elite's policies on the people and the manipulation of the masses. However, the mobilization of the masses and the reactions of the common people to high politics played a significant role in the nineteenth century, since the domain of politics expanded and was no longer restricted to the ruling elite.

These structuralist and elitist viewpoints have highlighted the role of the external dynamics in explaining the transformation that the Ottoman Empire experienced in the nineteenth century. Yet, as Chapter 1 will reveal, internal factors—such as native economic structures, local trading networks, the structure of Ottoman production, traditional guild organizations, local cultural structures, and local social classes—are also significant for understanding this process. For instance, the incorporation of the Ottoman Empire into the world economy did not erase the traditional guild organizations and the Muslim merchant class from social and economic life. The internal economic and social structure attuned itself to the transformation brought about by the world capitalist economy and the reforms of the state elite. Concurrence and resistance went hand in hand during this transformation process. Chapter 1 will focus on how these internal factors came together with the changing social and political context, as well as focusing on the place of Muslim merchants and working classes in this process. The literature within the framework of the World Systems Theory generally considers the non-Muslim bourgeoisie solely as a local agent of change. Although this approach is able to depict a significant element of history, it blurs the other parts of the picture. In these narratives, the ethnic clashes in the first quarter of the twentieth century appear as a reaction of nationalist cliques in the fashion of a conspiracy theory. The boycott movement, however, gives us the opportunity to look at the social background of this process.

Chapter 2 analyzes the emergence of the boycott movement as political weapon in the Ottoman Empire. The 1908 boycott targeted two foreign countries and was very much influenced by the fraternal atmosphere among the different ethnic/religious communities of the empire. The revolution set the stage for hope for a *bona fide* relationship between communities. A revival of Ottomanism and the Ottomanist discourse popularized the symbols of fraternity. This is why a boycott against Greece based on the Cretans' aspirations for a union with Greece was impeded. The Young Turks and the supporters of the new regime did not want to risk the newly constituted constitutional regime and jeopardize the fraternity between different communities. There was a large community of Greeks, both Hellenes and native *Rums*, living in the Ottoman Empire.

As a result, by declaring a boycott against Austria-Hungary and Bulgaria, a popular reaction was organized in which each community represented its support. The spontaneous protests espoused a constitutionalist path and did not turn against the regime. Because of the revolutionary atmosphere of the time, no particular political or social group dominated the boycott movement. The Ottoman government, the CUP, the merchants, workers, the different national organizations of the communities, and ordinary people from all walks of life had different agendas and interests within the boycott movement. For this reason, different social and political dynamics collaborated and competed with each other in a mixed social movement.

The boycott movement did not disappear after the Ottoman Empire and the boycotted states came to terms and concluded a treaty. The Cretan question was not settled and continued to create diplomatic problems between the Ottoman state and Greece, triggering popular reactions in nationalist circles. Thus, in 1909 a boycott was declared against Greece, although it did not last long. However, as the political and social environment of fraternity evaporated, a much stricter boycott against the Greeks was introduced in 1910 and lasted until the end of 1911. Although it was officially applied against Greece and its citizens, native Ottoman Greeks were also affected. This boycott contributed a great deal to the deterioration of the relationship between Muslims and non-Muslims. The 1908 boycott was partly implemented to unite different elements in the empire against a foreign enemy. However, the boycott against Greece aimed at the disintegration and differentiation of Muslim/Turkish and Greek communities. As a result, different problems between the two communities—from education to conscription, from churches to parliamentary issues—emerged due to the boycott movement. The details of the 1910–11 boycott will be analyzed in Chapter 3.

As the literature on Turkey has emphasized, the Balkan Wars had a deep impact on the Ottoman state and society. The loss of the lands in the Balkans and defeat at the hands of their former subjects shocked the Ottomans. The influx of Muslim immigrants into the Ottoman domains increased greatly, and Muslim/Turkish nationalism started to gain an unprecedented power in the Ottoman Empire. It was not a coincidence that the boycott movement began to openly target non-Muslim communities. At the end of 1913, thousands of pamphlets called on Muslims to support each other economically. Solidarity was preached to the Muslim community, while native non-Muslims were accused of betraying the empire. The governors began to express openly their discontent and dislike of non-Muslims to the foreign consuls. The Milli İktisat (National Economy) was redefined as a project for the progress and development of the Muslim/Turkish community, in opposition to the interests of non-Muslims.

Chapter 4 examines the widespread publications and general anti-non-Muslim agitation after the Balkan Wars. It then concentrates on the changing characteristics of the boycott movement and Muslim/Turkish nationalism. The violence that went along with the movement increased to an unprecedented scale. Unfortunately, this trend did not subside and left a pernicious legacy in World War I (WWI). The actions and assaults of nationalist gangs increased, particularly in early 1914.

Introduction

The boycott movement and the political and social environment that the revolution precipitated left its imprint on the political life of the Ottoman Empire. The mass politics that the ruling elite employed in governing the empire changed drastically. This change and its relationship with the boycotts will be discussed in the Epilogue. The 1908 Revolution paved the way for a turn in mass politics and mass mobilization in the Ottoman Empire. Two different mobilization patterns emerged: first, there was the mobilization of the masses from above, by the political elite. This was very much politically oriented and to a great extent employed by the nationalist organizations. The second pattern is the mobilization of different social classes for their particular interests. The transformation of the public sphere and the expansion of civil society prepared the ground for these different elements of mass politics. Demonstrations, mass meetings in public squares, mass campaigns, spectacles, parades, pageants, activities of civil societies, and elections became common aspects of daily life in the Ottoman Empire.

Last but not least, the scope and sources of this book should be explained. This study focuses in particular on the boycott movement that appeared against non-Muslims in the Ottoman Empire and its place within the transformation of mass politics between 1908 and 1914. Although the great majority of material included here refers to various instances of anti-Christian boycotts, it mostly refers to the anti-Greek movements. This is so because the open boycotting of native Ottoman citizens came onto the agenda only at the end of 1913 and mainly in 1914. Therefore, the boycott did not openly target native non-Muslims, but focused on the Greek state and its Hellenic citizens. The boycotting of native Greeks and foreigners other than Hellenes was an undesired outcome, according to the boycotters. The openly boycotted locals were those who had betrayed the empire; they might also be Muslims. Therefore, the boycott organization and network was very much established against the Greek community. Other non-Muslims, such as the Armenians, were not boycotted to the same extent as the Greeks, at least until 1914. The boycott against Armenians commenced mainly after February 1914. Due to this fact, there is not enough information on the boycotting of Armenians, whether in the archival sources or in the secondary literature. Even Armenian sources do not provide enough information, since Armenian scholars generally quote Turkish studies about the boycott.

Nevertheless, instances of boycotting other non-Muslims are also included in this study wherever information has been available. The boycott of Armenians became widespread during WWI and after. It was applied against those who had managed to survive the tragedy of 1915 and wanted to return to their homes in the Armistice Period. However, at this stage the boycott seems a rather less damaging weapon in comparison to the deportations, massacres and ethnic clashes, and has therefore not attracted the attention of historians. Furthermore, the boycott was a weapon generally used in peacetime. During the war years, nationalists had much more effective ways of eliminating non-nationals from the empire. Since the war created an entirely different economic and social environment, this study limits itself to the Second Constitutional Period before WWI, and focuses primarily on the anti-Greek mass mobilizations.

This book depends on a wide range of sources. Making use of a variety of primary sources is crucial, since nationalist historiography in Turkey is mainly based on Ottoman or Turkish state archives, and therefore narrates the past through the eyes of the state elite. Furthermore, a significant number of studies on the construction of nationalism and the formation of the Turkish Republic have been written to canonize the so-called national heroes. Even doctoral dissertations and studies authored by academics reproduce the nationalist lines of argument and historiography. Yet the longer this reproduction proceeds, the more these texts become a caricature of the classical nationalist narratives. In these works, the non-Muslim communities are portrayed as monolithic groups of people acting against Muslims and Turks under the command of their national leaders. These nationalist narratives not only depict the Muslim/Turkish community as a unified body, but also the non-Muslim communities as a nation without diversity. Therefore, the historical process is described as a struggle for survival in which one nation had to lose. In addition to this nationalist mentality, the use of a single type of archival sources contributes to this particular vision of history. In order to avoid such a single-minded point of view, this study is based on several contemporary sources.

State archives comprise one of the main sources of this book. The Ottoman, Greek, British and French state archives have left us with a substantial body of documents that present different viewpoints, making it possible to reconstruct the historical process from a variety of angles. Secondly, the periodicals of the time are also crucial sources of information. They not only convey details regarding the boycott movement, but were also an agent and a significant factor in the movement. Therefore, one should not consider these accounts objective or unbiased; for that reason, a variety of newspapers and journals have been included in order to allow different visions to emerge. This also helps to understand the viewpoint of a particular periodical. Since the boycott movement as examined here primarily involved the Muslim/Turkish and Greek communities, this book concentrates mainly on Turkish and Greek periodicals. This may help to overcome the one-sidedness of the nationalist narratives: there are many studies on the non-Muslim communities of the Ottoman Empire that do not use the material that these communities produced in their own language. Pamphlets, widely distributed in the Ottoman Empire, have also been taken into consideration in order to see how boycotters and nationalists utilized a certain discourse in order to mobilize the Muslim public.

CHAPTER 1

CLASS AND THE PROBLEM OF AGENCY IN THE OTTOMAN EMPIRE

The Ottoman boycott movement that appeared between 1908 and 1914 was a social movement composed of a variety of social and political actors. Political organizations such as the CUP, civil societies and different social networks, various social classes such as Muslim traders and working classes, professional classes such as public officials, teachers, lawyers and the like, and the Muslim public in general, all played significant roles in this movement. The modernization process and the integration of the empire into the world economy in the course of the nineteenth century brought drastic changes to the social and economic structure of the Ottoman Empire. The transformation of the public sphere and the emergence of a modern civil society in the empire paved the way for different sections of society to play their parts. Therefore, the public sphere and civil society, the political and social actors of the boycott movement, mass politics, modern ideologies and competing discourses are the main subjects of this book.

As a social movement, the Ottoman boycott movement made use of modern technology and embraced different agendas and interests of various sections of society. The main social actors—such as merchants, the working class, state bureaucracy, professionals and provincial notables—had vital roles in the boycott movement and the political and social life of the empire. An expanding public sphere and a flourishing civil society provided an opportunity for communication and organization between different social actors.

Non-Muslim Bourgeoisie and the State

One of the crucial features of Turkey's social history is the elimination of the non-Muslim population and the emergence of the nation-state succeeding the Ottoman Empire. This elimination process is considered in the historiography as if it were solely a political project. According to the existing literature on Turkey, the main actor in this process was the state or bureaucratic elite, with the political cadres of the CUP also playing a decisive role in these narratives. The main pillars of historiography treat the state and the state elite as the main agents of fundamental changes in the history of the Ottoman Empire and Turkey, thus neglecting the role of different social actors in history.[1] However, social and political phenomena like the Ottoman boycott movement afford us an opportunity to uncover the significance of these widely neglected social and political actors.

The Ottoman boycott movement was a crucial component in the process of eliminating the non-Muslim communities in the Ottoman Empire. In 1908, it emerged as an Ottomanist movement and targeted mainly foreign powers. Different foreign merchants and business activities of foreign countries in the Ottoman Empire—such as Austria-Hungary, Bulgaria, Italy, the United States and Greece—were affected by it. However, after 1909 and, particularly, 1910, the economic presence of non-Muslims in the Ottoman Empire gradually became one of the main targets of this political and economic protest movement. The movement slowly moved against native non-Muslims who suffered severely as a consequence. The incorporation of the Ottoman economy into the world capitalist economy had created favorable conditions for non-Muslim merchants, who started to operate under the protection of the Great Powers. When a Muslim protest spoke out against foreign states such as Greece, the native merchants acting under the banner of the Great Powers and those who could exploit the opportunities provided by the capitulations suffered as much as the foreign merchants. Yet, as the boycott movement strengthened its network and organization and as the resentment against non-Muslim communities increased, non-Muslim traders were also deeply affected.

Therefore, the *Milli İktisat* (National Economy), which advocated the development of the Ottoman economy, was not only an invention of nationalist intellectuals or the policies of state elites, but also a social movement involving different social actors. The literature on the Milli İktisat (National Economy), which will be analyzed in the following chapters, concentrates to a great extent on the intellectual history and does not take into account the social base of this process. The quest for the construction of a native industry, the abolition of the capitulations, and the economic development of Ottoman subjects became popular issues of the national economy during the Second Constitutional Period (1908–18). However, the Ottomanist element within this discourse and these practical policies evaporated, and the call for a national economy gradually culminated in a demand for the dominance of Muslim/Turkish element in the Ottoman economy. That is why, before entering into an analysis of social relationships that resulted in the Ottoman boycott movement, one has to evaluate the historiography on social class and the period in which the movement occurred.

The common analysis of the nineteenth-century Ottoman Empire focuses to a great extent on the relationship and the struggle between the non-Muslim bourgeoisie and the reforming state elite. Although there is some merit to this interpretation, this kind of bilateral polarization misses several significant points regarding social and economic developments. In the second half of the eighteenth century and particularly during the nineteenth century, the fundamental pillars of the Ottoman economy and society changed drastically. Historiography on the Ottoman Empire emphasizes two dynamics behind these fundamental changes. One of them was the integration of the Ottoman Empire into the expanding world economy; the other was the reform efforts of the modernizing Ottoman ruling elite. Two distinct social groups emerged as a result of these developments: the non-Muslim bourgeoisie and the modern state bureaucracy.

The increasing trade between Europe and the Ottoman Empire over the course of the nineteenth century stimulated the rise of the non-Muslim bourgeoisie, who played an intermediary role between the world markets and the majority of the small peasantry. Neither land nor agriculture was monopolized in the hands of a landowning class. The presence and persistence of small peasant producers was one of the main peculiarities of the Ottoman economy. This economic structure was the basis for the rise of a non-Muslim bourgeoisie.[2]

The predominance of small, independent family farms, particularly in the Anatolian agrarian structure, prevented the rise of a larger landowning class. The lack of a large landowning class in the provinces facilitated the recentralization of the agrarian order, attempts to modernize the state and the undermining of the power of the provincial notables (*ayans*).[3] As a result, agricultural production, particularly in Anatolia, was not based on a single crop, but on the export of various products.[4] Therefore, it was almost impossible for foreign investors and merchants to control small producers, because of their immense number and specialization in different products. Mediation between peasant farmers and the world market provided an economic opportunity, and it was the non-Muslim merchants who took advantage of this opportunity that resulted from both the expanding world economy and the agrarian structure of the Ottoman Empire.[5]

The small peasantry's domination of agriculture was not the only factor that triggered the rise of the non-Muslim bourgeoisie. It has also been claimed that non-Muslims, particularly Greeks, dominated the economy before the Ottomans came to Anatolia. Greek nationalism also contributed to this point of view, stating that trade was characteristic of the Greek community.[6] Although Augustinos has criticized such reductionist and essentialist evaluations, he has also underlined the significance of ethnic affiliations within the rise of a non-Muslim bourgeoisie.[7] Cultural factors, as well as various economic causes, played their part in the rise of the non-Muslim merchant class. European merchants preferred to consult with an intermediary native merchant class in order to avoid the instability of inter-state relationships. Second, foreign merchants had to pay the same internal tax as their Ottoman counterparts. It was only in the export taxes that they paid less and had an advantage. As a result, they began to avoid the more difficult internal trade relationships and left the field open to non-Muslim traders. Furthermore, as many scholars have asserted, the religious affiliations between Greeks, Armenians and Europeans reinforced the intermediary position of non-Muslim merchants.[8]

On the other hand, non-Muslim traders were also eager to take the initiative in this process. They managed to receive *berats*, a type of foreign passport that secured them a position above Ottoman law and regulations. The capitulations and *berats* provided Greek and Armenian merchants with legal extraterritoriality, as the official representatives of the Great Powers. These *berats* enhanced the position of non-Muslims in the economy at the end of the eighteenth and the beginning of the nineteenth century; during this period, the Ottoman state tried to balance the state of affairs by granting similar rights, first to non-Muslims under the title of *Avrupa Tüccarı* (European Merchant), and later to Muslims under the name of *Hayriye Tüccarı* (Benefaction Merchant).[9] However, these countermeasures were not enough to impede this process. As a result, the cultural capital of non-Muslim merchants, which provided them with cultural and linguistic proximity to foreign investors, increased their economic and political power within the economic and social structure of the Ottoman Empire.

The Greek historians Haris Exertzoglou and Elena Frangakis-Syrett have called our attention to the Greek bourgeoisie itself. They have claimed that the rise of the Greek bourgeoisie in the nineteenth century was due to their economic organization and trade network. For instance, Frangakis-Syrett has argued that when foreign merchants entered the Anatolian markets, they encountered already established Greek merchants and trade networks. Greek success, she has asserted, depended on a "tightly knit kinship organization" among the Greek merchant class and their knowledge of the inner-Anatolian markets, such as the customs and tastes of that market.[10] Similarly, Exertzoglou has claimed that free trade and commercial organization was more significant than the *berats* and the protection of the Great Powers in the rise of the Greek merchants in the nineteenth century.[11]

The non-Muslim merchants who played such an intermediary role in economic transactions mainly conducted four economic activities: collecting taxes, lending money, dealing with currency exchange and trade.[12] As Kasaba has argued, the non-Muslim bourgeoisie was not a full ally of foreign economic interests. They were also struggling against them in order to secure a better place in the economic network, trying to limit the power of both the government and foreign capital. As a result, they became one of the dominant forces in the Ottoman Empire in the course of the nineteenth century.[13] Likewise, Exertzoglou has contended that the Greek bourgeoisie was not a "comprador" class that worked for the benefit of European capital.[14] He has argued that they were not only involved in trade, but also in other areas such as banking, industry, mining, and the like. Apart from this mediating role, they also had to compete with foreign capital. Kasaba has also voiced doubts regarding the existence of a non-Muslim comprador class in Western Anatolia in the nineteenth century. For him, the fierce competition between foreign capital and non-Muslim merchants released the economy from the direct control of Western powers.[15]

The other reason for the non-Muslim bourgeoisie's rise to economic power was the gradual development of port cities and the formation of a convivial bourgeois lifestyle within these flourishing cities. There emerged a bourgeois class in port cities which adopted a new lifestyle, new consumption patterns and new customs according to a so-called "Western way of life." This peculiarity separated the non-Muslim merchant class in particular, and non-Muslim communities in general, from the Muslim population of the empire.[16]

This difference reveals the fact that "culture matters" when examining the conflicts between the non-Muslim and Muslim communities of the empire, particularly after the second half of the nineteenth century. The difference between the lifestyles contributed to the divergence and separation of the two communities. This cultural difference became the symbol of the rising non-Muslim bourgeois class, although their lifestyle was not shared by the entire non-Muslim population of the empire. The tension between the non-Muslim merchant class (as the champions of integration into the world economy) and the Muslim merchants (as the losers in this process) has not been sufficiently studied. It is quite apparent that the cultural traits of the non-Muslim bourgeoisie were the main ingredient of its identity. In the literature on Turkey, this lifestyle, identity and culture have been considered proof of bourgeois character: the Western lifestyle made this merchant class a bourgeois class. As a result, the bureaucrats of the Ottoman state and Turkey have been characterized by their Western lifestyles, and those sections of society without such cultural traits have been considered traditional classes, and have been depicted as being against any social and economic change. Different cultural characteristics might have played a crucial role in the formation of the social classes, but this remains a subject for future research.

Culture matters in the formation of a particular social class, but it is not possible to point to a single cultural feature as the main determinant of a social class. Therefore, a social class may have different cultural traits at different times and in different places. The historiography on the nineteenth-century Ottoman Empire has to a great extent focused exclusively on the relationship between the small peasantry, the central state authority and the rising non-Muslim bourgeoisie. As the small peasantry did not express itself as an agent, scholars have focused their attention only on the bureaucracy and the non-Muslim bourgeoisie.

Apart from the formation and the activities of the non-Muslim bourgeoisie, the main issues discussed in the literature on the Ottoman Empire are the activities of the state elite, their reforms in order to enhance the power of the state, and the creation of a modern bureaucracy to achieve this goal during the nineteenth century. In most studies, the state and the bureaucracy appear as the only actors in the historical analysis. This is why scholars refer to concepts such as the "state class," "bureaucratic class," or "bureaucrat bourgeoisie" in order to define the state as a social agent.[17] This point of view is also widespread amongst leftist intellectuals. For instance, Ahmet İnsel has pointed to the state elite as the sole agent, even treating the servants of the sultan (*kapıkulları*) as a social group that deeply influenced the bureaucrats of the twentieth century.[18]

It has been argued that a tension appeared between the Christian mediating merchants, as the actors of the empire's integration into the world economy, and the state bureaucracy. Keyder, for instance, has argued that this merchant class jeopardized the bureaucracy.[19] First, the social transformation that this class initiated posed a threat to the social legitimacy of the bureaucracy, by undermining the position of the traditional sectors in the Ottoman economy. Second, the bourgeois class was also a competitor in the process of surplus extraction from the small peasantry. Thus, while revenues and production in the Ottoman Empire increased, the bureaucracy's share was reduced.[20]

The relevant historiography has generally claimed that the conflicts between different social groups emerged due to ethnicity. Therefore, ethnic and religious conflicts in the Ottoman Empire are considered to be only a social question. However, scholars such as Keyder and Kasaba have put this view in another way. They have argued that there were class contradictions in Ottoman society; however, these were concealed by ethnic conflicts and did not engender a fully fledged consciousness. As a result, the reforms of the Ottoman elite, the creation of a modern education system and a modern central bureaucracy, as well as movements such as the Young Ottomans and the Young Turks, brought with them a rivalry between the Muslim bureaucracy and the non-Muslim bourgeoisie. This struggle between the Ottoman state and the non-Muslim bourgeoisie, and the elimination of the latter by the creation of a Muslim business class, are the arguments most widely accepted in the literature on the Ottoman Empire, which are questioned in this book.

Since the Turkish historiography is very much based on the controversy between the non-Muslim bourgeoisie and the Muslim bureaucrats, one should focus on one of the most extreme examples of these arguments. Fatma Müge Göçek introduced a new concept in order to grasp this relationship between the bureaucracy and the non-Muslim bourgeoisie.

With this concept, "the bourgeois class with two bodies," she argues that in the course of the nineteenth century a bourgeois class emerged with two components divided across religious and ethnic features. The Muslim/Turkish bureaucratic component of this fragmented bourgeoisie eliminated the non-Muslim commercial bourgeoisie and played an essential role in the construction of a new nation-state.[21] In line with the general arguments of the historiography on Turkey, she has claimed that the rise of centrifugal forces and the military defeats subverted the authority of the Ottoman central government. As a result, it decided to reform the state organization, resulting in the construction of a modern state. The ultimate aim was to enhance central authority: the institutional reforms, the construction of a modern bureaucracy and a modern education system were all put in force to build a more efficient administration. As an outcome of these efforts, two new social classes appeared that were different from the previous traditional elite of the empire: bureaucrats and intellectuals. The resources over which they began to acquire control were taken out of the hands of the sultan. The basis of this new bureaucratic elite was the human resources that depended on a Western education system. This modern education provided the newly growing bureaucratic bourgeoisie with cultural capital, which gave them a distinct social consciousness.[22] Eldem has also defined the rich bureaucrats who invested their money in the Ottoman Bank as a Muslim bourgeoisie.[23]

The second social group whose economic resources were derived from their economic relationship with the world market also withdrew themselves from the direct control of the sultan.[24] Their ethnic and religious affiliation did not lead them to undermine the sultan's power through the power they gained in the economic sphere. They were not able to form such a powerful social force.[25] Göçek has argued that this process brought to the fore a bourgeois class which was divided into bureaucratic and commercial segments. Furthermore, this separation also coincided with another division, based on religion. Their dual struggles with each other and with the sultan finally contributed to the demise of the empire. This fragmentation along religious and ethnic lines transformed into a polarization.

Muslim Merchants

There were other social actors (such as the working class, peasants and traditional guilds) whose activities and struggles had a significant impact on social and economic developments. Their efforts were effective in limiting the penetration of European capital into the empire and in bargaining for new legal regulations with the Ottoman state.[26] Alongside these lower classes, there were also a Muslim merchant class and the Muslim middle classes in the Balkans and Anatolia. Although they were generally depicted as the losers in these economic developments, they had crucial roles in economic and social life.

Class and the Problem of Agency

The old argument regarding the absence of a Muslim bourgeoisie in the Ottoman Empire maintains that the Muslims in the empire were indifferent to trading activities. This argument is based to a great extent on an article by Sussnitzki, which was translated into English in a volume edited by Issawi.[27] As Hilmar Kaiser has revealed, this article was written within the context of pre-WWI orientalist propaganda literature and has racist features. Kaiser has explored this literature in detail, and has shown how German orientalists depicted non-Muslims, particularly Armenians, as parasites and "bloodsuckers" in the context of German diplomatic interests in the Middle East.[28] This literature, and especially the article by Sussnitzki, not only illustrates non-Muslim Ottoman communities as exploiters of their country who abused Turkish tolerance, but also represented Turks as an ethnic group who lacked "racial aptitude for trade."[29] As a result of this argumentation, Germans considered getting rid of non-Muslims whom they saw as British and French allies, and collaborating with the Turks and the CUP who were in need of German help. Kaiser has also revealed how modern historiography, from Modernization Theory to Dependency and World-System Theory, reproduced this racist argumentation of German orientalist literature. However, one should also underline the fact that Turkish nationalists and the elite of non-Muslim communities repeated this argumentation endlessly in the last decades of the Ottoman Empire. As mentioned in this chapter, the non-Muslim elite attributed to their community a civilizing mission, by restricting trade and industrial activities to their own community only.

According to this widespread assumption, Muslims/Turks were apathetic about trade, commerce, banking, industry and so on. The Muslim/Turkish population consisted only of peasants and state bureaucrats or officials. This argument was repeated endlessly, also by those who wanted to create a Muslim/Turkish merchant and business class in the empire. Particularly after the 1908 Revolution, newspapers and journals were full of variations on this line of argument, and calls for the participation of the rich in commercial activities. One may consider this argumentation a representation of the truth, or the ideological discourse of a political and economic project, because the writers, elites and intellectuals who propagated this thesis were the ones who wanted the Muslim element to prevail in the economy. Therefore, the argument was always framed within the project of the *Milli İktisat* (National Economy).

The second point to be highlighted is the fact that the statistics cited in order to analyze the state of the Muslim bourgeoisie are the 1913 and 1915 Industry Statistics published by A. Gündüz Ökçün.[30] However, industry is not the only basis or determinant for the formation of a particular class. Moreover, industry was not the primary economic activity in the Ottoman Empire. Therefore, the Muslims' share in the industrial sector cannot provide information concerning the state of Muslim merchants in the economy. These statistics should be supported by data on the trading activities of the Muslim population. However, even these statistics on industry indicate that 19.6 percent (or roughly 1 in 5) of workshops were owned by Muslims/Turks.[31] This percentage also indicates that Muslim merchants active in industry could actually constitute a social group that could effectively support a social and economic project. Therefore, the Muslim merchant class should be taken into consideration as an agent in Turkey's history.

The historiography on the Ottoman Empire mentions the Muslim merchant class in two ways. First of all, due to the rise of the non-Muslim bourgeoisie, they lost their prominent place in international trade. As the Greeks and Armenians of the Ottoman Empire took advantage of the opportunities provided by an expanding world economy, the economic significance of Muslim merchants and provincial notables declined.[32] The loss of their position in the economy resulted in their total disappearance from the historiography on the Ottoman Empire.[33] Their disappearance corresponds with the common assumption on the social history of Turkey, which claims that the Ottoman Empire and Turkey in its initial decades lacked a Muslim/Turkish bourgeoisie. As Cemal Kafadar has argued, the claim that Muslims did not participate in trade is so widespread in the historiography that there is insufficient research on the subject, even on the periods before the nineteenth century.[34] According to the literature, it was only during WWI and under the Kemalist regime that a "nascent" bourgeoisie was created.[35]

CLASS AND THE PROBLEM OF AGENCY   23

Korkut Boratav has argued that the Muslim/Turkish bourgeoisie was nascent, unorganized and dispersed, and did not have much capital accumulation. Thus, he asserts that it had the characteristics of an *esnaf* (guild). Furthermore, it was to a great extent dependent on non-Muslim merchants.[36] Keyder claims that until the 1950s, the class issue did not play a significant role, and that this delay was due to the elimination of the Greek and Armenian populations. After they were gone, there was nothing by way of a Muslim bourgeois class.[37]

Muslim merchants, particularly in Anatolia, do not appear in significant numbers in Turkish scholars' social analyses of the Ottoman Empire. They have been presented as an impotent, scattered, almost dead social group who had no agency after the eighteenth century. As they were the losers in the process of integration into the world economy, their resentment regarding their decline is one of the only reasons for them to enter academic studies.[38] Although they constituted the social base of the protest movements against non-Muslim communities, their role has not been thoroughly investigated.

The second reason for this particular section of society to enter the narrative is in the study of the motivations and ultimate goals of the political elite. They have been mentioned in the context of the state elite and the Young Turks beginning to create a native (Muslim/Turkish) bourgeoisie.[39] It has been claimed that their existence and eventual access to economic power was directly related to the policies of the CUP, particularly during WWI. This time, Muslim merchants took advantage of rising Turkish nationalism and the elimination of non-Muslim communities. They were there to fill the newly emergent social gap. The economic and political policies of the CUP paved the way for the rise of Muslim provincial merchants. In this context, in Turkish historiography the Muslim merchant class has been depicted only as a dependent section of the society.[40]

As I have mentioned above, it has been argued in the literature that trading activities determined the general characteristics of the bourgeoisie, and that the empire lacked an industrial bourgeoisie. According to this argument, the non-Muslim bourgeoisie and the Ottoman bureaucracy were two rival powers in the Ottoman Empire during the nineteenth century. Furthermore, it has been claimed that the state bureaucracy lacked Muslim bourgeois collaborators in its struggle against non-Muslim merchants and, therefore, created such a class at the close of the empire, entirely liquidating the non-Muslim communities in the empire.[41] For instance, according to Keyder, society in general did not demand Turkification, apart from the bureaucracy. It was the Young Turks who attempted to impose this project from above.[42] Although the economic policies of the CUP played a decisive role in strengthening the position of the Muslim merchant class *vis-à-vis* the non-Muslim bourgeoisie, particularly in the Second Constitutional Period (1908–18), the Muslim merchant class was not a creation of the Young Turks and their economic policies.

Yet, in contrast to the claims of Keyder and Kasaba, who argue that the Ottoman Empire lacked an active Muslim bourgeoisie, it is possible to find traces of its existence even in their own studies. For instance, Keyder has argued that the Ottoman bureaucracy received support from Muslim traders and notables for their nationalist program. Muslim traders collaborated with CUP policies that intended to eliminate non-Muslims from the economy.

Furthermore, Keyder has asserted that, although Muslim merchants and guilds could not exploit the newly emerging opportunities created by the world economy, there was no decrease in their numbers. They continued to exist; however, their position in the economy became secondary.[43] Therefore, although it is evident that they lost power over the course of the nineteenth century, they continued to exist and did not disappear. For instance, Ahmad mentions several economic boycotts against non-Muslim communities; yet, he does not explore the activities of the Muslim merchants and notables, and repeats the general thesis of the "non-existence of a Muslim bourgeoisie."[44]

A study by A. Üner Turgay also depicts the existence and actions of the Muslim/Turkish merchant class in nineteenth-century Trabzon, although he concedes to the traditional argument in the historiography by underlining the fact that the foreign trade in the Black Sea was monopolized by the non-Muslims. However, he also mentions the Muslim resentment regarding the hegemony of non-Muslims in the economy. In his narrative, the Muslim merchant class, although they had lost their prominent place, appears as an active social group struggling through various means against non-Muslims. They not only established different economic ventures which were not carried out by non-Muslims, but also wrote protest letters to the governors. Their resentment was also recognized by foreign observers. These ethnic conflicts had their roots in the economic sphere, and both non-Muslims and Muslims were aware of the fact.[45] The resentment of Muslim merchants in the course of the nineteenth century was to be transformed into concrete action after the 1908 Revolution. Apart from the continuing existence of the Muslim merchant class in the provinces and the countryside, another significant point is that the prominence of the non-Muslim bourgeoisie was not permanent. Their position in the economy had its peaks and valleys.[46]

There are some exceptional studies that have mentioned the significance of the Muslim bourgeoisie and the Muslim middle classes, such as the work of Donald Quataert and Kemal Karpat. Quataert claims that, although international trade is easy to observe, it was never as important as domestic trade in the Ottoman Empire between 1700 and 1922, "both in volume and value."[47] He argues that some studies have overstated the significance of international trade, because it is "well-documented, easily measured and endlessly discussed in readily accessible Western-language sources."[48] Studies that over-emphasize international trade and world markets are mainly based on the secondary literature, or the archives of the Great Powers (such as Great Britain, France or the United States). Therefore, these sources do not reveal the role of Muslim merchants and domestic trade, which is not well documented. Although the flow of goods between and within different regions in the Ottoman Empire was crucial, it is impossible to quantify this trade. Quataert does not deny that non-Muslims were dominant in foreign trade and even surpassed European merchants, thanks to the *berats* they had obtained for the Great Powers; yet "domestic trade overwhelmingly outweighed the international," and it was the Muslim merchants who dominated trade between interior towns, trade networks, and the trade between port cities and their hinterland.[49]

Quataert has also underscored that, although guild manufacturing declined severely due to competing imports of cheap and high-quality foreign industrial products, the manufacturing structures and producers successfully adapted themselves to the changing environment. A shift occurred in manufacturing, which also altered their production preferences in different fields in which they could survive or compete more easily.[50] Both Muslim merchants and Muslim producers existed during the nineteenth century.

Kemal Karpat has also underlined the significance of the Muslim middle classes in the course of the nineteenth century. In contrast to other scholars who consider the state bureaucracy to be the initiator of Turkish modernization, Karpat takes into account "the success of Turkish modernization and its popular acceptance" due to the "internal social growth that produced a middle class."[51] Although he does not repudiate the notion that the sultan and his bureaucrats were significant actors in the political field, it was the new middle class that held the "true force." Thanks to the commercialization and privatization of the agrarian economy, a significant number of people engaged in trade of agricultural products. This contributed to the rising power of the small towns and its notables (*eşraf*).[52] Selçuk Akşin Somel provides numerous examples of how Muslim notables and merchants in the provinces contributed financially to the construction of an education system. Their contribution was vital in various cases.[53]

In her study on Istanbul textile merchants, Lorans Tanatar-Baruh indicates that, apart from a few large firms, it was small business owners who competed with each other in the market.[54] Her information was gathered to a great extent from the *Annuaire Oriental*, which forms one of the crucial sources for the economic history of the Ottoman Empire. She confirms the traditional assumption, by claiming that non-Muslims dominated the textile sector. However, she underlines the existence of a Muslim element. First of all, they had a small share of around 10 percent in the textile trade. At first sight, this share reveals that they did exist. However, Tanatar-Baruh adds that Muslims "were dominant in the trade of raw materials, such as cotton, or in a traditional branch of textile production."[55] Although they had a smaller share in the economy, Muslim merchants did exist in all sectors, and in some they held a significant share. She also underlines the fact that Muslim merchants gained more significance after the 1908 Revolution.[56]

Another scholar who has examined empirical data regarding the Ottoman bourgeoisie—such as the personal card catalogue of the Ottoman Bank—is Edhem Eldem. He asserts that, at 16.5 percent, the share of Muslims using banking services was low when compared to the empire's non-Muslim population. However, he also adds that this ratio "is probably higher than what most of the socio-economic models for the period would have predicted."[57] He demonstrates that the "surviving crafts of the time" were under-represented in the Ottoman Bank card catalogue; however, this sector was the part of economy in which most Muslim businessmen operated. Thus, one may still have reservations concerning the Muslim presence in the economy.

The presence of Muslims as actors in the economy is now gradually finding a place in the literature. For instance, Elena Frangakis-Syrett, an expert on the commercial life of Smyrna while concentrating on Greeks, has tried to underline the presence of Muslim merchants along with the non-Muslims in Smyrna's economy. She mentions both Muslim and non-Muslim trading networks when referring to native commercial initiatives.[58] It is not a coincidence that she refers to Gad G. Gilbar's study on Muslim large-scale merchant-entrepreneurs of the Middle East.

Gilbar questions the widespread claim that it was the local non-Muslims and foreigners who controlled the economy, and foreign trade in the Middle East in particular. He not only asserts that large-scale Muslim merchants were active in international trade even during the nineteenth century, but also that they invested in agriculture and industry. These merchants also turned into entrepreneurs and invested in "commercial agriculture, manufacture, modern industries, transportation and social services," such as education.[59] Gilbar also claims that, through the wealth they accumulated from their commercial and industrial investments, Muslim merchants found opportunities to influence the political developments in their countries, particularly in the early twentieth century.[60] Yet, to a great extent he concentrates on the "eastern crescent" of the Middle East, underlining the fact that the merchants' role in foreign trade in western and northern Anatolia and Egypt was limited. The place of Muslim merchants in foreign trade in the Western crescent was also relatively weak. The only exception was Beirut, where Muslim entrepreneurs flourished. For the port cities of western Anatolia and the Mediterranean, he repeats the traditional arguments as summarized above, and designates states as the main obstacle to economic and commercial development. Therefore, it was the rise of the nation-states after the 1920s that brought a halt to the convivial activities of the merchant class, just like the Ottoman state, which did not want a strong Muslim bourgeoisie as a power base.[61] However, his claims raise significant questions regarding the presence of a Muslim merchant class in the economy of the Middle East, and instigate new research on economic activities other than international trade with Europe and the port cities of the Levant.

In a similar manner, Ayhan Aktar makes use of the journal *Annuaire Oriental* in order to gather information regarding the economic activities and professions in Istanbul between 1868 and 1938. He draws attention to the regions that the *Annuaire Oriental* included. He notes that this collection also took into account traditional economic spaces—such as Eminönü, Kapalıçarşı and Sultanhamam—where Muslim traders were most likely to work. In contrast to these traditional places, Galata and Beyoğlu were dominated by native as well as foreign non-Muslims. Accordingly, there appears to have been a "dual structure" in Ottoman cities in the course of the modernization process during the nineteenth century.[62] Apart from underlining the dominant position of the non-Muslim merchant class in the process of the Ottoman economy's integration into the world markets, he also mentions that the traditional sectors did not disappear. Rather, they tuned in with this transformation process, and their existence is apparent in the "yellow pages" of the *Annuaire Oriental*. The information available in these sources reveals the fact that the number of *esnaf* in this traditional area did not decrease, but rather increased. For him, it was the guild organizations (which protected the *esnaf* from drastic changes) that dissolved. However, their members did not disappear and continued to operate in the market.[63] According to Aktar, these two distinct sections of society lived side by side but in isolation from each other, and had distinct cultures and tastes. Yet, at the beginning of the twentieth century and in the course of the Ottoman boycott movement, these two social groups were to come face to face.

Aliye F. Mataracı employs a different source that uncovers the existence and activities of the Muslim bourgeoisie at the end of the nineteenth and the beginning of the twentieth century. She analyzes the trade letters of a Muslim trading family. Three entrepreneur brothers who were settled in Rize, Istanbul and Manchester corresponded with each other while they executed their business. Although Mataracı is very much influenced by the existing literature that denies the significance of a Muslim merchant class, she contextualizes these letters as a sample "confirming the existence of a Muslim bourgeoisie dealing in trade within and without the boundaries of the Ottoman Empire."[64] Their identity, which was strongly defined by Islam and based on their relationship with non-Muslim merchants within the empire, is significant for this case study of the Ottoman boycott movement.

Similar to Göçek, Karpat also suggests that the Ottoman middle class was divided into two groups, in line with the ethnic and religious divisions within society. However, according to Karpat, the Muslim bourgeoisie did not consist of state bureaucrats, but rather of the provincial merchant class, landowners and notables. He also insists that the privileges that the non-Muslim communities acquired, thanks to the reform edicts of the nineteenth century, caused deep resentment amongst Muslims. The Muslim middle classes considered these reforms and privileges an economic freedom for non-Muslims, which they lacked. Like Quataert, Karpat argues that local retail trade was controlled by Muslims. The divide between the Muslim and non-Muslim counterparts of the Ottoman middle class widened because of the continuous immigration of Muslim populations from lost Ottoman lands. Not only did the ratio of Muslims in the population increase, but also the "cultural-ideological orientation" of this new middle class changed.[65] The rapid expansion of education, modern media and new forms of association provided the middle classes with the infrastructure to express their interests and transform their identities. Karpat views different ideological positions and programs, such as Islamism, Ottomanism and nationalism, as expressions of a growing middle class and their aspirations.[66]

As a result, it is possible to argue that there was a Muslim bourgeois presence in the countryside, with economic resources and an organized civil society. The modernizing reforms of the state elite—such as the construction of a modern education system, transportation, press, industry, voluntary associations and so on—also contributed to the power of the Muslim middle class. Different social actors who were also influenced by these novel developments had a deep impact on the historical process. First, there had always been different dynamics and groups within the state elite and the non-Muslim bourgeoisie with their diverging goals. Second, different sections of society—such as the working class, provincial Muslim merchants, the petty bourgeoisie and professionals—also played their parts. To exclude these groups and classes from an analysis would lead to misinterpretations; therefore, this book attempts to place the Muslim merchant class and working class into the historical context and evaluate their place within a social movement.

The Muslim Working Class

A constantly repeated theme of the historiography on Turkey is the lack of adequate information on the history of the lower classes in the Ottoman Empire and Turkey. This lack of information is due to the lack of a history (or even the existence) of working classes in the Ottoman Empire, according to most studies. Although numerous studies have appeared on the history of the working class in Turkey, younger scholars still refer to the "poverty" of the present state of the literature.[67] Scholars who are interested in the history of the working class in Turkish history relate this "poverty" to the mentality of the historians, as they are primarily preoccupied with the actions of the state and the political elite. This is why historians have not focused on the history of the working class.[68] Apart from this scholars who deal with labor history also mention difficulties related to the sources and archives, which are said to be unproductive.

Interest in labor history emerged when social movements grew and leftist political movements gained power in Turkey. Work that appeared in the 1960s and 1970s focused to a great extent on the history of the worker's movements and their organizations. Earlier research on working-class history had been left to amateur historians, journalists and union activists. Their studies brought to the fore crucial information concerning workers' movements and their first attempts at establishing unions and political organizations. Hüseyin Avni [Şanda] wrote in 1935 on the 1908 strike wave, which was one of the flourishing periods of workers' strikes in the history of the Balkans and Middle East.[69] He analyzed different aspects of the 1908 strikes, such as the actions in various industrial and service sectors, women and child labor, foreign capital, the suppression of the state, the political elite's treatment of the workers, the organizations of workers and so on. In 1951, Lütfi Erişçi published a booklet on the history of the working class in Turkey. His book is similar to Hüseyin Avni's study and focuses mainly on occupational and political organizations that emerged during the labor struggles.[70] Both writers contextualize the labor struggles in the Ottoman Empire and Turkey in relation to semi-colonialism. In addition to these two works, Kemal Sülker also mentions the history of the working class and labor struggles in his book on trade unions in Turkey.[71]

These early studies did not have a significant impact on the historiography of Turkey, although many of these writers' articles were also published in newspapers. However, as social and political movements in Turkey experienced a revival in the 1960s, activists and young scholars became more curious. Under these circumstances, two crucial studies appeared, one of them the continuation of Sülker's research, but in a much better organized version,[72] and the second by Oya Sencer [Baydar], who brought together information about workers' movements and their organization in unprecedented detail and scale.[73] Although for political reasons Sencer's PhD thesis did not result in her being awarded her PhD degree, her subsequent book was based on a survey of primary sources. The events surrounding this thesis and book also demonstrate why historians in university circles avoideded the study of working-class history.

The relationship between workers and socialists is another subject that these narratives have been concerned with. The studies of socialist Turkologists—such as Rozaliyev, Şnurov and Şişmanov—which were translated into Turkish during the 1970s treated working-class movements as a determined outcome of historical progress. According to this analysis, the industrialization process in Turkey had given birth to a working class that was to pioneer socialism in Turkey. Obviously, these books were only a Turkish variation in the field of international labor history. This is why they neither included detailed information, nor were they based on in-depth research.[74] However, they provide significant information and a particular point of view regarding labor history, at a time when historiography virtually ignored the lower classes and excluded them from the narrative. Numerous socialist periodicals published in the 1970s simplified and repeated the general findings of this literature. Although this political tendency paved the way for an academic critique of labor history for being reductionist, a significant amount of information was gathered as a result of this process.[75] Moreover, not all histories in the political journals were based on repetition. For instance, Zafer Toprak published an article in one of these socialist journals, thereby making a crucial contribution to the literature on the 1908 strikes.[76]

Most of these studies on working-class history in the Ottoman Empire and Turkey have concentrated on the activities of the trade unions, organizational initiatives, political struggles, the leaders' deeds and strikes. This tendency to limit working-class history to such fields is not peculiar to Turkish historiography; it is a universal trend in labor historiography.[77] Different facets of working-class history—such as daily life, gender, ethnicity and race, culture, religion, identities, and the like—have entered the historiography as novelties, particularly after the 1960s.

The working classes are mentioned in the works of the elite, as well as scholars, only within the framework of debates regarding socialist thought in Turkey. Intellectual history is one of the most developed areas in the historiography of Turkey, when compared to social and cultural studies. Historians and political scientists often mention the working class when analyzing socialist thought in intellectual circles. The literature asserts that socialism was restricted to a few personalities. This is because socialism did not have a social base in the Ottoman Empire; that is to say, an industrial revolution did not take place in the Ottoman Empire, and as a result there was no sizeable working-class population that would have triggered the emergence of a socialist ideology. There was nothing in the way of a capital–labor contradiction.[78]

These arguments take into account a particular definition of the working class. The narratives of Turkish historiography, to a great extent, assume the working class to be a population of men working in a modern industrial plant. Workers who operate in service sectors, such as transportation, are not even counted among the members of the working class. That is to say, a member of the working class is a blue-collar worker. Once more, this approach is not peculiar to the historiography of Turkey. Marcel van der Linden has argued that a significant number of interpretations on the working class are based on "free" wage-earners. He claims that the working class comprises different types of labor. Capitalist relationships may even be compatible with unfree labor. For him, the main point is the commodification of labor, and "this commodification may take on many different forms."[79]

Scholars who belong to similar schools of thought may have different definitions and classifications. For instance, E.J. Hobsbawm has pinpointed the end of the nineteenth century as the period in which a working class was formed. He mainly focuses on blue-collar workers operating in modern industry, who subsequently created a particular way of life and culture.[80] On the other hand, E.P. Thompson does not restrict his definition of the working class to industrial labor. His seminal work on the making of the English working class concentrates mainly on the experience of the eighteenth century, and ends at the very beginning of the nineteenth century. Thompson was interested in various formations of the working class as comprised of declining artisans and their experience and consciousness. He considered class as a historical phenomenon against the structuralist definitions, and uncovered how the workers were active and conscious participants in the process of their own making. This is why he concentrated on the real experience of the working class, through which they emerge as an agent in the historical process.[81] The port workers in the Ottoman Empire, "the heroes of the boycott movement," were also present in the formation of their class and, as this study will discuss in the following pages, their agency in this movement contributed to this process.

Although Thompson in his book occasionally referred to different sections of the working class—such as unskilled workers, casual laborers, paupers and agricultural laborers—he has been criticized for mainly concentrating on skilled artisans.[82] As mentioned above, this particular point is crucial at this juncture, since the literature on Turkey draws a sharp distinction between industrial laborers and artisans or guild workers.[83] The presumption underlying this distinction is the equation of capitalism with industrial revolution. Therefore, for many Turkish historians, it is nonsense to speak of capitalism, bourgeoisie and working class, since there was no industry in Turkey until the mid-twentieth century. For them, the Turkish case is a unique example from which notions such as class and social agency are absent.[84] However, as Sewell has argued, the class-conscious workers' movement was not an outcome of factories and industry until the 1871 Paris Commune. These workers were to a great extent artisans. However, he also underlines the fact that there no longer were any "traditional" urban crafts, since capitalism and new exploitative practices had already transformed crafts long before the invention of machinery.[85] Therefore, one should focus not on the level of industrialization, but on the development of capitalist relationships in the Ottoman Empire, in order to evaluate and analyze the social classes.

Christopher H. Johnson argues that proletarianization was not an outcome of technological development only. The division and specialization of labor, the increasing control over the means and knowledge of production, the disciplining of labor, and the existence of replaceable labor units were all there before the emergence of modern industry.[86] Therefore, before the industrial revolution, capitalism had already degenerated many artisans and journeymen into a proletariat. Producers had lost their ownership of and control over the means of production. This separation of producers from the means of production turned them into wage laborers.[87] Many master artisans lost their control over the means of production if they were unable to become capitalists. "Capitalism and proletarianization are two perspectives on the same historical phenomenon," and there were many different routes to the formation of a working class.[88] Furthermore, as Raphael Samuel once underlined, it was not only the factory system that, together with capitalism, emerged as a new mode of production, but also a proliferation of small producers. Samuel referred to the combined and uneven development of capitalism and revealed how steam-power and handicraft skills went hand in hand in mid-Victorian Britain.[89] That is to say, the absence of large industrial plants does not necessarily mean the absence of working-class formation and working-class movements. Turkish historiography has in general avoided exploring the history of labor and the lower classes, or the agency of different sections of society, because of evasion and theoretical assumptions. However, different theoretical backgrounds and approaches might also shed light on the history of different classes in the course of Ottoman and Turkish history. Crucial contributions in this vein are the articles by Sherry Vatter, who has written on the struggle of journeymen in Damascus. Her studies demonstrate that the structure of guilds or production based on artisanship did not represent obstacles to the emergence of a labor struggle and the appearance of a working class. Moreover, the traditional organizational structure of guilds and their traditional ideals facilitated and legitimized their struggle.[90]

Culture, Class-Consciousness and Islam

This study will show how different sections of society and different social classes played a central role in an empire-wide social movement, and represented themselves and their particular interests under the guise of national ideals. The actions of the port workers within the boycott movement, for instance, prove how a particular guild organization transformed itself within the modernization process in general, and during the boycott movement in particular. The port workers even succeeded in building an empire-wide network. One can argue that their tradition survived until the early twentieth century. Their legacy was not dead, contrary to the claims that guilds had vanished in the course of the modernization process. Yet, it is quite apparent that their organization and discourse also adapted well to the changing circumstances.

Unfortunately, the historiography of the Ottoman Empire and Turkey does not offer enough information for an analysis and evaluation of the transformation of the guilds' structure in the nineteenth century. Neither is there enough knowledge on how Muslim urban notables and merchants coped with this process of modernization and integration into the capitalist world economy. Thanks to the studies by Quataert, it is quite obvious that Ottoman manufacturing did not completely perish in the age of industrial revolution. As mentioned above, some sectors in the Ottoman economy were able to take advantage of the newly emerging opportunities, while others could not. As Quataert argues, although the position of the Ottoman Empire in the world economy diminished, its total production did not decrease. Manufacturing and production were able to transcend the regulations and confinements of the guild structure. He clearly shows that manufacturing is not necessarily machine-based production in a factory, and indicates how native traders adapted to the transformation process resulting from integration into the capitalist economy.[91]

As noted above, there is not enough information available on the Muslim/Turkish merchant class and urban notables. It has widely been claimed that Turkish history lacks a Muslim bourgeoisie comparable to the bourgeoisie found in Western history, a bourgeois class that struggled against the landed aristocracy and the state and finally brought democracy to its country. Yet, the literature on the emergence of capitalism in England and the revisionist literature on the French Revolution have also undermined these theoretical postulates.[92] Turkish historiography has assumed that the merchant class would have lived according to a Western lifestyle and, to a great extent, has looked for Western patterns of daily life and culture. As a result, private property, the process of commodification, commercialized social and economic relationships, and the transformation of lifestyle in a different manner did not enter the historians' agenda. In order to conduct an analysis of Muslim merchants, landowners and entrepreneurs, further research is needed, on their trading networks, their relationship with the foreign and non-Muslim bourgeoisie, their social relationships, their lifestyles, and their class discourse, all of which were to a great extent dependent on their Muslim identity.

Similarly, a significant number of German historians have criticized the German bourgeoisie for assimilating into the Junker culture and compromising with the Bismarkian revolution from above. As a result, for them, liberalism did not flourish in Germany when compared to west European patterns, and therefore Germany did not have a proper German bourgeoisie.[93]

Neither are French historians entirely enthusiastic about including the concept of the bourgeoisie into their narrative. They claim that the

French economy was dominated by agriculture and small-scale manufacturing. Therefore, for them, capitalism was marginal in the French economy until the second half of the nineteenth century. As a result, the French bourgeoisie did not exist. No particular social group called itself bourgeois, and this fact is a confirmation of this argumentation for some historians.[94]

Last but not least, Perry Anderson has also argued that the English bourgeoisie could not develop a coherent world view *vis-à-vis* the aristocracy. Because of its compromise with the aristocracy, the English revolution was the least bourgeois revolution. The superstructure stayed intact, and the pre-modern state system and anachronistic culture survived. Britain did not have bourgeois revolutions, as did Western European countries, particularly France. The revolution was never finished, and democracy did not mature in Britain, even in the 1960s.[95] I have referred to these studies in order to indicate that, even in the historiography of these countries, which are considered as ideal models in the Turkish historiography, the presence of a bourgeoisie is controversial in terms of economy and culture. These arguments depend on different definitions and understandings of the concepts and the intellectual discussions and agenda concerning a particular era.

Even though the structure of guild organizations in particular sectors had degenerated, paving the way for good fortunes in business, others succeeded in preserving their organizations, particularly those comprising laboring classes. They survived and continued to affect the social and economic life of the Ottoman Empire. The process of modernization and the integration of the empire into the capitalist economy were not smooth processes.[96] On the contrary, they provoked many different types of popular resistance, and social organizations with traditional roots, such as the guilds, found for themselves a space to act.

The historiography on working-class experiences in France and Britain indicates that the transformation of pre-existing discourses, popular and religious traditions, trade, and community solidarities played significant roles in class formation and the emergence of a class consciousness.[97] Yet, as Sewell has argued, these existing organizations and their traditional discourses also underwent a transformation and recruited Universalist arguments and vocabulary in order to include other workers or legitimize their actions.[98] In a similar vein, port workers in the boycott movement referred to their traditional rights, which they claimed to have had for centuries. Their guild organization facilitated their activities within the boycott movement. The balance of power in the national movement provided them with a shelter under which they were able to preserve significant elements of their traditional organization. Furthermore, thanks to the boycott movement and their political affiliations, they also strengthened their empire-wide network.

Moreover, they made use of nationalist arguments and presented themselves as representatives of Ottoman and national interests, and as defenders of the rights of consumers and people. They also cited the ideals of the new constitutional regime in defending their so-called traditional privileges in the Ottoman ports. Therefore, they were quite successful in developing a class discourse based on different cultural elements, while their positions in the harbors were undermined by capitalist relationships.[99]

New relevant information will help to create a better understanding of how people played a part in the making of their own history. Yet this book is not a study on class formation and class consciousness; it will only analyze the social origins of a popular social movement. Therefore, it focuses mainly on different patterns of mobilization and the agency of different segments of society. This study gives us an opportunity to see the Muslim merchant and working classes in action within the boycott movement. Their actions and their social movement prompt new questions regarding the formation of classes and culture, which was to a great extent based on Muslim identity. The answers to these questions may facilitate our understanding of the social basis of Muslim/Turkish nationalism, which was not only an intellectual current, but also a social and mass phenomenon.

CHAPTER 2

THE EMERGENCE OF THE ECONOMIC BOYCOTT AS A POLITICAL WEAPON, 1908

The young constitutional regime of the Ottoman Empire experienced its first diplomatic and political crises in the first week of October 1908. Austria-Hungary announced the annexation of Bosnia-Herzegovina, which it had occupied and ruled since 1878. The Berlin Treaty had left this county to the administration of Austria-Hungary, due to the fact that the Ottoman Empire was unable to police and maintain security in Bosnia, which was jeopardizing European security. As a result, although the Great Powers guaranteed the right to sovereignty of the Ottoman Empire, Bosnia and Herzegovina were left in the hands of the Habsburg Monarchy. After the promulgation of the constitution in July 1908, the Habsburgs wanted to cut the relationship between the Ottoman Empire and Bosnia and Herzegovina, even though it might have been an abstract tie. The revolution entailed a process of elections in order to form the long-suspended parliament, which would construct a tangible relationship between Bosnia and Istanbul, if deputies had been elected to the Ottoman parliament. Austria-Hungary annexed Bosnia-Herzegovina in order to prevent such a possibility.[1]

The Treaty of Berlin in 1878 created a self-governing Bulgaria as a semi-independent principality which became only a vassal of the Ottoman Empire. Numerous problems arose between the Bulgarian principality and the Ottoman Empire after 1878. Both political entities had different political designs for Eastern Rumelia and Macedonia. Bulgarian political elites worried about losing their influence in Macedonia. Moreover, they thought that the Great Powers might decrease their pressure on the Ottoman Empire for reform in Rumelia, which might strengthen the position of the Ottomans in the Balkans. Therefore, Bulgaria had similar fears to the Habsburgs after the declaration of the constitution, and declared its independence on 5 October 1908.[2]

In the historiography of Turkey, these two acts are considered the first political shock that the Young Turks and the Ottomans encountered after the 1908 Revolution. The Young Turks believed that all political, social and ethnic questions would be solved as a result of the revolution and the re-establishment of the Ottoman parliament, but this was not the case. Initially, the new regime encountered a strike wave in August and September 1908. The Young Turks managed to cope with this social problem, and were able to put an end to the strikes. However, the annexation of Bosnia-Herzegovina and the independence of Bulgaria represented a crucial political challenge to "Young Turkey," even though the political agenda of these states was not a surprise for the Ottoman elite and Ottoman public opinion (the elite's aspirations were quite well-known to the Ottoman public).[3] Austria and Bulgaria's acts were considered an offense against the new order and the recently gained "freedom" endowed by the promulgation of the constitution. Immediately after the above-mentioned declarations, spontaneous demonstrations and marches took place in Istanbul. These spontaneous popular reactions put the Ottoman government in a difficult position. The popular reactions were a continuation of the mobilization of Ottoman society, as it resulted from the revolution. The Ottoman government and the most powerful representative of the new regime, the CUP, were not in favor of a war. The CUP in particular entirely concentrated on the construction of the new regime. They were not willing to risk the newly acquired freedom for lands that had been lost long ago. Consequently, the spontaneous reactions of the Ottoman public and the reluctance of the government and the CUP to enter a war brought forth a new form of protest: the boycott.[4]

The boycott was a weapon that could satisfy the interests and demands of the social and political actors involved. Regarding the government, the boycott worked well in terms of driving mass reactions and protests along a much more reliable path. In terms of diplomacy, it was also useful in pushing Austria and Bulgaria against the wall. One of the first government statements came from Tevfik Paşa, the minister of foreign affairs: in an interview published in *İkdam* he underlined that the government was working, asking the people to stay calm and trust their government. He advised sobriety, patience and moderation on the part of the Ottoman public.[5] The CUP supported the boycott sincerely, since it was the best way to keep spontaneous reactions from a possible anti-constitutional political current. Other social actors such as workers and merchants also participated in the movement, which gave them the opportunity to realize their own interests and pursue their own agendas. Two factors played a crucial role in the construction of a social movement throughout the empire: these were the daily press and the flourishing civil organizations, which experienced a significant boom during the heyday of the revolution. They turned the boycott into a popular movement made up of different political and social actors with divergent agendas.

On the day of the interview with the minister of foreign affairs, on 7 October 1908, an article published in the newspaper *Servet-i Fünun* by Horasani (Ubeydullah Efendi) called on the Ottomans to impose a boycott against Austria and Bulgaria.[6] It was the first instance in which the term boycott was pronounced and proposed as a pattern of protest. Süleyman Kani (İrtem), then governor of Ohri, stated that the boycott was decided at a meeting convened for Muslim merchants and prominent members of the CUP in Cavit Bey's house in Istanbul. The meeting agreed that it was not expedient to declare a war against Austria and Bulgaria. According to Süleyman Kani, the merchant brothers Kazım Balcı and Ziya Balcı proposed a boycott against the two states. Talat Bey approved their proposition after they explained to him the way this protest weapon might operate.[7] Quataert has also referred to the action of several merchants in Salonica, who cancelled their orders from Austrian factories, as the first instance of a boycott.[8] However, one of the first complaints about boycotting actions was about the port workers' refusal to unload Austrian goods in Salonica. Their act was seen as an outcome of the influence of the CUP, which the committee denied.⁹ Therefore, it is reasonable to claim that the boycott was the result of different initiatives that probably coincided with each other.

People Take Action: Mass Actions and Public Demonstrations

On the evening of the day Bulgaria declared its independence, a popular spontaneous reaction spilled into the streets of the capital; newspapers wrote that two marching columns advanced toward the British Embassy, to thank Britain for not recognizing Bulgarian independence. The marching crowds sent a telegram to the ambassador who was in the embassy's summer residence in Tarabya. Later the same night, another group of protestors made up of Greeks, Armenians and Muslims congregated in front of the British Embassy. The crowd chanted "Long live the English Nation," while bearing Ottoman and Greek flags. The crowds thereafter continued to march and visit foreign embassies who did not recognize Austria and Bulgaria's actions. There was continuous reaction, and the Ottoman newspapers advised people to calm down: newspapers that held different political positions argued without exception that such a level of mobilization might lead to national weakness.¹⁰

These kinds of warnings did not have any impact on the popular reaction. One day after the protests outside the British Embassy, a similar demonstration was held in Beyazıt Square (where the Ministry of War was located). The gathered crowds encountered the minister of internal affairs, Hakkı Bey, and stopped him in order to receive information about the last developments between the Ottoman Empire, Austria and Bulgaria. The minister told them that the government was in charge; he wanted them to trust the existing cabinet. The protesting crowd continued its way to the headquarters of the CUP and cheered the committee members. One of the prominent figures of the committee, Bahattin Bey, addressed the crowd from the balcony and, like Hakkı Bey, recommended moderation. He also wanted them to trust the present cabinet. After he had finished his speech, the mass of protestors moved toward the Sublime Porte and expressed support for the government. Although these demonstrations were defined as "patriotic" and "national," the newspapers kept their distance from the crowds, as did Hakkı Bey and Bahattin Bey. The Ottoman press argued that ally states such as Britain did not give credit to demonstration or protest, but only to moderation, particularly to the "famous Ottoman tranquility"; however, the ambassadors approved of and praised these demonstrations in their declarations. They also congratulated the Ottomans for convening and acting together in fraternity. In one of these protest marches, a crowd of Muslim protestors headed by Hamdi Bey visited the Ottoman theaters, where they cheered for Greece and the Greek nation in return for their sincerity and friendliness. In one of these theaters, the crowd intervened and wanted the orchestra to play the Greek national anthem while it stand listening. The newspapers reminded their readers of the "Incident of '93" (the suspension of the constitution of 1878, which put an end to the First Constitutional Period) and argued that these protests and demonstrations might prevent the government from carrying out its duties. Moreover, it was argued that rallies and actions were an outcome of fever and thrill, rather than reason and logic. Therefore, they might have consequences detrimental to the "national dignity."[11] This elitist argument is reminiscent of the mentality of Gustave Le Bon.

Spontaneous reactions showed no sign of coming to an end and forced the elites to find new methods of channeling popular actions into a more secure path, compatible with the new constitutional regime. The CUP intervened at this point, setting up organized meetings throughout the empire. The local cadres and prominent figures in the provinces played crucial roles in organizing orderly demonstrations. One of these public meetings was held in Salonica, in Terakki Square, and was officially organized by the CUP. In a way, this meeting set the standard for the public meetings and demonstrations of the boycott movement that would take place during the Second Constitutional Period. Representatives of different religious communities addressed the gathered crowds in their own languages. At this particular meeting, speeches were delivered in Turkish, Greek, Bulgarian, Serbian, Wallachian, Ladino (Old Spanish), Albanian and French. The meeting agreed on three points, and these were approved by the applause of the people in the public square. These decisions were published in the name of the "People of Salonica," and regardless of whether they had been made before or not, therefore gained their legitimacy through the participation of the people. The meeting protested against Austria and Bulgaria, thanked the Great Powers and decided to pursue the struggle. However, it was also underlined that people should put an end to the street demonstrations. It was not what the Ottoman Empire needed at that moment, according to the speeches given at the meeting; what it needed was moderation and peace.[12]

These types of organized meetings were the best way to control the mobilization of the masses and at the same time to make use of it. They were orderly and safe compared to spontaneous street activities. Furthermore, the mobilization of crowds enhanced the legitimacy of the political designs of the elite. A Greek-language workers' journal published in Smyrna, *Ergatis*, stated that patriotic fliers were handed out before the meetings.[13] These bills confirm the organized nature of the meetings. Similar meetings occurred in various urban centers of the empire, during which speeches were given in several local languages, confidence in the Great Powers was expressed, moderation and peace were advised, and protest telegrams were sent to foreign embassies. These are the most often mentioned cities where meetings were convened: Manastır, Şam, Smyrna, Halep, Kastamonu, Kala-i Sultaniye, Üsküp, Adana, Trabzon, Yafa, Konya, Erzurum, Beirut, Aydın and İşkodra. Beirut was one of the vibrant centers of the boycott movement, where the demand to cut off all ties with Austria was proposed at a meeting. One of the protestors threw down his Austrian-made fez and wore a native one during the meeting against Austria; this action was reported to create a significant impact on the massed demonstrators.[14] More demonstrations were held in Beirut. The government sent telegrams to Beirut and informed the people there was no need for protest demonstrations.[15]

A meeting of 5,000 to 6,000 people was convened in Hürriyet Square in Manastır, similar to that in Salonica. The speeches were delivered in different languages, and protest telegrams were sent directly to the ministries of foreign affairs of the Great Powers.[16] The meeting in Konya was assembled on the initiative of three people: the religious scholar (*ulema*) Lokman, Mehmet Bey (the general secretary of the Administrative Council of the province, or *Meclis-i İdare Başkatibi*) and a journalist from local newspaper *Anadolu*. In a similar manner, it was argued at the meeting that a war against Austria and Bulgaria would probably turn into a disaster for the nation. To support a war was considered treason. The governor-general of Konya Province, who attended the meeting, stated that he would write to the government about how the people of Konya showed their tribute to empire and nation. As usual, the speakers addressing the people preached moderation and patience. The meeting ended with the slogans "Long live the Sublime State, England, France" and prayers for the patria, the nation and the CUP.[17]

On the same day as the Konya meeting, the meeting held in Smyrna's Konak Square was attended by thousands of people. Muslims, Greeks, Armenians and Jews protested in unity against Austria and Bulgaria. Çulluzade Halil Bey was elected as the president of the meeting and also wrote a telegram to be sent to the foreign embassies, which was read to the assembled crowd and generated great excitement. A commission was formed to send the telegram from the post office. A band played the "Hürriyet Marşı" (Anthem of Freedom) as the commission walked to the post office. The organized nature of the meeting and the existence of a band indicate that there had been preparations for the meeting beforehand.[18]

The meeting in Istanbul was more elaborately organized and, therefore, held somewhat later than in other towns. The meeting and its program was announced beforehand, and people were asked to obey the rules and the order of the demonstration. Slogans such as "We Want War!" were strictly banned. Ottoman newspaper articles reporting on the forthcoming meeting gave historical examples of the futility of war in defending the Ottomans' rights. Rowdy behavior was repeatedly condemned in the newspapers and announcements. The way in which Europeans held peaceful meetings was depicted in detail, and calls for moderation appeared again and again. At last, a massive meeting was held in Sultanahmet, where thousands of people gathered. Different religious communities, such as the Greeks, Armenians and Jews, as well as foreign communities such as the Hellenes, Serbians and Montenegrins, participated in the meeting. Speeches were given in a previously announced order. Celal Bey of the CUP, also the director of the Mekteb-i Mülkiye (School of Civil Administration), spoke first. After him, Mustafa Asım Efendi, as a member of the *ulema*, Kozmidi Efendi of the Greek community, Halıcıyan Efendi of the Armenian community, Ishak Efendi of the Jewish community, İsmail Hakkı, another member of the CUP, and the army mayor Mahmut Bey addressed the people in turn. The identity of the speakers clearly symbolized the Ottomanist ideal of the constitutional regime. In their speeches, the speakers argued that the Ottomans should not rise in revolt, as it was not appropriate in politics to act upon emotions rather than reason and logic. Different flags flew in the meeting square, and a Greek woman dressed in blue and white joined the meeting, bringing with her the Greek and the Ottoman flags side by side. This agitated the people, who chanted "Long live the Ottomans," "Long live the CUP," and "Damn the Despots!" The meeting, which was also photographed by foreign journalists for a cinematographic exhibition, ended with the prayer by an Arab participant.[19]

After Istanbul, protest meetings were convened all over the Ottoman Empire. In Tekfurdağı, thousands of peasants were mobilized and streamed from their villages to the town. Şerif Bey, a member of the local branch of the CUP, led the demonstration in front of the English consulate. In Kavala, 8,000 people gathered in the town center, and the benefits of a boycott against Austria and Bulgaria were announced in Turkish, Greek and Spanish. Similar meetings were held in Dedeağaç, Manastır, and again in Konya. In Trabzon, it was announced to the world via telegram that the people of Trabzon—Muslims, Greeks and Armenians—had begun a boycott. Parallel meetings organized in Cairo equally shaped public opinion in the Ottoman Empire.[20]

In Aydın, the Greek demonstrators began their march at the seat of the archbishop, before uniting with other protestors in the market place, from where they walked to the municipality together. There, the mayor also joined them, and the crowd visited the British and French consulates. Mithat Efendi gave speeches in front of the two consulates, and according to the Greek newspaper *Amaltheia*, many demonstrators wore local fezzes and *kalpaks*, which were made popular by the boycott movement.[21] The demonstrations and meetings before foreign embassies were a phenomenon that emerged in the initial days of the boycott movement.[22]

Although the protest movement and boycott occurred all over the empire, cities such as Smyrna, Beirut, Salonica and Istanbul were the liveliest centers of the demonstrations. Meetings were held several times in Smyrna, organized by a group of young men and repeating the rituals of earlier protest meetings, such as speeches in different languages, visiting foreign consuls, and so on. This particular meeting also repudiated the rumors regarding the clash of the Muslim and Greek communities of Smyrna. A very similar meeting was repeated in Beirut. In Jeddah, the crowd protested against Austria and declared that they never again would buy Austrian merchandise.[23] In Samsun, a local theater group, Samsun Osmanlı İttihad-ı Milli Kulübü (Samsun Ottoman National Union Club), presented a play in the city's port, in order to popularize the boycott among the lower classes. The play was a comedy about the contribution of the port workers, who were the most active social class in the boycott movement.[24] This play, staged in a public space, can be considered an example of political or street theater in the Ottoman Empire.

Several incidents that occurred during these meetings caused concern for the Ottoman elite. For instance, a group of Muslims convened in Fatih and marched toward the Yıldız Palace, where Sultan Abdülhamid II resided. They called for closure of the *meyhanes* (taverns) around Muslim quarters, a ban preventing Muslim women from walking around the city uncovered, and a ban on gambling. The crowd submitted their demands to the sultan who appeared in the window of the palace. This event, known as the "Kör Ali Incident," increased apprehension amongst the leaders of the new regime about a possible reaction against the constitutional government. This incident later became seen as a symbolic act in the secular historiography on Turkey. The newspapers claimed that these people had nothing to do with religion and the *ulema*, but were only illiterate people who had lost their privileges after the revolution.[25] It has been considered a forerunner of the 31 March Incident and an example of Islamic insurrection.[26]

Later, another protest demonstration held before the Fatih Mosque alarmed the Ottoman bureaucracy. Although the protest was organized by the Bosnians living in Istanbul, the police were ordered to stop the crowd if they marched toward the Yıldız Palace. The government did not want such an incident to be repeated.[27]

A similar event occurred in one of the demonstrations held in front of the embassies. A protestor by the name of Karamanlı Koçu wanted to lead the crowd toward the Galatasaray Jail in order to free a number of detainees who had been awaiting trial for a long time. However, Karamanlı Koçu was detained by the police, and this incident was referred to as an example of how these types of street actions might constitute a threat against the public order.[28] Apart from spontaneous demonstrations, other types of direct action also came onto the agenda and instilled amongst the elite a fear of the streets. Attempts were made to control the mobilization by means of newspaper articles and speeches from prominent figures: they wanted the people to protest, but within the limits they dictated. Most of the contemporary articles defined in detail how to participate in the boycott. The elite and the CUP considered boycotts to be a refusal to buy certain goods—that is to say, a consumer action. For them, to protest was to boycott. However, the launching of a boycott did not bring a halt to the street demonstrations, and for this reason, the number and scope of the organized meetings also increased, in order to control the mobilization of the people. As an example of an attempt to use the press to direct the course of the debate, the pro-constitutionalist satirical journal *Musavver Geveze* argued that not everyone had the right to free expression, since there were those able to understand and those who were not. As a result, not everyone on the street should be taken seriously; particularly not those who were not smart enough. For *Musavver Geveze*, if a country acted according to the decisions and will of the people, it would most likely lose.[29] For the Ottoman press, those who were able to understand were the parliament, the press and the CUP. This clearly reflects the elitist vision of the Second Constitutional Period.

Nevertheless, public opinion was not defined as passive or inactive, but rather was considered to be the driving force behind the boycott movement. The young regime's legitimacy ultimately derived from public opinion and the people. It was the nation that should decide and determine what to do in a civilized manner, rather than the mob. According to M. Ragıb, if the Ottomans wanted to spoil Austria's game, they should use the weapon of economic war; but this economic war should be executed in a moderate and peaceful way. Additional actions and demonstrations were not necessary for the national cause, and the Ottomans should fulfill their duties with moderation.[30]

However, these organized, pre-arranged meetings were not able to put a complete end to street demonstrations. Spontaneous reactions and night-marching became rare; instead, other activities prevailed. In Beirut, a crowd prevented an Austrian ship from anchoring and forced the ship to leave the port. Many posters and notices appeared on walls, propagating the boycott. The employees of an Austrian store, Gülizar Mağazası, wanted to remove them, but were confronted by passers-by. Bystanders turned into activists on behalf of the national protest and were ready to take action if necessary. In Beirut, rumors claiming that several shops had unloaded Austrian sugar from the port circulated among the population. A significant number of people gathered and inspected particular shops, and the packages of Austrian sugar that they found in several storerooms were returned to the ships from which they had been unloaded. Beirut certainly was one of the vibrant centers of the boycott movement. Apart from this inspection tour looking for Austrian sugar, a group of people convened in İttihad Square and visited theaters and cafes where singers performed, with the intention of suppressing the performance of Austrian actors and singers. The newspaper *Sabah* defined these protestors as "those who exaggerate in showing their *hamiyet* (patriotism)." Another group of people in Istanbul gathered in front of the Oroz di-Back store, which was rumored to sell Austrian products. The store manager hung Ottoman and French flags on his shop in order to appease the crowd and convince them that it did not belong to an Austrian. A merchant in Adapazarı was also threatened by a mob for importing goods from Austria, who told him that if he persisted in buying merchandise from Austria, he would also be boycotted.[31]

Another merchant in Kavala was similarly threatened: his shop was picketed by a crowd, and two Muslim women inside the store were pulled out by force. An official inquiry was launched regarding the incident, yet hundreds of people gathered once more in order to protest the inquiry and marched to the government office. They wanted the governor to dismiss the commander of the gendarmerie. The gendarmerie took preventive measures, and the crowd dispersed after a short while. The governor of Kavala responded by prohibiting street demonstrations and the picketing of shops, which provoked a major reaction: a mass of 10,000 people convened before the government office and protested the governor. They shouted slogans such as "We don't want the governor" and "We want to maintain the boycott." The central government took the reaction seriously, sending the governor (*mutasarrıf*) of Drama and the metropolitan district governor (*merkez kaymakamı*) of Salonica, Tahsin Bey, to Kavala to conduct an inquiry.[32]

A similar incident happened in Galata. Two students saw two Muslim women shopping in the Austrian Tring shop and shouted at them: "We are boycotting the Austrians, shopping in this store shows your *hamiyetsizlik* [not having public sprit/honor]." Upon this, the women started to scream, and a crowd gathered around them. The students were detained and taken to the Aziziye police station near the Galata Bridge.

In Adapazarı a direct action occurred that was typical of the Chinese boycotts mentioned in the introduction. A grocer who continued to sell Austrian sugar despite numerous warnings was punished by being paraded through the streets of Adapazarı in a handcart with his sugar packages. People shouted at him: "Boo to those who do not boycott!"[33] On 1 December 1908, a porter unloading an Austrian ship in Trabzon was attacked by a crowd. The merchandise he was carrying was not returned to the ship, but was burnt.[34] The boycott movement became increasingly violent. Again in Trabzon, when it was heard that a ship importing mushrooms from Austria had arrived, the mushrooms were burnt publicly.[35] Burning boycotted merchandise is a typical act of boycott movements everywhere in the world.

The picketing of Austrian shops was the most effective direct action of the boycott movement. The gathering of crowds before these shops increased the boycott's impact in the public sphere. People not only congregated in front of the boycotted shops, but also those that sold native Ottoman products. The wearing of Ottoman clothes and headgear, particularly native fezzes, became a fashion among the Ottoman population, and the mass consumption this entailed resulted in crowds in front of Ottoman shops. The gathering of people in front of Austrian shops—such as Stein, Mayer and Tring—at first resulted from curiosity, but groups of people soon started to harrass customers who continued to frequent these shops, and as such these groups turned into picket lines in the course of the boycott movement. Shops such as Stein were picketed even in Cairo, where Ottoman domination had disappeared long ago. The crowds chanted slogans against Austria and distributed leaflets in Arabic, Turkish and French, calling on people to participate in the boycott movement.[36] The *Musavver Geveze* depicted the picketing of Austrian stores on the front page of one of its issues.[37] This illustration shows that the Ottoman boycott was similar to other boycott movements in other parts of the world.[38]

The most spectacular direct action of the boycott movement was the so-called "Fez-Tearing Feast," which involved people harrassing each other on the streets, as Turks started to exchange Austrian-made regular fezzes with Ottoman-made ones.[39] The fez, the symbol of the Ottoman Empire and the Turks, was produced in great numbers in Austria in the nineteenth century. At the start of the boycott movement, the market-share of Austrian fezzes was so large that boycotters had to introduce different styles and colors in order to compete with Austrian merchandise and undermine their trade in the regular red fezzes. Austrian manufacturers specialized in cheaper and more basic products, which made them more vulnerable to tearing. Ottoman fezzes were different: some were white, while others came in different shapes. New types of hats which had their origins in antique Turkish culture were also invented (the *kalpak* and *arakiye* were such inventions). It was easy to recognize whether a fez was Austrian-made, or a new one popularized by the boycott, and it became a legitimate act to take the fez from the head of a passer-by and tear it, particularly in the main centers of the boycott movement such as Smyrna.

The most enthusiastic fez-tearing initially happened in Smyrna because the town was a latecomer to the boycott movement and had been criticized for its lukewarm support. As a result, the most active boycott society was formed in Smyrna, where it published the only boycott journal in the Ottoman Empire.[40] After the boycott had gained a prominent place in the daily life of the town, taking Austrian fezzes from people's heads became a popular grassroots action. The Salonic newspaper *Zaman* coined the name "Fez-Tearing Feast." A group of Cretans in Smyrna also organized a collective fez-tearing demonstration, during which they joined together in tearing their fezzes. Similar demonstrations also happened in Beirut. *İttihad* called fez-tearing an act of freedom of choice, reporting that it was a national movement resulting from the nation's free will. The old fezzes were thrown away. According to *İttihad*, people started to wear whatever headgear they could find, be it a *kalpak* or something else.[41] In Salonica, posters on walls and street corners, signed by *hamiyetmendan ahali* (patriotic people), called for the Ottomans to throw away their fezzes and invited them to wear a *kalpak*. After these posters appeared, groups gathered at the Sefa coffee shop and the coffee shops in front of the government house and tore up their fezzes. Many people at these meetings put on a *kalpak* in place of the fez.

The pages of newspapers such as *İttihat ve Terakki* and *Zaman*, which reported on the fez-tearing demonstrations and called for people to exchange their Austrian-made fezzes for native products, were stuck up on the walls as if they were posters. Such incidents and propaganda made fez-tearing popular in Salonica. But as fez-tearing became more common, violence also occurred. Port workers and youngsters caused clashes on the streets by taking fezzes from the heads of passers-by. For instance, on one occssion when they attacked a Muslim and took the fez from his head, he discharged his revolver in the direction of a group of people on Belediye Avenue. Fortunately, no one was shot. After these incidents, wearing a *kalpak* became widespread among the Ottoman population.[42]

Afterwards, port workers wore the *kalpak* when participating in national meetings and boycott actions. The newspaper *İttihad* described the image of people walking around with various types of hats as "carnival."[43] In Smyrna, people reacted against the fez-tearing. A Muslim officer in the province of Aydın, Ebu-el-Ahir Efendi, whose fez was taken from his head and exchanged for a felt *külah*, brought the case before the court. The Boycott Society claimed in its journal that the action of the young man who had removed the officer's hat was a result of rising national feelings. According to the boycott journal *Gâve*, Ebu-el-Ahir Efendi should have tolerated the youngsters instead of going to court. The Boycott Society threatened him with a personal boycott. *Gâve* suggested that if a boycott was pronounced against him, he might no longer work as a sergeant of the municipality in the province of Aydın.[44]

Extraordinary conditions in daily life, spectacular phenomena and exceptional developments represent significant features of social movements and protest actions. These types of spectacular actions in the context of social movements create their own symbols as well as extraordinary situations in daily life, which change the fundamental order of things. The tearing of fezzes and the preference for awkward hats produced an atmosphere of carnival, popularizing the boycott in Ottoman public opinion.

Many memoirs narrating this period mention the 1908 boycott movement, and unsurprisingly, almost all define the movement as a "Fez Boycott," describing the fez-tearing in detail. Ahmet Emin Yalman stated in his memoirs that many Ottomans wore *külahs* (conical felt hats), while many Ottomans went bare-headed in order to avoid becoming the target of a fez-tearing attack.[45] Hasan Ali (Yücel), who would become minister of education, was only a child in 1908; he wrote in his memoirs that he best liked his image in the mirror with a white *külah* on his head, as popularized by the boycott movement, which made him feel like an *efe* (a courageous bandit of south-west Anatolia). He felt like a volunteer ready to go to war, and mentioned that those who continued to wear old red fezzes were attacked by patriotic activists. He remembers that fezzes were thrown away on the streets.[46] Hilmi Uran referred to children on the street following those wearing a red fez, shouting, "Tear it down! Tear it down!" Many felt obliged to throw away their Austrian-made fezzes. Moreover, Uran in his memoir remembered a boycott committee visiting the Governor-General Rauf Paşa and giving him a boycott *külah* as a gift, as the committee wanted him to align himself with Ottoman public opinion.[47] Most of the memoirs describing this period refer to the boycott movement as well-meant but futile. Their evaluation is very much related to their overall consideration of the Second Constitutional Period or the 1908 Young Turk Revolution. It was only the more conspicuous aspects of the boycott, such as these festive actions, that they remembered of the movement.[48]

Fez-tearing demonstrations were also seen in other towns, such as Aydın. The Ottoman press very much supported these actions, which they considered an expression of Ottoman patriotism. For instance, the Greek newspaper *Amaltheia* of Smyrna endorsed these street actions.[49] However, the stance of those newspapers that had supported fez-tearing without reservation started to change with the increase in assaults and clashes on the streets, which disrupted public order and were therefore now condemned.[50] The Ottoman press argued that, once the picketing lines were lifted, the misery of the Austrian shops would become apparent; many articles asserted that in order to harm Austrian shops, it was also possible to write articles, hang posters, and address people. Using force to obstruct people who entered shops, or booing and shouting at people who left them, was said to be inappropriate, as well as contrary to legal codes. Furthermore, traitors or advocates of *istibdat* (autocracy) might mingle with the crowd. Therefore, citizens should watch out and not jeopardize the public order and the future of the freedom that the constitution had secured for the Ottomans. The Ottoman press called for the population to stay calm and act in accordance with the "Ottoman mildness" or "Turkish solemnity" (*türklüğe mahsus vakurluk*). It called these aggressive acts on the streets meaningless, unnecessary, excessive and "charlatanry." The press wanted the Ottomans to concentrate on the "economical awakening," which could really injure Austria.[51]

The moderation and sobriety that the Ottoman government and the CUP called for was not maintained on the street level. There were even instances of guns being fired during the demonstrations, something that probably terrified the elites. For example, a group of people were wandering around in Eminönü/Istanbul, making noise with drums and horns and firing their guns into the air. When they arrived at the Bahçekapı police station, they wanted to be enlisted as volunteers in the event of a war against Austria and Bulgaria. These acts were a challenge to the calls for moderation. Similar incidents were repeated several times in Beirut and Jaffa, where the boycott turned violent. The attacks against Austrian ships usually occurred in ports around Beirut. Apart from the ships, the Austrian post office in Jaffa was also attacked.[52] The violence, assaults and picket lines during the boycott movement caused fear among the elite, as it was thought that they might provoke an international intervention in the Ottoman Empire. The Ottoman government and the CUP tried to channel the protests and demonstrations into a more organized and planned mobilization. The newspaper *Sabah* used a rather odd argument in order to discourage picketing actions, claiming that those who appeared to shop in Austrian stores were not real customers, but actors who wanted to trigger an Ottoman reaction and provoke them into assaulting the shops; desperate store-owners would then demand compensation from the Ottoman government. Thus, *Sabah* argued that the Ottomans should stay away from Austrian shops.[53]

The elite's complaints regarding the mass mobilization at the grassroots level indicate the autonomous character of the popular movement. When a social movement happens on the street, it acquires its own momentum, and this triggered the elite's fear of the masses during the boycott movement. However, different segments of society had different expectations of the boycott movement, as did political actors such as the states and the political parties.

The Organization

There was a substantial increase in the number of civil organizations after the 1908 Revolution. The boycott movement did not lag behind, and set about creating an organization from its expanding network. This organization was an outcome of different intentions. First, it was seen as the best way to control the movement and the mobilized masses; therefore the elite of the Ottoman Empire, particularly the CUP, were in favor of the establishment of such an organization. Second, the activists working for the boycott needed an organization to implement their activities more easily. Third, the boycott movement in realizing its goals had to organize several particular social classes who occupied strategic positions. The first proposal for the formation of a boycott movement organization appeared in *Tanin*, with the argument that it was better for Ottoman merchants to form a union to publicize the names and addresses of the Austrian shops.[54] The newspaper *Millet* invited provincial merchants to act in accord with the boycotting merchants of Istanbul.[55] As the role played by workers and merchants became apparent, such propositions for an organization became widespread. *Tanin* repeated its proposal for an organization and claimed that they would probably lose if they did not unite within the boycott movement.[56]

These suggestions still continued to appear in the newspapers at the end of October.[57] A Boycott Union was established probably in the first days of November, and an anonymous manifesto written in three different languages was sent to the merchants and porters of the Black Sea region. This union was a convention of merchants that took place in Istanbul, and their decisions were about the rules and regulations of the boycott movement.[58] In the same vein, *İttihat ve Terakki* reported a similar meeting of merchants and similar decisions in Salonica, where a commission was constituted among the merchants to regulate boycotting issues.[59]

A similar declaration was made by the Boycott Society of Smyrna, announcing that a boycott organization had already been established, one day before the declarations in Istanbul and Salonica. The decisions of the Boycott Society were almost identical to those of other boycott organizations.[60] In Üsküp, a group of Turks, Bulgarians, Greeks and Jews came together in order to deal with boycott-related issues, and formed a similar commission that made similar decisions.[61] A newspaper article also appeared regarding the meetings and organizations of merchants which took place in various towns of the Ottoman Empire. These developments indicate that the initiative emerged from the merchant organizations within the boycott network.[62] The boycott organization dealt with a variety of tasks, and for this reason its members created a commission in order to handle the merchants' transactions, the Commission of Facilities (Teshilat Komisyonu).[63]

Another organization that appeared during the boycott movement was the Boycott Society (Boykotaj Cemiyeti), or Society of Economic Warfare (Harb-i İktisadi Cemiyeti). The Boycott Union was a merchant organization that included both Ottoman and foreign merchants who cut all their ties to Austria. The Boycott Society, on the other hand, was a larger organization. It aimed to propagate and organize the boycott throughout the entire empire. At this point, a problem of terminology arises. The Ottoman press used the terms committee (*komite*), commission (*komisyon*) and society (*cemiyet*) interchangeably; this leads to confusion about the character of these organizations, even leading to the impression that a single organization operated under different names. Furthermore, in small urban centers, there actually was one single organization that executed the different functions of a merchant union and a civil society organization. The subject is further complicated by the varied range of words used to refer to the boycott actions, such as curse (*lanetleme*), economic warfare (*harb-i iktisadi*), cut-off (*mukataa*) and ex-communication (*aforoz*). This complicated terminology makes it difficult to evaluate the structure of the boycott organizations. However, the functioning of the boycott movement indicates that there were two distinct organizations, particularly in the centers: one organized the merchants and the workers, and the other organized the Ottoman public and mobilized the masses.

Within a short time-span, the union registered many merchants and managed to obstruct the work of those merchants who were not its members. The society, however, focused its activities on spreading the boycott movement, organizing public meetings and conferences, hanging placards and posters, distributing leaflets, and sending declarations to government offices and foreign consulates.[64]

As mentioned above, Smyrna was criticized for being a latecomer to the boycott movement. The boycotters, workers and merchants of other towns even published articles protesting that the merchants of Smyrna were implementing the boycott only reluctantly. This prompted the boycotters to concentrate on organizing the merchants and influencing public opinion, and as a result, one of the most active boycott organizations appeared in this port city. The most remarkable venture of the Boycott Society in Smyrna was publishing an official newspaper,

Gâve, the only such journal to emerge during the boycott movement.[65] According to the journal itself, *Gâve* was in Smyrna to continue a holy war: the national economic boycott against Austria and Bulgaria.[66]

As the position of workers within the boycott movement became indispensable, *Gâve* increased its support for their actions. It also changed its subtitle, substituting "Political and scientific Ottoman journal of the Boycott Society published in Izmir" with "The Ottoman journal of the Boycott Society, published in Izmir to safeguard the interests of the ship-workers, boatmen, firemen, lightermen, porters, and other craftsmen and workers." The significance and the attachment of the workers exceeded that of the merchants within the boycott movement.[67] The affiliation of the Boycott Society with the port workers was to continue after the 1908 boycott, and the boycott organization would later become an organization of port workers in 1910 and 1911.

The Workers' Boycott: Oscillating between Strike and Boycott

After a short while it became obvious that a blockade of boycotted merchandise was the most effective way of boycotting. This could be maintained through merchants canceling their orders and port workers refusing to unload the goods. The Austrian protests regarding the boycott generally concerned the port workers. The Austrians claimed that the Ottoman Empire was acting contrary to international law by not preventing the porters' actions, and argued that they could sell their products, if only they could transport them from the ports to the hinterland. However, port workers were not officers, and they held traditional rights in the ports; it was therefore not possible for the Ottoman government to order the port workers to resume unloading boycotted goods. They were one of the most organized groups within Ottoman society.

The port workers were also an influential social class during the first wave of strikes in the Ottoman Empire in the 1870s.[68] Their struggle against the modernization of the ports was successful in the nineteenth century: they resisted the attempts of the port administration to modernize, managing to slow down the process, which they saw as undermining their existence, making lightermen, boatmen and porters obsolete.[69] The port workers worked at the heart of the economic network and occupied a strategic position in economic transactions.[70] The legacy of their struggle and their group's organized character in the ports endowed them with a strong position within the boycott movement.

The strategic place of port workers in the economy became clear during the first week of the boycott movement. Austrian ships arriving from Trieste were unable to unload their cargo in the main ports of the Ottoman Empire, such as Trabzon, Beirut, Jaffa, Kavala and Salonica.[71] In Salonica, the Jewish porters were offered twice their wages to unload the Austrian ships. However, neither porters nor lightermen unloaded the cargo. Similarly, the native Bulgarian port workers in the port of Salonica refused to unload 7,000 sacks of flour arriving from Varna in a Bulgarian ship. The ships of the Lloyd Company, which frequently visited Ottoman ports, began to leave without loading or unloading. In Beirut, the lightermen did not unload the merchandise and mailbags from an Austrian ship. The governor-general went to the port in order to convince the port workers, and it was only then that the mailbags were unloaded. Another Austrian ship in the port of Jaffa was not so successful in convincing the boatmen, and had to leave the port without taking on its passengers.[72]

The Armenian newspaper *Surhantak* reported that Austrian ships and vessels were arriving at and departing from Samsun empty. The Austrian consulate in Samsun complained to the governor about the boatmen of Samsun, but did not achieve anything. According to *Surhantak*, the Ottoman and Armenian clubs and civil societies of Samsun declared that they would no longer import goods from Austria, Germany and Bulgaria.[73] At the beginning of the boycott movement, port workers sometimes made allowances for Muslim merchants who had ordered goods from Austria before the declaration of the boycott. This merchandise was considered to be Ottoman, since it had already been paid for.[74] However, in most of these cases port workers had probably been persuaded by merchants or prominent figures of the respective town. For instance, the CUP intervened in several instances in order to persuade the port workers. These incidents confirmed the power of the port workers and the committee's influence over them.

In November, the boycott became altogether stricter. The tolerance for the Austrian goods that had already been bought and paid for was a contradiction, because the sale of these goods was also boycotted. Therefore, the merchants who successfully imported their goods had difficulties in selling them. In November, the port workers created an almost complete barrier against Austrian goods with their blockade in the ports. Their action enforced the boycott movement, making Austrian goods a scarcity on the Ottoman market.

However, several leaders among the porters unloaded Austrian merchandise during the boycott movement. For instance, four wagons of Austrian sugar were unloaded by the chief of tobacco porters. For this act, he was accused of treason; the porters sent telegrams to the Ottoman press and argued that they had been cheated by the Austrian merchants. In another case, the steward of customs for dried fruit, Ramazan Ağa, unloaded 150 sacks of Bulgarian cheese. He was condemned for this act and obstructed by two stewards from other docks, Mustafa Ağa and Hasan Reis, and their fellow workers. Yet, these two cases were only exceptions. If Austrian merchandise was found to have been unloaded by mistake, it would always be reloaded before its owner could move the merchandise from the customs, as once happened in the Sirkeci train station in Eminönü, Istanbul, where porters carried Austrian goods back to the train which had brought the merchandise into the city. Their commitment to the boycott movement made port workers popular national figures. The Ottoman press frequently praised them in news items and articles.[75]

Port workers were also active in detecting and inspecting merchandise that arrived in the Ottoman ports. There were many instances in which Ottoman porters and lightermen found Austrian goods hidden among other goods belonging to countries such as Britain, Italy or France. In one case, Kürt Ali Ağa, the head of the Istanbul porters, got angry at an Italian company that had hidden Austrian goods amongst its own shipment; he firmly stated that his porters would not unload the merchandise of this company, unless they fired their clerk. The porters also reloaded the cargo of the Italian company.

Leon Papazyan, the owner of the Mamulat-ı Osmaniye (Ottoman Products) shop, tried to convince the porters that the stove he had imported was a German and not an Austrian product, but was unable to persuade them. Numerous discussions and spontaneous negotiations took place between port workers and merchants in the harbors of the Ottoman Empire regarding whether merchandise was Austrian or German. The lightermen and porters were distrustful of any merchandise bearing German labels and reluctant to unload it.

The power of porters and lightermen increased in the ports over the course of the boycott movement. The Istanbul correspondent of *The Times* argued that public opinion feverishly supported the boycott and that neither the government nor the CUP could put a stop to it. Ali Ağa visited several Ottoman newspapers and claimed that merchants were trying to pass off Austrian merchandise as coming from other countries, denouncing them to the Ottoman public. A Greek steamship carrying Austrian merchandise was prevented from unloading its cargo and passengers, first in Istanbul and then in Trabzon. The ship returned to Istanbul where, again, neither passengers nor goods could be unloaded. Piles of merchandise from Austria appeared in many ports, as the port workers refused to touch them.[76]

The leaders of the port workers in Samsun also visited the local newspaper *Aks-ı Sada*. Two prominent figures among the boatmen there, Rıza Kapudan and Rauf Ağa, announced in the newspaper office that they would continue to boycott in a strict manner. The newspaper presented them and their fellow porters and boatmen to its readers as "Heroes of the Boycott."[77]

The lightermen of the Trabzon port sent a telegram to the Ottoman press describing how different transportation companies hid Austrian goods among their cargo. They declared that they would do everything to prevent Austrian merchandise from entering the Ottoman Empire.[78] The newspapers, which supported the actions of the port workers and published their telegrams, nonetheless warned them not to harm international trade, which might be against Ottoman interests. Port workers announced in their declaration that they were only obeying the orders of boycott organizations such as the Boycott Union. Yet they claimed in their telegrams that people wearing *kalpaks* had tried to deceive them by exchanging Austrian trademarks for Italian or German ones. Thirty-two lightermen signed a document warning the lightermen of other ports about these tricks.[79]

Port workers kept a close watch on political developments and carefully read the newspapers. They sent replies to newspapers whenever allegations were published against them. In some cases, they demanded that editors comment on their telegrams or events related to them. For instance, it was claimed that Ali Ağa, one of the most influential leaders of the port workers and the boycott movement, had started to collect money from the docks of Anadoluhisarı, Galata and Beşiktaş, as well as several theater companies, said to be in order to compensate the porters for their losses during the boycott. The port workers repudiated this allegation and took pains to make sure the Ottoman public did not believe such claims.[80]

Port workers also formed a network between different ports, communicating effectively with each other during the boycott movement. This network facilitated their mobilization and encouraged them to act. They utilized modern communication facilities not only for building the network and social movement, but also for congratulating each other. For instance, the porters and boatmen of Kala-i Sultaniye sent a telegram with their compliments to the chief steward of the porters and boatmen of Salonica. In this telegram, which was published in *Sabah*, the port workers of Kala-i Sultaniye considered themselves a significant part of the commercial war.[81]

The popularity of the port workers grew as the boycott movement gained power among the Ottoman population. The sympathy they acquired during the boycott movement revealed itself during a meeting that had been organized against the political designs to annex Crete to Greece. The appearance of the port workers at the meeting triggered excitement and thrilled the crowd that had gathered in the public square. The articles and commentaries in the newspapers and the people's treatment of the port workers were indicators of their rising popularity.[82]

This rising popularity increased their power in the ports. The Ottoman government, which was trying to come to terms with the Austrian government, forced port workers to relax the boycott.

However, the port workers refused to do so until the Austrians accepted the terms dictated by the boycotters. Clearly, different social and political actors had their own agendas in the boycott movement. The CUP and the Ottoman press in general supported the port workers' stance. The newspapers emphasized that the port workers were not employees of the state and could not be blamed if they chose not to work and earn money. They were poor and refused to earn money only because of their patriotism.[83] The official journal of the CUP, *İttihat ve Terakki*, reminded its readers that it was only the stewards and foremen of the port workers who could order them to work. The official journal of the Boycott Society, *Gâve*, also criticized the Ottoman government and repeated similar arguments, referring to the port workers' independence.[84] However, the foreman of the Istanbul porters, Kürd Ali Ağa, stated that it was the nation itself that had organized the boycott. Accordingly, the boycott could only come to an end if the Ottoman parliament endorsed the concessions that Austria would accept. Ali Ağa also asked for the approval of the parliament to be published in the Ottoman press.[85] In this, the port workers presented themselves as the representatives of the nation and the true interpreters of national interest.

The popularity and the position of the port workers in the boycott movement enhanced their power before the Ottoman state. Therefore, the state had to take a different path from the approach it had employed against the strike wave of August and September 1908. The government considered strikes as a threat to the public order and tried to repress them by force.[86] It was more difficult for the Ottoman government to control the port workers after the boycott movement. It should be underlined that the government referred to the port workers' actions during the boycott movement as "strike," whereas the port workers themselves referred to their strike-like actions as "boycott." Sadrazam Kamil Paşa, the Minister of Internal Affairs Hilmi Paşa, and the Minister of Zaptiye (security forces) Sami Paşa, used the words *grev* and *tatil-i eşgal* (strike) in their public statements.[87] These terms clearly point to the struggle between the government and the workers, and the significance of symbols in their negotiations. As will be explored below, the port workers realized that defending their rights under the shield of the boycott movement was an effective guard against the government. The struggle between the government and the port workers prompted initiatives in support of the workers. Apart from the articles published in different newspapers, several statements supporting the actions of the port workers were released. A number of these public proclamations were signed by several members of parliament, such as Arif Bey, Rıza Tevfik and Mehmed Salim (members of parliament for Gümülcine, Edirne and Karahisar-ı Sahib respectively). Meetings and demonstrations were also organized to encourage the boycotting activities of the porters and lightermen. Thanks to this support, the port workers were able to maintain their firm stance for the duration of the boycott movement. The minister of security visited the porters and lightermen before the gate of the Foreign Commodity Customs (Emtia-i Ecnebiye Gümrüğü) and informed them that their refusal to unload Austrian merchandise was against the law. The port workers underlined that their resistance was the result of their free will. The government could not force port workers to put an end to their actions, and the Administration of Customs (Rüsumat Emaneti), with the help of its own employees had to unload and carry the paper which it had bought from Austria.[88]

Religious cadres also issued a public declaration announcing their support for the port workers. The teachers of the Fatih Mosque (*ders-i amm efendileri*) sent a statement to *İkdam*, arguing that those who opposed the boycott movement were acting against the shari'a and patriotism (*hamiyyet*). They were praying for the porters and lightermen because of their patriotism.[89] A group of people living in the neighborhood of Dolmabahçe collected 1,059 kuruş and bought Kürd Ali Ağa a watch. The porters and lightermen of Galata went to the headquarters of the Boycott Society and renewed their oath to the boycott movement. Their act was celebrated in a public statement signed by 600 people.[90]

Interestingly, a merchant by the name of Monsieur Solari thanked the port workers who boycotted him. He managed to unload his merchandise with a little help from several officers, but was grateful to the port workers who had refused in a polite manner, which impressed him to the extent that he offered them a cash gift. This money was then donated to the Gureba Hospital, contributing to the port workers' rising prestige.[91]

Port workers also organized demonstrations in order to show their commitment to the boycott movement and stir up the emotions of the population. In Smyrna, the port workers, both Muslim and Greek, paraded through the streets, waving flags and shouting slogans such as "Long live the boycott!" and "Long live the Ottomans!" An Austrian ship belonging to the Lloyd Company encountered the resistance of Muslim and Greek porters. The workers began to march under the leadership of Aziz Ağa, the owner of a coffee-house, and proceeded from the Cordon to the Hunters' Club, and from the European Quarter to the Yemiş Çarşısı (Dried Fruit Bazaar). They ended up in front of the government house, but quickly dispersed to the coffee-houses across from the customs so as not to create a disturbance, although a few youths tore the fezzes of a couple of people during the demonstration.[92] The porters of Istanbul organized a similar march on the customs house of Galata. They congratulated each other for their contribution to the boycott. Carrying banners and playing drums and pipes, they visited the offices of those newspapers that supported their actions. On one of these visits, a columnist of *Sabah*, Samih Efendi, addressed the workers and promised them his newspaper's continued support. He claimed that the Ottomans could only be saved if they were as patriotic as the porters.[93]

The strife between the Ottoman government and the port workers intensified towards the end of January 1909. The Sublime Porte frequently informed the Customs Administration that there was no longer a need to boycott, since the government had agreed terms with the Austrians. However, the port workers's leaders declared several times that they could only end the boycott when the Boycott Society said so. Moreover, the parliament should also endorse the treaty between the two states. They also emphasized that they did not demand any compensation for their actions.[94] Yet, in February 1909, the resistance of the port workers and their coordination across the empire started to crumble. In several ports, Austrian goods were unloaded. In İnebolu, a ship arriving from Samsun was able to unload its sugar cargo after the porters briefly hesitated; they claimed that the bill of consignment bore the seal of the Boycott Society. However, on that very same day Austrian merchants were still unable to unload their merchandise in Istanbul. The ports of the Ottoman Empire sank into chaos.[95] It was only on 25 February 1909 that the Grand Vizier Hüseyin Hilmi Paşa could convince the Boycott Society that the government would sign the protocol with Austria within a day. The following day, Rıza Tevfik, one of the most influential political figures in post-revolution Istanbul, visited the port workers in the Istanbul and Galata customs houses and declared that the boycott had finally ended. The Boycott Society made a public announcement and informed the Ottomans that they had lifted the boycott.[96]

The end of the boycott is indicative of the power of the port workers both in the Ottoman Empire and within the boycott movement. The government could only put an end to the boycott after it had managed to convince the workers in the ports. The elite of the Ottoman Empire did not risk leaving a national movement only in the hands of workers. A day after the declaration was issued, it was still not easy to bring the port workers' boycott to an end. The workers refused to unload Austrian sugar, and only when they had been forced to do so by the police commissary Sadık Efendi was the sugar carried to the shops. However, the steward of the lightermen, Mustafa Ağa, tried to prevent the porters from carrying the sugar, claiming that the Austrian companies possessed their own barges and would violate the port workers' rights in the near future. He was asked to complain to the public authorities.[97]

After the decision of the Boycott Society and the CUP to put an end to the boycott, the workers carried on with their action. Although they claimed that they were continuing the boycott, their action more closely resembled a strike. The port workers fought for their class interests over the course of the five-month boycott. As mentioned above, they tried to frame their interests within the boycott movement after their strike had been suppressed in the strike wave of August–September 1908. For the workers, it was easier to draw attention to their particular issues in the context of a national movement. In the second week of the boycott movement, they opposed the 1879 regulations that determined their wages, which were based on piece work. The workers claimed that the capacity of their barges had been increased at least twice, but that their wages had remained the same; moreover, neither the municipality nor the port administration took responsibility for their problems. The port workers threatened the merchants with a strike, but were advised by the Ottoman press to be patient. But as their popularity rose and their power increased during the boycott movement, the port workers increased their wages. The newspaper *İkdam*, which supported the port workers' boycotting actions, found the new wages unfair. The port workers sent a reply to *İkdam*, arguing that a 20 percent increase was indeed fair, and mentioning that their costs had increased and that they had abstained from strike-like actions, which they defined as *serkeşane* (disobedient). They blamed the port administration and the Chamber of Commerce, which did not negotiate and agree terms with the workers. They legitimized their demands within the framework of the boycott movement, presenting their patriotic stance as a proof for their loyalty to their country. However, their demand for wages equal to those of the Dalmatian boatmen was considered illegitimate and refused by the Maritime Chamber of Commerce.[98]

Apart from their demands regarding wages, the port workers also asked for reform in their own organizations. Most of these demands were to do with the elimination of foremen, the stewards of the port workers who occupied the higher ranks of the guild bureaucracy. These were generally the *kahyas* and *kethüdas* and acted as referees amongst the port workers, or between the state and the workers. They had the right to punish them or even ban them from work.[99] These high-ranking officers in the guild organizations frequently abused their position and rights, and their privileges allowed them to dominate over the port workers. Therefore, the port workers took advantage of their increased power during the boycott movement by attempting to eliminate these men. For instance, the boatmen of Tophane and Mumhane gave a petition signed by many boatmen to the Sublime Porte, asking the government to fire İmdad Efendi, the *kethüda* of the boatmen. The government ordered the Ministry of Maritime Affairs to deal with the problem.

The customs porters tried to prevent the reassignment of Şaban Kahya to the post of the stewardship of porters. They marched to the Sublime Porte, requesting the withdrawal of his appointment. Accompanied by an officer, they were sent to the municipality. On another occasion, the lightermen wrote an open letter to the port administration to complain about Davut Ağa, the *tahsildar* (tax collector), who, as they claimed, oppressed the workers. The porters of Sirkeci also submitted a petition signed by 200 persons to the municipality, asking for Süleyman Kahya to be replaced with Ramazan bin Ömer. Their petition was accepted by the municipality.

After the boycott had ended, the lightermen of the Yağ Kapanı Dock submitted a petition to the grand vizier claiming that they had good reasons to carry on with the boycott. They denied the accusation that they were exploiting the boycott movement for their particular interests, and claimed that they had repudiated Austrian offers many times. They had two distinct claims regarding the boycott movement: first, the boycott was the result of their own free will. Therefore, it was up to them to decide when the boycott would end. Second, they referred to their traditional rights and the rights that they had obtained thanks to "freedom." They legitimized their demands within the framework of the constitution and the ideals of the new regime, claiming that their rights were curtailed under the yoke of *istibdat* (autocracy). As a result, their social and economic position deteriorated in comparison to that of foreign lightermen. They had to be content with secondary jobs and left the field open to the lightermen of foreign companies. Therefore, they were merely defending the rights that the constitution had bestowed on them. Furthermore, they referred to the rights that they had acquired since the reign of Mehmed the Conqueror (1444–7, 1451–81). Therefore, they not only invoked their constitutional rights, but also traditional historical rights that they had inherited from the past. The lightermen's document was signed by the prominent members of the guild and endorsed by the *tahsildar* (tax collector) of the Yağ Kapanı Dock to prove that the signatures were not forged.[100]

This lengthy reasoning reveals that the port workers were very conscious of their rights. However, Turkish historiography generally presents the protests or the reactions of the guilds and laborers as pre-modern remnants. This study argues that the port workers and their guild organization transformed themselves in this process and employed various kinds of argumentation in their discourses. Their network and traditional characteristics not only survived in the course of the nineteenth century, but also adapted to contemporary social and political developments.

The porters of the Istanbul customs house also entered into a dispute with the port administration. The workers claimed that the administration was trying to eliminate them from the port, despite their having worked there for centuries. During this long history, they had paid great sums to the administration. They also asked why the administration had in fact recognized their existence and their centuries-long traditions before. In a public notification, they declared that they would defend their legitimate rights against the administration with their blood. Their struggle was for the livelihood of the *amele-i milliye* (national workers). However, Istanbul's port workers did not defend the rights of the Armenian porters, who had been eliminated from the ports during the 1895–6 incidents. In 1829, during the abolition of the Janissary Corps, the Muslim porters had been eliminated from the ports for being their grassroots supporters. They were replaced mostly by Armenian porters who had already worked in the ports. However, after Armenian revolutionaries seized the Ottoman Bank in Galata, the Armenian porters were replaced by Kurdish ones. During the massacres of 1895, many Armenian porters were eliminated from the customs. The remaining Armenians had left the port due to excessive taxation.[101] After the promulgation of the constitution, Armenian ex-porters tried to return to their posts, but the present porters did not allow them to do so. The Muslim porters defended the new regime and the constitution, but refused to admit the Armenian porters who were also victims of the *istibdad*, the ancient regime. On this account, they resisted both the municipality and the Armenian patriarchate.[102]

As a result, the port workers gained a strategic position in the boycott movement. This position and their actions, which were presented to the Ottoman public as patriotism, secured them great popularity. They tried to take advantage of this popularity to reinforce their social and economic position in the Ottoman ports. They were successful in many cases and managed to eliminate several of the high-ranking guild members. They also tried to fortify their position in the customs house against foreign lightermen or porters, demanding wages equal to theirs for the same workload. They rejected temporal and provisional offers from foreign companies and tried to achieve structural change instead.

To this end, the port workers made use of the boycott movement. The traditional network between the Ottoman ports facilitated their mobilization process. Their organization functioned well in their fragile relationship with the Ottoman state, the foreign consulates, foreign companies, the port administration, the CUP, and the merchants. They were well aware of their organizational and economic interests, as was the case in the 1908 strike wave.[103] They utilized various means to achieve their goals. Port workers in the different ports of the Ottoman Empire had a positive relationship with the local newspapers. This relationship contributed to their popularity and strengthened the legitimacy of their sectional demands. Their good relationship with the CUP was another crucial element in their rising power. They constituted the street force of the Unionists during the Second Constitutional Period. However, they should not be considered servants of the committee. Süleyman Kani İrtem has asserted that it was Ferit Bey who established the relationship between the porters and the committee in 1908 and during the boycott movement.[104] According to İrtem, Ferit Bey stated at the outset of the boycott that the port workers should receive economic support in order to guarantee their loyalty. He wanted to save money for the workers through the Boycott Fund. The Boycott Society issued "Certificates of Boycott" and sold them to merchants; these certificates released them from the boycott. İrtem has claimed that Ferit Bey, as a member of the CUP, took money for the workers.[105]

Although the port workers had a strong network, widespread public support and good political relationships, they were not able to realize all their aspirations, particularly the economic ones. Thus, just after the end of the boycott, in early March 1909, they went on strike. The lightermen announced that they would strike in order to resist those Austrian, Russian and Italian companies that used their own barges and undermined the port workers' monopoly. Upon this declaration, a meeting was convened by the Maritime Chamber of Commerce, which also involved the representatives of shipping agencies. A commission was formed in order to deal with the issue, and it was decided to send a memorandum to the minister of commerce and public works, Gabriel Efendi. Meanwhile, with the end of the boycott movement, unity between the port workers started to crumble. A fight took place between the porters of the Yemiş Dock and the Çardak Dock. Many were wounded in this altercation. The Ottoman press, which had supported the workers for five months, considered the workers' new decision to be dangerous. The lightermen gave the foreign companies a week-long ultimatum to leave their barges under their control. Otherwise, they would go on strike. However, they did not mention the word "strike," but instead used the term "boycott." The foreign agents replied with a threat of their own: if the workers started a strike, they would boycott the Istanbul port. The port workers repeated their demands and argued that their only desire was to be treated equally to foreign lightermen. They gained partial success in this process, coming to an agreement with the Russian and Italian companies.[106] The port administration and the Ottoman government attempted to limit the number of port workers and thereby weaken their power in the ports. However, the port workers argued that such schemes were contrary to the principles of free trade, and sent a protest to the government and the Ministry of Public Works, containing 1,400 signatures. The government sent soldiers to the customs house, but did not attack the workers because of their peaceful demonstrations.[107] The workers' popularity made the authorities unable to suppress them.

Merchants during the Boycott: The Weakest Link

Ottoman merchants were considered a significant social element in the boycott movement, since it was they who imported Austrian merchandise into Ottoman domains. Besides, they were a vital component of the Ottoman economy. One of the ultimate goals of the boycott movement was to reinvigorate the national economy. Therefore, the boycotters asked them to stop importing boycotted items and instead to try to produce them within the Ottoman Empire. As a result, the genuine boycott (*hakiki boykot*)—that is, the development of the native Ottoman industry and economy—might materialize. It was thought that, if the merchants gave their support, the boycott's impact on Austria and Bulgaria would take hold more rapidly, at which point the actions of the port workers and the consumers would become unnecessary.

However, the Ottoman merchants, both Muslim and non-Muslim, were the weakest link of the boycott movement. Those who had business with Austrian companies were likely to lose out due to the boycott; on the other hand, a boycott was probably beneficial to those who imported goods from a competitor country. Therefore, during the boycott movement, boycotters and boycott organizations had to force Ottoman merchants to act in accord with the movement. Merchants who had good relations with the CUP and social links to national organizations were in favor of the boycott. Initiatives, public announcements and Ottoman merchant organizations grew up in order to transform the boycott into a widespread movement. They expected to earn a fortune from their relationship with the national political cadres and their engagement with the national movement. However, those who did not have direct links to the CUP and the boycott organizations were not particularly eager to adhere to the boycotting rules, unless the boycott movement provided an economic opportunity. This is why the boycotters were obliged to monitor and compel the merchants to obey the boycott regulations.

There were many merchants who tried to circumvent the boycott movement. Many Ottoman merchants were hard-hit by the port workers' boycott of Austrian shipping companies. They were advised to use Ottoman ships for import and export, but the capacity of the Ottoman shipping fleet was not enough to fill the gap. Merchants who had difficulties finding cheap transportation broke the boycott regulations. Nevertheless, the Boycott Union, which had been established in order to organize the merchant class within the boycott movement, became influential in a very short time span and made progress in enrolling merchants.

As mentioned above, Austrian merchandise which had already been bought by Ottoman merchants was considered Ottoman at the very beginning of the boycott movement. The boycotters allowed merchants to import Austrian goods for a certain period of time, as long as they had been ordered before the declaration of the boycott. The announcement of the boycott caused apprehension among the merchant class, and one merchant in Salonica wrote to the journal *Bağçe* to ask what he was to do with his Austrian merchandise. For him, to boycott these goods was to boycott the Ottomans themselves. According to the journal, Ottomans could only buy those goods if the Ottoman merchants could guarantee that they would no longer import anything from Austria or Bulgaria. This reply reveals the lack of trust between the boycotters and the merchants. There were rumors of merchants who continued to bring in goods from Austria under different titles. Therefore, *Bağçe* wanted merchants to put an end to their complaints and not to bother the Ottoman public opinion.[108] To consider the Austrian goods that were already bought as Ottoman was a theoretical solution to the problems of the Ottoman merchants. The mobilization of the Ottoman public was organized against this merchandise, and recognizing legitimate Austrian goods was practically impossible. The "Fez-Tearing Feast" highlighted the inconsistencies of this odd solution: Austrian fezzes that had already been paid for, and as such could be considered "Ottoman," were publicly torn on the streets.

One of the earliest boycotting calls on the part of merchants was made by a few big trading houses in Istanbul. This announcement was followed by a public notification from several merchants in Salonica who declared that they had already canceled their orders from Austrian factories. They also posted their declaration on the streets of Salonica. The text of this announcement, together with a call for a total boycott of Austrian and Bulgarian merchandise, was also published in the newspapers.[109] A group of prominent Muslim and Armenian residents of Karahisab-ı Sahib (Afyon) sent an open letter to *İttihad*, announcing that they would boycott even those who broke the boycott.[110] The *attar* (essential oil or perfume) traders of Konya convened in the Şeref Hotel and discussed the future of their profession. They decided to participate properly in the economic war against Austria and claimed that there were many Austrian goods among the merchandise coming from Smyrna. Merchants were advised to import from Britain in order to prevent cheating.[111]

The Ottoman press wanted Ottoman merchants to join the merchants who worked for the boycott. With most of the merchandise it was very difficult for the Ottoman people to understand which commodity was Austrian and which was not. Therefore, it was the merchants' duty to indicate the goods to be boycotted. They were also invited to inform on each other and expose those who stored Austrian merchandise in their warerooms.[112] The newspaper *Tanin* recommended that merchants establish an organization in order to regulate the boycott in the economic sphere. The Boycott Union was the result of such an initiative. Like the merchants of Istanbul, the tradesmen in Salonica, Kastamonu and Beirut canceled their orders. After a couple of weeks, the Austrian press claimed that the first excitement of the boycott movement had calmed down. These claims were met with several telegraphs from Ottoman merchants of various towns, which stated that they would never buy from Austria again. The purpose of these reactions was to indicate that the boycott was in progress and to stimulate a new impetus for the boycott among the Ottoman public.[113] The Muhabbet-i Milliye Ticaret Komisyonu (Love of the Nation Trade Commission) in Trabzon announced on 12 October that they would not buy from boycotted countries or transport with their shipping companies. Like the merchants of Konya and Trabzon, the notables and tradesmen of Bodrum convened a similar meeting. The meeting ended with the same conclusion: the boycott of the two countries.[114]

The merchants who organized themselves within the framework of the boycott movement continued their meetings, and this might have evolved into meetings of the Boycott Union. However, the commitment of the merchants to the boycott was quite different from the devotion of the port workers. In one of their meetings in the Merchants' Club, the Salonica merchants debated how they could contribute to the expansion of the boycott. They sought much more developed ways to restrain corruption and the tricks of businessmen. However, they criticized the blockade of an Italian company by the port workers when, as described above, the company was boycotted because of the Austrian goods hidden among its cargo. In the meeting, the merchants stated that this was a result of over-enthusiastic patriotism, and decided to warn the port workers.[115] Two different social classes within the boycott movement had different perceptions of boycotting. Merchants who imported goods from countries other than Austria and Bulgaria promoted the movement. For instance, Petro Papasoğlu announced in the newspaper *İttihad* that he had started to import fezzes from Belgium only to compete with the Austrians. He wanted the Ottomans not to confuse them with the Austrian ones and underlined the fact that he did not encounter any difficulty in the customs, which proved that his products were legitimate and deserved to be consumed.[116]

Market prices started to increase after the declaration of the boycott, particularly of basic consumer goods such as sugar. It was claimed that the rise was the outcome of the boycott, which had caused scarcity in the market. It was also seen as a consequence of the greed of merchants who had stockpiled goods in order to sell them more expensively; this second claim represented another way of profiting from the boycott. The most significant import item from Austria was sugar. Its prices increased by at least 15 percent after the boycott began. The Ottoman press accused the merchants of not being patriotic when a national movement was taking place, and expressed the view that they expected nationalist traders to decrease their prices in order to support the poor, particularly for the approaching Ramadan feast. According to the Ottoman press, such merchants were identical with the Austrians, and deserved to be boycotted. It was claimed that there were only 15 merchants who imported sugar from Austria. Ten of them were non-Muslims, and only 1 Muslim out of 15 tried to seek an alternative to Austrian goods. The press called on the merchants to unite and not to increase prices, but to boycott the Austrians.[117]

Therefore, the Ottoman press had reservations when it came to the Ottoman merchants. *Aks-ı Sada*, a newspaper in Samsun, compared them with the port workers and argued that the merchants did not entirely adhere to the boycott movement. According to the newspaper, the merchants were storing goods, thereby increasing the prices on the market. Moreover, they did not try to import goods from other places in order to decrease prices. *Aks-ı Sada* argued that people were infuriated about this situation, and there were rumors of attacks on shops that were said to be full of Austrian goods. This statement was like a threat to the merchants of the town.[118] The influence of the press on society increased over the course of the boycott movement. For instance, *Aks-ı Sada* continued to voice criticism of the merchants who were nothing but speculators. The newspaper claimed in one of its issues that there were merchants in Samsun who had imported goods from Austria and hidden them in their shops, and that the newspaper knew their names and addresses. Such news coverage made several of the merchants anxious and forced them to make a public statement about their merchandise. A native merchant, Kefelizade Asım, wrote to *Aks-ı Sada* and confessed that he had imported and had been able to unload Austrian merchandise. He claimed that he had paid the price before the boycott and had done everything he could to return the goods to the producer. He promised the Ottomans that he would donate the profit he earned on these goods to Ottoman educational institutions. Although he asserted that he had not violated the boycott rules, he nevertheless felt obliged to spend money for the public good.[119] For him, it was the only way to preserve his legitimacy.

Similar to Kefelizade Asım, Hacı Mustafa and Hüsnü Efendi visited the office of the newspaper *İttihad* and confessed that they had imported sugar from Austria. They too argued they had ordered the sugar before the boycott, and were fortunate in successfully convincing the journalists. Kemal Caferi Bey, whose name was publicized as that of a traitor, also confessed that he had 278 sacks of sugar in his shop, and he too asserted that these had been imported before the announcement of the boycott. These confessions reveal that the boycott movement and the threats of inspection had their impact on the merchant class. Kemal Caferi Bey promised not to import Austrian goods again. His sugar was seized by the boycotters and he was saved by enrolling in the Boycott Union. He donated eight sacks to the hospital in order to repair his ruined public image.[120]

These merchants were not alone or exceptional; many Ottoman merchants found themselves between a rock and a hard place. The owner of the Kramer beerhouse was mentioned as traitor. After he had been denounced as an unpatriotic Ottoman, Kramer announced that he was ready to fulfill all the obligations dictated by the Boycott

Society, and would even break off old relationships. Kramer signed a commitment letter for the Boycott Society, and *İttihad* advised him to post the advertisements of the Boycott Society on his window in order to protect him from boycotting activities. As a result, a tradesman who had a long-standing relationship with Austrian firms was obliged to cut all ties. Another company, Arara ve Mahdumları, also rescued itself by joining the Boycott Society. Meanwhile, rumors began to circulate that might have emerged as a result of competition. For example, it was claimed that the Papa Dimitriyu brothers were importing Austrian goods. However, the Dimitriyu brothers had a good relationship to the boycotters, so it was immediately announced to the Ottoman public that the Dimitriyu brothers were reliable and trustworthy. Hayim Franko made use of his affiliation with the boycott movement as an opportunity for advertisement, proclaiming that he had only British and Italian goods in his store. The certificate of the Boycott Society on the door of his shop also proved his patriotism, and therefore consumers had every reason to buy from him. A group of merchants from Aydın also wanted the merchants of Smyrna to prove their loyalty to the boycott if they wanted to continue to do business in their town.[121] Israil Salomon was accused of importing Austrian goods. He refuted the allegations and claimed that his merchandise had been approved by the Administration of Customs, as they were of German and not of Austrian origin. He underlined that he was a "truly Ottoman" (*cidden ve hakikatten Osmanlı*) merchant. His goods had been inspected by the merchants' commission. The accusations were a result of illiteracy, but his honor was under suspicion. He promised to burn all of his merchandise before the Administration of Customs, if someone could prove that they were of Austrian origin. Moreover, he assured that he would donate 1,000 lire for the public good.[122]

Several other merchants informed the Ottoman public about cheating traders. These denouncements were made in order to demonstrate their loyalty to the boycott, with perhaps the added motivation of advertising their names and trademarks. For instance, the owners of the Louvre Store announced that the glassware generally thought to be Italian actually came from Austria; this was appreciated by the

Ottoman press. Likewise, the İpekçi Brothers proclaimed that Austrian manufacturers were proposing to send merchandise via the Austrian postal service, as if they were samples. The İpekçi Brothers warned Ottomans to be distrustful of these kinds of tricks; their behavior presented an ideal role model.[123] However, lack of trust between the merchants and the boycotters resulted in a number of inspection initiatives. One of these initiatives was launched by the Bosna Hersek Cemiyet-i Hayriye-i Osmaniyesi (Society of Bosnians), another in the Anatolian provinces, including Bursa. They offered a prize to those who informed them of the addresses, trademarks and methods of merchants who brought Austrian goods into the Ottoman Empire. The society would also meet the expenses for denouncing their names to the Ottoman public.[124] The controlling mechanisms expanded as the boycott progressed, and merchants accused each other of raising prices or importing boycotted goods. Moreover, as mentioned above, the merchants of different towns blamed each other. Similar to the merchants of Aydın, a group of merchants in Kavala sent a telegram to the Ottoman press, claiming that the tradesmen of Smyrna were indifferent to the boycott movement. This is why Smyrna became one of the centers on which boycotters started to concentrate.[125]

Merchants from different provinces announced that they would no longer work with the Austrians, even two or three months after the beginning of the boycott. This might appear to be a contradiction, since it meant that they had continued relationships prior to their announcements. Yet these public notifications were made to indicate that the boycott was still ongoing. Merchants usually convened a meeting and decided to issue a declaration signed by each participant. This kind of news was used to create the impression that the boycott was expanding throughout the empire.[126]

The boycott movement tried very hard to organize the merchants within the boycott. Its ultimate goal was the flourishing of the national economy, which was defined as "genuine boycott." However, numerous clashes occurred between boycotters and merchants. In many towns, the port workers refused to work for those merchants who were claimed to be bringing in Austrian goods and whose shops had been attacked by activists. For instance, in January 1909 many incidents occurred between boycotters and merchants. In these incidents, merchants were attacked by groups of people, and their merchandise was returned to customs. Merchants who resided in towns where the port workers were less powerful, such as Babaeski and Tekfurdağı, were luckier. Merchandise that arrived via train was transported to the towns of the interior by cars.[127]

Thus, the merchants, who were considered the most crucial element of the national economy, did not as a social class entirely dedicate themselves to the boycott movement. Social classes do not act *en bloc*, and always comprise several distinct categories, based on societal, cultural, ethnic, religious and regional differences. Therefore, those merchants who had well-established relationships with Austrian business circles were reluctant to act in accordance with the boycott movement. Merchants who felt safe or free of risk did not hesitate to trade with the Austrians. Meanwhile, merchants who were engaged in the national movement, and sought to make their fortune through it, remained loyal and worked hard for the expansion of the boycott movement.

The Popularization of the National Economy

One of the crucial aspects of the era after the 1908 Revolution was the rise of the idea of the national economy and the prelude to concrete national economy policies. It is apparent that an economic activity such as a boycott would have a significant impact on these thoughts and policies and, vice versa, would have been influenced by them. Therefore, it is not a coincidence that the nucleus of the national economy thesis and policies can be detected in a social movement that emerged in the immediate aftermath of the revolution. As a popular movement, the boycott influenced all sections of Ottoman society, and different symbolic, ideological and political demands related to the national economy appeared in the public sphere.

One of the controversial issues of the 1908 boycott to occupy the minds of the boycotters was the durability of the movement. The boycotters were aware that it had to end someday, and therefore it was crucial to improve the native industry, in order to rescue the empire from economic dependence. They tried not only to persuade Ottoman consumers to buy native and "national" commodities, but also "national" merchants to invest in industry. Although protectionism and building a national industry through high tariffs was not discussed, the boycott movement opened up the argument that the Ottomans should produce their own commodities in order to replace foreign ones.

Thought regarding the national economy that appeared during the boycott movement can be placed in two categories. First, there was the tendency to stop buying or even using Austrian goods. It was argued that they should be substituted by native equivalents, whatever the ultimate consequences. According to this attitude, Ottomans were expected to choose local goods, even if the quality was poor and the price high. Boycotters encouraged Ottomans to buy Ottoman goods, claiming that people would get used to wearing the native *külahs* instead of Austrian fezzes, even if this type of headgear might seem strange at first. If sugar was scarce in the empire, then Ottomans should replace it with honey or molasses. On behalf of their *hamiyyet* (patriotism, public sprit), Ottomans should tolerate untidy clothes and inferior goods. Otherwise, the Austrians might easily mislead and deceive the Ottomans by resorting to political and economic tricks.[128] This tendency was not widespread and can only be detected in the emotional articles written to mobilize the populace. An example would be the Greek journal published in Smryna, *Amaltheia*, which stated that to buy foreign goods was to finance the bullets of the enemies used against the Ottomans. It argued that even buying from friendly countries (such as England and France) was not sufficient for the boycott. The ultimate goal should be the development of the domestic industry.[129]

The second category was a much more moderate stance. Its advocates also wanted the Ottomans to produce their own goods, but with reservations: they objected to the use of rudimentary and inconvenient commodities that were considered inappropriate for Ottomans. The ultimate goal was that Ottomans should find native substitutes for the boycotted merchandise or produce these goods domestically, but the manufacture of these native equivalents or the invention of national commodities was not possible in the short term. Therefore, for example, French and English sugar could be bought, even if it was much more expensive. Russia was also referred to as an important alternative country from which merchants could import sugar. Merchants began to import goods such as cotton, sugar and matches from Russia, and this development pleased the boycotters.[130] This classification is presented here to facilitate an understanding of the different positions that emerged over the course of the boycott movement. This never appeared as a conscious debate, with two sides and advocates in the public sphere; these were only two different attitudes and suggestions related to the national economy at the time.

The demand for the development of a domestic economy and indigenous industry can be defined as a transition period. These goals had always existed in Ottoman economic thought, even before the 1908 Revolution. There had been preliminary attempts to create an industry in the Ottoman Empire in the nineteenth century, although they did not culminate in an industrialization process.[131] The motto of classical liberalism, *laissez faire, laissez passer*, maintained its hegemony in the economic thought of the Ottomans. Yet, after the 1908 Revolution, during the rule of the CUP, *étatisme* and protectionism started to gain favor among the elite and the population. The 1908 boycott movement emerges as a significant link between these two eras, and as a crucial transition period.

However, during this period it was frequently underlined that commerce was free and that all should respect it as such. Moreover, the state should not intervene in the boycott movement and the economy; calls for protectionism through high tariffs were scarce. On the other hand, the Ottomans began to think about the development of the Ottoman economy, as it was widely accepted at the time of the boycott movement that it was hard to compete with the European economic powers via economic means. At this point, various non-economic methods entered the scene. Emphasis was put on the mobilization and education of the Ottoman public, and the movement provided an opportunity for this cause. Because of the boycott, debates about the national economy, which had previously been confined to textbooks, became widespread in the public sphere.

Therefore, in order to deal a blow to Austrian commerce, the Ottomans began to think about producing the previously imported goods within the empire.[132] As an alternative to damaging Austrian commerce in the short run, manufacturing commodities in domestic industries was praised as "genuine boycott" by the boycotters and the Ottoman press. Moreover, the need for governmental encouragement, support and help for the Ottoman economy became a popular issue in the debates on the national economy. The Greek journal of Smyrna *Amaltheia* wanted the government to be active in creating and consolidating national industries, calling on the citizens to encourage and even force the government.[133] The economic patriotism that the boycott brought to the agenda and that popularized domestic products was considered an opportunity. Faruki Ömer declared that such an opportunity did not happen every day, and it was up to the Ottomans to take advantage of it.[134] Historiography on Turkey views WWI as a significant occasion for the national economy to come into existence. Yet the boycott movements starting in 1908 were also a crucial political and cultural incentive for the merchants and tradesmen to contribute to the national economy.[135]

The boycotters and the Ottoman elite attributed little significance to direct state investment. For them, it was not the lack of capital that caused the under-development of the domestic industry, but rather inconvenient political and social circumstances, the lack of entrepreneurial spirit, scientific know-how and skills in society. Thus, during the boycotts of the Second Constitutional Period the Ottoman press addressed the wealthy, encouraging them to invest.[136] In its articles on the boycott, the newspaper *Anadolu*, published in Konya, expounded on the need to build factories. The articles on the economic condition of the province, written by a reporter who had toured throughout Anatolia, emphasized the need for mechanization and industrialization. For him, the production of the world-famous Uşak carpets was heavily impaired because of counterfeiting and speculation. Development of trade and industry was considered sufficient to remedy the situation. *Anadolu* was also concerned with the financial aspect of industry, claiming that an economy without finance was nothing but "shooting without powder," or "navigation without current or wind." For *Anadolu*, the financiers should be "honorable," "high-esteemed" and "virtuous" persons. Muslim identity was not counted among the characteristics of a financier, since the atmosphere of fraternity among religious communities was still strong: the emphasis on Muslim identity would become crucial only after 1910. The Ottoman Bank was illustrated as a negative example, while the newly established Konya banks were cited as productive initiatives for the national economy.[137]

The relationship between the Ottoman Empire and Austria was occasionally evaluated in terms of dependency and exploitation. The journal *Musavver Geveze* argued that 50 percent of the goods that were imported from Austria were in fact Ottoman products. It claimed that Europeans bought commodities such as wool and cotton which the Ottomans despised, which allowed the Austrians to buy them for nothing, yet they processed and refined them, only to sell them back to the Ottomans at inflated prices. Since the Ottomans were unable to produce independently to meet their needs, they were obliged to buy from foreigners.[138] This reasoning would have an important place in Turkish political thought and intellectual history.

Articles appeared in the Ottoman press addressing the youth, advising them to work for the construction of factories, even if they did not have sufficient capital. Famous foreign companies and success stories that had started with a small amount of capital were given as examples. The under-development of the domestic industry was also the result of the population's unfounded dependence on foreign goods. The newspapers argued that, if the Ottomans preferred native goods, then both existing and newly established factories would develop rapidly. The view that the Austrian Lloyd Maritime Company prospered thanks to the Ottoman ports, passengers and money was frequently used to support this argument. Preferring Ottoman merchants, establishing Ottoman businesses, encouraging Muslim entrepreneurs, tolerating temporary shortages, and keeping money within the empire all became current issues during the boycott. As a result of the boycott movement, an Austrian shop in Tünel/Istanbul was closed; the newspapers called on the Ottomans to continue their boycott by opening an Ottoman shop in place of the Austrian one. This was pointed to as a possible future course and the natural outcome of people's patriotism.[139] A group of 50 young Ottomans convened a meeting and formed an organization called *İktisadiyun Fırkası* (Economy Party) in Smyrna.

They held a meeting in Karantina and shot a group photograph of themselves wearing white fezzes. The photograph was also printed as a postcard to propagate the boycott in the Ottoman Empire.[140]

A couple of days after the announcement of the boycott, people gathering around foreign shops in town centers and the appearance of various types of headgear made the boycott more visible and concrete in the public sphere. The first explicit advocation of the use of native products was an open letter sent to *Sabah* by the Menfaat-i Millet Cemiyeti (Committee for the Benefit of the Nation). In this letter, Ottoman goods were defined as "holy," even if they were primitive. On the same day, *Anadolu* called on the people of Konya to buy Ottoman goods, if they were patriotic enough to do so.[141] In many articles and news items, Ottoman merchandise were described as "sacred," and "pure," whereas Austrian goods were mentioned as "rotten," "inferior" and "corrupt."[142] The Smyrniot Greek journal *Ergatis* defined Austrian stores as "damned places."[143]

The alternative types of headgear that appeared in place of the fez became the symbol of the boycott movement and the national economy. The Austrian-made fez was initially replaced by a fez made in Feshane or Hereke, the fez factories of the Ottoman Empire. Yet, as mentioned above, different hats appeared on the streets, such as the *arakıyye*, the *keçe külah*, the white fez and the *kalpak*. Many state officers announced in the newspapers that they had started to wear a *kalpak* instead of a fez. Postcards were sent to offices of the central administration, advising them to wear the new *serpuş-ı milli* (national headgears) in the parliament's opening ceremony. The Ottoman government also approved of the *kalpak* as an alternative to the fez and allowed the officers to choose one or the other.[144] Following the government's permission regarding the choice of headgear, there was a public debate on the headgear of the bureaucrats, and the state imposed new dress regulations on its officers. The *kalpak* became mandatory for policemen.[145] *Amaltheia* claimed that the Greeks had already exchanged the fez for the new hats. Even the Greeks in the provinces had started to wear the *kalpak*, according to *Amaltheia*.[146]

These debates and the official change to the dress code clearly demonstrate the effect of the boycott and the motivation it created among the masses. *Tanin* welcomed these new developments with the slogan "New Fezzes for New Turks."[147] The idea of using new hats was also a way of competing with foreign economic powers. The Ottoman press claimed that the Austrians knew nothing about the *kalpak* and the *keçe külah*; the Ottomans, on the other hand, were accustomed to these hats, which had existed in Anatolia for centuries, and this fact was to facilitate their production. It was also easy for merchants and artisans to give these hats a national character. The Ottomans were at an advantage in terms of the market competition related to these new hats.[148] This is why the new headgear was greeted by the journal *Musavver Geveze* with the following sentence: "Against the red fezzes of the *istibdat* (autocracy), the new era of liberty has the white fezzes."[149]

Edhem Nejat proposed the invention of a "national headgear" in the form of the *kalpak*. The main focus was on competing with the Austrians, so it was one or the other, and the Ottomans should find for themselves a hat that would facilitate their economic development. Ancient types of headgear, such as the *arakiyye* and the *külah*, might easily be adapted to become the national hat. It was no coincidence that the term *icat* (invention) entered the vocabulary of the Ottoman elite in this regard. Like Edhem Nejat, in his articles on the history of the fez Ahmet Rasim also referred to the concept of invention during the boycott movement. For him, it was easy to invent a style of headgear compatible with Ottoman taste. The newly emerging hats were evidence of this search. Mühendis (engineer) Nevres underlined the significance of the invention of a national headgear in writing an analysis of the development of the Ottoman national economy.[150]

It should be noted that the fez went hand in hand with the notion of invention in the course of Ottoman history. The fez is a typical example of the "invention of tradition" in the Ottoman Empire.[151] It was adopted as official headgear in 1823 by Sultan Mahmud II, and it ended up becoming the symbol of "Turkishness" all over the world. It was introduced to the Ottoman Empire as a requirement of modernity, but ironically enough, was abolished in the Republican Era, again as a necessity of modernity. The alternative hats that appeared during the boycott movement were ancient types of headgear which had almost disappeared from daily life in the Ottoman Empire.

The boycott movement created "new necessities which were handled by the old models."[152]

However, the fez and other headgear were not the only merchandise with which the boycotters dealt. The Ottoman press and the boycott organization tried to alert the Ottoman public regarding other Austrian goods such as swords and medical equipment. Detailed information about the Ottoman factories appeared in the Ottoman press. For instance, it was reported from Manisa that half of the population was already wearing the *kalpak* or *keçe külah*, and that a local firm, the *Manisa Mensucat-ı Dahiliye Şirketi*, was producing better fabrics than its European counterparts. Initiatives to establish businesses and factories started to appear frequently in the Ottoman press. A revived Konya vermicelli factory proposed to provide rice for the troops stationed in Konya, rather than importing it from Trieste. A group including *ulema* and merchants announced that they were thinking of building a factory in Konya. Existing factories, such as the one at Hereke, also wanted to take advantage of the atmosphere created by the boycott, and increased the number of advertisements in the newspapers.[153] The atmosphere created by the boycott movement paved the way for initiatives regarding investments. To this end, an organization called Mamulat-ı Dahiliye Teavün Cemiyeti (Domestic Products Aid Society) was founded in Smyrna. The ultimate goal of the organization was to encourage this atmosphere.[154] The Osmanlı Kibrit Şirketi (Ottoman Match Company) was also established in Smyrna, with the aim of relieving the Ottoman Empire from its dependency on foreigners. The necessary machinery and equipment were ordered on 26 November 1908, and it was announced that its construction would finish within one month. The company also declared that it would donate 4 percent of its revenue to the CUP.[155]

The advertisements and the content of the announcements started to change with the 1908 boycott. Ottoman companies underlined that they were selling the products of the motherland. They emphasized that they were national businesses and could protect consumers from the tricks of foreigners. Foreign businesses also made public proclamations in order to distinguish themselves from the Austrians. Several of these foreign companies declared their nationality and hung their national flags over their windows. For instance, the Olympus Palace in Salonica published an announcement that covered the entire back cover of the journal *Bağçe*, stating that they were not selling Austrian beer. The advertisements of the Hereke factory and shops that sold Hereke products appeared on the pages of the Ottoman newspapers and journals.[156] Being Ottoman became fashionable, and this laid the foundations for the rise of the national economy.

The boycott movement also aimed to develop Ottoman businesses and organizations in the service sector. It was declared that those who continued to send or receive their parcels via the Austrian postal services would be exposed to the Ottoman public.[157] However, the increase in the demand for Ottoman postal services caused problems, since the national service was not sufficient, but demand continued to increase throughout the boycott. People's complaints regarding the problems they faced in using the Ottoman postal services resulted in the government appointing additional personnel to Mersin; similar demands for the development of the Ottoman Post Office came from Samsun.[158] These complaints indicate the boycott movement's impact on the emergence of a national economy in the Ottoman Empire.

During the boycott movement, the Ottoman government tried first to limit and then to put an end to the boycott actions. The mobilization of the masses on the streets and the actions of the port workers infuriated the political elite. However, they were also using the movement to ensure a compromise with the Austrians. The boycotters, on the other hand, demanded a final concession between the two states, which would be ratified by the Ottoman parliament. On 26 February 1909, the day of the signing of the agreement between Austria and the Ottoman Empire, Rıza Tevfik, one of the prominent political figures of the time, announced the end of the boycott in the ports. The following day, the press announced this declaration to the public. The Boycott Union also stated that the boycott had ended without the ratification of the parliament. The protocol was approved on 5 April 1909. The port workers tried to prolong the boycott movement, but their strike-like actions also halted in March 1909. The boycott finally ended, only to re-emerge again in autumn of 1909, for a short while, against Greece. The Cretan Question triggered a reaction among the

Muslim population, and the 1908 experience had taught them about an effective means for their cause. Yet, a strong boycott movement against the Greeks, and against non-Muslims in particular, emerged only after 1910. Then the Ottomanist boycott movement transformed itself into an effective tool used for the elimination of Christians from the Ottoman Empire. The events and processes following 1910 are the subject of the subsequent chapters.

CHAPTER 3

THE SHIFT FROM FOREIGN TO "INTERNAL" ENEMIES, 1910–11

During the 1908 boycott movement, a boycott against Greece was proposed following the declaration of the Cretan Assembly in favor of unification with Greece. This proposal worried the elite of the new Young Turk regime because it was the height of the 1908 Revolution and such an act against Greece would probably damage intercommunity relationships in the Ottoman Empire, which had a significant number of Greek citizens. The prominent figures of the boycott movement, and particularly the CUP, did not want to risk the newly created atmosphere of fraternity. Nonetheless, the Young Turk regime had significant problems both with Greece and the Ottoman Greek community. The 1908 elections, for instance, revealed this tension between different communities and the political groups representing them.[1] The boycott movement of 1908 did not include Greece as a target, a decision that was helped by Greece's attitude, as it did not dare to affirm the proclamation of the Cretans.[2] Therefore there was no boycott called against Greece at that time, although there was rather a weak call for one.[3] Still, the Cretan Question persisted as one of the pressing issues during the Second Constitutional Period. This is why during the autumn of 1909 a boycott against Greece related to the Cretan Question returned to the agenda.[4]

The Cretan Question

The Cretan issue emerged as a diplomatic question after the independence of Greece in 1829. Over the course of the nineteenth century, numerous riots and upheavals in favor of a union with Greece occurred in Crete. The concessions that Crete received from the Ottoman Empire did not diminish the struggle of the Greek Cretans and the tension between the Christian and Muslim inhabitants of the island. The Pact of Halepa gave semi-independent status to the island under the rule of a Christian governor in 1878. However, the Ottoman Empire was unable to control the island, and the 1896 revolt paved the way for a war between Greece and the Ottoman Empire. Although the Ottoman Empire won the war, Crete became an autonomous state under the administration of Prince George of Greece, thanks to the intervention of the Great Powers.[5] The tie between Crete and the Ottoman Empire was only a diplomatic recognition of Ottoman rights by the Great Powers; in practical terms, the island was detached from the empire.

The Cretan Question remained one of the important issues for Greek and Turkish nationalists. The Ottoman Turkish press informed the public about the incidents in Crete after the 1896 revolt, and a mobilization took place in the Ottoman Empire to lend support to their co-religionists. However, the administration of Abdülhamid II did not allow this mobilization to grow, and the propaganda on the Cretan Question was left in the hands of the Young Turk movement in exile.[6] The Greek Cretans' dissatisfaction with the rule of Prince George culminated in the 1905 Therrisso Uprising, which was also an indication of the rise of Venizelos (a Cretan leader) in Greek political life.

After the 1908 Revolution, the Cretan Question became one of the prominent issues in the Second Constitutional Period. The boycott against Greece and the Greeks came on the agenda in May 1910, and did not disappear again until November 1911. In 1910, Cretan officers were officially asked to take an oath of allegiance to the king of Greece. In May, the deputies of the Cretan Assembly also took an oath of fidelity to the king of Greece. However, there were 16 Muslim deputies in the assembly, and they refused to do so, causing a political and diplomatic crisis which only passed when the assembly was suspended. This prompted a great reaction in the Ottoman Empire, and hundreds of meetings were convened in towns all over the empire in order to protest against Cretan Greeks and Greece. These mass meetings prepared the ground for a boycott at the end of May 1910. Furthermore, in April 1910 Crete elected Venizelos to the Greek parliament, and this also had repercussions in the Ottoman Empire. The election of Venizelos to the Greek parliament by Attica in the August 1910 elections and his becoming the prime minister of Greece in September 1910 gave the boycott a new impulse.[7] The final political and diplomatic crisis that triggered a reaction in the Ottoman Empire and affected the boycott movement was the crisis in the appointment of *kadıs* (Islamic judges) to Crete. The Cretan Greeks refused to accept the Ottoman Empire's right to appoint a *kadı* there. In May 1911, this issue became a political crisis and was utilized by the boycott movement to galvanize the emotions of the Muslim people in the Ottoman Empire. The Cretan Question could only be solved after the Ottoman Empire's defeat in the Balkan Wars and after *enosis* had been made reality and endorsed in diplomatic circles.

Meetings, Direct Actions and the Mobilization of Society

The proclamation of the boycott against Greece coincided with a general wave of meetings regarding the Cretan issue in most urban centers across the empire. A number of these meetings were spontaneous and vibrant, while others were officially organized and contrived. Between May and June 1910, the newspapers were filled with reports regarding these meetings, about how they were convened, who gave speeches, what the speakers said, and how the meetings had been organized. The mobilization process that they triggered made a crucial contribution to the boycott movement, galvanizing the nationalist sentiments of Muslim public opinion in the Ottoman Empire. The mobilization consisted of direct actions, volunteer enlistment initiatives, agitation and an upsurge of emotions. This national atmosphere paved the way for the boycott, for picketing, the obstruction of economic activities, and blockades.

Traditional Turkish historiography has framed these kinds of meetings as spurious undertakings of the CUP or the Ottoman government, but a general look at this mobilization process depicts a different scenario. In several towns, meetings were organized with the direct support of the CUP, but elsewhere the level of mobilization instilled fear in the elites, the members of the CUP, and particularly the Ottoman government. The elites tried to constrain the meetings and the mobilization of the masses in these particularly passionate towns.

One place where such a meeting was held was Manastır. There, Ferid Bey, a prominent member of the CUP, publicly criticized the meetings, underlining their "fatuity," which he said was entertaining Europe. His speech was received with displeasure. This meeting is significant for the analysis of the boycott movement, because it produced the first public plea for a boycott against Greece. It was convened in the Place de la Liberté (Hürriyet Meydanı), and sent a telegram to the government, demanding that it issue an ultimatum to Greece and threatening a general boycott of Greek merchandise. The British consul, Arthur B. Geary, claimed that the meeting had been organized by the CUP, yet Ferid Bey's speech indicates that there were different views among the members of the committee. Delegates of different nationalities convened at the municipality.[8]

As mentioned above, there were hundreds of meetings in almost all provinces and towns of the Ottoman Empire. In most of these meetings, the crowds gathered in a central public place and sent telegraphs to the governors, the Ottoman government and foreign embassies, protesting the political developments regarding Crete. The reading of these telegraphs consumed a significant amount of time in the Ottoman parliament. Therefore, the parliament decided to read only the names of the towns that had sent the telegraphs.[9]

The speeches during these meetings were delivered in different languages. For instance, in Üsküp the speeches were in Turkish, Bulgarian, Serbian and Spanish, but according to the British consul they were exact translations of each other. This gives the impression that the meetings were organized by a particular political power. From the Üsküp meeting, we can infer that tensions between different communities also had an impact, as Albanians were not invited to the meeting in this town.[10]

In a large open-air meeting in the Place du Dix Juillet (10 Temmuz Meydanı) of Salonica, several thousand people gathered to protest the Cretan issue, but the Bulgarians refused to attend. The meeting was an orderly one, since it was officially organized by the Union and Progress Clubs. Yet, the British consul—like consuls in other towns— underlined the fact that most of the crowd was comprised of the lower classes. A few hundred people came from the neighboring town of Langaza. According to the report of the British consul, everything was pre-arranged, and after a short while the crowd quietly dispersed. In addition to the government and the foreign embassies, the meeting also sent telegrams to the mayors and the *ulema* of Pristina, İpek, Dakova, Ghilan and Prizren. These very telegrams might have prompted similar meetings in those towns. Furthermore, similar meetings were held in Drama, Serez, Kavala, Katerina, Tikveş, Avret Hisar and Langaza. In Resne 4,000 people gathered in order to protest the oath of the Christian Cretans.[11]

A protest meeting was convened in the courtyard of one of the principal mosques of Edirne, where about 2,500 persons participated in the demonstration. As was typical, the participants included the head of the Muslim community, a member of the local branch of the CUP, and representatives of the non-Muslim communities, such as a Bulgarian teacher, the secretary of the chief rabbi, and a Greek grocer.[12] The participation of non-Muslims in these meetings was also a confirmation of their Ottomanness. *İttihad* congratulated a merchant in Denizli, Dimiloğlu Mihalaki, who gave a speech at a meeting in which he claimed that Crete was the honor of the Ottomans.[13]

These meetings were held in order to draw the attention of the Ottoman public to the Cretan Question and to provoke the mobilization of the ordinary people on behalf of the national cause. Therefore, a year later, when the boycott began to be applied in a more severe way, another similar meeting was convened once again in Edirne. Four thousand people were present at this meeting, where a Turkish lawyer, an Armenian teacher, a prominent member of the Jewish community, and a Kurd addressed the crowd. The British consul claimed that it was more an organized meeting than a spontaneous expression of popular opinion. Moreover, he claimed that the municipal police visited the bazaars and shops in order to "invite" people to the meeting.[14] It was evident that a new stage in the boycott movement coincided with a mass meeting.

In Beirut on 25 May 1910, like in many places in the Ottoman Empire, a large crowd congregated in one of the main streets, carrying banners with slogans such as "Crete or Death." Similar to other meetings throughout the empire, rather temperate speeches were delivered. Only Sheikh Mustafa Galayani threatened Greece with war, a siege of Athens and the capture of King George. According to the report of the British consul, the people gathered in the square did not show much enthusiasm. The meeting dispersed after several telegrams had been sent to the embassies, the ministries and the grand vizier. Similar meetings were held in Sidon and Haifa. The British consul underlined the support of the government officers in organizing these meetings.[15]

It was thought that these meetings were organized following the instructions of the Ottoman government, which wanted to enhance its position concerning the Cretan Question. The British consul stated that the meeting in Damascus had an "air of artificiality" and, therefore, "a large proportion of the crowd which had been shepherded with flags and bands from the poorer quarters of the city, dispersed long before the 'speeches' were over."[16] His choice of terminology should be underlined; the derogatory attitude of consuls towards the actions of the lower class and the people in general are the main reason for considering the boycott actions as a conspiracy of the government or the CUP. This mentality was prevalent amongst the Ottoman elite, and dominates today in the circles of historians who write on these issues.[17] The Greek periodicals in the Ottoman Empire and Greece also employed a similar reasoning in their evaluation of the boycott movement. For them, a nation should not hand over its official policy to a flock of porters. *Embros* (an Athens newspaper) argued that after the promulgation of the constitution in 1908, the claim that freedom is nothing but an empty cry became prevalent in the Ottoman Empire. It was only the Young Turks who employed such methods in Europe, and it was only in Turkey that the weapon of the boycott became very popular.[18]

In some towns, these gatherings worried the Ottoman central bureaucracy. A telegraph sent by the meeting convened in Mihalıçık/ Ankara threatened the Ottoman government: condemning the acts and claims of the Greek king on Crete, the leader of the meeting, Necib, stated that they had started to enlist volunteers in order to fight those who wanted to take Crete from the Ottoman nation. They would meet with the citizens at the Sarıköy train station and not depart from the telegraph office until they received a definite word of assurance concerning the Cretan issue. That was not all; he also declared that the volunteers would seize the Sarıköy train station. The Ministry of Interior Affairs warned the governor of Ankara about the volunteers and a prospective seizure of a train. The governor appeased the Interior Ministry, saying that the crowd had already dispersed thanks to the operations of the local governor and the gendarmerie sent to the town.[19]

The Ottoman government was usually interested in the meetings that triggered the mobilization of the masses, or direct actions, or at least claims of a potential loss of official control on society. Thus, when the meeting in Kula/Aydın declared that they would form a large unit in order to get rid of and punish those who irritated and terrorized the Ottomans, the government wanted the governor to stop such initiatives.[20] Most of the meetings lasted one day, but in some places, their duration and number increased in a short time. In Margiliç/Yanya, the meetings took off with drums and flags and continued with enlisting volunteers, but did not come to an end. After three days of mobilization, some of the volunteers planned to march toward the center of the province, and the excitement and agitation continued at a high level. The governor-general ordered the local governor (*mutasarrıf*) to disperse the people by force if necessary and wanted him to reassure people that the government had the power to defend Ottoman Crete.[21] It is not clear if the crowd in Margiliç was dispersed by force, but that was definitely the case in Kuşadası/Aydın, where the gendarmerie used bayonets to disperse a crowd who blockaded a Greek ship in the port.[22]

The commander of the gendarmerie in Limni/Cezayir Bahr-i Sefid was not as fortunate, since the soldiers under his command were not eager to disperse the crowds. The officers were afraid of an assault on the non-Muslims of the town and wanted to stop the boycott mobilization. Yet, the crowd that had already gathered spat in the commander's face.[23] The officers had reasons to fear such an assault since such instances occurred in other towns of the empire. For instance, the Greek community of Jaffa was attacked during a meeting about the Cretan issue.[24] However, the gendarmerie officer in Limni was harshly criticized by the daily press in Salonica, particularly by the newspaper *Rumeli*, which had formerly condemned the excessive acts of the boycotters.[25]

The mobilization during the meeting in Adapazarı did not subside quickly either, so the Ministry of the Interior requested the *mutasarrıf* to move from İzmit to Adapazarı in order to deal with the masses. The *mutasarrıf* informed the government that the excitement had died down after he had contacted the local governor (*kaymakam*) and the notables via telegram, but the central government was not satisfied with his reports and sent him to Adapazarı. The report that he sent from Adapazarı clearly depicts the mobilization of different segments of society. At first glance he had realized that the town was full of peasants, but it was not only the peasants or the lower ranks, but also the town's notables and prominent persons who had met in order to demonstrate on behalf of the Ottoman Empire's rule in Crete. The emotions of the crowd were galvanized, yet thanks to the imam's calming sermon during the Friday prayers, the 30,000 people acted in a restrained manner. However, although the meeting in general was temperate, the crowd's decisions were daring and audacious: if the government showed any kind of weakness in defending Crete (which was claimed to represent the honor of the Ottomans), the people would stand up and take action.[26]

As mentioned above, the enlisting of volunteers emerged in different parts of the empire during the meeting wave of 1910. These initiatives and newly formed organizations tried to communicate with each other, but did not develop into a full-fledged society, due to the government's undertakings. A telegraph regarding the enlistment initiatives was sent to Diyarbakır from Trabzon, signed by the leader of the Trabzon Volunteer Society (*Gönüllü Cemiyeti*) on behalf of the *müftü* and the mayor.[27] (The Volunteer Society was formed on the day when 30,000 convened in Trabzon.) The same telegram was also sent to Erzurum. By informing the other towns about their enlisting activities, the people of Trabzon called on these other towns to do the same. The governor of Erzurum, Celal, warned the government that this type of initiative might agitate the populace, and the Ministry of the Interior asked the local officers why they would permit such telegrams to be sent.[28]

The ministry also warned the post, telegraph and telephone administration regarding these types of telegraph, the latter informing the former that after a meeting in Konya many inciting telegrams had been sent to different parts of the empire.[29] One of these telegrams had been received by a meeting convened in Smyrna. The meeting in Konya launched an initiative to raise funds for the enrolment of volunteers for a war with Greece, and the president of the Konya committee invited the *müfti* of Smyrna to start a similar movement. The telegram informed them that 50,000 volunteers were ready to march against Greece on behalf of their 50,000 co-religionists in Crete, and they were begging the people of Smyrna to join them. This call was met with great enthusiasm: the meeting in Smyrna replied that the entire Muslim population of the province of Aydın was ready and had begun to form volunteer battalions.[30]

The meetings held in the towns of the province of Aydın sent telegrams to the government and the newspapers of Smyrna, informing the public that they were enlisting volunteers. These initiatives were not anonymous, as the telegrams were signed by the heads of similar organizations. The commander of the national troops in Manisa, Sülayman Sırrı, wrote that they had already formed a volunteer battalion and were ready for a military mobilization.[31] The head of the Volunteer Society, Tevfik, wrote to the government that they had started to enlist volunteers in Urla.[32] The telegram of the commander of the national battalion of volunteers in Nazilli was very detailed: Sadettin Bey reported the number of volunteers and their commanders for each district of Nazilli. He mentioned eight different districts (such as Yılara, Arpaz and Kuyucak) and claimed that the total number had reached 3,985 volunteers in a very short time.[33] Enlisting initiatives also took place in Denizli, Foça-i Atik and Menemen.[34]

The same telegram was also sent to Diyarbakır by Emin Efendi, the president of the Konya Volunteer Committee, on the same day. The governor-general of Diyarbakır summoned a meeting of Muslim and Christian notables, as well as the mayor and the *müfti* of the town. It was held at the municipality building and it was decided to ask the government's view on the issue. The government informed the governor-general of Diyarbakır that they were working to maintain Ottoman rights and that volunteers were not needed at that moment.[35] The most active volunteer committee was the one in Konya, which tried to control volunteer enlisting activities in Edirne as well. The British consul of Edirne informed the embassy that the meetings of the volunteer committee in the town were held at night and that a considerable number of people had already enlisted. He was informed that a telegram from Konya had asked how the movement was proceeding in Edirne. The answer was that Edirne was in a position to furnish 40,000 volunteers.[36]

An enlistment initiative also occurred in Serez/Salonica; the notables of Serez visited the governor of Salonica in order to learn whether the government had given its consent. The government replied quickly, banning any kind of activity.[37] A similar event took place in Çatalca/Edirne, where a committee had been formed and had started to organize volunteer units. A number of these volunteers also applied to the local government in order to be sent to any prospective war. The Ministry of the Interior warned the *mutasarrıf* of Çatalca that the government was not in need of volunteers.[38] A volunteer organization also appeared in Manastır, and it was claimed that the initiative had received the consent of Niyazi Bey. This volunteer initiative went hand in hand with the boycott mobilization.[39] Most initiatives seemed to fizzle out after the first excitement; yet the British consul of Smyrna informed his ambassador that the enrolment of volunteers in the province was still ongoing and that there was great enthusiasm among the Muslim population. Feverish meetings continued to occur in Manisa, Denizli and Nazilli.[40]

Boycotting was a weapon used during peacetime, but this does not necessarily mean that it lacked violence. In different types of boycott movements across different countries, various forms of violence have occurred repeatedly. Although the main goal of boycott movements is to persuade the public to abstain from consuming certain merchandise, often other types of obstacle are also employed: picketing and ostracism are the main enforcement vehicles and these may be performed either in peaceful or violent ways. Both vehicles were utilized during the Ottoman boycott movements, particularly in eliminating certain merchants from the market.

Tellals (public criers) played a significant role in proclaiming and publicizing the boycott at first. However, they were used not only to announce the boycott, but also to watch the boycotted shops and guard the picket lines in later phases of the movement. The latter function was crucial, since the main announcement of the boycott was done anyway by the periodicals and the publications of the Boycott Society. *Tellals* made the declaration of the boycott audible in public places with their cries, and monitored the boycott with watchful eyes.

References to such *tellals* mostly appear in the complaints of the Greek Orthodox community. The Greek Orthodox patriarchate complained about the boycott in Akhisar/Aydın in order to attract the government's attention to the problem. It claimed in a telegram that the boycott had been announced by the public criers and that it was the Ottoman Greek shop-owners that suffered the most, having to shut down their stores.[41] In Erzurum, it was the public crier who announced the meeting held before the Government House. As was the case in many towns, the mayor, a cadet and a non-Muslim representative spoke about and condemned the encroachment on the territorial integrity of the empire.[42] Similarly, it was *tellals* in Preveze/Yanya who declared that the boycott against Greek ships was to begin after 9 June. The head of the porters at the customs house had declared the boycott to the trade agencies, but the announcement was done publicly by criers.[43]

After the *tellals* had proclaimed the boycott, it was the turn of the boycott movement's watchmen, who tried to ensure that Greek shops would be ostracized. In most places, they used coercion and threats whenever they felt it was necessary. Watchmen appeared in front of Greek shops, particularly in the Muslim quarters of Smyrna, keeping customers away from the stores. Greek shops were also marked by particular signs so that the Muslim public could easily recognize them as such.[44]

Cretans emerged as a street force against the Greek shops, particularly in the port cities of the Mediterranean such as Smyrna and Antalya.[45] Bands of Cretan Muslims marched through the streets of Smyrna and compelled the Greeks to either shut down their stores or renounce their Greek citizenship.[46] If they refused to do so they were beaten. One one occasion, Cretans who had gathered at the port to prevent communication between a Greek steamer and the shore annoyed the Greek consular dragoman, who lost his temper and fired three shots toward the Cretans, thereby weakening the position of the Greek consul with the boycotters and the Ottoman government.[47] In Antalya, Muslim Cretans entered several Greek shops, telling the owners that they had started the boycott, and mobilized other Muslim artisans and merchants against the Greeks.[48] In Kala-i Sultaniye, two Ottoman Greeks were allowed to disembark from a ship of the notorious Destouni Company, so that they could attend the funeral of a relative. However, when a private boat took them to Konak Square, 300 people, led by Muslim Cretans, convened to protest.[49]

A Muslim Cretan damaged the property of a Greek coffee-house keeper in June 1910. The leader of the local boatmen's guild in Beirut, Scharkawi, was arrested because of his support for this Cretan. Tension between the boatmen of Beirut and the government grew during these incidents.[50] In October 1910, a group of Muslim Cretans, who were defined as "a band of hooligans" by the British consul, blocked the Greek steamer *Elli* from docking at the quay of Smyrna; their leader Akif had even offered armed resistance.[51]

It was not only small businesses, but also banks that suffered during the boycott. The Bank of Athens in Kavala/Salonica was claimed to have been besieged by armed men who prevented customers from entering.[52] However, the *mutasarrıf* of Drama/Salonica denied this claim and confirmed only the existence of a peaceful boycott.[53] This attitude on the part of a local governor was typical during the movement, as will be discussed below. The picketing and sieges sometimes achieved their goal. For instance, a Greek leather merchant, Grigor Aleksiyu, had to close down his shop in Edremit/Hüdavendigar due to the pressures of the boycotters, and after a year diplomatic and administrative correspondence relating to his case was still continuing.[54] The picketing of Greek stores by groups of boycotters was one of the most often underlined facets of the boycott to be mentioned in the Greek newspaper *Embros* published in Athens.[55]

The Ottoman government sent a decree to all provinces about incidents of enforced picketing around shops of Ottoman citizens during the boycott, requesting that governors put a stop to these actions.[56] Before this general government warning, only the governor of the province of Konya had informed the Ministry of the Interior that they had succeeded in reopening the shops that had been forcibly shut down in Antalya.[57] However, a year later Greek shop owners were still complaining about their shops being picketed, claiming that not even their relatives were able to enter their shops. The shop of the Greek consul's dragoman was also boycotted, and the boycott was only lifted after the dragoman had resigned from his post.[58]

After the first months of the boycott, claims regarding violence and coercion occurred more and more frequently. This happened for two reasons. First, the boycott became stricter, and the movement expected a rigorous application of its rules. In general, coercion is always used to enhance consent during boycott movements, and the Ottoman boycott was no exception. Second, the victims of the boycott put forth claims regarding violence during the boycotting activities. They did so to attempt to stop the boycott by appealing to existing laws, because a boycott was legitimate and legal only if it was applied in peaceful terms. The neutral attitude of the Ottoman government was based on the boycott's peaceful character. Thus, by referring to instances of violence, the victims of the movement tried to force the government and the Great Powers to stop the boycott. The Greek daily *Embros* reported instances of attacks and coercion from the first week onward.[59]

Such a conflict between the factions occurred in Burhaniye/Hüdavendigar. Workers employed in an olive grove whose owner was a Greek citizen were attacked by a group of armed men. The local governor (*kaymakam*) refused to believe the story of this attack and informed the Ministry of the Interior that a Muslim who was afraid that his olives would be damaged had interfered with the workers, because the owner had not been around. Moreover, according to the governor, the true reason for the owner's complaint was the boycott of his grove, which he maintained had been applied peacefully. Meanwhile, in Burhaniye the olives of Trikoplidi, a Greek citizen, were purchased by a Muslim, but his workers were attacked, and this time one of the workers received a head injury. The *kaymakam* wrote to the government that it was not certain if this had been an attack by the boycotters, or a quarrel between the workers.[60] In Ulucak/Smyrna, a case of arson occurred. The owners of the olive grove there were a Greek citizen and three Ottoman Greeks, and the peasants who tried to extinguish the fire were forcibly prevented from doing so. The Greeks of Manisa could not harvest their entire crops, and the doctors and pharmacists were expelled from the town.[61] The British consul in Smyrna also made it clear that in the interior regions the boycotters made use of force. For instance, a British subject was prevented from harvesting his figs and grapes, because the boycotters were under the impression that he was Greek.[62] The Greek consul also emphasized that in the hinterland of the port cities and towns, where the power of the central government was weaker, the boycott was much stricter.[63] This was also asserted by the French consuls in their reports. Accordingly, the government lost authority and power as one travelled from the Aegean coast toward inner Anatolia.[64]

In Ayvalık, when Hacı Atnasi sold his olive grove to an Italian citizen, the farm was besieged and its workers and watchmen expelled. The *kaymakam* of Ayvalık informed the Ministry of the Interior that Atnasi had not sold the olives, but the farm, and that it should not be possible to boycott a grove owned by an Italian. There were instances in which the victims of the boycott sold their properties— such as shops, ships, farms, and the like—to foreigners in order to rescue themselves from the boycott movement. Nevertheless, in many cases the boycotters continued to boycott sold properties, if they believed that the transfer of property had been a trick. The Boycott Society expressed its suspicions regarding these sales to the British consulate in a meeting, and accused foreign embassies of protecting Greeks.[65] Hence, the new Italian owner continued to be boycotted, leading to the Italian embassy consulting the Ottoman Ministry of Foreign Affairs.

The Ayvalık boycotters also besieged Greek shops by placing men in front of them.[66] The picketing of shops in Ayvalık destroyed the Greeks' business in the region. Panaghiotti Pantaleon, who wanted to transfer his Greek Pantaleon Oriental Navigation Company to a British liability company, confessed to the British consul that "the boycott had naturally quickened his desire to transfer his property to a British company."[67] Another Greek entrepreneur, Andrico Plaska, officially named his employee Alexander Scoudamor (a Maltese and British subject) as the owner of his butcher shop. Furthermore, Scoudamor claimed compensation because of the boycott and entered his name on the list of the British Embassy. Therefore, the boycott turned an employee into a so-called shop owner in order to avoid the boycott and to claim compensation.[68]

The transfer of navigation companies also caused problems between the United States and the Ottoman Empire. The Hacı David Company was sold to a US citizen and operated under the American flag in 1909. However, the crew was Greek. On one of the company's ships, a fight occurred between the crew and recently discharged Ottoman soldiers. The fight had begun with the passengers' reaction to the low quality of the company's service, but quickly transformed into a national question. The company was notorious for their bad service and had become symbolic of the exploitation of Ottoman customers. It was claimed that the Greek crew and the captain were insulting the Ottoman people. The main actors of the boycott movement, the port workers, considered the fight a humiliation of the Ottoman nation by the company, and began a boycott against the company in January 1911 in the Ottoman ports. The US Embassy lodged a protest with the Ottoman government, but the boycott only stopped when a boycott against another American company, Singer Sewing Machines, was organized. This incident clearly shows how a mundane issue of daily life could turn into a national problem, and how the transfer of a company to a different nationality could also be perceived as a trick.[69]

The Ministry of the Interior warned the provinces of Aydın, Halep and the region of Karesi on 30 November 1910 about placing picketers in front of shops and forcibly preventing people from working. The pickets led to the Ottoman state having to pay compensation to foreign businesses, and the government wanted to put an end to these payments, hence it wanted local governors to punish such activities. This document proves that there were such cases and that the state did pay compensation for these acts.[70] However, the Ottoman state soon tired of claims for compensation, and in 1911 began to refuse responsibility for losses incurred because of the boycott.[71] The boycott movement and the position of the local governments did not change drastically, even a year later. A British citizen by the name of Charles Wilkinson encountered significant difficulties with the boycott movement. He rented a farm from a Greek called Tricoupis and continued to employ Greek workers and officers in his field. The farm was probably leased to him because of the boycott movement, and the remaining Greek workers attracted the boycotters' anger. They attacked Wilkinson's farm and wounded his workers.[72] The British Embassy warned the Ottoman government about this matter and wanted it to pay compensation for the losses. At first the local governors refused the claims, as they had done in similar cases. However, the farm was attacked twice more. Finally, the British vice-consul in Ayvalık forced the consul-general of the province of Aydın and the British Embassy to make the government put pressure on the local bureaucrats regarding the Wilkinson case.[73] After the third attack and the resulting injuries, the Ministry of the Interior wanted the *mutasarrıf* of Karesi to send a report about the inquiry, yet the local governors still did not reply with any urgency, forcing the Ministry of the Interior to write again to ask about the outcome of the investigation. The investigation was expanded from Burhaniye to Ayvalık and Edremit, and several of the offenders were arrested and the notables and prominent people in these towns admonished.[74] Although the case was considered closed, Wilkinson's farm was attacked a fourth time. This time, both crops and production facilities were destroyed and burned.[75] This last attack indicates the power of the boycott movement and the reluctance or incapacity of the local governors to deal with the boycotters.

Similarly, an Italian citizen in Ayvalık could not harvest the olives he had bought, because a group of armed men blockaded his entrance to the olive grove. The Greek Embassy continued to report acts of violence to the Ottoman government. One of these reports claimed that the boycotters had seized the crop of a farm owned by the Greek Karali, and consequently the gendarmerie took into custody 20 people who had been frequenting the Greek consulates in Kavala/Salonica and in Alasonya/Manastır.[76]

Like many nationalist boycotts in different parts of the world, the boycott organizations in the Ottoman Empire also established inspection teams in order to control whether shops were selling Greek goods. In one of these inspections in Salonica during the first month of the boycott, bottles of Greek cognac sold in a Jewish grocery shop were destroyed. The Jewish owner was also "severely thrashed" when he tried to protest, according to the British consul's report.[77]

A Russian merchant in Giresun had imported barrels of cognac from Piraeus, but the Boycott Society did not allow him to transport the cognac from the port to his shop. Boycotters told him not to remove the boxes with the barrels from the customs house, threatening to break all the barrels if he did so; when he had his own porters carry the cognac, a crowd of people attacked them, broke open the barrels and poured the cognac into the sea. Although the importation of cognac had become a public issue and the embassy interpreters and the police were there, no one could stop the crowd.[78] In communication with the government, the governor of the province of Trabzon claimed that the local police force had secured the transportation of the cognac to the shop. He confirmed that an attack had taken place, that a barrel was broken in the incident, and that he was secretly investigating this incident. This secrecy indicates that the governor was also afraid of public opinion.[79] The direct actions and assaults of the port workers were generally motivated by their defense of their monopoly rights in the ports. In the first day of the boycott, two workers were beaten because of unloading goods from a boycotted vessel and working in place of the porters.[80]

Greek newspapers from Athens were also boycotted in Smyrna, particularly in March 1911. The boycotters received information that a Russian steamer was due to bring Greek newspapers from Piraeus, which would then be distributed to the town from the French Post Office. When the newspaper vendors started to carry the newspaper packages off the ship, the boycotters attacked and confiscated the newspapers. Most of them were destroyed. However, the boycotters were not content with this attack and attacked and destroyed the shop of a newspaper dealer. The police arrived after the attack had ended and detained the owner of the shop, a Greek citizen by the name of Panos Anastasopoulos, and his employee Grigorios Kefalas, from the island of Sakız/Chios. The Governor-General Nazım Paşa expressed his regret regarding the incident and maintained that he did not approve of such actions. However, he also wanted the newspaper dealers to suspend the import of Greek newspapers from Greece at least for a while. The detained boycotters and the Greeks were released after a short time.[81]

Another similar incident that took place in Smyrna involved a British subject by the name of Fritz Vadova, who imported goods from Greece via a steamer of the then famous Austrian Lloyd company. He was unfortunate, since the new, stricter wave of the boycott movement made the merchandise questionable, even though it was carried on a non-Greek steamer and owned by a non-Greek subject. The customs duty of the goods was paid, and the boxes were loaded on the carts. However, the Boycott Committee interfered and threw the goods on the street, where they stayed for days. The governor-general ordered the chief of police to deliver the goods to the owner, but he did not fulfill his responsibilities. The British consul reported that the governor-general's orders were disregarded and that he was helpless.[82]

A German company was confronted with the Boycott Society because they rented a tugboat whose personnel was Greek. The Boycott Society forcibly obstructed the loading of the German company's wine barrels, and another 30 people prevented fish owned by another German merchant from being loaded onto a Greek ship.[83] Therefore, even foreign merchant experienced the boycott of Greek merchandise if they had any relationship whatsoever with Greece or the Greeks.

As well as *tellals*, picketing lines, coercion and watchmen, the boycott movement made use of posters, stickers, signboards and placards in order to enhance the application of the boycott and to point out targets in advance. For example, to indicate whether an establishment was Greek, the Boycott Society chalked the word "*Yunani*" on shopfronts.[84] The Bank of Anatolia also suffered from having the sign "*Yunanlıdır*" ("it is Greek") hung on its entrance. It took almost a month for the bank to get rid of the signboard on its entrance, after they put pressure on the public authorities.[85] The posters on the walls and windows of shops kept customers away and ruined the business of the boycotted targets. Within the first month of the boycott, a number of shops across Istanbul that were owned by Greeks closed down due to the absence of customers. Most of the owners complained to the Ottoman government about the offensive and humiliating posters on their walls. Dimitri Grasas closed his two shops in Beşiktaş; Filanga and Mandilas closed their wine house and restaurants; the Habiri brothers closed their grocery in Beylerbeyi; and Nikola Arayoyoani, Dimitri Borla and Nikola Galanis closed their stores in different parts of Istanbul.[86]

The owners of a drapery store in one of the main streets of Salonica ventured to erase the boycott marks on their wall. However, Kerim Ağa appeared with his men and threatened to cut the owner's throat if he dared to wash off the sign again.[87] The shop owner sought protection from the police, but decided to close his store after failing to receive any official protection.[88] The Central Boycott Committee of Salonica published an announcement in *Rumeli* that disapproved of such acts of violence (thereby confirming their existence), and also condemned writing on public walls and the imposition of boycott signs on shop windows. The Boycott Committee wanted the police forces to prevent these kinds of actions, which were not in line with the "honor and dignity of the Ottoman nation."

The newspaper *Rumeli*, considered to be the official voice of the CUP in Salonica, proposed leaving any kind of "rowdyism to the sons of Plato." The newspaper called on the public to be firm and serious and act in a polite manner. *Rumeli* even condemned persons who chalked the word "boycott" on storefronts and demanded certificates of nationality.[89] Another store was more fortunate in another incident: the owner managed to paint over the boycott mark under the eyes of the police. This was after the publication of the Boycott Society's announcement. The newspapers *Rumeli* and *Yeni Asır* approved of removing boycott marks, but also underlined the need for a "firm maintenance of the boycott against the Greeks."[90] However, in one of its declarations published in *İttihad*, the Boycott Society of Smyrna wanted the Ottomans not to buy from Greek stores that had been marked.[91] Therefore, it referred to these markings and signs as a fact.

The boycott was generally announced via public placards hung in various parts of Ottoman towns. For instance, in Salonica, at the very beginning of the boycott, a notice in Turkish and French was placed in various parts of the town. The declaration on the walls invited patriotic citizens to defend their country and defined what a boycott really was.[92] The Greek newspaper *Proodos* complained about the posters plastered all over Bursa, as well as the leaflets that were playing on the emotions of the Muslim public.[93]

Pamphlets started to appear depicting the sufferings of the Muslims in Crete. These types of publications were effective in mobilizing the sentiments of the Muslim public. *Girid Kurbanları* (Victims of Crete) was a pamphlet written by Naziktir Muzaffer which told stories about how the Muslims of the island suffered at the hands of "the savage Greeks" (*vahşi Rumlar*).[94] The dichotomy of "savagery and civilization" was frequently used in the discourse of the boycott movement. The Greeks of Crete and Greece were described as acting in an uncivilized manner, whereas the Ottomans were fighting against them in accord with the requirements of civilization.[95] According to *Girid Kurbanları*, Muslim women and children were killed "barbarously," and their murderers, who were "thirsty for Muslim blood," insulted their honor. The pamphlet narrated the escape of a group of Muslims from Greek gangs during the Greek insurrection, ending with a description of the massacre of the group and the rape of the women by the Greeks.[96]

Two other pamphlets on Crete were published in the course of the boycott movement, both on the main characteristics of the island, particularly the history and geography of Crete. *Girid*, for instance, focused on the presence of Islam and the Muslim community and their heritage on the island.[97] These types of publications attempted to construct a link between the island and the Muslim population in general.

The pamphlet entitled *Girid: Mazisi, Hali, İstikbali* (Crete: Its Past, Present, Future) was largely about the history of Crete. In addition to offering a historical narrative, the pamphlet included illustrations depicting the sufferings of Muslim Cretans. For instance, in one of these pictures a Muslim girl aged about ten was depicted with her arm cut off by "savage Christians."[98] The term *hıristiyan* (Christian) was preferred by the writers of the narrative, rather than *Rum* or *Yunani*. This usage might have enhanced the Islamic discourse of the movement. Another photograph showed an eight-year-old child whose head and legs had been wounded by Christian Cretans.[99] The news from Crete quoted in newspapers depicted similar sufferings on the part of the Muslims in Crete. It was claimed that Greeks turned mosques into taverns, killed unborn children (*cenin*) in their mother's womb, insulted Islam and humiliated and abused Muslim women.[100]

The government was still receiving complaints from the Greek Embassy concerning provocative posters in 1911. The boycott movement and the means of publicizing the targets went hand in hand. The Boycott Society generally announced the targets and goals in newspapers.[101] However, the boycott movement on the whole insisted on using posters since it made the movement publicly visible. According to one primary source, the Greek Embassy protested about the posters pasted on Greek shops in Kala-i Sultaniye (Çanakkale-Dardanelles), and the indifference of the local governor to the issue.[102] Fliers calling on the "Ottoman people" to boycott were distributed in Manastır. Although these handbills were not stamped – so they were not registered and were therefore illegal – they were openly distributed: the French consul reported that officials did not intervene.[103] These fliers were widely used to propagate the goals of the movement. The names of the Greek merchants and shops were usually announced in the newspapers, but this kind of leaflet was used to galvanize the sentiments of the public. For instance, such a handbill, disseminated by the boycotters in Kala-i Sultaniye, wanted Muslims to cut their relationships with the Greek merchants, causing panic among the Greek population of the town.[104]

A significant feature of the placards is the fact that the Ottoman bureaucracy considered them illegal. According to the Ottoman government and the local governors, placards on the walls of the shops were not compatible with the "peaceful" character of the boycott movement. Publishing lists of the names of firms and shops as boycott targets in the newspapers was not an assault, but posting placards on particular walls or windows was considered coercion and thus in many places the government wanted local governors to tear them down. For instance, the governor of Salonica informed the government that the placards posted in Serez had all been taken down, but that it was not clear who had posted them. The lists in the newspapers were generally published by the Boycott Society, which called on the Ottomans to be watchful and active, informing them of those Greek citizens whose names did not appear on these lists.[105] In contrast, the placards and posters on the walls were generally posted anonymously, and this is why it was difficult to find out who had posted them. In Serez, the placards were taken down, but no one was caught for having put them up.[106]

In Bursa, numerous posters appeared on the walls, and there was also a boycott against the Greek consul, who was not even able to find a car for his own transportation. The Greek Embassy referred in particular to the widespread placards when reporting the assaults on Greeks in different parts of the Ottoman Empire.[107] In Ayvalık, the boycotted Greeks were prevented from harvesting the olives that they had bought; this mobilization against them was achieved by means of the placards posted everywhere in the town. The non-Muslims of Ayvalık were terrorized by the placards and by being yelled at by men on the streets, leading them to request help from the government.[108] An American shipping company which suffered from the consequences of the boycott movement in İskenderun/Aleppo also referred to the placards there.[109] In Mersin, a placard signed by the Boycott Society of Mersin remained in place on the main road of the town for two days. The text of this poster was provocative and tried to incite the Muslim population against Greece, calling on them not to forget the experiences of the Muslim Cretans. According to the poster, Muslim girls were raped and mutilated, with their noses and ears sent to Athens. It also threatened those who frequented the Greek cafes, declaring that the names of these "shameless" persons would be published in the fourth edict of the society.[110]

The Boycott Society

The Boykotaj Cemiyeti (Boycott Society) and the Harb-i İktisadi Cemiyeti (Society of Economic Warfare) was founded in the first days of the 1908 Ottoman Boycott. It was organized spontaneously in the course of the boycott, and its branches were formed concurrently all over the empire. The 1908 boycott lasted roughly six months during the chaotic political atmosphere of the 1908 Revolution; because of this chaos, like many organizations that appeared in this particular era, it was not a legal society. After the introduction in 1909 of legal regulations regarding public meetings and organizations, civil societies were taken under the control of the government, and many nationalist organizations which acted on behalf of the public good were established according to these regulations. However, although the main body of the Boycott Society did not disappear following these regulations, it did not become legal either. It was present during the brief boycott of August 1909, but only emerged as a full-fledged mass organization after 1910. It was active in the main centers of the empire and had flourishing branches in numerous towns. The organization and activities of the Boycott Society were part and parcel of other national organizations—such as the Donanma Cemiyeti, the Müdafaa-i Milliye Cemiyeti, and so on. Yet, apart from those organizations, it was never legalized since its main body of operations was at the fringes of what was lawful. As mentioned above, most of the activities of the boycotters were considered part of the secret pursuits of the CUP. Although the support of the CUP, particularly its lower ranks, was evident in the boycott movement, the activists and leaders of the movement also gave their activities an official air in order to legitimize or legalize their interventions. For instance, the leader of the Boycott Society in Preveze/Yanya, Mehmet Ali Efendi, interfered with consumers as if he had an official, authorized responsibility. This state of affairs was the main subject of complaints, apart from the acts of intervention against consumers.[111]

The basic feature of the boycott, encouraging consumers to refrain from buying certain goods, was the only legal action of the movement. However, in order to obtain the loyalty of consumers, to transform the movement into a mass mobilization and to increase its effect, the

Boycott Society performed many illegal actions, which gave it a mysterious, secret and amorphous character until its demise. In most places it was dominated by the port workers and their structural hierarchy. In some centers, the young cadres of the CUP were active in its branches. The Muslim notables actively involved in national organizations such as the Donanma Cemiyeti were vigorous participants in the boycott committees of provincial towns.

The activities and the members of these different national organizations intersected in small provincial towns in particular. Over the course of the boycott movement, its opponents frequently complained about the excessive activities of Cretan Muslim immigrants and concealed support by officials and nationalist organizations. The consul of Greece in Antalya stated that the president of the local Donanma Cemiyeti, Zeki Bey, was also a prominent member of the Boycott Society. He belonged to the Cretan immigrant community, which was the most passionate social base of the movement in Antalya. The Donanma Cemiyeti, the government office and the civil registration office were close to each other, and Zeki Bey regularly moved between these offices. Therefore, when a Greek citizen decided to gain Ottoman citizenship, the boycott on his business was immediately removed. The division of labor between the boycotters and the official administration was well organized and worked fast, according to the Greek consul of Antalya.[112] Thus, the national organizations active in the course of the Second Constitutional Period supported the cause of the boycott movement. Elsewhere, the branch of the Donanma Cemiyeti in Diyarbakır put up posters in the town's most prominent places to try and attract public attention to the Cretan issue: "If they (the protecting powers) do not give us our rights, if committing an injustice they attempt to take Crete, we shall dye every side in red blood" was written on the placards.[113] The official journal of the Donanma Cemiyeti also published articles and nationalist poems endorsing the goals of the boycott movement.

The formation of the boycott committees in the provinces had different dynamics. Some of them were established as a result of the initiative of central boycott organizations in Istanbul or Salonica, while others were formed spontaneously in the course of anti-Greek demonstrations on the Cretan issue. For instance, in Ergiri/Yanya a boycott committee was organized and the meeting in the public square dispersed after its declaration. The Boycott Society in Yanya, on the other hand, had been established beforehand, and it was only obeying the orders of the Boycott Society in Istanbul.[114] The governor of Aydın was informed at the very beginning of the boycott movement that the initiative was brought onto the agenda by newcomers to Smyrna.[115] There is no exact information on how the boycott started in various places, or who the first activists were. The consul reports indicate that there were many local committees all over the empire that ordered the strict application of the boycott.[116]

The lively activities and network of the Boycott Society at the very beginning of the boycott in 1910 prompted the Ottoman government to intervene. The Ministry of the Interior wrote to the Administration of Public Security, noting that there were two boycott committees functioning as if they were formal societies, and reminding them that no such civil societies had been approved by the government and that it was therefore the duty of the state to forbid those who acted outside the law.[117] Before this decree, the Ministry of the Interior had refused to intervene with the Boycott Society at the request of the Tram Company, which had been threatened with a boycott if it refused to dismiss its Greek employees. The Ministry of the Interior stated that it could not establish contact with an illegal organization.[118] Both the Tram Company and the port administration in Smyrna continued to struggle with the demands of the boycotters to dismiss their Greek employees.[119]

Nevertheless, during the course of the movement, the government did have to communicate with the boycott organizations, but it was not consistent in doing so. For instance, in the same week when the government refused to contact the Boycott Society, it informed the governor of Beirut that it had forced the Boycott Society in Istanbul to order its branch in Jaffa to relax the boycott. However, it became obvious later that nothing had happened and that the boycott continued as it had before. At first it was claimed that the Society of Economic Warfare in Istanbul had sent an order that the boycott should be applied in the manner permitted by the government.[120] The Jaffa

Boycott Committee decided to ask the Beirut Boycott Society what to do. They stated that they would also consult the Beirut branch if they received orders from the capital. Later, it turned out that neither the Boycott Society in Istanbul nor the Beirut Boycott Society had sent such restrictive orders. The British consul in Beirut argued that the boycott in the city had started because of the encouraging telegrams of Kerim Ağa from Salonica.[121] The Boycott Committee on the island of Lemnos, which was largely composed of Muslim porters and boatmen, referred to a letter that they had received from the Kavala Boycott Society.[122] Therefore, each boycott committee maintained contact with a boycott organization in the central towns of the empire.

As a result of this network between boycott organizations in different parts of the empire, the decrees of the government became more frequent and stricter in tone. The Boycott Society tried to force various institutions to obey its boycott regulations: for instance, the Boycott Society of Smyrna threatened the Istanbul Regie Administration with a boycott if it failed to dismiss its Greek employees within five days. In November 1910, the Ottoman government was still trying to limit the movement. A telegram that the Ministry of the Interior sent to the province of Aydın argued that although the Boycott Society was neither a legal nor an official organization, it should at least be based on public opinion and the common will; but on the contrary, the society was using coercion in the application of the boycott.[123] From this it is apparent that the government was willing to tolerate a peaceful but illegal organization. However, the boycott organizations did not obey the Ottoman government, and the Ottoman state was caught between the boycotters and the Great Powers.

The most visible members of the Boycott Society were the port workers and activists who prevented trade transactions in the towns. The society's image was that of a secret committee, made up of a crowd of low-class persons. To redress this, the Boycott Society sent a declaration to the foreign consuls, saying that their organization consisted of prominent elected individuals, who were obeying international law and civilized regulations. The declaration claimed that unlawful actions were rare despite massive participation on the part of the lower classes, and this proved that the boycott was controlled by these elected committees; the rumors regarding the illegal actions of the boycotters were only Greek tales.[124] The Boycott Society in Smyrna also published declarations in the newspapers, stating that the Ottomans should not pay attention to those who acted on behalf of the Boycott Society without showing their stamped documents. The organization claimed in these declarations that those who opposed the boycott movement had recruited agents to act illegally and unlawfully in order to create a bad image for the society.[125] Rumors regarding anonymous and undated threatening letters sent to particular institutions and firms forced the Boycott Society of Smyrna to announce that they had nothing to do with these intimidations. The society wanted the Ottomans not to believe those who did not have special Boycott Society certificates.[126] Even the Boycott Society itself had to publicly disapprove of threats and coercion. However, the activities of the boycott organizations increased and expanded over the first six months of the movement. In one of its declarations, the boycott organization stated that the newspaper *Alsancak* was its official journal.[127] Furthermore, the Greek consul of Smyrna also complained about this particular journal.[128]

According to a British dispatch, the Boycott Society had three vital functions: preventing communication between Greek vessels and the shore; not allowing goods that did not bear the seal of the committee; and preventing the public from entering "Hellenic shops." The British Embassy closely watched the boycott movement, as did the other consuls, because it was affecting all foreign interests. For instance, according to a consular dispatch, Greek shops were stocked with British goods. Therefore, the Boycott Society and the British consul in Smyrna were often in contact with each other. In one of these meetings, the Boycott Society of Smyrna promised the British consul that all facilities would remain available to British trade.[129] The British ambassador in Istanbul depicted the boycotters as an "illiterate Turk of the lowest class" with a "fanatical spirit." Since the actions of the port workers played a vital role in the movement, it was considered a lower-class movement.[130] This was also an argument to belittle the movement.

In the port cities, it was the port workers who took the leading positions in the boycott organizations. However, in cities such as

Edirne, different professions also took the initiative. There, a dealer in second-hand goods who was also a prominent figure in the politics of the town was the chief of the boycott committee.[131]

The Ottoman state feared the diplomatic pressure of the Great Powers and the potential compensation it might have to pay for the losses of the merchants. The most urgent problem was unloading foreign merchandise from Greek ships and disembarking Greek passengers. The Ministry of the Interior not only underlined the fact that the Boycott Society was an illegal organization, but also wanted local governors to restrict the activities of the local boycotters, such as refusing the telegrams signed by the boycott committees, and unloading merchandise with the help of gendarmerie.[132] The telegrams going back and forth between different boycott organizations and from the central boycott societies to the branches are indicative of a strong network.

When the boycott movement entered a period of fresh intensity in March 1911, the organizations informed their dependent communities by making use of the available communications technology. The British consul in Smyrna reported that the central boycott committee of the province sent its instructions regarding the new decisions for the strict application of the boycott via telegram. In this report, the consul underlined the fact that these new instructions emanated from the general center of the organization in Salonica and, as such, it was the Boycott Society of Salonica that directed other boycott organizations and the movement in general.[133] The French consul in Smyrna also referred to the influence of Salonica over his town. He wrote to Paris that several delegates from Salonica had visited Smyrna; following this visit, the boycott, which had been quite relaxed for several months, started to become more strictly applied, and a number of violent incidents occurred.[134] Although we do not have enough evidence to prove such a claim, it is certain that there was a hierarchy among the network of boycott organizations.

Information regarding the boycott societies exists which allows us to conclude that they were organized according to the administrative units of the empire. For instance, a report by the Greek consul of Aydın, who took a close interest in the activities of the organization, stated that the Central Boycott Society for the province had resigned, so an election would be held in order to form a new one. The Boycott Committee of Smyrna was asked to nominate five people, who would convene a meeting in which the central boycott committee of the province would be elected. It was this committee that was to administer the boycott in the province.[135] This was not the first time that the Boycott Society in Smyrna had changed its administrative staff. Nine months before this election, the committee of directors had resigned due to their workload, and the committee changed.[136]

The Ottoman state tried to limit the boycott to Greek merchandise that came on board Greek ships, but the boycott societies were trying to be much stricter. The Boycott Society of Istanbul (Dersaadet Boykot Heyeti) wrote to Mustafa Ağa, the head of the porters of the oil entrepot, ordering him not to unload goods from Greek ships. They also wanted to be informed regarding any shipments loaded onto these vessels. Two days later, the society sent another telegram, requesting that the oil barrels should not be unloaded and that the owner of the goods be directed to the Boycott Society.[137]

However, the Boycott Society exhibited diverse attitudes, and had a number of negotiations with the shipping agencies. One of the shipping companies sailed under the Greek flag even though most of its share was owned by British capital. The company and the Boycott Society settled on an agreement: if the company's ships hoisted a British flag while they were entering the port of Smyrna, they would not be boycotted. This is significant because it shows that neither the Ottoman governor-general of the province of Aydın nor the British diplomatic representatives were enthusiastic about defending the rights of the company, since it was sailing under the Greek flag. When a ship of the company forgot to hoist a British flag, the boycotters blocked it from unloading at the quay, and the British consulate forwarded the company's appeal to the Greek consulate.[138]

Apart from the Boycott Society and the boycott committees, there were other organizations, such as the Boykotaj Teshilat Komisyonu (Boycott Commission for Facilities), which facilitated the boycott. These types of organization were generally formed by merchants, and issued a particular certificate that protected merchants from the boycott. This is why in different periodicals there were different signatures under the declarations concerning the boycott.[139] The first of the declarations of the Salonica Boycott Society announced that a certificate had been printed in order to avoid any misinterpretation regarding Ottoman Greek citizens who were officially exempt from the boycott. The certificates were distributed by Kerim Ağa within 24 hours of the merchants submitting their names, addresses and a description of their trade, and paying 10 kuruş.[140] The Boycott Society of Smyrna announced that the certificates were free of charge, encouraging merchants to request a certificate in order to protect themselves from the boycott.[141] The society called on merchants to request a certificate in almost all declarations published in the newspapers. The Boykotaj Teshilat Komisyonu in Smyrna operated under the umbrella of the municipality; therefore, an illegal commission acted under one of the town's major institutions.[142]

It was neither feasible, nor would it have been sufficient, to limit the access of the boycotters to the telegraph offices in order to restrict their communication and empire-wide organization. The Ministry of the Interior was still complaining about the correspondence between different boycott organizations and branches on 31 July 1911.[143] On the other hand, the newspapers were very effective in distributing knowledge concerning the boycott. The boycotters utilized the daily press in advance, in order to guide their own organization and influence public opinion. The second wave of intensity in the course of the 1910-11 anti-Hellenic boycott movement was also triggered by newspaper articles and announcements in March 1911. The local press, particularly in the towns, was very effective in disseminating and propagating the decisions of the boycott organizations.[144]

For instance, in Mudanya the port workers paid close attention to news from Salonica. The most popular boycott leader in 1910 and 1911 was the leader of the port workers in Salonica, Kerim Ağa. The boatmen of Mudanya intensified the boycott based on the news they received through the newspapers of Istanbul and Salonica, and also made contact with the boycott organizations in these centers. Therefore, the government was forced to ask these organizations to write to Mudanya, to persuade them to loosen the boycott. However,

Kerim Ağa's declarations inspired the boycotting activities of port workers generally.[145] Thus, the Ottoman government tried to put pressure on Kerim Ağa and block his entry to the quay of Salonica.

Muslims versus non-Muslims: "Our Greek Citizens are Exempt from the Boycott!"

Although the emergence of the boycott movement in 1910 was a political and popular reaction to the Cretan Question, it should be contextualized within the framework of the phenomenon of the Milli İktisat (national economy). As it will be argued in the following chapters, the national economy emerged first as a theory and started to be put in practice during the Second Constitutional Period. After the 1908 Revolution, the national economy came onto the agenda as a proposition for the development of a native Ottoman economy. However, as the political ideals of the revolution and the atmosphere of fraternity started to evaporate, the content of the Milli İktisat was Islamized. The discourse and policies of the Milli İktisat began to propagate the enhancement and advance of Muslims against the alleged hegemony of non-Muslims in the economy.

Turkish historiography considers this shift to be a result of the political aims of the Turkish elite, or the project of nationalist political organizations. Popular social movements such as the boycott uncover the other side of the story, however. These movements contributed to the nationalization of the Ottoman economy, and different sections of society played their parts within this process. As a result, it becomes possible to draw a much more detailed picture of the social origins of this political project. For instance, in the declaration of the Trabzon Boycott Committee, the first principle was "the boycotting of Greek residents in the country." The economic activities of Greek merchants came next.[146] Similarly, the Smyrna Boycott Society stated in one of its numerous declarations that the boycott should harm the interests of the Hellenes, so that they would be forced to migrate "first by their own will."[147] This indicates the boycotters' intention of eliminating Greeks from the empire, not only in economic but also in demographic terms.

Within this context, Islam, as an ethnic marker and identity, also played a crucial role, since the notables and port workers who were the main actors of the boycott movement were also Muslims. This is why both national and Islamic references were used during the boycott movement in order to justify the ultimate cause. Islamic arguments were also utilized to galvanize the sentiments of the Muslim population and legitimize the movement in the eyes of the Ottoman Muslim public. The active presence of Muslim notables and the Muslim working class within the boycott movement created a frustrated relationship between different communities of the Ottoman Empire. As a result, although the boycott only targeted Greece and its economic presence, the Ottoman Greek community started to suffer as well. The boycott became a crucial weapon in the elimination of non-Muslims from the economy in particular and the society in general.

The boycott declaration by the Boycott Society insisted on the fact that the boycott was against the Greeks of Greece (*Yunanlı*), not the Ottoman Greeks (*Rum*).[148] The notice published by the Boycott Society of Salonica in most of the town's newspapers highlighted this fact. This declaration warned the Ottoman public that "our" Greek "Ottoman fellow countrymen" were exempt from the boycott. Moreover, in order to avoid any misinterpretation, the Boycott Committee printed certificates for non-Hellenic merchants; these would be handled by Kerim Ağa, the head of the lightermen's guild.[149] However, the rumors and claims regarding the boycott of *Rums* immediately became the subject of public debate, just after the announcement of the decision to boycott. Articles in Turkish newspapers denied such claims and condemned such actions, if indeed any had taken place.[150] Yet, it was not easy to discern Greeks who were citizens of Greece from Greeks who belonged to the Ottoman Greek Orthodox community. As mentioned in the first chapter, many Ottoman Greek merchants took on the citizenship of various European states in order to facilitate their trade in the course of the nineteenth century. Following Greece's independence from the Ottoman Empire, it became one of the states that gave citizenship status to Ottoman people. Therefore, there were many Greek merchants who held Greek citizenship at the same time as being members of the Ottoman Greek community.

The Shift from Foreign to "Internal" Enemies   121

The Ottoman Greek press reacted to the boycott movement with the claim that a boycott against Greece would harm the interests of the Ottoman Greek community, and at the outset stated that the Ottoman state and economy would be damaged as well. They questioned the argument of the boycotters that Ottoman citizens were exempt from the boycott. The Greek press quoted articles and comments from the Turkish press, which stated that the Ottoman Greeks should certainly be exempt from the boycott.[151] The newspaper *Proodos* put forth three points: first, goods imported from Greece were mostly sold in the shops of Ottoman Greek merchants. Second, it was the Ottoman Greeks who generally found employment in the stores of Greek citizens. Third, the citizens of the Kingdom of Greece and the Ottoman Greeks were tied to each other not only by trade networks, but also by family relationships. *Proodos* wrote that there were many cases in which husband and wife, cousins and even brothers and sisters possessed different citizenships.[152] Therefore, the newspaper warned the Turkish press and the boycotters that a boycott against the Greeks of Greece would naturally harm the interests of Ottoman citizens. It was not only the newspapers but also Ottoman bureaucrats who occasionally warned the Ottoman public about family ties between *Rums* and *Yunanis*. The governor-general of Smyrna, Mahmud Muhtar, addressed a group of boycotters in a local club of the CUP, underlining the blood and friendship ties between Greeks.[153]

For instance, there was the confusing case of the owner of a mill in Uzunköprü/Edirne who was boycotted. He spoke mainly Greek, was only able to write in Greek, was married to a Greek woman, and operated a second mill in the neighborhood, which was his wife's property. However, contrary to the claims of the boycotters who placed notices on the wall of his mill and forcibly prevented customers from entering his establishment, he was not a Hellenic subject, but a British citizen of Maltese origin. The British consul and the governor-general of Edirne worked hard to convince the boycotters of his British citizenship. It was not until mid-November 1910 that the boycott on his mill was revoked.[154]

In another case, a small eatery close to the quay of Salonica was boycotted, based on the claim that its owner was a Greek. However, it turned out that the owner of the restaurant was the brother of the manager, who was actually a US citizen. Therefore, the boycotters came up against the dragoman of the US consul.[155] Considering these cases, it is not a great surprise to come across a family whose members each held the citizenship of a different country. In Menemen/Aydın, John Koundouros intended to purchase land for tobacco cultivation. However, his family ties made this purchase rather interesting: his brother was the president of the Cretan Executive Committee, the arch-enemy of the boycott movement. He bought a large piece of land between Menemen and Old Phocea, but in the name of his nephew Adam Adamopoulos, who was an American citizen.[156] A Greek citizen by the name of Nikolaos Haciargiriou, who lived in Antalya, applied to the Ottoman civil registration office in order to receive Ottoman citizenship because of the boycott movement. His brother Pandeli was already an Ottoman citizen.[157]

On the other hand, many Ottoman Greeks were neither Ottoman citizens nor had any official registration anywhere else, in order to avoid tax burdens. The legal status of Greeks also caused serious problems in the Ottoman parliamentary elections in 1908, when many Greeks were denied suffrage. Hence, after the declaration of the boycott against Greece, distinguishing who was an Ottoman Greek and who was not became a disputed matter. For instance, several activists who picketed the Greek stores in Antalya claimed that they were also boycotting those Greeks who were advocates of Greece, which was in itself an ambiguous claim since deciding who was working for Greece and who was not was quite subjective.[158] The Boycott Society of Smyrna complained about Ottoman Greeks who had been raised believing in the idea of a larger Greece. The organization criticized not only the *Yunanis*, but also those who had a Greek mentality.[159] The Turkish newspaper *Tercüman* accused the Ottoman–Greek newspaper *Proodos* of betraying the country, because it wrote against the boycott movement. *Proodos* replied that patriotism was not a monopoly of the majority.[160] It was not only *Proodos*, but almost the entire Greek-language press that was accused of being an advocate of Greece or the Greek national idea. Both the Turkish press and the declarations of the boycott societies claimed that the Greek-language press incited native

Greeks against the Ottoman Empire. The Smyrna Boycott Society, meanwhile, referred to the Turkish press in one of its declarations as the "true interpreter of all Ottomans."[161]

The Islamic and national discourse employed by the boycott, together with the mobilization of the Muslim section of Ottoman society, turned the movement into a conflict between Muslims and non-Muslims. Therefore, in an article published in *İsopolitia*, Harisios Vamvakas, the member of parliament for Serfiçe, brought up the concept of *müstemin* to refer to people who came from abroad and resided in the empire. Their ethnicity and religion were not different from that of the citizens of the Ottoman Empire, and they were contributing to the economy of the country. Harisios referred to the Islamic law and claimed that the *müstemin* who did not act against the interests of the Ottoman state should remain under its protection. A boycott against them was damaging to the interests of these Ottoman subjects who had intense economic and commercial relationships.[162] For him, the boycott should not be considered an outcome of patriotism, since it was harming the economy of the empire. Therefore, Harisios underlined the interrelation between Ottoman citizens and *müstemins* and tried to use an Islamic discourse in reasoning against the social movement.

Clashes between Muslim and non-Muslim communities were not absent over the course of Ottoman history. In Lebanon in particular, serious conflicts occurred between different communities during the nineteenth century. Tension between different ethnic groups also emerged after the heyday of the 1908 Revolution. Rumors of massacres circulated among different religious communities and made the relationship between communities increasingly precarious.[163] This is why Beirut and its hinterland became one of the centers of the boycott movement, where ardent instances of direct action occurred. In its first week, the boycott in Beirut was not particularly passionate. However, on 17 June 1910, after the Friday prayer, a significant crowd of people gathered in one of the main mosques of the town. Sheikh Abdurrahman Selam led a procession, followed by a man dressed up as a janissary with a sword, another holding a Koran, and two men with green banners. The march ended in a square, and several rousing speeches were given.

Although the demonstrations were in general moderate, Greek shops were forced to close and two were damaged.[164]

The Greek consul in Smyrna was also concerned about the proclamations and declarations of the boycott committees and the speeches held in clubs and mosques. He claimed that these speeches were provoking the fanaticism of the Muslims against the Greeks.[165] The French consul in Smyrna claimed that the *khodjas* in the mosques were teaching the people about why and how to boycott; these "lessons" were repeated in the speeches in the clubs and on the streets.[166] The foreign consuls were very watchful concerning the sermons in the mosques and the behavior of the religious cadres. However, regarding the mobilization of the Muslim population at the grassroots level, the Ottoman state apparatus did not pay much attention to the mosques, because nothing truly threatening occurred in or around them; only in a few instances during the boycott movement did the imams or sheiks play a part in the mobilization of the masses. Therefore, such claims were rather related with the Orientalist perspective of foreign observers. The Ottoman government was more afraid of the lower classes.

The French consul in Rodos (Rhodes) reported that the Muslim population of the island was fanatically against the Greeks and that was why they faithfully supported the boycott. The consul emphasized that even the moderate Muslims had told him that they would declare a holy war if the European states supported the Cretan Assembly.[167] The Greek community, particularly the elite, complained about the predominance of the word *gavur* (infidel) in daily life; the mobilization during the boycott movement probably did increase its usage in the nationalist discourse. Mihail Sofroniadis claimed that *gavur* was used in order to point out non-Muslims, even though the new constitutional era had promised fraternity between different communities.[168]

Posters on the Cretan problem that were hung by the Donanma Cemiyeti in Diyarbakır caused fear of a massacre among the Christian population. According to the British consul, although the Cretan Question was not a popular issue, a massacre of non-Muslims and plundering of their property might nevertheless have resulted.[169] Therefore, even a nationalist discourse based on Islamic arguments or addressing the Muslim population provoked fear of a clash between different communities.

Although Bulgaria had gained its independence, there were still tensions between Muslims and Bulgarians in both Macedonia and Thrace. Moreover, the newspaper *Embros* mentioned an economic war between Bulgarians and Turks, as these two communities did not frequent each other's shops.[170] The killings, murders and assassinations between the two communities paved the way for an undeclared boycott. The Ottoman government grew alarmed by the emerging tensions between different communities. It warned the ministries and all provinces of the empire that a discourse based on Islam or Christianity was contrary to general Ottoman interests.[171] The government warned the Ottoman public and the governors twice within the same month: although the boycott movement was the outcome of people's *hamiyyet* (patriotism), some instances of assault had taken place against Ottoman non-Muslim subjects, which had the potential to lead to a general clash between Muslims and Christians.[172] In May and June 1910, during the wave of meetings against the Cretan Assembly's oath of allegiance to the king of Greece, tension between Greeks and Muslims rose. Even in towns such as Edirne, where there was no clash or outward hostility, the relationship was no longer friendly.[173]

As a result, it can be claimed that the boycott movement that commenced in May 1910 was officially against the Greeks of Greece, but very quickly expanded to the Ottoman Greek merchants. There is significant evidence to support this claim. For instance, the Ottoman Ministry of the Interior sent a third order to all provinces, underlining the fact that the protest was indeed expanding to the economic activities of Ottoman citizens and their shops. Unlike the previous two orders, this time the ministry also wanted its order to be published by the Ottoman press.[174] The governor of Konya, in line with the Ministry of the Interior's statement, considered the boycott dangerous since it might trigger a clash between different communities.[175] In the province of Yanya, the *mutasarrıf* of Preveze was worried during the first weeks of the boycott because the population of his town was largely composed of non-Muslims, and he too feared that the boycott might lead to a clash. The government informed the governor of Yanya that nothing would be more harmful to national interests than a conflict between Muslims and non-Muslims.[176] The great majority of the town was Greek Orthodox and, therefore, a boycott against Greece was also harmful to the trade of Preveze, which depended on business relations with Greece. Thus, it was the Albanians from Margariti and the Bosnian immigrants who enforced the boycott.[177]

During the wave of meetings and demonstrations against Greece regarding the Cretan issue, a number of incidents occurred that caused much fear not only among the Greek Orthodox community, but also other Ottomans. For instance, in Kala-i Sultaniye a Muslim preacher by the name of Mehmet Efendi spoke against the Greeks and claimed that it was not only the Cretans who had sworn fidelity to the Greek king, but all Greeks who resided in the Ottoman Empire. He argued that it was a sacred duty for Turks to eliminate the empire's Greeks and that he himself would kill 20 of them. Cevad Bey (a prominent political figure in town) protested against this kind of language and withdrew from the council that had been formed to organize the meeting at which Mehmet Efendi spoke. This fanatical speech alarmed the Greek community of the town. The British vice-consul claimed that there was no genuine "patriotic sprit" among the Muslims, but that such speeches, particularly by a preacher, might cause clashes between different communities.[178]

One of the targets of the boycott were the Greek employees of various corporations and institutions. Even non-Muslims employed by the state were boycotted. For instance, in November 1910, the Ministry of the Interior sent a warning to the governor of Aydın concerning the boycott of a non-Muslim state official in İnegöl, considering this action improper.[179] The most visible aspect of the boycott movement was the picketing of Greek shops, which caused anxiety among state elites, and led them to warn the local authorities that such actions would probably lead to a clash between Muslims and non-Muslims.[180]

An instance of such tension occurred in Tarsus (Mersin) and provides an insight into how such conflicts took place in daily life. A Greek citizen, an employee of the Ottoman Bank, was said to have insulted a crowd which had gathered to protest Crete's declaration of union with Greece. According to a report sent to the Ministry of the Interior, the

Greek official showed his contempt for the crowd by saying: "Here they are, the mob, they think that they will turn European public opinion against us." The report claimed that the same officer had also humiliated several of the Muslim merchants who had acted in accord with the boycott, and that this humiliation was about to create an "undesired event." The first encounter between the employee of the Ottoman Bank and the meeting was a coincidence, but clearly illustrates how such a confrontation may have emerged: the Ottoman Bank subsequently became a boycott target, even though the report did not particularly point out the employee as a Greek citizen, but as a person who served the interests of Greece (which in itself is a rather vague statement).[181]

In another incident, a transportation commissioner of the Ottoman Anatolian Railways, Kostaki İnceoğlu, was said to have gathered together 130 Muslim porters who worked for him to ask where they had learned how to boycott. He fired all of them, telling them to boycott a different business, and in so doing, provoked the reaction of the Turkish press. *Tanin* published an article criticizing the commissioner, claiming that he had betrayed a country that had fed him and his ancestors. This article was then republished in the pages of *İttihad* in Smyrna. The article advised the Ottoman public not to consider him an Ottoman, since he preferred Greece to the country where he earned his livelihood, and neither should Anatolian Railways ignore his behavior.[182] However, it soon became apparent that Kostaki İnceoğlu was in fact innocent and that the rumors about him had been the result of a scheme against him. He had had a problem with one of the porters, and his enemies used the boycott to spread lies about him. *Tanin* and the Boycott Society officially apologized to the commissioner.[183] Such schemes, with the aim of ruining specific persons by spreading lies related to the boycott movement, were not uncommon; foreign merchants in particular complained about them.[184]

Another incident occurred in Smyrna, where a captain of the Pantaleon Company was said to have insulted his Muslim workers. The port workers probably refused to unload the ship because of the boycott; however, the newspapers reported that the captain would only employ port workers to unload his ship on the condition that they convert to Christianity. He was also said to have insulted the workers by wondering when they finally would exchange the hat for the fez and thereby become proper human beings. The newspapers reported this incident both as a consequence of the boycott and a humiliation of Islam.[185]

Tension between Muslims and non-Muslims also occurred in Yanya. This time, the complainants were the non-Muslim notables of Preveze, who reported several instances of assault against Christian children. They claimed that their most sacred possessions had been damaged and that they had been humiliated and attacked in the middle of the bazaar. The governor of Yanya informed the Ministry of the Interior that several of these assaults had actually been provoked by Christians. According to Governor Mustafa Zihni, the primary reason for the increase in the tensions between different communities was the boycott movement. Sailors, merchants and their consul were also mentioned in the reports of the governor.[186] As mentioned above, tensions between different communities occurred in Lebanon in particular. For instance, in one incident during the Bayram holiday, two people were killed and eight wounded. As a consequence, the boycott movement became more and more terrifying for both elite and commoners.[187]

The discourse of the boycott movement in 1910 and 1911 was still based on Ottomanism; the movement legitimized its actions by referring to the general interests of Ottoman society, which is why the Cretan Question was always at the center of the debate and the apparent target was Greece. Yet, as mentioned above, the discourse also oscillated between Ottomanism and Islam. Muslim identity emerged as a distinctive reference point that distinguished this boycott from the 1908 Ottoman boycott. In practice, and contrary to the official claims of the boycott movement, non-Muslims other than Greek citizens were also affected by the movement.

Georgios Bousios (Yorgos Boşo Efendi), the member of parliament for Serfiçe, stated in one of his articles that the boycott declared against Greece in practice included the Ottoman Greeks. He wrote that one group of Ottoman citizens had raised doubts regarding the Ottoman identity of another group of Ottoman citizens; the Boycott

Society wanted non-Muslims to prove their Ottoman identity by issuing a certificate. He reminded his readers that the Ottoman nation was not only made up of porters and lightermen. For him, every non-Muslim was a potential subject of Greece if the Boycott Society had not confirmed otherwise. He also asked why the Boycott Society had not met with prominent Turkish, Greek and Armenian members of the commercial communities.[188] *Embros* (Athens) reported that the Ottoman Greeks of Salonica had been asked to wear a fez instead of a European hat in order to prove their Ottoman identity. The newspaper article underlined this paradox and reminded its readers that during the 1908 boycott they had been asked to get rid of their fezzes.[189] The newspaper tried to stress the idea that the boycott was against the Greek world in general.[190]

The Greek Orthodox patriarchate complained to the Ministry of Justice that the Greek community in Akhisar/Manisa suffered greatly from the boycott. According to the patriarchate's report, the Boycott Society had proclaimed a boycott against the Ottoman Greek community by recruiting a number of *tellals* (public criers). Furthermore, they had posted guards in front of Greek stores in order to block customers from entering. As a result, a number of Greeks had had to close their shops, and their business had been wiped out.[191] The main reason for the boycott against the Ottoman Greeks was the presence of two teachers with Greek citizenship in the Greek school, and another Greek citizen working in the Greek Church. After the declaration of the boycott, they had been dismissed by the Greek Orthodox community. However, the boycott did not cease, because these three Greek citizens did not leave the town. According to a telegram sent to the Ministry of the Interior by the notables of the Greek schools, the Boycott Society had announced that even those persons who talked to these three Greek citizens would become a boycott target.[192]

In this case, the local ranks of the Ottoman bureaucracy did not repudiate the existence of such a boycott against Ottoman Greeks, and informed the government that they were doing their best to stop it. Usually, these types of claims were denied by the local governors. The British consul in Smyrna, Henry D. Barnham, blamed the Greek population who "think and talk of nothing else but this Cretan Question and who by their actions do everything to provoke the Turks."[193] The French consul of Cidde (Jeddah) wrote a similar statement regarding the relationship between Muslims and Greeks. According to him, the Greeks of the town were in a dangerous mood; he claimed that they were provocative in their talk and their behavior. On the other hand the Turkish officers were arrogant and did not have good intentions towards the Greeks.[194] These reports clearly prove how the Cretan issue affected the daily lives of the common people belonging to different communities.

The recruitment of Greek citizens, or any other relationship with them, could provide grounds for a boycott. Therefore, the Ottoman Greeks were on the alert, since there were many Greek citizens within their community who worked in various jobs, as teachers and skilled employees in the service sector. Regarding this employment, a rather harsh polemic emerged between the Greek and Turkish press of Smyrna over the course of the boycott movement. One of the hotly debated issues was that of the Greek teachers who taught in Ottoman schools. The Turkish newspapers claimed that they were provoking the Ottoman Greeks against the Ottomans and that this was undermining the unity of the Ottoman Empire; they asserted that as a result of this education, the Ottoman Greeks preferred Greece to the Ottoman Empire. The Turkish newspaper of Smyrna, *İttihad*, wrote that these Greek citizens should be expelled from their institutions by force, if they were not fired by the Ottoman Greek community.[195] *İttihad* claimed that the state of the Greek community was harmful to the Ottoman Empire, since most of the Greek press of Smyrna was in the hands of Greek citizens.[196]

Such convoluted problems regarding Hellene-Greek versus Ottoman-Greek identity also occurred in the agricultural sector. Boycotters prevented the workers on the farm of İbrahim Ahmed Efendi from carrying out their duties. The reason for this boycott was the alleged Greek identity of İbrahim Ahmed Efendi, who guaranteed the government that he was an Ottoman citizen from Beyşehir. He reported that he was considered a Greek citizen because he was from Beyşehir. The governor (*mutasarrıf*) of Karesi quoted the reply of the governor (*kaymakam*) of Edremit, stating that the workers did not boycott because they did not want to.[197]

There were many instances of non-Muslims being boycotted instead of Greek citizens, especially in the province of Aydın. Therefore, the consuls of the Great Powers in Smyrna decided to act collectively if the interests of foreign subjects other than Hellenes were threatened by the boycott movement.[198] The consuls excluded Greek citizens from their protection and thereby admitted the legitimacy of the boycott. This is the reason why most documents regarding boycott activities in the Ottoman archives relate to the affairs of foreign citizens other than the citizens of Greece.

For instance, the lighters and boats that were boycotted in the port of Smyrna, particularly during the spring of 1911 when the boycott was strictly applied, did not belong to a Greek but to an Italian citizen. In one case, the police detained five Ottoman citizens thinking them to be Greek citizens; the grand vizier in a subsequent telegram to the Ministry of the Interior particularly underlined the fact that the persons claimed to be Greek citizens were indeed Ottomans.[199]

Ottoman Greek merchants also had to struggle with the boycott movement. For instance, one of the owners of a flour factory in Dedeağaç complained that the flour that he had sent to an Ottoman citizen in Kavala, Nikola Pavlo, by means of an Ottoman steamship, was boycotted by the port workers. The *mutasarrıf* of Drama and the governor of Salonica wrote to the Ministry of the Interior explaining that the boycott was due to the Greek citizenship of the factory owners. The intervention of the Ottoman government helped to prove the Ottoman citizenship of the owner, Yani of Kırkkilise. However, in the same week flour produced in his factory was boycotted in Gümülcine and in several other towns in the province of Edirne. Once again, he sent a telegram to the Ministry of the Interior and, after offering his thanks for the government's previous intervention, asked the ministry to intervene once more, but this time with the governor of Edirne. In this telegram, he also underlined the fact that the documents he had received from the Dedeağaç Chamber of Commerce confirmed his Ottoman citizenship.[200] In the case of two beerhouses with Ottoman shareholders, the Boycott Society of Smyrna left the decision to boycott to the Ottoman citizens.[201] However, in many cases, to entertain any kind of relationship with a Greek citizen was enough cause to be boycotted.

The cigarette papers produced by Anastasyadi in Galata for the benefit of İzmir's Greek Hospital was also the target of a boycott; their importation to İzmir was prohibited by the boycotters. There were many instances during the boycott movement in which rolling papers, matches and tickets were boycotted because they carried illustrations of the Greek king, the Greek flag or other national symbols. However, there is no mention of such an illustration in Anastasyadi's case: the only reason for this boycott was his citizenship. The minister of commerce and public works wrote to the Ministry of the Interior and confirmed Anastasyadi's Ottoman identity based on the official documents that Anastasyadi had submitted.[202] The governor of Aydın sent a report and disavowed the existence of such a boycott. According to this report, there was a boycott of another cigarette paper brand in Manisa, but it was discontinued after it became apparent that its owner was an Ottoman citizen. Like so many others, this report also revealed that the boycott was applied to many Ottoman citizens.[203]

The greatest damage was done to the maritime sector of the Greek economy. It was easy for the boycotters to closely watch the Greek ships that regularly visited the Ottoman ports. An Ottoman ship company owned by non-Muslims also suffered from the boycott movement because of a ship that they had bought from a Greek company. In 1910 and 1911, there were many instances of Ottoman companies purchasing boycotted ships. These were usually bought by Ottoman Greeks and subsequently became a target. The general director of the Banque de Mettelin and the Guruci Company sent a telegram to the government, stating that they had purchased the ship in place of an old ship and that it had been registered with the Ottoman port administration. However, the Ottoman flag that the ship flew did not rescue the company, and it failed to extricate itself from the boycott.[204] The İzmir Boycott Society prohibited the companies' transactions between Ottoman ports.

The Boycott Society was very suspicious of the transfer of goods from Greek citizens to Ottoman citizens. Such a transfer of property occurred in Üsküdar, where two Ottoman merchants by the names of Trinidisi and Yorgi bought a pasta factory whose former owner had been a Greek citizen. The Ottoman merchants announced their purchase in the newspapers *İkdam* and *Proodos*, but the Üsküdar Boycott Committee regarded this transfer of property as fake, and Trinidisi and Yorgi sought help from the government in order to rescue themselves from economic ruin.[205] Similarly, several markets and shops in Üsküdar were boycotted, even though the owners of these shops were Ottoman citizens. They claimed that this boycott was without reason and cause.[206]

The Destouni Line, which had greatly been affected during the initial days of the boycott movement, passed into the possession of an Ottoman subject. Its steamers began to operate between the ports of Salonica and Istanbul. However, one steamer of the line, *Anghelike*, was boycotted even though it was carrying Muslim refugees from Bulgaria, "on the grounds that the sale to the Ottoman subject had not been a bona fide transaction". The boycotters only allowed the passengers to disembark, and the ship could only depart for Kavala and Dedeağaç with the help of Kerim Ağa's written instructions, which informed the lightermen of these two towns that the ship might unload its cargo but should not be allowed to reload.[207]

The boycott usually targeted the trading and economic activities of Greek citizens, but since it was a popular movement, several strange instances also happened. In Adana, one of the actors of the Turkish Drama Company was boycotted and the performance stopped. The police reported that the boycott was applied only for one night, because the player was a Greek citizen, but the director of the theater company, İsmail Behçet, denied this and assured the Ottoman public that the actor was an Ottoman citizen.[208]

The blockade of Greek shops was one of the chief direct actions of the boycott movement and appeared in the first week of its existence. An official report on one of these events from İzmir revealed that Ottoman shops were included amongst those that had to be closed down because of the picketing.[209] Attacks on Greek shops in the marketplace were not new in the Ottoman Empire, as increasing tension and conflicts between different communities had already led to harassment. Before the declaration of the boycott, several Ottoman Greek shops had been disturbed by crowds who convened to protest about new developments regarding the Cretan Question.[210]

The picketing of Greek stores was the most effective form of direct action during the boycott movement. A merchant in İzmir, Philip Kotlidi, had opened a new shop in Menemen, but it was boycotted with the claim that he was a citizen of Greece. After a month and a half, he complained to the government that the governor's orders in his favor had failed. In his complaint, he confirmed that he and his ancestors were Ottomans and had served the Ottoman motherland. What is crucial in his report is that he referred to the boycott as being motivated by the explicit interests of a few individuals.[211] That is to say, he pointed out the existence of competition and rivalry. In the same month, but this time in Bergama, the farm of Fotiyadi was seized by the boycotters; Fotiyadi's son, a teacher at the Heybeliada School of Theology, assured them that his father was a citizen of the Ottoman Empire. He asked how the estates and assets of Ottoman citizens could possibly be boycotted and pleaded with the government to send orders on his father's behalf to the province of Aydın.[212]

The Aegean islands were densely populated by the Greek community, and this made their economic situation quite precarious. Their close relationships with Asia Minor were sometimes cut, and the blockade caused significant economic damage, particularly to the small islands that were dependent on the mainland. The Chamber of Commerce in Midilli (Lesbos) convened a meeting to debate the negative effects of the boycott on the trade of the island. Two Muslim members of the chamber proposed forming a boycott society in order to regulate the boycotting activities. They claimed that such a committee could inspect the merchandise and prevent non-Greek merchants and goods from being boycotted. However, the suggestion was declined; instead, the merchants decided to send telegrams to the Ottoman parliament and ask for help.[213]

The president of Midilli's Chamber of Commerce sent a telegram to the member of parliament for Midilli, Panayotis Bostanis, complaining about the boycott of their island in Edremit. An Ottoman merchant had sent goods to Akçay, but had been blocked in the port of Edremit. He reported that many merchants were complaining about the boycotting activities. Seven non-Muslim notables sent a telegram to the Ministry of the Interior, proclaiming that the boycott in Ayvalık had extended to Ottoman businessmen. This complaint regarding the boycott of Ottoman Greeks was signed by several local Greek citizens.[214]

Because the boycotting of the merchants of Midilli did not end following this complaint, the vice-president of the Midilli Chamber of Commerce, Apostol, sent a telegram to the government in order to inform them that, in Dikili, Ottoman commodities sent to Ottoman merchants by Ottoman ships were still being boycotted. The Greek consul also informed the Foreign Ministry of Greece that in March of 1911 the boycott in Dikili, Akçay, Edremit and Kemer had been very strict, to the extent that one of the captains of these ships could obtain not even a glass of drinking water at the port.[215] Apostol informed the government that the boycott appeared to expand to Bergama; as a result the merchants of the island were facing bankruptcy.[216] The governor of Aydın informed the government that as soon as the Boycott Society had learned that the owners of the goods were Ottomans, the merchandise had been carried to the stores.[217]

However, the complaints of the Midilli Chamber of Commerce did not end, and the officials continued to send telegrams regarding the boycotting of the island, including to the member of parliament for Midilli in Istanbul, in order to air their grievances. The situation deteriorated, since in Edremit and Dikili the boycotters declared that they would also boycott those merchants who brought commodities from Midilli. Thus, the Ministry of the Interior wrote to the governor of Aydın that such a boycott of an Ottoman island should be banned, although the *mutasarrıf* of Karesi reported that the complaints of the Midilli merchants were only based on their anxiety and worry.[218]

The National Economy, Muslim Merchants and the Working Class

One of the most significant features of the Second Constitutional Period (1908–18) was the rise of the Milli İktisat (National Economy). Thoughts concerning the development of a native industry became quite popular immediately after the promulgation of the constitution in 1908. After the political atmosphere of fraternity had started to evaporate, the Young Turks put forth specific policies in order to enhance the position of Muslims and Turks within the economy. The mobilization of the public for the national economy was also a significant aspect of this process, yet this aspect is generally disregarded in the historiography on Turkey. The economic boycott was a political weapon to mobilize the masses and create a shift in public opinion. Thanks to the boycott, the masses, workers, merchants and notables participated together in politics. Demands for the construction of a native industry were followed up by criticism of foreign domination within the Ottoman economy. The capitulations were considered one of the ultimate reasons for Ottoman backwardness. Non-Muslims became one of the targets of critics arguing in favor of a national economy. The boycott turned towards them, becoming a social movement whose aim was the elimination of non-Muslims from the empire's economy. The 1910–11 boycott movement was an important link in this transformation.

The general discourse of the boycott movement after 1908 was based on Ottomanism. However, during the 1910–11 boycott, Islamic and Turkic elements also took their place within this discourse. At that time, Ottoman Greeks and Armenians were not yet targeted, but were included in the definition of "us." Whenever a Greek citizen was to be replaced by an Ottoman citizen in a particular economic sector, the replacement still might have been an Ottoman Greek or Armenian. At the same time, it was also widely claimed that Muslims constituted the most backward element within the economy. In daily life, the border between Ottoman Greeks and Hellenes was sometimes crossed, as the boycotters sometimes included the Ottoman Greeks when they eliminated Hellenes from the Ottoman Empire. To be a Greek citizen or to have any affiliation with them became disastrous for merchants during the boycott movement. Thus, merchants like Yorgaki İstradi were afraid of being associated with Greek citizens. He wrote to the newspaper *İttihad*, refuting the rumors that he had been entertaining relationships with the late Alexander and a person by the name of Kasmati.[219]

The boycotters and the writers who defended the boycott referred to the Ottoman Empire as the land of Muslims. For instance, Fahri wrote in *İttihad* that Greeks who wanted to be Greek citizens or to defend the interests of Greece were free to leave the country if they wanted to. Nobody forced them to live in the Ottoman Empire, and it would be better if they left the "Turkish land."[220] In the same issue, M. Sai wrote that wealthy Ottomans should take advantage of the opportunity of the boycott movement and invest in the sectors left by the Hellenes. He wondered why the Ottoman Greeks and Armenians did not run the taverns in the port of Smyrna, which were entirely owned by foreigners. M. Sai addressed the Muslims in particular, whom he wanted to invest in the economy, in small enterprises or in the newly formed Cemiyet-i Müteşebbise (Society of Entrepreneurs) in Istanbul. He claimed that it was a social responsibility for the wealthy to invest, and that the poor and the workers had rights to their wealth.[221] Yet Muslim notables made different kinds of investments in the Ottoman Empire and competed with foreigners. For instance, before the commencement of the boycott in 1910, Tiridzade Mehmed Pasha stirred up trouble among the Oriental Carpet Manufacturers in Uşak. The carpet company accused him of inciting people and producers against the company. The British consul even claimed that he was provoking a boycott of the company's shipments.[222] A year earlier, Tiridzade Mehmed Pasha had been accused of boycotting a yarn-dying factory in Uşak. However, the governor of Uşak informed the government that foreigners considered his initiative to establish a national company for carpet trading preparations to be a boycott. Therefore, there were instances of rivalry between Muslim merchants and notables on one side and the foreigners on the other, but also instances of collaboration.[223]

The investments of Muslims attracted the attention of the Turkish press. Berberzade Hafız Ali Efendi who had grocery stores all over the province of Aydın decided to open a new shop in Smyrna. *İttihad* praised his enterprises and his personal qualifications and reported on his plans concerning Smyrna. *İttihad* claimed that Smyrna was desperately in need of such a respectable Muslim grocer whom Ottomans could trust. They would no longer be obliged to give their money to foreigners, particularly to Greek citizens. The newspaper also underlined the fact that Hafız Ali had already donated a significant amount of money to the navy. Such a donation was considered one of the most significant nationalist acts of the time.[224] Therefore, Berberzade Hafız Ali constituted a proper role model who invested, donated to national charities and competed with foreigners.

The foreign consuls and Greece claimed that the boycott was harmful not only to Greece, but also to the Ottoman Empire itself. Both the internal and international trade and economy were damaged because of the boycott movement. It was also claimed that, as well as the merchants, the workers in the ports of the Ottoman Empire also suffered economic loss. Although these statements were not entirely incorrect, the boycott movement had a different motivation: the construction of a national economy, in which the Muslim and Turkish elements would prevail.

The newspaper *Proodos* argued that not only Greeks would suffer from the boycott, but also Turkish merchants. Everybody had to pay more for transportation and had difficulties in finding vessels to carry goods. Therefore, the "primitive weapon" of the boycott was harmful to the economy of the Ottoman Empire in general.[225] However, the boycotters and the Turkish press had a different point of view; they concentrated on eliminating the Greek element from the economy. Therefore, the French consul in Rhodes had been right when he claimed that the boycott's aim was the elimination of the Greek element from the empire. He stated that there was a new power gaining strength in Turkey. This new social force was protected by the CUP and the official authorities, but it was not identical to them.[226] For instance, a branch of the Orient Bank in Soma/Smyrna was boycotted because of its Greek director. The boycott of the bank was denounced by the governor-general, the local head of the police department, and even the representatives of the CUP. Yet, these initiatives were not enough to put an end to the boycotting of the bank.[227]

The Greek press paid attention to the emphasis that Turkish periodicals placed on the national economy. *Proodos* quoted *Jön Türk*, which claimed that the boycott was paving the way for the enlargement of the Ottoman trading navy. *İkdam*, on the other hand, claimed that Greece had prospered thanks to earnings from the Ottoman Empire. Accordingly, Greece had great interests in the empire, but was not treating well the Ottomans on Greek soil. Therefore, it was the Ottomans' duty to cut all relationships with Greece.[228]

The French ambassador was also right when he claimed that the Jewish community of Salonica and their Turkish fellows had benefited from the perpetuation of the boycott movement.[229] He repeated his assertions seven months later, when the boycott was applied more strictly after March 1911. The French consul in Salonica reported to the French ambassador in Pera that the newly formed Donanma Cemiyeti and the boycott movement had organized a specific division of labor. Both had close relationships with the CUP. Both Jews and *dönmes* (Jews converted to Islam) were active in these organizations. According to his report, the Donanma Cemiyeti was to play a crucial role in taking over the coast navigation that had been done by Greek vessels before the boycott. This is why Jewish and Muslim merchants were looking forward to replacing Greek trading activities between the Ottoman ports. The report stated that the new motivation within the boycott movement had been provoked by this particular social class.[230]

The British ambassador in Athens in his annual report referred to "the underlying desire to make Ottoman and especially Salonica merchants profit at the expense of Greek trade."[231] A year later, the British annual report made the same claim. The boycott harmed the interests of its most active social group, the lightermen. The British ambassador wrote that the "lightermen found themselves victimized for the benefit of Turkish and Jewish ship owners."[232] The most active social group of the boycott movement, the port workers, helped Ottoman ship owners tremendously in their competition with foreign ones. The foreign naval transportation companies complained to the Ottoman government that the boatmen demanded more money from the customers of foreign ships. By doing so, they indirectly compelled customers to travel on Ottoman ships. The Ottoman government wrote to the governor-generals of the empire's coastal provinces to instruct them not to allow such illegal actions of the boatmen in the ports. Nevertheless, the government described the act of the boatmen as "genuine boycott" (*hakiki boykot*) in its dispatch to the provinces. The concept referred to a distinct way of boycotting which would pave the way for the establishment of a national economy.²³³ Therefore, the Ottoman bureaucracy was well aware of the movement and its specific goals and terminology. Similarly, *İttihad* called on the Ottoman public to join the boycott not only as an occasional weapon, but as an everlasting economic war. As a result, no one would be able to insult their religion, nation and honor.²³⁴

Peros Kalambelis, an executive manager working in the Dardanelles, wrote to the Ministry of Foreign Affairs of Greece and claimed that it would be impossible for Greeks to extricate themselves from the boycott, because the Turks had learned the merits and advantages of such a weapon and were ready to utilize it whenever necessary. Henceforth, the boycott would be the Sword of Damocles for the Greeks.²³⁵

The French consul in Salonica repeated his social analysis several times when writing about the boycott movement. In September 1911, he also referred to a Cretan Muslim ship owner who played a significant role in the formation of the Donanma Cemiyeti in Salonica. He had lobbied the mayor of Salonica in order to receive institutional support. His efforts towards creating a boycott movement and a civil navy organization were successful in eliminating the Greek flag from the Ottoman ports in a short period of time, according to the French consul. The consul also underlined the fact that the Donanma Cemiyeti was made up of Muslims, rather than being an Ottoman union.²³⁶

Marquis Pallavicini, the Austrian ambassador in Istanbul, also told the French ambassador in Vienna that the boycott was a stroke of luck for the big interests. Having experienced the boycott in the Ottoman Empire since 1908, he stated several times that it was the Boycott Society who had power over the movement, and not the government or the CUP.²³⁷

The lightermen, stevedores, porters and boatmen were the main actors of the boycott, particularly in the port cities of the Ottoman Empire. They were the most organized social group of the boycott movement. Their declarations and activities constituted the main aspects of the movement. The main spokesman of the movement was the head of the lightermen in Salonica, Kerim Ağa. The head of the lightermen in Istanbul was also the movement's head and its main spokesman in the capital.²³⁸ Yet, it was not only the porters in the ports but also the porters in towns inland who played a crucial role in the movement. This is why the Boycott Society of Eskişehir thanked these "boycott heroes," and particularly their head, Ömer Onbaşı, and the head of the carters (*arabacılar*), Arap Ömer Ağa.[239] The boycott societies generally acted as anonymous organizations, and it was always the port workers who spoke on behalf of the boycotters. However, the port workers were also under the control of the boycott organizations. At the beginning of the boycott movement, the port workers of Istanbul took an oath of allegiance to the boycott before the Boycott Committee.[240]

The foreign consuls and the non-Turkish press despised the port workers and claimed that it was a shame for the Ottoman state to leave politics and diplomatic affairs to the hands of porters and lightermen.[241] At first sight, the tone of such remarks was not particularly contemptuous. *Proodos* asked in the first days of the boycott why the duties of statesmen and diplomats were left to the port workers.[242] However, in the later phases of the boycott, disdain turned into mockery and insults.

Kerim Ağa, for instance, was portrayed in the Greek press as if he was the master of commerce in the Ottoman Empire. He was depicted in illustrations and cartoons as an ugly Oriental figure, sitting on a pillow, smoking a *nargile* (hookah) and giving orders to the workers around him.[243] In a short period of time, he became one of the most famous persons of the empire. He was regularly mentioned in the political and popular press and became the subject of diplomatic correspondence. Several times he was detained and sent to jail, but he did not lose his power in the port of Salonica, or his influence over different ports of the empire. His relationship with the CUP and his position as head of the most powerful guild of the empire facilitated his dominance in trade. Likewise, the heads of the port workers elsewhere appeared as prominent figures of their towns in this period. For example, in Antalya, where a significant number of Cretan immigrants were living, Süllü Ağa and Fehim Ağa emerged as significant political and social agents. They not only played a crucial role in the anti-Greek boycotts, but also carried their struggle into the national movement, even in the Armistice Period.[244]

The Turkish press also published polemic articles against the boycott movement. Most of the newspapers and journals were for the movement. However, there were a handful of newspapers that criticized the actions of workers or the role that they played in the movement. For instance, a polemic emerged between the two major newspapers of Trabzon, *Meşveret* and *Tarik*. *Tarik* criticized the dominance of the port workers and particularly Kerim Ağa in the boycott movement. *Meşveret* replied that it was the boatmen who exhibited nationalist sentiments. The newspaper asserted that Kerim Ağa, Ahmet Ağa and Hüseyin Reis had brought up the issue of Ottoman union for public opinion, and that they sacrificed their interests for the national cause. Therefore, they should be applauded and not criticized. If the boycott had been organized by elites, pashas and *beys* instead of persons like Kerim Ağa, it would have lasted only two days, the newspaper claimed.[245] The new Italian consul who arrived in Salonica in August 1911 was amazed by Kerim Ağa and his men's role in the boycott movement and the power of the port workers.[246]

The port workers on the Ottoman quays—such as porters, lightermen and boatmen—were a well-organized social group who pressed for their economic and social rights in a variety of ways, from boycott to strike, over the course of Ottoman history. The boycott movement gave a legitimate "national" argument to their struggle. As mentioned above, they gained significant social rights thanks to their struggle during the 1908 Ottoman boycott. Before the declaration of the boycott in 1910, the port workers behaved in similar ways. For instance, on 3 April 1910 the boatmen of Haifa, while escorting passengers to steamers, once halfway between the shore and steamer demanded three times the sum they had agreed upon with the passengers. This was not an isolated incident, since other boatmen came to help when travelers wanted to take boats to the steamer on their own initiative. Yet, the travelers were desperate when they encountered an organized group of boatmen. Two of the offending boatmen were arrested and the case was brought to court; however, from the point of view of the consuls the inquiry was unsatisfactory, because the boatmen were soon released again. As the British consul in Beirut underlined, the boatmen were an organized corporation in all Levantine ports, and such a vain inquiry might be "a dangerous precedent highly discreditable to any Government."[247]

The boatmen utilized these mass mobilizations and national campaigns in order to strengthen their social conditions. Thanks to their boycotting activities, they consolidated their position *vis-à-vis* the state, the trading companies and the Port Company. Their active presence in the movement facilitated the confirmation of their traditional rights in the ports. The governor-general of Yanya and the governor of Preveze asked the Rüsumat Müdüriyet-i Umumiyesi (Public Administration of Customs) about the legal status of the port workers. If the workers were not organized as guilds and were paid wages in return for their work, they should be considered officers. That is to say, they could not participate in the boycott movement since they would be a part of the state apparatus. However, if they were organized as a guild and worked for fees, they would have the monopoly in the ports and customs.[248]

The Ministry of the Interior tried to undermine the boatmen's traditional rights, since their social power instilled fear in the elites. They had good reason to be afraid. The Cretan porters in Smyrna, for instance, considered the boycott a suitable occasion to strike against the shipping agents and the lighter owners. This was an opportunity to abolish an agreement made by the government on their behalf. This agreement limited the number of Muslims among the porters to one-third of their total number.[249] The British consul in Smyrna reported that the governor-general of the province of Aydın thought of summoning the boycott leaders and threatening them with punishment based on the law on strikes.[250] Therefore, the governor also considered a significant part of the boycott activities as workers' actions. The boycott movement also provoked the Zonguldak mine workers. In order to support the port workers of Ereğli, who were boycotting a Greek ship, the miners also stopped their work in the mines. As a result, the Greek ship was without adequate coal supply. As a consequence, a crisis arose between the mine company and the workers, and the company threatened the workers with a lockout. This decision also frightened the local governor and the government, since 5,000 workers would then be ready to march to the city center. The Ministry of the Interior also feared that, if these workers were to march into the city, great disorder would probably follow. Thus, the ministry ordered the local governors to prevent such a lockout. Furthermore, the Ministry of the Interior wanted the governors of Bolu, Zonguldak and Ereğli to restrict the mobilization of the workers in the port, in transportation and in the mines. The governors replied to the ministry that the government should send additional troops to the region, in case it became necessary to apply force. Therefore, the boycott of a Greek ship in Zonguldak over a very short period of time led to great excitement and chaos.[251]

In the end, the Ministry of the Interior was unable to limit the monopoly of the port workers. The Administration of Customs confirmed the monopoly rights of the port workers one month later.[252] The Nezaret-i Umur-ı Bahriye (Ministry of Naval Affairs) also affirmed the rights of the lightermen, stating that foreign companies did not have any rights of transportation.[253] This monopoly was the main pillar of their social power, and is why there were numerous incidents of porters threatening porters newly hired by the foreign companies on the Ottoman quays. In Jaffa, the old porters pushed the newly hired ones into the sea.[254]

Irrespective of their power, the port workers were losing money because of the boycott movement, since they did not have a fixed income and their wages depended on the amount of work they did. This is why, in Smyrna, the Boycott Society had to threaten several porters, lightermen and carters who unloaded Greek merchandise. In a declaration, the Boycott Society stated that an Ottoman should not work for the enemy, even when he was starving. There is evidence that there were port workers with Greek citizenship who tried to work nevertheless. The port workers who were threatened by the Boycott Society in this case may have been non-Muslims, but this was the only case in which a group of port workers was criticized during the boycott movement.[255]

In most towns, the port workers were the only social group that fought for the boycott, even though they lost wages when they refused to unload goods and passengers from the ships. One source of revenue that they did have was the certificates printed in order to prove merchants' identity. These certificates were sold for 10 kuruş and provided a small budget for the movement. Moreover, the inspection teams of the boycott organization, who inspected the shops and stores, were said to force merchants to "pay for their protection against boycottage." These sources of income did support the livelihood of the port workers to a certain extent.[256] The newspaper *Embros* also claimed that these certificates were invented to fill the pockets of Kerim Ağa, who had lost his commissions because of the refusal to unload Greek merchandise. According to the Greek journal, this was the new source of income for "generous and ascetic" Kerim Ağa.[257] The boycott organizations also established a fund (*sandık*) to support the port workers.[258] Moreover, there were initiatives to raise money for the benefit of the port workers. The inhabitants of Mustafapaşa in Istanbul collected 328 piasters and handed the sum over to the porters and boatmen in order to support them at the very beginning of the boycott. *Proodos* guessed that these donations may have increased in the later phases of the boycott movement.[259]

The State and the Boycott Movement

The Ottoman government held contrasting attitudes toward the boycott movement. First of all, an effective boycott against Greece would have put economic pressure on the country and reduced its aspirations regarding Crete. The Cretan Question galvanized the emotions of the Ottoman public and put pressure on the government. The boycott movement channeled the pressure toward a different target and was therefore useful for the government in terms of politics and diplomacy. At the beginning of the movement, the members of the government employed the argument of the local governors and low-ranking bureaucrats who said that the boycott was the outcome of the free will of the people. The Ottoman government even referred to Venizelos's candidacy for the Greek parliament as a provocation that triggered the patriotism of the Ottomans.[260] Grand Vizier Hakkı Paşa gave the Greek ambassador Gryparis a furious reply when the latter criticized Ottoman coercion and violence, stating that he was unable to prevent the anger of a people provoked by Greece.[261]

The first evaluations of the boycott movement by the Greek press held the Ottoman government responsible for its emergence. It was claimed that the government was too weak to deal with the Cretan Question and wanted to use the boycott in order to put pressure on Greece.[262]

The mobilization of the Ottoman public increased day by day, and the expansion and intensification of the boycott undermined the government's control of society. For instance, an old *Khodja* in Bornova (Bournabat)/Smyrna convened a meeting in one of the *medreses*; several soldiers of the Bournabat garrison also participated. He preached to the gathered crowd about a Holy War and prayed for the destruction of the new regime, which he condemned as the "arch-enemy of Islam." He referred to the incidents in Crete as proof of his claims.[263] He was arrested the following day; this incident shows that the government did consider such mobilization as dangerous to its existence.

The boycott movement employed coercion in different parts of the empire, and the trade of other countries was also negatively affected in the course of the boycotting activities. The government also started to fear a clash between Muslims and non-Muslims, and the governor-general of the province of Aydın addressed the similarity between the *Rum* and the *Yunani*. When the governor visited the City Club in order to give a speech on the boycott, he underlined the fact that the Ottoman Greeks and Greek citizens both had the same religion and language. Furthermore, their similarity was complicated by inter-marriage. Most of the merchants in the region had Greek citizenship. Therefore, he warned the boycotters to be cautious regarding possible clashes between different communities.[264] Elsewhere, Talat Bey, minister of the interior and a prominent member of the CUP, advised the head of the Boycott Union in Istanbul to put an end to the boycott.[265] Rumors of the end of the boycott began to circulate in political and diplomatic circles, and news items reporting its demise even appeared in foreign newspapers.[266] In response, the Boycott Society frequently published declarations in local newspapers, proclaiming that the boycott had not been lifted.[267]

At first, the Ottoman government had tried to prevent the emergence of the boycott movement. It had sent orders to Trabzon and Samsun/Canik, declaring that such a boycott against Greece was not needed since the government was taking the necessary steps. According to the government, the boycott would probably give a bad impression among the European public and so was contrary to the general interests of the country.[268] However, the government did not manage to halt its emergence; the local governors informed the government that the port workers, merchants and people were acting in accord with the boycott. The governor of Trabzon wrote to Istanbul that it was the strong emotions of the Ottoman public that had triggered the movement. The Ottoman government took steps to stop the boycott, but this only provoked a reaction from the Boycott Society: the Smyrna Boycott Society, for instance, published a declaration stating that the government advised them to stop the boycott. This declaration proclaimed that they harmed neither the interests of foreign citizens nor the Ottoman Greeks, and that they therefore had a right of expression to call on people for a peaceful boycott against Greece. Contrary to the demands of the Ottoman government, the Boycott Society wanted the Ottoman public not to relax the boycott.[269] The Boycott Society repeated its claims regarding the government's anti-boycott attempts and condemned the actions of several governors in a number of declarations.[270]

Since the government could not impede the emergence of the beycott movement, it tried to regulate and limit it. There were two courses of action available in order to deal with the problem. First, it sent orders to the local governors to attempt to ensure the implementation of the law. The doyen of the consular corps in Smyrna visited the governor-general of the province of Aydın and thanked him for his support. In this meeting, the governor showed the doyen a telegram that had just arrived from the Ministry of the Interior, instructing him to utilize every means to stop the boycott. However, the British consul in Smyrna underlined the fact that, four days after this meeting, the governor-general had still not been able to do anything about the boycott movement. He asserted that the movement "was sustained by a feeling of hatred against the Greeks on the part of the Mohammedans which increased as time goes on."[271] The British consul in Salonica also thought that the Ottoman government at last understood that the boycott had gone too far, and that the excesses of the boycott organizations were "not only illegal but inexpedient."[272]

The second course of action used by the government was to put pressure directly on the Istanbul Boycott Society. In June 1910, the government even forced the Boycott Society to send specific orders to its branches in different provinces. In this order, the Boycott Society limited the boycott exclusively to Greek merchandise on Greek ships.[273] The Boycott Committee in Trabzon on 21 July 1910 declared the regulations in line with the government's limitations. The British consul in Trabzon claimed that the declaration had been issued by the Boycott Society of Salonica. According to these regulations, any foreign merchandise on foreign vessels and non-Greek merchandise on Greek ships were exempt from the boycott. Yet, Ottomans were banned from using Greek vessels or having any kind of economic relationship with Greeks of Greece.[274]

Although the Boycott Society assured the government that they had indeed sent such an order, the events after June 1910 do not confirm this. (One of the significant aspects of the relations between the society and the government is the fact that the government dealt with an organization that legally did not exist; this aspect will be analyzed below.) The government repeated several times the argument that the Boycott Society should send its order to the provinces,[275] requesting that the boycott movement stay within the economic sphere—that is to say, a boycott consisting only of the consumers' refusal to buy certain goods.[276] Not even the actions of the porters and lightermen in the customs were included in this definition.

The Great Powers protested to the Ottoman state when their merchants faced difficulties as a result of the boycott movement. The official definition of the boycott gave rise to claims on the part of foreign merchants whose interests had been damaged.[277] For instance, in one of these complaints the ambassador of Austria-Hungary underlined the fact that their merchants had trusted the Ottoman state's word and sent their merchandise to the Ottoman Empire; hence, the damage caused by the boycott should be paid by the government.[278]

Thus, the Ottoman government continued writing to the provinces to remind the local government of the official limits of the boycott. After a while, the government requested the local governors to compel the boycotters, if necessary by force, to act within those limits.

The Shift from Foreign to "Internal" Enemies 149

In September 1910, the government became stricter and took measures against the boycott movement: in an order sent to the province of Salonica, the government allowed the local governor to use the gendarmerie to prevent the boycott's negative effects. According to this telegram, international trade had been badly damaged, and the damaged interests of the foreign merchants undermined the honor of the Ottoman state. The most famous and popular character of the boycott movement, Kerim Ağa, was banned from entering the customs house and the quay.[279]

The reason the government became firmer in September 1910 was because, after a brief period of relaxation in August, the boycott movement had become more aggressive again. In August, most of the ships carrying foreign (other than Greek) merchandise and Greek goods on foreign ships did not experience many problems due to the boycott. However, at the end of August, a Greek ship in Preveze encountered a blockade of the port workers. Several hundred people, including Cretans and *hodjas* (Muslim preachers), convened a meeting in order to support the boycott of the port workers.[280] Kerim Ağa called a meeting of lightermen, porters and carters and declared new regulations regarding the application of the boycott—that is, an enlargement. Henceforth, all foreign merchandise on Greek ships and all Greek commodities in any vessel were to be boycotted.[281]

This is why the government decided to put pressure on the boycott movement. However, resorting to police force was not an easy decision. M.H. Clonarides & Co. Ltd. a company established in Greece but registered in Britain, was sending barrels of beer from its brewery in Piraeus; it had been boycotted since the commencement of the movement, but the situation became intolerable in November 1910. Its beer barrels were lying in front of the customs house of Smyrna, and the company tried to carry them into town. However, their porters were stopped by 40 to 60 boycotters, and the company requested help from both the governor-general and the British consul. Obliged to leave the barrels behind in order to wait for help, they found them standing in a row the next morning, pierced and empty. The British consul assured his protection of the remaining barrels. Yet when the porters began to load the barrels on a cart, a group of boycotters arrived, pulled the horse away, and once again unloaded the barrels. The British consul returned to the office of the governor-general and witnessed his distinct orders to the chief of police to use force in the event of any further hindrance. The consul then went to the customs house for the third time. The chief of police and a dock-porter who was also the representative of the Boycott Committee negotiated the loading of the barrels, and the police asked the British consul if it was possible to postpone the loading until the following day, since the boycotters had already forcibly removed the company's carts. Then, hand-pulled carts were brought to the quay, but the boycotters threw them into the sea in front of the consul and the chief of police. When the consul asked the chief of police to carry out the orders of the governor-general, the chief replied that he had no orders at all, and sent a policeman to the governor to ask for further instructions. At last, the policemen afforded sufficient protection to allow the barrels to be moved in the evening. The British consul complained to the embassy that no one had been arrested and that the police had not intervened even when there had been force. The reason for such hesitant behavior was the fear of spilling blood. Although most of the British reports claimed that the government had no authority over the boycotters, the British consul in this case asserted that the acting governor had an "ill-concealed intention to act hand in glove with the boycotters." He demanded additional pressure on the Sublime Porte to send more stringent orders to the governors in the province of Aydın.[282]

The government kept reminding the local government of the limits of the boycott throughout 1910 and 1911.[283] The Ministry of Foreign Affairs, which was under pressure from the Great Powers, also tried to reduce these limits, claiming that the Ottoman state should defend the interests of foreign merchants, even if they were Greek. However, the Great Powers could not act collectively to stop the boycott because they had different opinions regarding the movement. Austria-Hungary was reluctant to become involved.[284] Therefore, the Ministry of Foreign Affairs forced the Ministry of the Interior to take measures against the boycott movement.[285] The orders of the Sublime Porte had an effect on the boycotting of foreign merchants at the end of 1910. Although the offenders who had been detained were released after a very short time, the complaints of the British merchants barely increased.[286] The Ottoman government's telegrams underlined that, if the boycotters trespassed beyond these limits, the governors should resort to armed force. However, the government continued to send similar telegrams, and was still telling the governor to act in accordance with the gendarmerie regulations in November of 1911, at the end of the 1910–11 Boycott wave.[287]

Greece, other foreign states and the Greek press made two incompatible claims regarding the attitude of the Ottoman government towards the boycott movement. First, it was claimed that the government had lost its power in the face of the acts of the "mob" of port workers. This was also an argument to force the government to impede the actions and mobilization of the port workers throughout the empire. On the other hand, it was stated repeatedly that in fact the Ottoman government was responsible for and had orchestrated the boycott movement; the real power belonged to the Young Turks and the Boycott Society, and the leaders of the movement were nothing but their hand puppets.[288] Although the Ottoman government and the elites in general took advantage of the boycott movement, one cannot claim that it was under its control. The French ambassador wrote several times that it would be unfair to claim that the government was encouraging the boycott movement; rather, it did not have enough power to prevent the movement, although it wanted to limit it.[289]

The provincial governors and other ranks of the local bureaucracy did not pay much attention to the warnings of the central authority. They largely tolerated and overlooked the boycotters' excesses, sometimes trying to explain the reasons and motivations behind their actions and to legitimize them. If the Ottoman government did persist in their orders, then the local bureaucrats ignored them. The central government had to insist very strongly in order to get results. One has to be aware of the fact that there were divergent attitudes concerning the boycott movement in different ranks of the state bureaucracy.

The main argument employed by local bureaucrats was that the boycott depended on the free will of the people and should be considered within the framework of free trade. Therefore, the government had no right to intervene in the market and compel consumers to buy certain goods. A report sent to the Greek Foreign Ministry in the second year of the boycott movement demonstrates that these kinds of reply from local state officials had become typical when consuls visited them, and it was in vain to expect any reaction from them against the boycott movement.[290]

The *kaymakam* (district governor) of İskenderun/Aleppo informed the governor of Aleppo that he had no right to interfere if there were no incidents of violence. Furthermore, he emphasized that Greek firms could hire independent porters or use their own boats to load or unload their merchandise.[291] The governors of the province of Hüdavendigar, Kütahya and Salonica all maintained that the boycott was only the decision of people not to consume certain goods and, therefore, an outcome of people's will.[292] The French consul in Rhodes had problems in defining the main character of the boycott movement. The governor-general and the general secretary of the province asserted that it was the right of the people and the workers not to work if they so wished. Moreover, the general secretary told the consul that the Ottomans had learned about the concepts of strike and boycott from the Europeans, and they were only imitating the West.[293]

The arguments and negotiations surrounding the general character of the boycott movement between the British consul of Edirne and the governor-general of that province lasted one year. The governors of the province stated that there were no laws prohibiting peoples' participation in the boycott and that the government was therefore not responsible. For their part, the boycotted businessmen and the consul claimed that a certain segment of the population had been subjected to force. In one instance, the government had not placed a notice declaring that a mill owner was not Greek, but British. According to them, the government should have posted gendarmes before the mill where boycotters were keeping customers away, and it should not have allowed the boycotters to post on the wall the notice that declared the owner as a Greek.[294]

When the Greek shops were forced to close, Smyrna's acting governor Tevfik Bey (who was the director of the educational department and the president of the local branch of the CUP) issued a declaration in which he approved the boycott movement. He also mentioned that all acts of violence, such as the forced closure of shops, would be punished.

Furthermore, he convened a meeting with the editors of the daily press and advised them to take a moderate and calming stance regarding the movement. He warned them not to inflame public opinion.[295]

The local governors in the province of Trabzon informed both the governor-general and the local vice-consuls that there was nothing that could be done regarding the boycotting activities, since they were peaceful actions by the local people.[296] The *kaymakam* of Zonguldak added another restriction to the existing limitations: although the boycott was carried out by the people and the workers, and although the government had no right to intervene, the workers should not be allowed to crowd the public squares in the center of the town. A public march to the center would have indicated that there was public and official encouragement behind the boycott, according to the *kaymakam*. Therefore, the boycotters were not allowed to use violence and coercion, and the workers were not allowed to use tactics similar to a strike. The bureaucracy and the elite were cautious and anxious regarding the mobilization of people on the street.[297]

The governor of Beirut warned and advised the boatmen of the city who held the monopoly in the port and refused to unload French products. Whether to load or unload merchandise was their free choice, since they were not officers or servants of the state. They either had to be convinced or forced to do so, as the governor could not achieve their compliance, and he informed the government that he would take recourse of the law as well as regulations concerning the freedom of trade and work.[298] He also published a notice on the instructions from the Sublime Port, in which he repudiated claims that the British Empire had an unfriendly attitude toward the Ottoman Empire regarding Crete. The government was competent in dealing with the question;[299] however, it was not easy to act since the united boatmen were a powerful group in the town. For instance, the governor of Yanya and the *mutasarrıf* of Preveze informed the government that unlawful actions, such as preventing the passengers of Greek ships from disembarking, and instigating disorder, should be punished. However, the governors hesitated to take action, because of the social origins of the movement. They wanted the Ottoman government to confirm the need to take action and send specific orders regarding the blockades.[300] Similarly, the second vice-governor of Trabzon informed the government that he had advised the mayor and the head of the Boycott Society regarding the actions against the Bank of Athens. Still, he asked the government what to do if the boycott representatives did not accept the terms that he dictated to them.[301] Thanks to the efforts of the French consul, the Boycott Society conceded that the Bank of Athens was a French enterprise and published a declaration in a local newspaper, *Meşveret*, saying that they did not want to harm the friendship between the Ottomans and the French. To this end, they declared that the boycott against the Bank of Athens was over.[302]

In Kala-i Sultaniye, the boycotters claimed that some of the ships sailing under the Russian flag were in fact Greek ships. Therefore, the *mutasarrıf* of Kala-i Sultaniye had no choice but to write to the port administration in Istanbul to ask whether these ships had been sold to a Russian company or not. He hesitated to take action against the boycotters because of their social power and legitimate position in society. The posters advertising the boycott movement about town also became a subject of criticism. The governor defended the posters to the Greek vice-consul, arguing that they were only hung in the neighborhood of the boatmen and could not be considered as violence. Therefore, a local bureaucrat in Kala-i Sultaniye did not put pressure on the boycotters, but accepted their demands.[303] This official treatment provided space for the movement.

In the course of the boycott movement, the government was generally unsuccessful in forcing the local governors to prevent the excessive actions of the boycotters, particularly the port workers. In September 1911, the Ottoman government was still sending orders to the coastal provinces, requesting the local authorities to apply the legal regulations.[304]

It was not only the power of the boycott movement that forced the local bureaucracy to side with the movement. The local officials favored the boycott and usually tried to legitimize the boycotters' excesses. A most intriguing case was that of a public prosecutor who accused a French citizen, Jan Rolan, of not acknowledging the Boycott Society; this was an illegal organization, but a prosecutor still accused a person of not recognizing it.[305]

The Shift from Foreign to "Internal" Enemies   155

The local governors did not approve of coercion and force, but they did try to explain the reasons behind them. The *mutasarrıf* of Antalya informed the central government that, although the closed Greek shops had been reopened and the aggressors detained, the vice-consuls there still complained about the boycott. The *mutassarıf* emphasized that the French consul of the town was the son of a Greek doctor, and that the consuls' complaint might therefore have been related with their Greek identity or their philhellenism.[306] The director of the civil registration office in Antalya, Hüsnü Efendi, told Nikolaos Haciargiriou, who applied for Ottoman citizenship, that the nation and the government together were boycotting the Greeks and that they would force all Greek citizens on Ottoman territory to assume Ottoman citizenship. If they did not assume Ottoman citizenship, then the government would send the Greek consulate back to Greece. He claimed that the boycott would end only then.[307] However, the report of a Greek manager from the Dardanelles claimed that Dimitri Liyakos, who had already applied for Ottoman citizenship, was unable to get an exemption from the boycott; his coffee-house was besieged by the boycotters, and his customers had been expelled.[308]

The governor of Preveze also referred to the British consul as an advocate of Greek interests and claimed that he had been trained in Corfu.[309] The governor of Adana informed the central government that the boycott against a theater company had been limited to one night only, trying to diminish the significance of the movement and therefore the reaction of the government.[310]

The *mutasarrıf* of Karesi informed the government about the secret ambitions and goals of the boycotted parties in Edremit. According to the governor, the Greek owner of a farm rented his land to a British citizen, but still could not escape from the boycott. Moreover, the governor claimed that the farm was close to the sea and that the boycotted party was planning to kidnap the tenant and extort money from the government in order to compensate for the damage caused by the movement. The *mutasarrıf* of Karesi informed the government that he had given the necessary orders to impede such plans. It is evident in this case that the governor took measures not against boycotting activities, but against a prospective intrigue of the boycotted persons.[311] There were also false claims for compensation. The British consul reported that in Smyrna several of the British subjects who applied for compensation were "looking upon this idea of compensation as an easy way of making profits."[312]

The Greek consul visited the governor of Aydın to inform him about the picketing of the Greek stores and Greek citizens who could no longer buy goods to cover their most urgent needs. The governor replied that the order for this boycott had been given by the Boycott Committee of Salonica and that they could do nothing but wait. The governor thus referred to an order by the Boycott Society as if it were legitimate and procedural. The committees of the boycott movement and the Boycott Society were illegal organizations, and their legal status was underlined in many official documents. However, the governor of Aydın did not hesitate to follow their orders.[313]

A typical example of the local governors' approval of the boycott movement and the Boycott Society occurred in Balya/Karesi. The Boycott Society declared a boycott against an Ottoman mine corporation, calling for the dismissal of Greeks from the mines. The *kaymakam* of Balya emphasized that the society had not acted against the law. He confirmed that he approved of the dismissal of the Greeks, but added that the boycotters had not harmed the production and business of the firm. The reply of the *kaymakam* and the *mutasarrıf* of Karesi read like a defense or legitimization of the Boycott Society. However, the vice-president of the mining corporation, in the telegram he sent to the Ministry of the Interior, complained about the boycotters' persistent harassment of the employees and the mines. He was worried that the violations of the law would ruin their business, which employed more than 2,000 Ottoman workers.[314]

The *mutasarrıf* of Bolu claimed in his report to the government that the complaints of the Greek ships that they could not buy coal from Ereğli were groundless. He argued that the main reason for these complaints was not the boycott, but their greed for money from the insurance companies. This allegation was also contrary to his former report about the case. In that report, the *mutasarrıf* concentrated on the boycotters and assured the government that he and the *kaymakam* of Zonguldak were taking preventive measures. However, even in that report they had underlined that the boycott movement was the expression of the people's free will and consisted of peaceful actions.[315] The *kaymakam* of Ereğli was also accused of not helping a Greek ship that experienced problems: it had started to sink about 65 m from the coast, and it was claimed the *kaymakam* had not allowed the boatmen to help the sailors and passengers.[316] Three months later, the Ministry of Foreign Affairs and the Ministry of the Interior were informed in greater detail about how the ship was rescued.[317]

The most obvious defense or praise of the boycott movement, the Boycott Society in particular, appears in a report of the Administration of Public Security. This report maintained that the Boycott Society was the outcome of national enthusiasm and sentiments. It was not governed as a society, but as a voluntary movement. Therefore, the state of affairs was under control, and an outburst was not too likely.[318] Similarly, the mayor of Istanbul referred to the report of the *mutasarrıf* of Üsküdar, saying that a boycott against a factory was consistent with the official limitations on the boycott. However, he only referred to the statement of the local boycott committee in his reply. Typically, he stated that there was nothing he could do about the boycott, since it was an expression of national emotions, repeating the reasoning of the boycott movement.[319]

The local governors were not only sympathetic towards the boycott movement, but were sometimes also its members. The government sent a warning to the province of Edirne, because in Mustafapaşa the *kaimakam*, the judge and the member of the court were all on the board of directors of the Boycott Society. The Ottoman government had to remind them that the state and its bureaucracy should stay impartial in the face of the movement. There were many grievances regarding the damage caused by the boycott, but the authorities to which the victims would apply were in fact part and parcel of the movement.[320]

For example, the governor of Smyrna advised the head of the Tobacco Regie that they should solve their problem via negotiations with the Boycott Society. The Boycott Society encouraged the illegal marketing of tobacco in the city, and the Regie tried to stop this initiative. The governor brought the society and the Tobacco Regie together in his office and asked them to reach a compromise: although the Boycott Society was not a legal entity, it was asked to negotiate in the office of the governor-general. When the government ordered the arrest of those boycotters who encouraged the illegal marketing of tobacco, the vice-governor replied that the telegrams sent by the Boycott Society were anonymous (in most cases, it was the deputies or the vice-consul who replied to the government, not the governors themselves). Therefore, he claimed that they did not know whom to detain. As a response, the Ministry of the Interior reminded the authorities of the province of Aydın that it was easy to find out who had sent the telegram from the post office. As mentioned above, the governor-general himself had met the representative of the Boycott Society in his office; therefore, it was obvious that local bureaucrats aided the Boycott Society, even when it was acting against the law.[321]

In Ergiri/Yanya, the Boycott Committee was under the leadership of the mayor. A meeting was convened in the public square of the town, and 200 Muslims and non-Muslims announced a boycott against Greek merchandise. The Boycott Committee was composed of five Muslims and five non-Muslims. The Ottoman government informed the governor of Yanya that a meeting could only be convened within the limits of the law, but that this kind of organization was not acceptable.[322]

At the time when the 1910–11 boycott wave came to an end, the famous Turkish author Süleyman Nazif was the governor-general of Trabzon. In one of his reports to the government, he touched upon the boycott issue and summarized his view: if boycott was a means to realize the national interest, he certainly would have advocated it. However, the state's politics of trade, and the trade of politics, had been left in the hands of the porters and boatmen because of the boycott movement. The rise of the power of the port workers was not a promising development for the empire.[323] He stated that the damage caused by the boycott also harmed the interests of the Ottoman Empire, both politically and economically.[324] However, he did not take any action against the boycotters, unless they turned violent. He advised a Swiss merchant to hire his own boats and assured him that no one, particularly not the port workers of Trabzon, would obstruct him.[325]

Although the ranks of the local bureaucracy gave clandestine support to the boycotters, the Boycott Society in Smyrna complained about the interference of the government and the police. This was due to the dominant nature of the boycott in the city. Since the boycott was more extensive in Smyrna, the pressure on the boycotters was also more intense.[326] Several of the members of the Boycott Society were even detained, and this triggered a reaction from other boycott organizations in the region. For instance, the Tire Boycott Commission sent a telegram to Smyrna to ask why the organization in Smyrna did not protest, saying that the oppression of the national interests and the protection of foreigners should finally come to an end. The Tire Boycott Commission asked the commission in Smyrna what activities they planned for their next meeting. Clearly, the network of boycotters was working well. This network and the social origins of the boycotters were putting pressure on the Ottoman state apparatus. The following day the Boycott Society announced in the newspaper that their friends who had been arrested a couple of days ago had been released.[327] However, the tension between the boycotters and the local bureaucrats did not decrease, because of the picketing activities. The police force and the gendarmerie intervened in the picketing, resulting in scuffles between the boycotters and the gendarmerie. This prompted the Boycott Society of Smyrna to publish a declaration, asking whether the police's duty was to defend and to serve the Hellenes in the Ottoman Empire or not. The society stated that there was great social pressure on them to protest to the government through mass meetings because of the negative attitude of the police forces.[328] The government and the local governors had reasons to fear the social power of the boycott network.

CHAPTER 4

THE MUSLIM PROTEST: THE ECONOMIC BOYCOTT AS A WEAPON IN PEACETIME, 1913–14

Before the Balkan Wars, boycotts had been organized against European countries and their economic representatives in the Ottoman Empire. However, as demonstrated in the previous chapter, the non-Muslim Ottomans also suffered from the boycotts. Their losses went hand in hand with the rise of Turkish/Muslim nationalism. Although Ottoman citizens were never openly targeted in the boycott movement's statements, political and economic developments in the nineteenth century had paved the way for a clash between different religious and ethnic communities. As is widely argued in the Turkish historiography, Turkish nationalism eventually gained unprecedented power in the empire after the Balkan Wars. Thenceforth, Turkish/Muslim nationalists increasingly excluded native non-Muslims from economic and social networks.[1] In this context, by late 1913 the boycott movement was explicitly promoting solidarity within the Muslim community, and had began excluding non-Muslims by early 1914.

In this chapter, I will analyze the widely distributed pamphlets that were aimed at Muslims and called for economic and social solidarity. The distribution of leaflets and mass propaganda for a national economy coincided with the revival of the boycott movement. The discourse and the organization of the movement directly targeted non-Muslims and advocated Muslim dominance in the economy, which it was hoped would pave the way for full power for Muslims/Turks in the Ottoman Empire. Because of the violence among different communities that accompanied the boycott (and was the subject of public discussions and diplomatic negotiations), the role played by Muslim gangs in the movement became as significant as the mobilization of the masses. In the course of the boycott movement, different political and social actors competed and negotiated with each other. The boycott organizations were generally made up of local notables, local bureaucrats and immigrants. The government and the CUP were in favor of the boycott movement, but at the same time tried to control it. The non-Muslims who suffered from the boycott, particularly the Greeks and the Armenians, tried to publicize their problems with the international public. Thus, the patriarchs of these communities put pressure on the Ottoman government by communicating with the Great Powers. The Great Powers and their diplomatic representatives were much more involved in this phase of the boycott than in previous cases. For this reason it is crucial for the study of the boycott movement to understand the struggle and relationships between the Great Powers, the patriarchates and the church network, the CUP and its social base in Asia Minor, Muslim/Turkish nationalist organizations and their cadres, and the masses of Muslim immigrants flowing into the Ottoman Empire from the lost territories.

The Political Milieu

The boycott movement came to different towns of Asia Minor around February 1914, targeting Ottoman Greeks in particular and, to a lesser extent, Armenians and Bulgarians. In order to grasp the general characteristics of the boycott movement in 1914, it is important to understand the contemporary social and political agenda. Apart from the general devastating social consequences of the Balkan Wars, which deeply influenced Ottoman Society, there were also political and diplomatic problems that the Ottoman elite used in order to galvanize the sentiments of Muslims in the Ottoman Empire.

Before the declaration of WWI, the Ottoman press closely followed the formation of the alliance among the Great Powers. Apart from the issue of the balance of power, Ottoman public opinion was almost exclusively occupied by two crucial diplomatic questions. The first was the Islands Question (*Adalar Meselesi*), which was so significant that newspapers included a special column reserved for news and comments regarding this matter.[2] It concerned the controversy about the sovereignty rights of the Ottoman Empire and Greece over the Aegean islands. The dispute continued until July 1914, when the two states came to terms with each other as they realized that the world was approaching a great war.[3] However, until then the issue continued to cause tension between the two countries.

The second problem between Greece and the Ottoman Empire was the question of Macedonia. The plight of Muslims in Macedonia provoked nationalist and religious sentiments among Ottoman Muslims.[4] Therefore, the Macedonian Question is significant for understanding mobilization patterns and discourses related with the boycott movement. The Ottoman Turkish press utilized the issue to stir up national and religious sentiments. Voluminous news items and many rumors appeared regarding the persecution of Muslims in the newly lost Macedonia. The misery of the immigrants who were constantly flowing into the Ottoman Empire fueled the resentment of Muslims.[5]

In a confidential memorandum, the British consul W.D.W. Matthews reported that the educated Turks were convinced that the loss of the islands of Lesbos, Chios and Samos to Greece would result in the "disintegration of the Turkish possessions in Asia." The CUP considered the islands a threat to the motherland, Anatolia.[6] The Turkish press blamed the Great Powers for their injustice toward the Turks and for not keeping their word to "assist Turkey to consolidate her position in Asia," and, according to the memorandum, asserted that these islands would be a base for Greek gangs to agitate and launch attacks on Asia Minor, as had happened in Macedonia. Matthews also referred to the extremist and chauvinist views in newspapers such as *Tanin, Köylü* and *Tasvir-i Efkar*, which incited anti-European and anti-Greek feelings among Muslims. These newspapers reported on a daily basis about ill-treatment of Muslims in Macedonia and on the islands, according to the British consul. The stories most often quoted in these articles were of the hoisting of a Greek flag over the *mihrab* (prayer niche) of the Hagia Sofia, the conscription of local Greeks into the Hellenic fleet, and the embellishment of Istanbul for the prospective arrival of the triumphant Greek King Constantine. The memorandum stated that these claims were nothing but baseless allegations that instigated Muslims' sentiments against Ottoman Greeks.[7]

The Islands Question and the Macedonian Question created an unstable atmosphere for the Ottoman Greeks since both issues were related to Greece. Furthermore, the Ottoman/Turkish press published news of the atrocities and assaults of Greek gangs on Muslim villages, or of the lessons taught in Greek schools, or of the state of Muslims in places densely populated by Greeks. These rumors circulating among the Muslim population increased the tensions between the two communities and facilitated the mobilization of Muslims against Ottoman Greeks during the boycott movement.[8]

Among the Turkish elite, and particularly the CUP, there was widespread fear of an invasion of Asia Minor. The presence of non-Muslims in Thrace and along the coastal regions was considered a threat. Therefore, the CUP probably wanted to replace non-Muslims with Muslims, whom they considered to be more loyal.[9]

To sum up, there were sufficient reasons for great tension between various elements of the Ottoman Empire. The Ottoman parliamentary elections, which took place between the winter of 1913 and the spring of 1914, were the final contributory factor to this uneasy social environment, which gave rise to numerous incidents between the CUP and prominent members of the Armenian and Greek communities.[10] Therefore, the social and political milieu legitimized the actions of different segments of Muslim society and the cadres of the Turkish nationalist movement, who wanted to improve the social and political position of Muslims *vis-à-vis* non-Muslims. The stage was set for agitation against non-Muslims.

Pamphleting the Muslim Public

At the end of 1913, numerous pamphlets were handed out for free, aimed at the Muslims and Turks of the Ottoman Empire. The aim of these leaflets was to bring about an economic revival of the Muslim population, which was hoped to rescue them from the "merciless hands" of the non-Muslims who were working against the empire. The discourse on the national economy became more critical of the economic inferiority of Muslims *vis-à-vis* the Christians. Mehmed Reşid, the governor of Karesi, wrote in his diary on 30 July 1913 that national sentiments were on the rise and that a national economic awakening was taking place among the Muslim population of Edremit. During his visit, he also underlined that the Muslims of Edremit and Burhaniye were in need of a national bank for their economic progress. He claimed that Muslims had started to compete with the Christians.[11]

On the one hand, it was claimed that it was still primarily non-Muslims who profited from the current state of the economy. Non-Muslims were professionalized in different crafts, while the Muslim population constituted their consumers and bought only from them. Non-Muslims became wealthy thanks to the money that Muslims spent. On the other hand, non-Muslims used the money they earned against the interests of the Ottoman Empire. That is to say, non-Muslims, and particularly the Greeks, were betraying the country, by economically supporting Greece with their endowments and donations.

As a result the boycotters' discourse shifted and began to directly target non-Muslim Ottomans. This idea became prevalent among the Ottoman elite and was echoed in the news, articles and commentaries of the Turkish newspapers. Pamphlets addressed to Muslims tried to popularize this new concept of the Milli İktisat (National Economy) among the Muslim and Turkish lower classes. At least four pamphlets were published in 1913 and 1914 in Istanbul, and another one in Smyrna in 1914. In fact, the four pamphlets published in Istanbul are to a great extent identical and offer almost the same structure, so it is possible to talk of different versions of a particular text. Thousands of these leaflets were distributed for free, both in Istanbul and in the provinces. They had very similar titles: two of them were named *Müslümanlara Mahsus* (Especially for Muslims), and the others were titled *Müslümanlara Mahsus Kurtulmak Yolu* (A Path of Salvation for Muslims) and *Müslüman ve Türklere* (To Muslim and Turks).[12] There may be several other versions, since the short versions do not include the lists of merchants that were attached to these pamphlets to help

Muslim consumers in finding Muslim businesses.[13] Secondary information regarding these pamphlets indicates that some of these short versions did enclose a list.

The authors of these leaflets were anonymous. However, thanks to the publication of the diary of Ahmet Nedim Servet Tör, in which he wrote about the day-to-day life of his little daughter Nevhiz, we now have ample information about these pamphlets.[14] Ahmet Nedim was a civil bureaucrat working in the Ministry of War who published patriotic and nationalist pamphlets and poems in order to generate a mobilization among the Muslims and Turks after the Balkan Wars.[15] His brother Edib Servet Bey was among the ten members of the *heyet-i aliye* (sublime board) of the CUP before the revolution.[16] This fact, and his being an officer in the Ministry of War, indicates that the state and the CUP had a much more active role in the boycott movement after the Balkan Wars.

The first of these booklets was *Müslümanlara Mahsus*.[17] Ahmet Nedim first mentions this pamphlet in the diary entry of 10 November 1913, as an excuse and apology for not concentrating on the diary for about two months. He summarizes the introduction of *Müslümanlara Mahsus* in order to explain to his daughter the reasons why he embarked on such an endeavor. The "articles in the newspapers and other publications on *milli iktisat* were inexplicit and obscure and therefore were not effective on people," writes Ahmet Nedim. Therefore, he decided to address Muslims directly in order to force Muslim merchants, artisans and tradesmen to "spend their capital" within the empire and to induce Muslims to buy native products. He wanted to reach those people who were largely illiterate, did not read newspapers and did not have money to spend on books. This is why he handed out the pamphlets for free and wrote in a very simple and basic Turkish.

At first, he distributed 2,000 copies. The pamphlet attracted so much attention that there was a second print run after a very short time, this time of 20,000 copies. To the second edition he added a list of merchants. He mentions that the preparation of the pamphlet took almost a month. On 10 November 1913, he considered printing another 100,000 copies. Ahmed Nedim was content with the demand for the pamphlet and the attention it had garnered among the people.

He was also very happy since he had heard of the bankruptcies of five or six *Rums* (Ottoman Greeks) in different quarters of Istanbul.[18] Ahmed Nedim claimed that the publication of the pamphlet inspired an *inkılab-ı iktisadi ve ticariye* (economic and commercial revolution), and it was a source of pride to him that the pamphlets and their contents became a subject of daily conversations among ordinary people.[19] The Greek consul in Ayvalık reported to the Greek Foreign Ministry that government agents throughout the country had tried to entice Muslims to participate in the boycott movement, by distributing booklets that provoked Muslims against the Greek population.[20] The Greek newspaper *Embros*, published in Athens, also reported of leaflets that instigated Muslims around Smyrna.[21] These sources indicate that these pamphlets succeeded in reaching Muslims in different provinces.

It was not only the pamphlets of the boycott movement that inflamed Muslims against Greeks, but also booklets written with less specifically economic motives. For instance, the metropolitan bishop of Ephesus claimed that a book called *Kavm-i Cedid* (The New Nation),[22] which supposedly cursed Jesus Christ, was provoking Muslims.[23]

Müslümanlara Mahsus begins by reminding its readers of the terrifying defeat of the Balkan Wars. Although Edirne and the areas around Kırkkilise were taken back, the general loss of territory was tremendous. The pamphlet mentions lost towns such as İskeçe, Salonica, Yanya, Manastır and İşkodra, also the Aegean islands and the lakes, rivers, fertile plains and forests that these embraced. The Muslims in these towns and regions were abandoned and destitute. Even the wealthy now led miserable lives. Children were begging on the streets, and some of them were serving *rakı* to enemy soldiers in the taverns.[24]

Compared to *Müslümanlara Mahsus*, *Müslüman ve Türklere* has a much more bitter and fierce tone and echoes the sentimental articles in contemporary Turkish newspapers. It begins by referring to the "rotten skins" and "carved eyes" of Muslims in the lost lands, then goes on to talk about the enemies who killed their brothers with bayonets, raped mothers and sisters, and afterwards drank wine.[25]

The pamphlet published in Smyrna was much more moderate compared to the others. *İzmir Tüccaran ve Esnefan-ı İslamiyyesine Mahsus Rehber* (A Guide for Muslim Merchants and Artisans of Smyrna) avoids a provocative tone, being written in moderate language in order to convince its readers.[26] This pamphlet was not free of charge: revenues from its sale went to the Donanma Cemiyeti, a typical nationalist act of the time. It includes a detailed list of merchants and artisans of Smyrna and Aydın. This guide also refers to the Balkan Wars as a turning point in Ottoman history, which have enabled the Muslims/Turks to see developments more clearly. The pamphlet explains to its readers why trade and money are crucial for a nation, and its writer expresses gratitude for the economic and commercial awakening among the Turks and Muslims. As well as the list of merchants at the end of the leaflet, several examples of Muslim entrepreneurs are cited in order to depict what Muslim wealth should accomplish. The pamphlet mentions Mehmet Rasim Bey, who constructed a textile factory in Tarsus/Adana with a capital of 100,000 lire.[27] Mehmed Rasim also had an agent, Bosnalı Suhadlizade Abdullah Hilmi Bey, indicating that Muslim merchants not only constructed factories, but also built a business network within the empire.

The pamphlet heralds newly emerging national companies in Konya, Istanbul and İzmir. Like in other leaflets and publications in Turkish periodicals, the significance of grocers is highlighted, with most of the population in Asia Minor dependent on the network of Greek grocers. Therefore, the emergence of Muslim grocers is seen as a vital development for Muslim/Turkish nationalists. This is why *İzmir Tüccaran ve Esnefan-ı İslamiyyesine Mahsus Rehber* does not employ the term "boycott" for the new entrepreneurship of Muslims in the economy and trade. For the writer, this is a struggle for living; a struggle for survival. The leaflet employs the notion of "catching up" by stressing the preference of non-Muslims for their co-religionists. The writer claims that Turks, at last, have taken the economy and the trade of the country into their own hands and will genuinely and actually own them.[28] These arguments, which would also prevail in the discourse of Turkish nationalism, were a call to reconquer the country. In terms of trade and commerce, Muslims and Turks had virtually been asleep, which reduced them to the level of slavery in their own country. Therefore, Muslims should help each other and particularly those who were rich should invest in the economy and come together to establish banks.

All pamphlets attributed the responsibility for the atrocities that they describe to those who hoisted foreign flags, and ultimately to those Muslims who surrendered themselves to the non-Muslims by buying from them and making them rich. The Muslim merchants could not compete with their non-Muslim counterparts because of the "silly preferences" of Muslim consumers. Non-Muslims were "sucking the blood of Muslims," and as a result Muslims were "financing the bullets that kill their co-religionists." These ideas became prevalent among the Turkish elite in the course of the boycott movement. For instance, the medical students Behçet Salih, Mahmut Halit and Mustafa Muzaffer delivered public lectures on hygiene in the province of Aydın and repeated the arguments of these pamphlets. The acting British consul-general in Smyrna, Heathcote Smith, quoted a part of their lecture in his report: "We are broken hearted at finding you Muslims are still asleep. The Christians, profiting from our ignorance, have now for ages been taking our place and taking away our rights. These vipers whom we are nourishing have been sucking out all the life-blood of the nation. They are the parasitical worms eating into our flesh whom we must destroy and do away with. It is time we freed ourselves from these individuals, by all means lawful and unlawful..."[29]

The cost of Muslim consumer patterns was allegedly 5,000 Muslim lives in Rumeli. The leaflet warns its readers that they would be next and that it was their turn to suffer, if they did not change their habits. Otherwise, the caliphate and the Turkish sultanate would not prevail, and the coat of the Prophet would be trampled under the feet of the *gavurs* (infidels).[30]

At this juncture, the warship *Averof* entered the discourse. The *Averof* was bought by the Greek navy from an Italian shipyard and became its flagship. For at least three reasons, this armored cruiser (*thorakismeno katadromiko*) was crucial for the rising Turkish nationalism. First, in spite of bargaining with the producer, the Ottomans had not been able to buy the ship.[31] Second, the *Averof* played a significant role in the Balkan Wars and particularly in the Ottoman defeat. Third, a Greek benefactor by the name of Georges Averof had donated a large amount of money and thereby facilitated its purchase. *Müslümanlara Mahsus* claims that the Ottoman army could not exit through the straits to help Salonica and the islands and, therefore, could not stop the Greek army, ultimately because of the *Averof*.[32]

How was it possible that a small state like Greece was able to buy such a battleship, but the Ottoman Empire was not? The pamphlets underlined the fact that in Greece it was not the state, but the nation who bought such battleships. This argument was very popular among the Ottoman elite and gave rise to the establishment of the Donanma Cemiyeti (Navy Society) in 1909. Furthermore, the pamphlets pointed out that the battleship was bought by a *Rum*, Averof, who was not a Greek citizen, but an Ottoman Greek from Görice (Korçe in Albanian). The leaflets express regret that Ottoman citizens helped the enemy; *Müslümanlara Mahsus* asked: "How many citizens are there whose hands we shake and whom we see every day and who work day and night to endow to Greek government."[33] Georges Averof's donation was proof of non-Muslim treason, which matched news of other non-Muslims who regularly gave to Greek charities. In fact, Averof was not from Görice, but from Metsovo (also on Ottoman territory) and had at a young age migrated to Egypt where he made his fortune with a business based in Alexandria. By the time the Greek navy bought the cruiser, Averof (1815[8]–99) had already passed away, and it was not him personally but his charitable foundation that contributed the donation.

The name George M. Averof was utilized in nationalist discourse to mobilize the Muslim public to shop only from Muslim merchants. According to the pamphlets, every penny given to non-Muslims became a bullet aimed at Muslims. This is why the pamphlets argued that they should not earn any money, or at least Muslims should not pay any money to them. Instead, the native economy should be supported. It is important to mention here that, in relation to the attitude toward non-Muslims, a fundamental shift occurred: until 1912 non-Muslims were not excluded from the definition of "us" within the discourse of the boycott movement. During the 1910–11 boycott movement, non-Muslims were also invited to invest in the development of native production. However, after 1913 they were no longer treated as a constitutive element of the empire and were excluded from the national economy. This shift in emphasis was not completely new, but it only became apparent and spoken about at that point.

The pamphlets warned Muslim consumers about the marketing tactics and strategies of non-Muslims: how they decorated their windows, how they treated their customers, how they convinced people to buy from them, how they followed fashion, and so on.[34] Non-Muslim shops did not employ Muslims because they only wanted to support their co-religionists. They hired Muslim workers only for menial tasks, which did not cost much in terms of wage expenses, because they considered Muslims and Turks stupid and foolish.[35] The first part of *Müslümanlara Mahsus* and *Müslümanlara Mahsus Kurtulmak Yolu* ends with a call to the people, warning that *Müslümanlık* and *Türklük* (Muslim and Turkish communities) were perishing because of their own negligence. Therefore, Muslims should start to think about their future and strive to become merchants themselves and amass fortunes. If they only proceeded on this path, they could protect their nation and religion.[36] The pamphlets also informed their readers that Greece was working to buy another battleship, the *Konstantin*, and half of its cost was to be paid by Ottoman Christians. The leaflets claim that, if Muslims had frequented Muslim shops, there would have been wealthy Muslims who could purchase one or two battleships for the Ottoman navy. And if Muslims were to succeed, then Christians would no longer be able to take over "the Ottomans' beautiful countries" where mosques were now turned into barns and churches and the tombs of dervishes washed with wine.[37]

The pamphlets urged Muslims to buy from Muslim and Turkish stores, because after the loss of Rumelian territories, Anatolia and Istanbul were next. Therefore, people should stop paying money to Christians who welcomed and cheered for the enemy soldiers and showed them where to find Muslim houses and Muslim women in the lost Ottoman territories. Compared to the other pamphlets, *Müslüman ve Türklere* was much stricter in its tone. The anonymous writer admonished Muslims who criticized others for their clothes: native products might be tasteless, rough and dull, but of course they were better than a probable occupation and the loss of the remaining lands–Those who continued to wear luxurious clothes would probably wear them as fancy dress, dancing before the infidels while these drank their *rakı* and wine. The pamphlet ends with a threat: Muslims who enter Christian stores will be prohibited from doing so with warnings, threats and force. In the end, the writer tells Muslims and Turks to repeat the following oath:

> I will never shop from Christians. If I do so, I am dishonest and a bastard and deserve every kind of curse and insult.[38]

These pamphlets also include stories intended to motivate the Muslim public to buy native products. *Müslümanlara Mahsus* tells a story of an English lady in Egypt who gave a lesson to her Muslim servant regarding the national economy. The wife of Lord Cromer, the British viceroy in Egypt, gave 1 lira to her Muslim servant to buy a bolt of unbleached muslin from a particular store. However, her servant brought her a better and cheaper fabric, but from a different store. The lady became angry and told the servant that the fabric was not English, but a French product, and the store where he bought it was probably not English either. Therefore, she declared, although she had paid 1 mecidiye less, her nation had lost 1 lira, and her nation's loss was her loss. As a result, the servant who had served in the house for five years was dismissed. The story ends with a commentary on how even a very wealthy lady thinks only about her country, even for 1 mecidiye.[39]

Müslümanlara Mahsus Kurtulmak Yolu contains a different story, the story of Selanikli Ayşe Hanım (Mistress Ayşe from Salonica). As stated in the text itself, the touching and tearful story of the Maraşoğlu family was included in the leaflet in order to teach the public a lesson. Ayşe Hanım—whose father, husband and children had been killed by Greeks in Salonica—went for a walk in Istanbul. She was shocked when she came across the store of the Gramatopoulo Brothers, the Binbir Çiçek Mağazası (Store of One thousand and One Flowers). As is repeatedly described in these pamphlets, there was an employee at the door, kindly inviting prospective customers into the shop. Ayşe Hanım also discerned Muslim women inside the store who had taken off their veils and did not hesitate to show their powdered necks. Ayşe Hanım also entered the shop. The owner and salesman tried to advertise their products to her, while she slowly moved around the store. She asked whether the person to whom she was talking was Gramatopoulo himself, and when he confirmed that he was, she asked if he had a brother in Salonica who owned a similar store.

Ayşe Hanım then told the Muslim shoppers her story and the story of who the Gramatopoulo in Salonica were. Nikolaki Gramatopoulo had escorted Greek soldiers to Ayşe Hanım's *konak* (mansion). The soldiers then killed her servant and mother. Ayşe Hanım hid, until Nikolaki saw her and ran toward her, saying "Oh my beautiful young woman. I want you, you!" She escaped over the roof and hid in the house of an Austrian lady. Upon hearing her story, the shop owner began to quarrel with Ayşe Hanım. Yet she continued to address the Muslim women: enemies bought their weapons thanks to the help of non-Muslim Ottomans. After the invasion of Salonica, she saw military cars with inscriptions stating that these had been presents from the Greeks of Istanbul, Smyrna, Bursa and Samsun. She asked women how they could buy from non-Muslims who worked against the Ottoman Empire. Finally, the Muslim women understood the truth and left the store, thanking Ayşe Hanım.[40]

Ahmet Nedim attached a list of merchants to the Pamphlet in order to indicate that it was possible to satisfy all needs by buying from Muslim traders only. He left blank spaces within the list to give the readers the opportunity to add missing names of Muslim merchants, so that Muslims themselves could actively create a perfect list: he stated that Istanbul was a large city and that it was almost impossible to collect the names of all Muslim businessmen. He was also happy that, thanks to the economic awakening among Muslims, many new Muslim shops, stores and companies had appeared. He wished for one of the *vakıf hans* (apartment blocks containing offices and shops) built in Istanbul to be reserved for Muslim and Turkish producers and merchants only, so that customers would immediately know where to go.[41]

Ahmet Nedim was still working on new editions of *Müslümanlara Mahsus* at the end of January 1914. On 28 January 1914, he wrote in the diary for Nevhiz that he had just completed editing a new, improved version of the pamphlet. He defined his endeavor as "propagandism" and stated that the pamphlet would be distributed to Istanbul and Anatolia in two or three weeks.[42] This date also coincided with the renewed boycott movement. The effective propaganda activities for a national economy and the extensive distribution of pamphlets for an awakening of the Muslim and Turkish public resulted in its revival after the Balkan Wars, and the movement came to a head, together with complaints of non-Muslims, in late February and early March of 1914.

The Ottoman 1913–14 boycott movement was, like most others, directly related to notions of economic nationalism, economic revivalism and the development of a national economy. The number of Muslims in the economy started to increase over the course of the Second Constitutional Period, particularly after the Balkan Wars. The boycott was a crucial factor in this increase, and it was no coincidence that Hüseyin Kazım took this into consideration in his open letter to the Orthodox patriarch, who had complained about the movement. In this pamphlet, which constitutes a significant document of the boycott movement, Hüseyin Kazım tried to legitimize it by referring to the state of Muslims in the economy.[43]

The pamphlet begins by referring to the dispute between the Greek Orthodox patriarchate and the Ministry of Justice. The Greek patriarch had proclaimed that he would consult different means and ways to solve the problem, if the boycott movement did not stop. For Hüseyin Kazım, this statement implied the intervention of the European Great Powers. He argued that there had been many instances in Ottoman history of these powers interfering in Ottoman politics. Furthermore, there was much evidence pointing to the collaboration of the patriarchate and Athens.[44] He touched upon the issue of the capitulations and how they had impoverished the empire. At last, Muslims and Turks had started to learn how to earn money and to produce. According to Hüseyin Kazım, the patriarch wanted Muslims to remain poor while Greeks earned money and made donations to the Greek navy.

Hüseyin Kazım claimed that it was the Muslims who constituted the poor of the empire and this was why they had to learn how to earn money. In his view, Muslims were now merely trying to imitate the Greeks who only did business with and employed their co-religionists: with the boycott, Muslims were doing the same, by buying from each other. However, their preference was to do this without violence, force and illegality. He claimed that no violent act was possible, since the government would not allow such a thing to happen.⁴⁵ The boycott was merely the awakening of Muslims. Hüseyin Kazım asked his readers whether Greeks would shop from a Greek or a Muslim grocer. He asked whether they acted in line with their patriotic duties. He implied that Greeks did not donate to the Donanma Cemiyeti (Navy Society) or buy shares in national organizations, particularly national companies. Therefore, for him, the movement was not even a boycott, but a duty and revival of Muslims. It was only with the disaster of the Balkan Wars that Muslims understood their backwardness in the economy and decided to improve themselves. Now, they were starting to invest and learn how to earn money. Hüseyin Kazım claimed that, within the space of two or three months, approximately 450 new Muslim stores had opened in Istanbul.⁴⁶

Hüseyin Kazım argued that similar acts in foreign countries were regarded as patriotic activities, whereas such nationalist endeavors in the Ottoman Empire were considered the acts of crowds, rowdies and fanatics.⁴⁷ He reminded his readers of the atrocities that the Muslims encountered in Macedonia under the Greek yoke: how the Greeks killed their co-religionists, how they raped Muslim women, and how they destroyed the houses of their Muslim neighbors. The Ottoman Greeks who donated to the Ottoman fleet and participated in the national mobilization were exceptions. Therefore, for him, Muslims should decide to support each other.⁴⁸

Similar thoughts concerning the need for a national economy were common in the contemporary Turkish press. For instance, a leading article published in *İkdam* claimed that the movement about which the Greeks were complaining was not a boycott, but a type of solidarity.⁴⁹ According to *İkdam*, Muslims would no longer work as public employees, but rather invest in industry and trade; they would become productive and earn their own bread. The newspaper repeated the argument that Muslims in general did not work hard, but were the slaves of the state, and that they left business activities to non-Muslims. Furthermore, *İkdam* claimed that, as Muslims started to become entrepreneurs, non-Muslims began to worry: Europeans would from now on prefer Muslims as trade partners, because they could be trusted without any reservation and, as a result, the Armenians and Greeks were alarmed. For *İkdam*, there was enough food in the empire for everyone, and Muslims would act in line with Armenians and Greeks, who did not employ or work with Muslims and preferred their co-religionists.[50] At the same time as motivating the Muslim public to undertake an economic revival, the propaganda activity resulting from the boycott movement also aimed at restricting non-Muslims' economic transactions. For instance, 15 tile-making factories in Menemen were destroyed in June 1914; Nicolas Kaydachi's losses ruined his business.[51]

The term "awakening" was a metaphor that the rising discourse of the *Milli İktisat* frequently employed. The emergence and the expansion of the boycott was also considered a sign of this awakening during the Second Constitutional Period. The Greek patriarchate, on the other hand, repudiated the claim that the boycott would lead to the salvation of the Turkish people from economical slavery. Rather, the boycotting of Greeks was against the economic interests of the empire. The economic and social status of the Greeks was a result of tradition and system, and it was the preference of the Turks to specialize in the fields of administration and military, which removed them from the economy. Therefore, it was the Greeks who undertook the civilizing mission and dealt with trade. Since the Greeks had deep roots in the economy, it was futile to attempt to remove them from the sector.[52] The patriarchate claimed that the government would prevent a possible catastrophe, since the destruction of such a loyal and hard-working segment of society was contrary to the interests of the state.[53]

However, the Turkish press of the time passionately supported attempts to build a national economy in which the Muslim/Turkish element would dominate. For instance, the formation of Muslim companies and partnerships was announced in *İkdam* with praise and admiration.[54] Turkish nationalist organizations likely played a crucial role in the rise of the *Milli İktisat* and the expansion of the boycott network. For example, *Türk Ocağı*, which was constituted in 1912 and was one of the first influential civil organizations of early Turkish nationalism, wanted newly established Turkish and Muslim businesses to send in photographs of their shops and offices.

The organization planned to facilitate the formation of a network and to encourage solidarity between Turks and Muslims. *Türk Ocağı* declared that it planned to exhibit these photographs to the people, contributing to the development of national trade by making use of "effective advertising."[55]

"Henceforth Goods to be Purchased from Muslim Merchants"

The 1914 boycott movement started around February. The British consul-general in Smyrna, Henry D. Barnham, reported on 18 February 1914 that the distrust between Muslims and non-Muslims was increasing for several reasons. In Smyrna, Greeks were put under pressure by "frequent expulsions on trumped-up pretexts, by forced contributions to the fleet, by the prohibition to wear or display any colors that might suggest they were not Ottoman subjects and by a close police control over all their actions."[56] On the other hand, in the interior of the province, a "systematic boycott" against Greeks and Armenians appeared, according to the report. In Manisa, Muslims and Greeks were forbidden from entering the shops of non-Muslims. Those who dared to do so were beaten. Barnham claimed that the boycott movement was influenced by the CUP and that the envoys of the committee were provoking people everywhere. He also referred to eyewitness accounts of two Englishmen travelling in the province who asserted that cruel boycotting was happening "under the eyes and with the assistance of the gendarmes." The consul concluded his report with the statement that the relationship between Turks and Christians was worsening, compared to the two past generations. He argued that the Turkish press was also instigating the Muslim public against Christians. They even wanted people not to salute Christians and to act as if they did not exist.[57]

A report that the French ambassador submitted to the Sublime Port also provides information regarding the early phases of the boycott movement. From the outset, the movement engendered violence. Instances of violence had occurred occasionally during the 1910–11 Boycott, but now, after the Balkan Wars, started to appear with greater frequency. Both Ottoman public opinion and international diplomatic circles became used to incidents associated with the boycott, but the patterns of violence changed. Both the targeted non-Muslims and the foreign consuls conceded that the boycott was in principle a refusal of the consumers to buy from non-Muslims, but they complained over and over about the violence that went along with the boycott. The report of the French ambassador also described these violent acts. In one instance, an Ottoman Greek merchant by the name of Stilyanos Yordanou sent 32 sacks of sugar to Sadizade Hasan, through the agency of Deveci Emin. However, Emin was stopped 5 km from Bandırma by four armed individuals who seized the sacks, which were worth 50 lire. The boycotters tore the sacks with a knife and ruined the sugar by pouring petroleum on it.[58] Deveci Emin, who had carried the sugar, was attacked because he transported something that belonged to a Christian. The merchant Sadizade also received a threatening letter, warning him to break off his relationships with Christians. The letter was signed by *Vatan Fedaileri* (Guards of the Homeland).[59]

In another incident, again in the region of Bandırma, another agent was captured by an armed gang on 25 February. This time, one of the camel drivers was wounded and a donkey killed. Two days later, the merchant Nikolayidis sent flour from Bandırma, but the camel convoy was held up about an hour down the road. The camel drivers were "persuaded" by disguised armed men to go back to Bandırma and return the flour to Nikolayidis. The Greek merchant informed the local governor in Bandırma about the incident, who advised Nikolayidis not to send any goods without informing him. However, although the governor and the commander of the gendarmerie assured him that the road was safe, his goods were seized once again on 11 March. This time, the gang consisted of 15 men with covered faces who were armed with Martini rifles; they scattered his merchandise on the ground. By the time the gendarmerie arrived in the district, the villagers had already looted the goods.[60] The merchants Anagnostou and Vasiliyou also experienced similar misfortunes; their camel drivers were threatened with death, and the boycotters handed their manifestos to them.[61]

The report also mentioned several other incidents that took place in Smyrna. Two were boycotts against Ottoman Greeks. On 4 March, five Greeks and, on 8 March, a woman with her child were prevented from disembarking in the port of Kuşadası. The report claimed that the officers in the port and the policemen were responsible for this incident. The husband of the woman with the child did his best to disembark his family from the ship, but without success. On 9 March, Muslims assaulted a Greek quarter in Old Smyrna where more than 400 Greek families were living, leaving many wounded. These types of claims continued to appear in consular reports and non-Turkish newspapers, revealing the tension between Muslim and non-Muslim communities.

However, in addition to the acts of violence, there were also typical and universal patterns of boycotting in the report. For example, on 15 March several students of the İttihat ve Terakki Mektebi (School of Union and Progress) and the Sanayi Mektebi (School of Industry) held a protest in front of the Greek shops and stores in the bazaar of Smyrna. During the demonstration, the owners of the shops were ordered to remove any signs and objects that reminded people of their Greek nationality. The boycotters were most sensitive to the national colors of Greece, white and blue. The students broke the shop windows when the owners resisted their orders. On 21 March, two boycotters poured petroleum on a donkey carrying merchandise belonging to a Greek. The owner of the goods, Yanko Pavlidis, consulted the police, but received only the advice that the boycotters were protected by high-ranking officers and it was therefore impossible for the policemen to stop them.[62]

The Greek Orthodox patriarchate reported in the *Ekklisiastiki Alitheia* that the commercial boycott became most widespread in the empire at the end of February. It was publicly announced in mosques, public squares and bazaars. Merchants and people who wanted to continue commercial relationships with the Greek Orthodox community were warned and threatened. The merchandise of Greek traders was destroyed, and the Greek population was replaced by Muslim immigrants.[63]

In Edirne, the boycotting of Greek and other non-Muslim dealers was particularly strong in February and early March 1914. Its intensity decreased in April, until severe clashes between different religious communities and the emigration of local Greeks occurred in May and June 1914. However, even during the boycott movement's weak period Muslims were warned that they would be better off dealing with their co-religionists. On the other hand, many non-Muslim merchants had already left the province because of the Balkan Wars, and the agriculture – the main base of commerce in Edirne – was not productive enough for trade.[64] Moreover, due to the boycott movement, the situation of those merchants who were still working deteriorated. Still, Muslims opened grocery shops in the poorer quarters of the town after the Balkan Wars and still did so in the spring of 1914 in spite of all the political and economic crises, according to the quarterly report of the British consul of Edirne.[65]

There are two significant points that should be highlighted in this context. First, the picketing of non-Muslim shops and the terrorizing of customers had also been part of the boycotts before 1914, but the intensity, persistence and frequency of these boycott acts increased. Second, the support of the local bureaucracy for the boycott movement became much more obvious. For instance, a crucial change took place in the bureaucratic hierarchy of Smyrna after 1913. This change became one of the main complaints of non-Muslims during the boycott movement. In 1913, Rahmi Bey, who was known for his strict Unionist identity, became the governor-general of the province of Aydın. Moreover, Emin Efendi (the former gendarmerie officer of Serez and the new head of the gendarmerie in Manisa) and Çerkez Eşref Efendi (Kuşçubaşı) arrived in Smyrna from Serez, and their activities were considered proof of the committee's association with the boycott movement and Turkification policies. Their activities were not only against non-Muslims, but sometimes also against Ottomans who were not ethnic Turks. For instance, in one of his dispatches the British consul-general in Smyrna reported their anti-Albanian policies in the province of Aydın. He underlined the fact that the expulsion of Albanians increased after their arrival and attached a detailed list of Emin Efendi's and Çerkez Eşref Efendi's activities.[66]

It is also possible to trace the increasing intensity of the boycott and the local support for the movement in the incidents that occurred in Kayseri. Usually, boycotters engaged in preventing Muslims from entering non-Muslim shops would verbally warn the customers, but sometimes they also pulled them from the shops by force. Such acts increased, and as a result policemen detained several aggressive boycotters and sent them to court. However, although the aggression was evident in these instances, the judge released the suspects. The governor of Ankara wrote to both the local prosecutor and the governor and warned them concerning the release of the suspects. The governor-general feared that such a verdict would encourage similar acts in the near future. The local governors replied that these acts were not a crime according to Ottoman law and asked for a document to be provided that showed that these acts were a crime. The local governors also asked the Ministry of the Interior whether these aggressors should be send to court or not.[67]

The official journal of the Greek Orthodox patriarchate, *Ekklisiastiki Alitheia*, began to publicize these acts when they became prevalent in the Ottoman Empire. According to the reports of the metropolitan bishop of Ephesus, many watchmen were placed in front of the doors of Christian butchers in particular. He reported that boycotters had placed notices with insulting remarks about Christians in 40 different places in Neo Kesaria (Niksar) and Parthenio. The peasants who came to the town to shop were pulled from Greek stores and taken to Turkish shops. He also wrote about a marching band in the bazaar that sang anthems and propagated the boycott. The committee collecting money for the navy also called on citizens to take part in the boycott movement by playing drums.[68]

Sokratis Prokopiou mentioned in his memoirs that Muslims were harassed in Uşak whenever they attempted to enter the shops of the *Rum* community. There were watchmen armed with sticks and knives. Overnight, Greek names were removed from shop signs.[69] The boycott movement was no longer confined only to the Hellenes of Greece, but everything Greek openly became a target. Even the Greek alphabet and the Greek national colors became a target.

The Armenian merchants of Bandırma also complained about the indifference of the local bureaucracy regarding their complaints and grievances about the boycotters. The telegram that they sent to the Ministry of the Interior was signed by 41 people. They asserted that it was almost impossible to pursue their business and pay their taxes under such circumstances; it was only a matter of time until they had to close down their shops. They appealed to the grand vizier for help, stating that they were the "uncoupled sons" (*evlad-ı gayr-ı müfarık*) of the Ottoman fatherland.[70]

The merchants' situation did not change so they sent another telegram to the government, this time with 46 signatures. They claimed that, although they were among the most loyal subjects of the Ottoman Empire, Muslims had been provoked against them. They complained about boycotters beating and injuring Muslims who wanted to buy from Armenian shops, pouring petroleum on Armenian merchandise and destroying Armenian goods. Several Muslim customers had been forced to return what they had bought. The telegram also emphasized that the boycotters walked up and down in front of Armenian stores and warned "poor people" in advance that "henceforth, goods were to be purchased from Muslim merchants." The merchants claimed that they had suffered great losses in the past three months and repeated that the local bureaucracy took no notice of their complaints. This time, the Armenian merchants and tradesmen requested at least precautionary measures against the boycotters' attacks on their businesses.[71] The situation of the Armenian merchants was deteriorating day by day; thus, they—who identified themselves as *zavallı Ermeniler* (poor Armenians)—expressed that they would be satisfied as long as the boycott movement's worst offenses stopped.

These complaints regarding the boycott movement were not restricted to individual initiatives of non-Muslim merchant communities. The Armenian patriarchate also conveyed the grievances, anxiety and fear of Armenian merchants to the Ottoman government. The patriarchate, having been briefed by Armenian delegates (*murahhas*), wrote to the Ottoman government on 16 March 1914, stating that Armenians had been boycotted and that there were many people picketing their shops. The customers of Armenian merchants were threatened by these aggressors, while the boycott movement grew due to the government's inactivity. The provocation against Armenians undermined the unity of the different elements of the Ottoman Empire, and for this reason the patriarchate urged the government to take action immediately.[72]

As was the case in previous boycotts, many foreign merchants also suffered economically. For instance, a Marmara Express ship, which belonged to a French company, was not able to unload its cargo and land its passengers in the port of Bandırma. The government sent a decree to the local governors asking them to investigate whether any incidents against non-Muslims had occurred. The government ordered the local bureaucrats not to permit such aggression. The government also underlined that the boycotting of ships belonging to the Great Powers was not permissible and should be banned because of potential diplomatic and political problems.[73] Therefore, one may claim that the government's priority was not to protect its non-Muslim subjects, but foreign powers.

Nevertheless, the government's policy also differed toward various foreign countries. The Greek Foreign Ministry stated in its dispatch to the Ottoman Foreign Ministry that Greek ships arriving from Chios were blocked in Ottoman ports due to the plague epidemic on the island. The Ministry of Foreign Affairs asked the Ministry of the Interior whether these claims were true, since Ottoman, French and Italian ships were freely sailing between the island and the Ottoman mainland.[74] The governor-general of the province of Aydın, Rahmi Bey, confirmed that the passengers of ships arriving from Chios were not permitted to land due to the plague epidemic, as a precautionary policy. Rahmi Bey wrote that the ban had been removed a short while before and that there was no longer a particular ban for Greek ships arriving in his province.[75]

It was not only the Armenians and Greeks who suffered from the boycott movement, but also the Bulgarians. The rather effective application of the boycott forced the ambassador of Bulgaria to complain to the Sublime Porte, informing the Ottoman government that the boycott against Greeks had started to include Bulgarians. The embassy also attached a list of Bulgarian merchants whose business had been damaged by the boycott movement.[76]

As a result, the Ministry of the Interior wrote to the provinces where the boycott movement was particularly strong, requesting that the governors investigate the situation and, if Bulgarians had really been affected, prevent further damage.[77] This telegram was sent to İzmit,

Hüdavendigar, Canik, Karesi, Kala-i Sultaniye, Bolu, Aydın and to the minister of the interior, Talat Bey, who was in Manisa at the time.[78] Talat Bey was traveling through Thrace and western Anatolia in order to deal with the rising social tension among the different communities. In these almost identical telegrams, the Ministry of the Interior asked governors to protect the Bulgarian merchants mentioned by name from the boycott movement. The governors replied to this telegram by submitting information regarding the Bulgarian merchants in their localities. Most of them claimed that there were not many Bulgarian merchants and that there was no boycott against Bulgarians. Several governors also sent information concerning the mentioned Bulgarian merchants.[79]

This correspondence regarding the boycotting of Bulgarian merchants reveals that the bureaucracy took the boycott of Ottoman Greeks, and Greeks in general, for granted. The orders sent from the capital prohibited the boycotting of particular communities or nationalities, but not boycotting in general. It was only at the beginning of July 1914 that such orders were sent to the provinces, after the movement reached its peak. Compared to the boycott against other non-Muslim communities, the one against the Bulgarians was limited, since there were not many of them in the Ottoman Empire.[80] However, the boycott against them indicates that after 1913 the boycott movement targeted all non-Muslims.

As the relationships between Muslims and non-Muslims deteriorated, an International Commission of Inquiry was formed and travelled throughout western Anatolia, following the minister of the interior, Talat Bey. The commission, which consisted of British, French, Austrian, Russian, Italian and German members, set out on 20 June 1914 and concluded its travels on 11 July 1914. The report of the British member of the commission, the consul Matthews, provides detailed information regarding the anti-Greek movement in Asia Minor. In villages and small towns, the primary outcome of the movement was the migration of Greeks *en masse* to the larger towns and cities. Dozens of reports appeared concerning Muslim assault on non-Muslim villages or neighborhoods. This created significant problems in terms of housing and providing a livelihood for these non-Muslims.

Many Greeks migrated from the towns near the western coastline to the Aegean islands, such as Lesbos, Samos and Chios. Particularly after February 1914, panic occurred among the Greek community; this was echoed in the correspondence of the Greek Foreign Ministry. Some of the Greeks also complained about the Greek consuls whose efforts were ineffective *vis-à-vis* this catastrophe. M. Konstantinidis wrote directly to Venizelos to lodge a complaint against the Greek ambassador and demand help.[81]

The Ottoman officers claimed that the emigration of Ottoman Greeks resulted from active Hellenic propaganda. They referred to propaganda documents such as Greek maps, which, according to them, had provoked the mass migration of Greeks to Greece. For instance, a *müdür* by the name of Salim Efendi informed the British consul Matthews in Trilye (Zeytinbağı/Mudanya) that not long ago they had arrested a Greek reserve officer who was engaged in propaganda activities. By contrast, the notables of the Greek community claimed that Muslim gangs were attacking their villages and driving off their cattle, which brought about the exodus of the Greeks.[82] Reports of murder and rape were not common, but looting was widespread according to these claims. There were also rumors of the killing of Greeks in order to attract the attention of the international public to the problems of non-Muslims. For instance, there were reports that several Greeks, including a priest, had been killed in Gürüklü (around Mihaliç–Karacabey/Bursa). When the British consul reached the village, he found out that no one had been killed, but that the village had been plundered.[83]

Although not very common, murders and rape did occur in Anatolia. For instance, the British consul saw the corpses of Greeks in Başköy/ Bursa, where people had also been shot and injured, and several women had been raped. The gangs that had attacked the village consisted of Muslims of the region whom the village inhabitants knew. They argued that the aggressors were Circassians and Gypsies. The inhabitants of Başköy and other like villages began to depend for their subsistence on the aid and charity of Greeks living in larger towns. According to the report, a significant number of Greeks in villages such as Çatalağıl, Eskice and Uluabad had left their villages. (Similarly, the Greeks of

Seyrekköy, Gerenköy and Ulucak now lived as refugees in Menemen.)[84] The British vice-consul in the Dardanelles, Palmer, stated that there were 2,000 refugees in Erenköy. Their position was not improving, and they were entirely dependent on the help of their community since they had lost all their possessions.[85]

The governor of Mihaliç, Cemil Bey, claimed that the corpses that Matthews had seen were those of two Greeks who had committed suicide. The public prosecutor stated that ten Muslims had already been arrested and reported to Matthews that in Başköy six Greeks had been killed, one wounded, and two had committed suicide. Nine Muslims had also been killed in the clashes there, yet these Muslims were from different villages; this fact indicates that they were attacking the village.[86] The governor left Mihaliç for Kurşunlu, where two Greeks had been killed, in order to hold an inquiry.

The engineer of a mill told Matthews that the raids on Greek villages were organized by the commandant of the gendarmerie, Captain Abdülkadir. He claimed that Abdülkadir received the larger share of the plundered goods and possessions. The public prosecutor and an army captain by the name of Alibeyzade Raşid Bey (of Circassian origin) also played a significant role in the looting. Raşid Bey was told to collect the sheep from the plundered villages in Emreköy. The engineer argued that the pillaging had been done by gangs of Muslims whose members were natives of the region.[87] In Foça and Yenifoça, the commission observed the marks of axes on the doors of buildings; as far as possible, these were removed under the supervision of Hacim Bey (the police chief of Smyrna). As a result of these violent incidents, the public prosecutor Şükrü Bey informed the commission that Giritli Ferid Efendi (the governor of Foça), Mehmed Efendi (the local commander of the gendarmerie), Talat Bey (the commander of the gendarmerie in Menemen) and Cafer Efendi had been arrested and sent to be court martialled.[88] On the other hand, officers such as Mehmet Efendi, the governor of Soma, whom the British consul and the Greeks considered a protector of Christians, was dismissed; at the same time, Muslim refugees were settled in Greek houses.[89]

As in many coastal towns, all the Greek residents of Foça and Yenifoça had already left their towns and escaped to the islands close to the mainland. The Greek consul repeated the often-mentioned claim of Turkish officers that the Greeks were forced to sign a declaration stating that they were leaving the country of their own free will and that they would not make any claims on their possessions.[90] Yet, there were also cases that stood in stark contrast to such attitudes. The Greeks of Menemen informed the international commission that the Muslims of Çukurköy had refused to take part in the attack on Seyrekköy, thanks to the efforts of the imam of the village.[91] The British consul attached to his report a document for a Greek worker, Kosta from Urla, who was working on the construction of the macadam road of Çeşme. The document was addressed to the leaders of the gangs and soldiers in the area and asked them not to prevent his passage to Urla. This document, signed by Karabinazade Ali, indicates that the gangs and soldiers controlled the roads.[92] According to the Greek consul, houses and shops were pillaged in May, and Kato Panoiya was totally devastated. The Christians in Urla and Çeşme considered migrating since they had heard that there were more *muhacirs* coming to their district.[93] The British reports state that particularly in late May and June 1914 looting, expropriation and injury took place against the local Greeks, causing them to flee western Anatolia.[94]

The anti-Greek movement appeared in the form of boycotting in larger towns such as Bursa, Manisa, Bandırma, Aydın, Smyrna, Ödemiş, Köşk, Aziziye, Nazilli, Bayındır, Tire and Soma. The fundamental trait of the boycott was the picketing of stores and shops. The mobilization of the Muslim public for the boycott movement and for Turkish nationalism in general occurred after the Balkan Wars. Even Muslim women started to play a role on the streets in the course of the boycott movement. As mentioned above, the boycott pamphlets also called on Muslim women to take action. On 4 May 1914, a Muslim woman with her children denounced a group of Greek youngsters who were singing in Greek. The Greek consul asserted that they were singing Smyrniot songs; however, the Muslim woman complained about them to the police because they might have sung the Greek national anthem or songs in the name of King Konstantin. One of the debated issues of the day was the singing of Greek national songs that praised the king and revealed the singer's loyalty to Greece. Therefore, the youngsters were detained by the police.[95] On 5 May, the watchmen on the picket line were replaced by watchwomen. Muslim women started to take part in the boycott movement by preventing customers from entering Christian shops around the mosque of Hisar in Smyrna.[96]

Non-Muslims complained mainly to the local branches of the CUP and the local authorities. They identified the Circassians in particular as perpetrators who had played a role in the boycotting on the street. For instance, on 11 June 1914 in Bursa they broke the windows of Greek shops and beat the owners. The goods in the stores were also destroyed. Afterwards, Greek shops remained closed. Just before the arrival of the international commission, the police wanted the Greeks to reopen their business. However, a great majority of Greeks refused to do so, which allowed the British consul Matthews to observe the outcome of the boycott movement in Bursa.[97] Since there were cases of emigration and clashes between different communities, the actual boycotting was considered rather calm after May 1914. For instance, the report of the commission stated that "no serious incidents had occurred but a strict boycott" in Manisa. For Bandırma, it was reported that "there had been a panic at Panderma during the preceding 10 days but nothing serious had occurred. A boycott was being enforced against the Greeks."[98] The boycott rapidly succeeded in interior regions such as Simav, where all Greek shops were reported on 27 June as having already closed down due to the severity of the boycott movement.[99] The boycott actions were always accompanied by violence. It was reported that in Torbalı/Smyrna the agents of the Boycott Committee carried out the boycott by means of violence and intimidation. The public prosecutor, Şükrü Bey, ordered the arrest of Mehmet and Bilal Usta, who were considered responsible for the violence, and they were sent to be court martialled in Smyrna.[100] Even in major cities such as Istanbul armed gangs appeared, preventing customers from entering Greek stores. A Greek report claimed that 200 youths armed with knives prevented Muslims from entering Greek shops.[101] The Greek consul in Ayvalık stated that the owners of the Greek shops began to refuse to serve Muslim customers in Edremit, in order to avoid trouble.[102]

The violence resulting from the boycott was the logical outcome of the regulations of the movement. As elsewhere, in Aziziye/Smyrna, the boycotters urged Muslims not to buy from Greeks; this demand turned into a ban, and Greeks were no longer allowed to sell their products in neighboring Muslim villages. When a Greek gardener refused to comply, he was beaten and his arm broken. The boycott evolved along similar lines in different villages and in the towns of the region, such as Değirmencik, Ayasoluk (Selçuk) and Karapınar. It was not only Greeks who were beaten if they did not adhere to the rules, but also Muslims. A Muslim in Karapınar who bought from a Greek shop was beaten and had petroleum poured on his purchases. One person threw a stone into the compartment of the train in which the members of the commission of inquiry were sitting while they traveled from Karapınar to Köşk. Şükrü Bey, who was traveling with them, sent a telegram from the next station to inform the authorities in Karapınar about the incident.[103]

In Köşk/Aydın, the boycott was provoked by posters depicting Greek cruelties in Macedonia. Two active members of the Boycott Committee had arrived in the town from Smyrna, but boycotting was not restricted only to their activities. The mobilization of the people and the actions of the local notables in the towns also played a significant role in the boycott movement. For instance, in Akça (Söke) the orange trees of the Greek Yovan were cut down. The gardener Simeon in Akça also complained that his trees had been cut down and that his Muslim neighbors cut off his water supply. The house of Yorghi Themopoulo was burned and his property looted by the locals. Greeks could no longer go to their fields. Although the Greek stores had remained open, Muslims were prevented from entering. In Nazilli, the leader of the boycott was at the same time the police commissar and land assessor from Istanbul. In June, notices were distributed to the Greek neighborhoods, advising them to leave the town. If not, then great misfortune would befall them. The notice was signed by "The Nation."[104]

It was the *kadı* Ahmet Efendi, who also served as the treasurer of the town, who proclaimed and triggered the boycott in Bayındır. A meeting in the club of the CUP also played its part in the formation of the movement there. In Tire, the boycotters' leasers were the notables of the district: Mehmet Bey, Tokatlıoğlu İsmail Efendi, Derebaşlı Molla Mehmet and Hacı Ramiz Bey. The report of the commission underlined the fact that they were all natives of Tire and had a good relationship with the governor of the town, Muhtar Bey.[105] Another report stated that Tokatlığolu, a Cretan immigrant, had attacked Muslim workers who were employed by Greeks.[106] It was also the notables who gathered the Muslims in the mosque and incited them against the Christians in Kula, according to a report of the Greek consul.[107]

Prokopoui writes in his memoir that Deli Ahmet (Ahmet the Mad), the leader of the boycott in Uşak, made a great fortune thanks to the movement. Nazım Bey and the governor-general Rahmi Bey also visited him when they came to Uşak. They called him Ağa (chief), in reference to the famous boycott leader Kerim Ağa. Deli Ahmet exploited the opportunity provided by this network and the boycott movement, and entered the carpet business.[108]

A lawyer, Refik Bey, played a crucial role in the emergence of the boycott in Ödemiş. He gave a speech before the government office (*konak*) of the town, urging Muslims to take revenge on the local Greeks for the crimes of their co-religionists in Macedonia. The governor of the town was also present during the speech. A gang of Muslims, whose chief was Sarıköylü Hasan Efendi, had attacked Greeks several times, according to the complaints of the Greek priest of Ödemiş, Papa Nicola. Sarıköylü Hasan Efendi was arrested, but managed to escape. Apart from him, Fahri Efendi, a member of the Administrative Council of Ödemiş, and a former police commissar were among the leaders of the boycott movement.[109] In the region around Ödemiş and Sarayköy, three more people appeared as gang leaders who, in a report of the British Acting Consul General Heathcote Smith, were described as brigands: Ödemişli Ömer, Giritli Hüseyin and Büyük Emin Mustafa.[110] The Greek consul on the island of Meis (Kastelorizo) informed his ministry that the shops of the Christians in Asia Minor were closed down. The ties between the island and mainland had been cut due to the boycotting activities. However, since Meis was a small island, it was unable to sustain itself. The consul named several persons who played active roles in the boycott movement in the region: Kubrukçuoğlu

Süleyman, Nail Efendi (the forest watchman), Çolak Hasan, Giritli Ali, Gökçe Mehmet, Aptullah Efendi, Nazmi Sarıoğlu and Hasan Kurdaroğlu.[111] Their roles, their names and their occupations lead naturally to the discussion of agency within the boycott movement.

Banditry and Agency in the Boycott Movement

As the violence related to the boycott increased, practices of banditry were also employed by the boycotters. In 1914, the boycotters' actions extended beyond the outskirts of towns, and violent acts employed in the cities (such as picketing and intimidation) changed: as they were carried to the countryside, these actions evolved into banditry. Banditry had a significant tradition, particularly in Asia Minor, and this tradition and its symbols were available for the boycotters to employ as strategies. Boycotters appeared with guns or rifles and covered their faces; no longer did they only force the merchants' agents to return the merchandise, but they ruined it or left it behind to be looted. Therefore, in 1914 boycotters turned into bandit characters and were also called *başıbozuk* (irregulars), a term generally used for brigands, even in British documents.[112]

A number of state officers seized the properties of non-Muslims, and so did local notables who had probably been rivals of those who had left. The ownerless estates were generally taken over by the thousands of incoming Muslim refugees from the lost territories. In one often-mentioned incident, the Muslim Cretan army led a Muslim *muhacir* to the house of Tombalacı Evanghelos in Karantina and ordered him to take possession. According to the British report, the Muslim immigrant did so. These acts resembled instances of social banditry, although they were conducted within a nationalist framework. Yet, these bandit-like actions were also based on personal interests. For instance, on the same day as the house of Tobalacı Evanghelos was transferred to a Muslim, in the same town the wife and mother of Nicolas Arvaniti were beaten, and their jewelry stolen.[113]

It was not only in the reports of the foreign consuls or the Ottoman state's correspondence that instances of violence found mention. In his book on the Turkish nationalist movement in Western Asia Minor,

THE MUSLIM PROTEST 191

the nationalist historian Nurdoğan Taçalan has claimed that the boycott alone was insufficient to eliminate non-Muslims from Turkey. Therefore, nationalist organizations started to terrorize non-Muslims and tried to force them to leave the country. He underlined the activities of Kuşçubaşı Eşref, who organized Turkish gangs and attacked Greek villages, particularly around Söke. According to Taçalan, Turks were doing the same as the Greeks had done to Muslims in Macedonia. They had expelled Muslims to Anatolia, and Turkish nationalists were now making room for the newcomers. Therefore, for him boycotting and deportation are two sides of the same coin and were the last resort in the struggle of the Turkish nation for survival in Asia Minor.[114] Taçalan has claimed that the deportation of the Greeks was organized by a particular committee comprised of Pertev [Demirhan], Cafer Tayyar [Eğilmez] and Mahmut Celal [Bayar]. The *Rums* of Smyrna were not disturbed, since they were under the protections of the Great Powers, but other *Rums* in provincial towns were harassed by various means.[115]

Agency in the boycott movement was unclear, both to foreign observers and to the victims themselves. Non-Muslims and foreign consuls laid the blame for the movement and the concurrent violent acts with the CUP and its members. However, they were not certain in their assertions. The report of the British consul Matthews—who had traveled with the international commission to the villages, towns and cities of western Anatolia for 20 days—referred to the suggestions of German officers who found the presence of Greeks on the coast of Asia Minor dangerous and advised their expulsion. Matthews claimed that this advice removed the last hesitations of the government. However, the expulsion of Greeks was not directly ordered by the central government, but only approved. According to him, the government wanted to get rid of the Greeks only by means of intimidation, but not violence or bloodshed. The governor-generals of Bursa and Smyrna were active in the anti-Greek movement, but their orders were enthusiastically followed by the minor officers, civil, military and semi-military.[116] In a report to the British foreign minister, Edward Grey, the British ambassador L. Mallet claimed that he had the impression that the grand vizier, Said Halim Paşa, and the minister of naval affairs, Cemal Paşa, were ignorant of the actions against the local Greeks, particularly the incidents that occurred in areas around Istanbul, such as Pyrgos (Kemerburgaz).[117] The Greek Orthodox patriarchate accused the Ottoman government and state officers of failing to prevent the boycott movement and encouraging emigration. Segments of the bureaucracy and the Turkish press were inciting illiterate people against the Greeks. Therefore, the patriarchate blamed the government, the state officers and the people for various reasons.[118] Another article claimed that the mobilized people belonged to the lowest classes who had turned into fanatics.[119]

The British consul in Edirne reported that the governor-general of the province and the minister of the interior had had a conversation via telegraph on the issue of Greek emigration. The minister of the interior was said to have instructed the governor-general to stop the molestation and encourage the emigration of Greeks. Thanks to these instructions and their execution by the local governors, such as the *mutasarrıf* of Kırkkilise (Kırklareli), the movement seemed to come to an end for a while. However, the entire Greek population of Vize had already emigrated at that point, and there were still reports about the killing of Greeks.[120] In his quarterly report on the province of Edirne one month earlier, the British consul had reported that the government had been willing to create an entirely Muslim population in this region.[121]

The protest and the flow of Greeks to Greece reached such an extent that the minister of the interior, Talat Bey, had to travel to Thrace and western Anatolia. Cavit Bey, the minister of finance, who stood in for Talat Bey in the capital, made a statement to the newsapaper *Tan* in which he claimed that it was the mass emigration of Muslims from Macedonia that had caused problems. He stated that 24,400 people had immigrated from Salonica to Thrace between 17 March and 10 May 1914, and asserted that, had these people not been forced to leave their land, nothing would have happened in the Ottoman Empire. The native population had not upset the order anywhere in the empire, according to Cavit Bey. For him, the ultimate goal of Talat Bey's visit was to prevent any clashes between immigrant Muslims and native Greeks.[122]

The violence against Greeks increased in a very short time and forced the government to take action against the chaos resulting from the anti-Greek movement. Talat Bey even visited the small towns and villages located on his travel route. In each settlement, he addressed the people and tried to inculcate trust in the Greeks. For instance, he spoke at a train station to the people waiting for a train who planned to leave the town permanently. Talat Bey convinced them to stay and return to their houses.[123] However, the same Talat Bey wrote to Tekirdağ requesting that the governor immediately deport to Greece the Greek peasants who were crowded in the port.[124] The most active centers of the boycott movement coincided with the areas of highest Greek emigration. The boycott was strictest in Smyrna and the towns in its hinterland, such as Menemen, Foça, Urla, Bergama and Ulucak. Bithynia and Mysia, to the south of the Marmara Sea, were the second center of the boycott movement. Third was Thrace.

Due to the mass emigration of Greeks, many small towns were depopulated in a very short time. The political situation and the ceaseless appeals of the Greek Orthodox patriarchate put pressure on the Ottoman government, and it sent a decree to the province of Aydın at the end of July 1914 requiring the governor-general to stop the boycott movement against the Greeks to prevent their emigration. Yet the governor-general of the province of Aydın, Rahmi Bey, replied to the Ministry of the Interior that it was impossible to boycott Greeks since there were no Greeks left in Ayazmenci.[125]

During his travels, Talat Bey also dealt with the incidents that occurred while he was on the road. The Greek Orthodox patriarchate sent a telegram to report that Ayvalık was burning. An investigation showed that in one of the villages of Ayvalık four houses were burnt in one night. The owners of the houses and the remaining population decided to emigrate, but were persuaded to stay. The Greeks of Burhaniye were resettled in their town and assured their security. The Ottoman officers brought the metropolitan bishop of Karşıyaka with them to a train station in order to convince the Greeks not to leave the country.[126]

The patriarchate and the church network in the Ottoman Empire also tried to influence social and political developments. Due to the strained political and social atmosphere and the boycott movement of the spring of 1914, the relationship between Muslims and the Greek

Orthodox community deteriorated. This culminated in the crisis between the Unionists and the Greek Orthodox patriarchate. The patriarchate decided to shut down the churches and suspended education in Greek schools, arguing that the Greek population was under risk. Another reaction of the Greek population was the migration of Greeks from small settlements to bigger towns and cities. Greeks firstly fled from villages to cities such as Istanbul and Smyrna, and then emigrated to Greece. This was also an opportunity to attract the attention of the Ottoman government and the international public to the situation of the Greeks in the Ottoman Empire.

The inclination of Greeks to leave their homes was not always directly related to the boycott movement, which was just one element of a general political and social atmosphere. It is not a coincidence that news about the emigration of Greeks appeared in the Ottoman press at the time when the boycott was in its initial phase.[127]

The Greek Orthodox patriarch and the two administrative bodies of the Greek community, the Holy Synod and the National Permanent Mixed Council, convened to take action regarding the "critical situation that the nation faced." The patriarchate submitted an official report to the constitutional government, the content and message of which were summarized in the official journal of the patriarchate. It was the duty of the constitutional government to defend the rights of its subjects, according to the patriarchate, and the "so-called economical independence of the Turkish people which demands a so-called spontaneous awakening" was just an alibi, a "demagogical claim." Such awakening and salvation could not be realized by destroying and robbing the Greek nation; such independence was not attainable by placing armed guards in front of Greek stores, forcing Greeks to leave the country, and distributing pamphlets that preached hatred against the Greek Orthodox community. Economic salvation might come only as a result of free trade and free economic activities. The report stated that Greeks were not against the development and commercial progress of the Turkish people, but rather the violence, lawlessness and mistreatment targeted at them. The report declared that, as the "strongest native element" of the country, who "had historical rights, the Greek Orthodox community would not permit this transgression."[128]

The Greek Orthodox patriarch visited the minister of the interior, Talat Bey, together with his commission, and issued a memorandum. Talat Bey promised to take preventive measures. The delegation then visited the minister of justice, İbrahim Bey. Although he affirmed the content of the memorandum, he regarded the protest expressed in it as improper; for this reason, he did not accept it, and the patriarchate did not insist on the issue. However, the two administrative bodies of the Greek Orthodox community convened and decided to cut their relationship with the Ministry of Justice. The patriarchate informed the grand vizier about their decision.[129] However, in the end the Greek Orthodox patriarch and the commission visited both the grand vizier and the minister of justice and received reassurance regarding the safety of the Greek nation.[130]

In order to persuade the Greeks to stay in the Ottoman Empire, the government took action to try and prove that it was sincere about maintaining security. For instance, on 16 June 1914 more than 40 Muslims were detained, and the governor of Ayvalık was dismissed from his post due to his incompetence.[131] One day later, the precautionary measures (which were considered by the newspaper *İkdam* to be a challenge to those who acted against Greeks) were extended: the governors of Foça, Ayvalık and Biga, the administrators of the districts of Gömeç and Barbaros and the gendarmerie captain of Çeşme were removed from their offices; two military officers and 100 peasants were sent to the court of martial law (*divan-ı harb-ı örfi*); and the newspapers *Anadolu, Köylü* and *Lareforum* were suspended due to their provocative publications regarding the immigration of Muslims.[132] However, in general the Ottoman government did not change its stance and continued to blame Greece for the disorder in the Ottoman Empire. Therefore, in addition to punishing public officers, the government also submitted a memorandum to Greece, addressing Greek atrocities committed against Macedonian Muslims. According to the government, the main reason for these atrocities was the flow of Muslims into the Ottoman Empire.[133]

In the province of Aydın, Talat Bey, while traveling with Governor-General Rahmi Bey, gave orders to the local officers and admonished the Muslim and non-Muslim populations in the towns of Nazilli,

Aydın, Söke, Tire and the like. In one of his speeches there, a non-Muslim interrupted him and complained about the boycott. In his reply, Talat Bey warned the notables of the town that the boycott had a harmful impact on the economy of the country and he wanted it to end.[134] Talat Bey returned to Istanbul on 27 June 1914, but the boycott was not lifted after he had left the region, so the government continued sending orders for it to end. Moreover, the minister of the interior demanded the symbolic punishment of an aggressor as a public example. He wrote to Rahmi Bey that it was evident from the report of the public inspector, Şükrü Bey, that everybody knew about the suspension of the boycott, and therefore he wanted the governor-general to execute an aggressor who had committed a murder and to punish a few other boycotters who had gone too far.[135] The government sent similar telegrams to different provinces to try and prevent a continuation of the boycott. Such a telegram to Menteşe affirmed that governors should stop the boycott and also the emigration of the Greeks. Vice Police Inspector Kadri Efendi was dismissed from his post.[136]

Many officers were removed from their position because the government was unable to halt the boycott movement, due to their support. For instance, the report sent to the governor of Lazistan stated that the guards of the Regie and public officers had taken part in the picketing of Greek stores.[137] However, further government orders attest that these official precautions were not successful in stopping the boycott: for instance, a telegram sent again to the province of Aydın and the governor-general reiterated that the continuation of the boycott was harming state interests as long as political negotiations were ongoing. The central government repeated its demand that the local officers put pressure on those responsible for the boycott movement, underlining that some of its prominent members should be punished. The government had become quite desperate, and this was clearly reflected in its discourse. The last telegram asked the governor to stop the boycott by any means possible, "at least for the moment."[138]

It was not only to the province of Aydın that the government sent such orders, but also to districts such as Lazistan. The government told the governor of Lazistan that the boycott should first be relaxed and then completely stopped.[139] Similar orders to ban the boycott and punish aggressors were also sent to the provinces of Edirne, Adana and Hüdavendigar and the districts of İzmir, Bolu, Çatalca, Canik, Karesi and Kala-i Sultaniye.[140] All these telegrams were ignored, so the minister of the interior sent orders again and again: on 14 July 1914, Talat Bey repeated his orders, emphasizing that the abolition of the boycott was in accord with state interests and that those who could not stop the movement would be dismissed.[141]

In spite of this, it should also be underlined that after the Balkan Wars the CUP, and particularly Talat Bey, had decided to clean the country of those who they thought had betrayed the empire. This was a strong statement, since it was made by Halil Menteşe, a prominent political figure in the CUP and the president of the Ottoman parliament; in his memoirs, Menteşe confirmed that Talat Bey had decided to eliminate the Bulgarians and Greeks.[142] Yet, when it came to the Greeks, this was not easily accomplished, since the government was not in favor of a war with Greece. Therefore, the government and the Ottoman bureaucracy did not plan to intervene or take part in the deportation of Greeks from Thrace and western Asia Minor. The CUP and its network were to manage the mission. Halil Menteşe also argued that Talat Bey's travels were arranged in order to convince the consuls of the Great Powers that the government was trying to calm the prevailing nationalist fever and to diminish the reaction of foreign consuls. It was claimed that the Greeks were leaving the country because the Balkan Wars had greatly disturbed them. As a result, the committees terrorized the native Greek population, giving them no choice but to flee Anatolia, while Talat Bey and the governors acted as if they tried to stop their citizens. Halil Menteşe stated that 100,000 Greeks from Thrace and 200,000 Greeks from around Smyrna had left their homeland as a result of this policy before WWI. The governor-general of Edirne, Hacı Adil Bey, the governor-general of Aydın, Rahmi Bey, and Celal [Bayar] helped Talat Bey in this plan. Hacı Adil Bey was assassinated by a Bulgarian and Greek gang while inspecting the deportations, and his son was also killed in this attack.[143]

This account reveals that the Unionists employed a double correspondence, public and secret, in governing the empire. The official state correspondence gives the impression that the government was not involved in the deportation of non-Muslims and tried to prevent the harassment by punishing the local bureaucrats. Hüseyin Kazım's pamphlet, as mentioned above, was confiscated by the Administration of Public Security—or at least, such an official statement was made publicly.[144] However, memoirs of Unionists and Turkish nationalists, memoirs of victims, and documents from the archives of other states show a different picture.[145] Taner Akçam has very clearly shown how this dual mechanism worked in the Aegean region and Thrace after the Balkan Wars during the deportation of the Greek population. He sees these events as a preparation for the catastrophe that would take place during WWI.[146]

Yet, this should not lead us to a conspiracy theory of the sort claiming that the mission was executed by a group of nationalist *komitadji*. On the contrary, these different accounts point to a broad social and political network and the extensive social base of the CUP. On the other hand, the mobilization of the Muslim public was not total and absolute. This is why victims were always blaming gangs, committees, or prominent leaders of the national movement. For instance, Dimosthenis Stamatios underlined the fact that it was not the average Muslim population, but the boycotters who attacked them. It was the boycotters who provoked the Muslim mobilization. His and his family's relationship with the Turks was good. His family sold tobacco and salt in Tatarti/Salihli, and most of their Muslim customers continued to buy from them. Those who wanted to remove *Rums* from the economy were the CUP and the boycotters.[147] Similarly, Prokopiou, who has been mentioned above, also claimed that the Muslim majority was against the boycott.[148] Kiriakos Miçopulos said that it was the immigrants who provoked the boycott of non-Muslims during which his family lost its possessions, particularly the flour factory, in Kermasti (today's Mustafa Kemalpaşa/Bursa). Thanks to the operators and the foreman of the factory, who refused to work without their boss, the father of Miçopulos, the family was able to return to their town.[149] It is noteworthy that this story is based on a rigid differentiation between natives and newcomers.

There were also high-ranking local bureaucrats who opposed the boycott movement. One of these was the governor of Adana, Hakkı Bey, who in contrast to other Ottoman bureaucrats was strongly critical. When the Ministry of the Interior sent out a decree on 18 June 1914, the governor-general was the only one to respond. He replied with a long and detailed report on the same day, indicating an immediate reaction. He wrote that the boycott at first was very active in Adana for ten to fifteen days. (That is to say, the boycott around Adana started only after it gained prominence in western Anatolia. The boycott spread to different regions in the Ottoman Empire, but did not start simultaneously.) Although the boycott commenced quite late, it became powerful over a very short period; as a result, the governor advised a total suppression of the movement. The governor revealed his discontent regarding the boycott movement with the terminology he employed to describe the boycotters in his report: "brainless," "simple-minded," "imprudent," "injudicious," and "lack control of their emotions."[150] Hakkı Bey warned that boycotting was akin to playing with a delicate weapon, and might have disastrous results for the country, which was in a financial and political crisis. According to the governor-general, the Ottoman Empire tried to heal the material and moral casualties caused by the Balkan Wars. Probably, he was annoyed about the interference of ordinary people in politics and state affairs: the autonomous character of the boycott movement irritated many state officers.

Hakkı Bey stated in his report that Adana was a region of farmers and that the buyers of their products were to a great extent non-Muslims. If these buyers stayed away because of the boycott movement, then the prices would collapse, and the peasants and the treasury would lose out in the process. Hakkı Bey asserted that the boycott movement could not succeed with empty words. The boycott forced weak and poor peasants into a fight against a strong enemy, a fight they would probably lose. This argument was a typical response of the opponents of the boycott movement, since the weapon was generally utilized by the weak against the strong; it is unsurprising therefore to find the same argument being used by a high-ranking Ottoman bureaucrat.

Another significant point in Hakkı Bey's report is his reference to a telegram that was sent from Smyrna to the merchants of Adana. This information indicates that the boycotters and Muslim merchants were connected by a communication network throughout the empire. (It also reveals their organizational capabilities, like the claims made about the merchant Mehmed Rasim in the boycott movement's pamphlets, as mentioned above.) Hakkı Bey stated that the precautionary measures implemented by him alone could not put a stop to the boycott, which was harming the interests of anybody involved in industry and trade; these official measures should also be used in other major boycott centers, such as Smyrna, in order to prevent the expansion of the movement. He repeated this intention not to tolerate the boycott movement in Adana in another dispatch to the Ottoman government, referring back to his detailed report that he had sent on 18 June 1914.[151]

According to the confidential memorandum written by the British consul Matthews, the Muslim population in general was reluctant to cut their relationship with the Greeks, and it was the CUP that undertook the task "on behalf of the nation." Yet one should also be aware of the attitude of Matthews, who claimed in the memorandum that "an order or a permit is required as a preliminary to almost any action." Therefore, he was looking for an order, claiming that it was circulated to the local branches of the CUP in the second half of May 1914. Boycott committees, made up of government officers and groups of Muslims, were formed at the beginning of June. Therefore, Matthews was not entirely sure who was responsible for the excessive acts of the boycotters, since in the end he again alluded to the government losing control of the situation.[152]

Likewise, the Greek consul in Ayvalık argued that it was the officers of the state who encouraged and protected the boycott, although he maintained that this was hard to prove. However, he did not assert that the officers and the boycotters were the same people. He also mentioned the support that the boycotters received from the Turkish guilds and the unions of Turkish merchants, saying that it was these institutions that paid the wages of the boycotters.[153] Another report of the Greek consul claimed that the boycott was initiated by an organization, the Society for Pan-Islamic Union.[154]

The social and economic milieu also contributed to the decisions of Muslim merchants to cut their ties to non-Muslim traders, by making it precarious and economically unsound for them to continue their business with Greeks. The general social and economic atmosphere might have forced some of the Muslim merchants to come to terms with the boycott movement, even if they were not really enthusiastic about it or did not belong to the network of the *Milli Itkisat*.

The most frequently mentioned actors were low-ranking bureaucrats, such as local governors (*kaymakams*), police officers, gendarmerie, directors (*müdürs*) of various official institutions, and local gangs. These gangs mostly consisted of Muslim immigrants. Over the course of the 1910–11 boycott movement, it was the Cretans who were most active, particularly in port cities. After 1913, the Macedonian *muhacirs* (immigrants) joined them. The flow of Muslim immigrants into Asia Minor provided the street-level force to the boycott movement. They were eager enough to play their part after an exhausting journey. In addition, a political group generally described as the extremist section of the CUP came to the fore in 1914. Nazım Bey was considered one of the prominent members of this group, along with Rahmi Bey in the province of Aydın.

In a conversation with the British consul Matthews, Rahmi Bey stated that Muslims in general and Muslim officers in particular were touched by the stories of ill-treatment of *muhacirs* at the hands of Greeks in Macedonia. Therefore, Rahmi Bey told him, "it was no wonder that local Greeks had been subjected to aggression," and that he would not have been astonished if this aggression appeared in Smyrna. For him, "it was too much to expect gendarmes or police sent against the Moslems to carry their orders, so strongly did they sympathize with their brethren in Macedonia." He repeated his point of view also to the metropolitan bishop of Philadelphia (Alaşehir), and it was also published in the journal of the Greek Orthodox patriarchate.[155] Therefore, the highest-ranking bureaucrat of the region considered the movement, the violent incidents, and the indifference of the security forces to be legitimate.

Nazim Bey, who was regarded as the organizer of the boycott movement, argued in another conversation with the consul that the nation was imbued with the "sentiment of hatred"; therefore, it was impossible for the government to put an end to the anti-Greek boycott.[156]

The British acting consul-general Heathcote Smith also argued that many moderate-minded Turks believed that they had to express their hatred against Greeks to prove their patriotism.[157]

To a great extent, the historiography on Turkey sees all Unionists as if they were state officers, *komitadji*, or soldiers. However, the CUP had members and supporters from different segments and classes of society. For instance, one of the prominent members of the CUP, Ali Bey, who was also a leader of the boycott movement in Edremit, had an olive oil factory and various stores.[158] The diary of the *mutasarrıf* of Karesi, Mehmed Reşid, who visited Ilıca/Edremit on his trip to the region, also refers to the factory of Ali Bey. It was one of the four factories of the region owned by Muslims.[159] However, it has generally been the bureaucrats whom the contemporaries and historians have taken into consideration.

Heathcote Smith reported in July that Rahmi Bey was imbued with blind and bitter hatred of the Greeks, and therefore was likely to tolerate anti-Greek violence in the coming war. In a personal conversation, he implied to Smith that the Greeks would probably be sent to the interior regions for strategic reasons. Yet, the same report stated that, thanks to the efforts of Rahmi Bey, who traveled to the interior towns of the province, the boycott ceased in late June and early July. He also informed the consul that in Torbalı several Turks had been "bastinadoed" for continuing to boycott contrary to his orders. Although the buying and selling resumed to an extent, the region was unsafe for its Greek inhabitants.[160]

The governor-general also confessed to Smith that the Circassian ex-brigand Eşref Bey and his brother Sami Bey were beyond his reach. According to Rahmi Bey, Eşref, who was living in Cordelio (Karşıyaka/Smyrna), had armed the Cretans in his entourage and was strongly supported by the minister of war, Enver Paşa.[161] Hence, there were different power centers among the anti-Greek movement. As a powerful man, Eşref Bey had special relationships with foreigners. For instance, he protected a European merchant who had large interests "up country" and gave him a personal letter of safe conduct in order to save him from any kind of nationalist intervention. He also gave a guard to a European who was a friend of the British consul-general in Smyrna. When this guard was dismissed in July 1914, the British consul deduced that the boycott was to relax.[162]

Yet, it should be highlighted that a mass mobilization did take place within the movement, since there were numerous incidents of cattle theft, injury, seizure of land and houses, pillaging of gardens, and thousands of people emigrated. In Marmara, in the province of Aydın, after the street criers had proclaimed that the boycott should end, Muslims were carrying grain that they had bought from the mill of Sophocles Panavogolou, but on their way from the mill boycotters attacked them and tried to drive them back.[163] This incident also indicates the will of the people, the power of the governors and the point at which they came into conflict with the boycott organization and its leaders. As a result, and as distinct from the previous boycotts, the political groupings and gangs were much more visible than the groups of merchants and port workers. This was so because the level of social mobilization increased and social relationships deteriorated. A group of Muslim notables seems to have taken advantage of these ethnic clashes and made a fortune out of this turmoil.

EPILOGUE: THE BOYCOTT MOVEMENT AND MASS POLITICS IN THE SECOND CONSTITUTIONAL PERIOD

The Popularization of Politics and the Shift in Mass Politics

Popular participation in politics emerged in the Ottoman Empire over the course of the nineteenth century. The Ottoman state began to intervene in the daily life of its subjects as it modernized social, economic and political structures and institutions. Mass politics and social mobilization of the masses were modern devices that the elite of the empire utilized in order to cope with the new needs of politics. As the relationship between the state and its subjects changed drastically, and different kinds of networks emerged among the people, the domain encompassed by politics expanded. These changes required new politics, through which state and society transformed each other.

A variety of changes took place in this period that allowed this transformation to happen: the incorporation of the Ottoman Empire into the world capitalist market, the expansion of market relationships within the empire, the formation of middle and professional classes, the modernization of the civil and military bureaucracy, and the emergence of modern communication technologies, a modern education system, the daily press, and different social and political networks and organizations. The expanding public sphere provided a space in which new politics could take shape. Within the emerging mass politics, different sections of Ottoman society found appropriate and effective ways in which they could represent themselves. The Ottoman state also exploited the formation of the modern public sphere as a means of ruling society. This gave the emerging mass politics two dimensions. On the one hand, it provided an opportunity for the elite to rule its citizens: new governing policies were put forth to ensure the consent of the people and secure the legitimacy of the political and social system. On the other hand, different classes and social groups took advantage of the changing public sphere to participate in politics in new ways. In order to evaluate this change it is important to define the concepts of public sphere and civil society; this is also necessary in order to clarify one's position in Turkish historiography, because a significant number of scholars object to the use of these terms in the Turkish or Middle Eastern context.[1]

A public sphere provides the space and the opportunity for a social movement or a mobilization process to emerge in an extended arena where people do not have face-to-face relationships. A modern public sphere is a social realm in which people imagine communities. On the other hand, pre-modern publicity, which Habermas calls "representative publicness," depended on concrete visibility and was directly related to the court.[2] However, the definition is the subject of a vivid debate. Habermas has argued that the public sphere is a realm that mediates between the private realm of the family and civil society (where commodity exchange and social labor take place) and the sphere of public authority, the state.[3] For him, the public sphere has two crucial dimensions: rational–critical discourse, and openness to popular participation.[4] Furthermore, the public sphere is not only immune from the intervention of the state authority, but also constituted against the state. Therefore, both the market, which belongs to civil society, and the state are outside it. Since the state is not included, there is no coercion in the public sphere, and free rational discussion can take place among the people. Public opinion emerges from communication and rational discussion between people.[5]

Habermas's approach and definition have been harshly criticized; these criticisms can be classified under two points. First, his definition of the bourgeois public sphere is seen as idealized, for the openness and free accessibility that he attributes to it. Negt and Kluge have argued that Habermas ignores the concomitant exclusionary mechanisms at work, by which the bourgeois public sphere blocks "all those sections of the population that do not participate in bourgeois politics because they cannot afford to."[6] While Negt and Kluge concentrate mainly on class structures, Landes and Ryan depict different exclusions by focusing primarily on the gender relationships of the bourgeois public sphere.[7] Secondly, Habermas has been criticized for overlooking the existence of public spheres other than the bourgeois one, such as alternative or counter-publics. Negt and Kluge, for instance, describe the "processing of social experience" and the "proletarian context of living as it exists," and highlight the presence of different publicities.[8] In addition, Fraser has depicted how feminists have built "subaltern counterpublics" with their own journals, bookstores, publishing companies, social and cultural networks, lecture series, research centers, conferences, conventions, festivals, and the like. These alternative institutions have helped women to decrease their disadvantage within the "official" public sphere.[9]

Habermas omits these two significant traits of the public sphere, and considers the flow of interests into this realm to be a form of degeneration. He has mainly accused "the pressure of the streets" for the degeneration of the public sphere.[10] As Hill and Montag have argued, his analysis is very much related to his defense of social democracy within the context of the Cold War and his "acceptance of capitalism as an absolute horizon," the "fear of the masses," and "the restriction of politics to parliamentary politics."[11] This is significant, since the historiography on Turkey is also very much influenced by the conservative mentality of many scholars. The literature on Turkey to a great extent equates the public sphere with civil society. It has widely been claimed that civil initiatives and democracy in non-Western societies are weak. Civil society was something that emerged in spite of state authority. It was a domain of freedom, free trade and autonomous organizations that developed against the authority of the state. Therefore, as Mardin has asserted, these concepts are considered a "Western dream" and "part of the social history of Western Europe."[12] According to this point of view, Turkey has had a strong state tradition that has strangled civil society, leaving no room for different sections of society to play their part. As argued in the first chapter, the agency of social groups outside of the state structure has been excluded from the historiography on Turkey. This also is the case when it comes to the concepts of public sphere and civil society. The fundamental elements of this book—mass politics, social mobilization patterns, social movements, and the agency of different sections of society—did not exist in Turkey's history, according to this perspective.

However, İslamoğlu has raised the question of whether it is empirically possible to identify state and society as separate domains actually interpenetrated by each other. Abbot, in a similar vein, has claimed that a weak civil society might result from a weak rather than a strong state.[13] An "overriding antagonism between state and society" paves the way for an essentialist analysis for different societies. An individual or a civil society free from state intervention is only a liberal conception of civil society. The definition of democracy derived from this conceptualization is also based on liberal ideology.[14] Therefore, as the subject of this book indicates, the expansion of the public sphere, the flourishing of civil society and the centralization of state power go hand in hand. One should not attribute essentialist characteristics to the concepts of the public sphere and civil society, viewing them only as the domain of democracy and freedom. As Trentmann has argued, these notions are paradoxical: "While it may open doors for freedom and plurality, it may also bring in some cases suspension of tolerance and mutual recognition."[15]

The discussion of these concepts is crucial, since the literature on Turkey to a great extent avoids employing concepts, underlining instead the unique character of its history. Although different countries and societies do have crucial differences in their histories, scholars cannot recruit different concepts and categories for each society. This particularism leads Turkish historiography to "essentialist" or "exceptionalist" evaluations, while trying to avoid reductionism. There are also endless differences and variations in the history of each society and country, which may require further particular conceptualization. Yet, essentialism precludes comparisons between different cases and complicates the understanding of different societies. Making use of the concepts of social sciences and debating their definitions and meanings may help to uncover the uniqueness and peculiar features of particular cases.

In this study, the public sphere is employed to describe a social space in which different sections of society can express themselves, where the relationship between different classes takes place, and the relationships between individuals, people, state and civil organizations occur. It is the social realm and space that provides both face-to-face and imagined interactions between different social actors. Civil society, on the other hand, is used in order to refer to the notion of agency. It is employed in order to refer to the initiatives of social and political actors in a society, such as civil organizations, associations, unions, classes, individuals and the spontaneous actions of the ordinary people. There are different dynamics in the transformation of the public sphere and the emergence of civil society in the Ottoman Empire of the nineteenth century. Different ethnic or religious communities and different social classes competed with each other in the expanding public sphere, and influenced its structure. The state was a crucial actor in the formation and regulation of this modern space. Yet reciprocally, it was also deeply influenced by other political and social actors.

As mentioned above, various new political practices allowed broad sections of society to play their part in the expanding public sphere. Official and public holidays, the invention of "national" celebrations, the use of new political symbols, campaigns of imperial or national charities, different acts of public benevolence, and imperial and national anthems were some of the significant formal elements in this newly emerging mass politics.[16] Some of its other more general features were elections, economic boycotts, strikes, social and political organizations, the total mobilization of the society during wars, mass sport activities, commercialized mass entertainment, and mass spectacles. One of the main practices of the new politics was the social mobilization of people.

Mass politics began to acquire prominence over the course of the nineteenth century in the Ottoman Empire. As is widely claimed in the literature on Turkey, the Imperial Edict of the Rose Chamber (1839), starting at the beginning of the Tanzimat period, paved the way for a structural transformation of Ottoman imperial institutions and society. As a result of this reform process, the notions of public opinion emerged as crucial realities that the elite had to take into account in their manner of rule. This is why the early modern state began to show interest in the opinion of its subjects on political issues and, as a result, began to become involved in the daily life of its subjects.[17]

The monarchs no longer represented themselves as semi-divine rulers, but rather as paternalistic father figures who worked for the well-being of their subjects. They put forth new policies in the public sphere, in order to obtain the loyalty of the people who were now considered citizens.[18] Fundamental elements and devices of mass politics took concrete, practical form during the reign of Abdülhamid II. During these years, although the policies of the state did not go further than demanding unilateral conformity from the Ottoman public, they began to take public opinion into account. In other words, while the social mobilization of people in public spaces did not emerge as an official policy in this period, the elite of the Ottoman Empire tried to legitimize their power in the eyes of public opinion with the help of new devices, such as charity campaigns, in which ordinary people could participate. The state did not want ordinary people to gather as crowds in the streets, but to find different ways to contribute and participate. Legitimization policies increased in variety during the second half of the nineteenth century.[19] The elite resorted to these devices in order to obtain the loyalty and consent of the Ottoman public, and the public sphere provided the space in which these new mass politics could emerge.[20] The 1908 Revolution brought about change and a turn in mass politics and social mobilization patterns in the Ottoman Empire.

The 1908 Revolution marked the beginning of a new era. During the Second Constitutional Period, there occurred clear-cut instances of mass politics and social mobilization patterns. The change in mass politics was due to the rise of the CUP, which attributed great significance to the mobilization of the masses and the participation of different sections of society, such as workers and merchants, in politics. Nationalist celebrations, lively civil associations, voluntary organizations, mass movements and the flourishing daily press provided ordinary people with an opportunity to voice their opinions. The particular problems and interests of different segments of society turned into public issues. Henceforth, these were openly debated. Therefore, mass politics and social mobilization practices during this period had a bilateral character, in which state and different sections and classes of society played reciprocal roles, in contrast to the general characteristics of the previous era.

In the previous era, the masses had been kept passive and motionless. The affirmation of their consent and loyalty was enough for the elite. The congregation of crowds in public places was rare, and the direct mobilization of the masses on the streets was not employed by the political establishment. One of the main traits of the period after the 1908 Revolution was the mobilization of masses in public spaces. Studies that have collected visual material on the 1908 Revolution reveal that the most spectacular phenomenon after the revolution was the gathering of crowds in public places.[21] Mass parades, marches, public meetings, demonstrations and street actions became ordinary instruments of politics. Even funeral ceremonies after political assassinations turned into political mass protests in which thousands participated. Since the Second Constitutional Period was an era of wars (with the Italo–Ottoman War in 1911–12, the Balkan Wars in 1912–13, and WWI), the mobilization of the Ottoman public emerged as a significant issue for the elite.[22] Protesting against foreign states was no longer exclusively the domain of the diplomats, but also entered the realm of public meetings: mass demonstrations to protest against the Great Powers became a well-known phenomenon during the rising Muslim/Turkish nationalism after the 1908 Revolution. Inter-ethnic friction also erupted in large-scale clashes, as nationalism spread among the Ottoman population. National issues were no longer restricted to intellectual circles, but became public issues that affected the daily routines of ordinary people.

At this point, it should be underlined that there are different patterns of mass mobilization. One is the mobilization of different segments of society from below, to claim their rights; the other is the mobilization of the society from above. The 1908 Revolution paved the way for both of these mobilization patterns. The mobilization of the masses from below was what made the promulgation of the constitution a revolution. The narratives on the revolution generally depict it as a *coup d'état* of young military cadres who would thereafter dominate politics; it is seen as the root of military intervention in politics. This orthodox view therefore defines it not as a revolution, but as the promulgation of the constitution. The first problem with this view is that it neglects the revolutionary struggle of different ethnic groups, such as the Albanians, Bulgarians and Armenians. Second, it ignores the actions of the lower classes all over the empire. The CUP was prevented from taking full control of the revolution due to the mobilization of ordinary people on the street. It was not a simple transition from one political system to another, or simply the promulgation of a constitution: 23 July 1908 marked a political revolution in which different political, social and ethnic groups played their part, and was a turning point that drastically changed the order of things in the Ottoman Empire.[73] However, the mobilization patterns from above ultimately prevailed in the course of the Second Constitutional Period as the CUP gained power.

Following July 1908, the Ottomans resorted to different types of action—such as strikes, boycotts and mass demonstrations—and many people participated in these new types of politics. After this turning point in the history of the Ottoman Empire, they expressed their social and political demands in mass demonstrations and in the Ottoman press, which had freed itself from the censorship of Abdülhamid II. The abolition of censorship had more impact on the Muslim/Turkish community, since non-Muslims had had a much more vibrant press before, yet the 1908 Revolution did also bring about a boom in the number of non-Muslim periodicals and organizations.[24] Ottoman people started to organize meetings and establish organizations. As Tunaya has stated, politics became accessible, allowing ordinary citizens to express their opinions.[25] One of the main reasons for this vibrant political life following the promulgation of the constitution was the chaotic political situation after the revolution.[26] From the very beginning of the Second Constitutional Period, Ottomans filled the streets and public squares and started to build mass organizations. The CUP, the initiator of the constitution, could not control or dominate the political life of the empire. It gained more power after the counter-revolution of the 31 March Event (13 April 1909), and became the most powerful organization in the empire after the Babıali *coup d'état* in 1913.

Between 23 July 1908 and 13 April 1909, when the 1908 boycott took place, there was an optimistic atmosphere in the Ottoman Empire regarding the ideals of the constitution: Equality, Freedom, Fraternity, Justice and the *ittihad-ı anasır* (union of ethnic/religious elements— that is to say, Ottomanism). As is widely accepted, the CUP could not come to power just after the promulgation of the constitution, because it lacked senior members who had a significant reputation, being composed of low-ranking military and civil officers who initially thought that they were incapable of assuming power. Furthermore, although the CUP was the leading agent in the promulgation of the constitution, it was not organized throughout the empire.[27] The Young Turks sought to mobilize public opinion and initiate action in order to attract support for their policies. This necessitated the mobilization of the population from above, and compelled the CUP to find different means to this end.

The CUP sought to become more active and strong in parliament; as a result, the first elections were held in a tense political atmosphere. Both these elections and the 1908 Ottoman boycott revealed the significance of a development that appeared after 23 July: public opinion and mass politics. The elections to the Ottoman parliament always became an occasion for mass politics, a point which has not been adequately dealt with in the literature.[28] The political struggle between the different communities and different political groups revealed itself in election campaigns. For instance, the 1912 elections earned the name "battered elections" (*sopalı seçimler*) after they developed into an open clash between different political groups, and the CUP suppressed different political attitudes and organizations during that time. The 1914 elections were held under the absolute hegemony of the Unionists, and the tension between the different religious communities contributed to the emergence of the boycott movement against non-Muslims in 1913–14.

Mass politics also allowed the emergence of social movements within particular social classes, such as the working class. The constitution was followed by an unprecedented wave of strikes. Workers organized many demonstrations in August and September of 1908 and refused to work until their demands were met. This was a significant moment in Ottoman history, which saw workers struggling for their interests all over the empire. However, further research is needed to uncover the relationships and the networks among the workers of the Ottoman Empire. These working-class mass actions ended on the initiative of the CUP.[29] The other significant feature of these actions was the generally fraternal atmosphere of the 1908 Revolution. The nationalist and ethnic divisions among the Ottoman working class did not matter during the 1908 strike wave.[30] Its goals were mostly based on economic demands, and ethnic divisions did not impede its struggle against the companies.

Such a widespread strike wave never recurred in the Ottoman Empire after 1908. However, as I have argued in previous chapters, workers found an opportunity to express themselves in other social movements, such as the boycotts of 1908 or 1910–11. For instance, the port workers whose demands had been suppressed by the Ottoman government during the strike wave of 1908 successfully presented their interests in the 1908 boycott, an Ottomanist movement that helped them acquire certain rights. As they proved themselves to be the most powerful social base of the boycott movement from 1908 to 1911, they enhanced their position in the economy.

It was not only the workers that pursued their interests; women, who were traditionally kept distant from political life, began to come onto the public scene in the course of the Second Constitutional Period.[31] Women emerged and participated in the social life in a more deliberate way. They began to appear in theaters and at public concerts, and to represent themselves in the public sphere. Primary education for girls became mandatory in 1913. Since the Second Constitutional Period was an era of wars, the recruitment of women into the workforce facilitated their entrance into public life. They published journals, formed societies, and did participate (albeit very little) in the 1908 boycott. Ottoman women also came onto the scene as activists within the workers' movements, as happened in Bursa in 1910.[32]

Women were also able to find a particular place for themselves in both the discourse and movement of nationalism.[33] Within the rising Muslim/Turkish nationalism, women occupied positions that gave them an opportunity to become active.[34] During the boycotts of 1910–11 and 1913–14, women had different functions. In the first place, they were considered to represent the honor and purity of the nation. Moreover, there were instances of women denouncing actions that were against the rules of the boycott at a grassroots level. They also functioned as the protagonists of nationalist stories told during the boycott movement. Although their place in the division of labor was confined according to gender lines, it is still possible to hear their voices.

One of the significant aspects of mass politics was the boom in the number of civil organizations and societies established and organized by Ottomans after the 1908 Revolution.[35] Voluntary organizations and civil societies were crucial elements of the social and political life of the Second Constitutional Period. Numerous organizations emerged with a variety of goals, including philanthropy, national economy, education, nationalism and sports. These organizations popularized politics and increased the participation of ordinary people in public life. Apart from the organizations of the boycott movement, flourishing civil organizations such as the Donanma Cemiyeti played a significant role in the making of the boycott movement. The economic organizations of Muslim merchants, nationalist associations and semi-official organizations supported each other and contributed to the emergence of a Muslim/Turkish nationalist popular movement.

After the 1908 Revolution, and particularly after the joyful revolutionary days of fraternity, the relationship between the different religious and ethnic communities deteriorated. Competing nationalisms affected the daily life of the Ottoman people and undermined cooperation between different communities. Although there had already been numerous instances of ethnic violence over the course of the nineteenth century, clashes, struggles, hostilities and strife became one of the fundamental aspects of the Second Constitutional Period.[36] Economic boycotts and Muslim protests against non-Muslims, which were relatively peaceful actions compared to ethnicity-based atrocities, were another expression of this ethnic tension and fed into rising Muslim/Turkish nationalism. The rise and strengthening of a Muslim/Turkish bourgeoisie became one of the main aims of Turkish nationalism and the boycott movement after 1910. Muslim notables, the state elite and wealthy Muslims also took advantage of this process and contributed to the movement.

To sum up, different actors in Ottoman society began to express themselves more widely, and the masses found an opportunity to take action. The CUP successfully mobilized the masses in order to enhance its status and reinforce its political power, usually legitimizing its policies and actions by presenting them as the demands and interests of the Ottoman nation. Social movements represented an opportunity for the CUP, and by mobilizing the public, it headed off possible opposition to the new regime. It not only used devices such as boycotts to organize the Ottomans, but also established local organizations. To accumulate more power, the CUP sought legitimate public support for its policies. Particularly after 1908, when the weapon of the boycott was turned against non-Muslim communities, the mobilization of Muslim and Turkish Ottomans became inevitable in the course of the Second Constitutional Period.

Mass Politics, the National Economy and the Boycott Movement

The declaration of the boycott against Austria-Hungary and Bulgaria in 1908 coincided with a wave of mass public meetings and mass spectacles. Crowds of people marched and chanted slogans against these states and defended the sovereign rights of the Ottoman Empire regarding Bosnia-Herzegovina and Bulgaria. The targets of these marching crowds were the foreign embassies. These actions were followed by spontaneous demonstrations and meetings, instilling fear amongst the elites of the Ottoman Empire. The government, the CUP and the Turkish press tried to control the mobilizations of the crowds on the streets and to appease their nationalist sentiments. The same social phenomenon was repeated in the initial phase of the 1910–11 boycott movement: the elites exploited the widespread public support, but at the same time were afraid of the mass mobilization after it reached a certain level.

The Young Turks were worried about the possibility that the masses might turn against the young constitutional regime, and that their energy would be utilized by reactionaries. They were very much influenced by the thoughts of Gustave Le Bon, whose fear of the masses depended on the belief that masses and crowds played only subversive and ruinous roles in society.[37] Thus, the Young Turks did not ban the mobilization of the masses, but rather tried to manipulate and control them by means of organized and orderly public meetings and demonstrations. The prominent figures of the CUP and its local cadres were not entirely absent from the first reactionary spontaneous demonstrations. However, these actions were not under their control. The contemporary newspapers claimed that these meetings were the largest in scale and extent, after the promulgation of the constitution. As a result, the first reaction of the elite to these meetings and the mobilization was a call for sobriety and moderation to those who were already on the streets. The Ottoman press praised the so-called famous "Ottoman temperance."

The meetings and demonstrations that followed these spontaneous reactions were well-ordered and planned, and *tellals* (public criers) were recruited to announce their time and place in advance. Banners, flags, drums and posters were widely used in the public sphere during the boycott movement. These instruments of mass politics facilitated the popularization of the movement and its symbols. Posters, signs and stickers were designed to simplify the basic demands of the boycott movement. These should be considered symbolic signs and marks, rather than plain texts; the symbolic, simple language on these posters was instrumental in reaching ordinary people who were to a great extent illiterate.[38] These posters were hung in public places and rallied the Ottoman public regarding national issues, or advertised the targets of the boycott movement, such as Austrian stores in 1908 or Greek shops after 1910. Boycott targets and foreign observers, such as diplomatic consuls, took these public notifications very seriously and often complained to the Ottoman government, fearing that they would provoke the Muslim population. There were not many complaints about the lists of targeted merchants published in the newspapers, but much more fear resulted from similar lists posted on public walls.

EPILOGUE   217

Both the Ottoman state and the foreign consuls considered this imagery an assault and coercion during the 1910–11 boycott movement.

Fliers, hand-bills, leaflets and pamphlets were also used in order to attract the attention of Ottoman citizens to issues related with the boycott movement. The state of Muslims in Bosnia-Herzegovina and Bulgaria in 1908, the sufferings of Muslim Cretans in 1910–11, and the misery of Muslim immigrants from the Balkans after the Balkan Wars enhanced the mobilization efforts of the boycotters. Many publications appeared concerning the state of Muslims in the lost territories, calling Muslims to action. These pamphlets contributed to the rise of Muslim/Turkish nationalism and reinforced Muslim identity. In the first instances of the boycott movement, the pamphlets and fliers announced the targets of the boycott movement: that is, the persons or companies to be boycotted. By the last phases of the boycotting wave, however, the announcements were all about the Muslim stores where a proper Muslim should shop: there was no longer a particular non-Muslim target, and as a whole they were positioned *vis-à-vis* Muslims.

Flags, banners, placards, pamphlets and fliers were also widely used in well-organized meetings. Public speeches at these meetings were held in the different languages of the Ottoman communities. The meetings were convened in many of the empire's urban centers, and the representatives of different religious communities participated. This was arranged to underline the official fraternity policy of the new constitutional regime. The same variety of communities participated again in the meetings against the Cretan National Assembly and against Greece in 1910 and 1911. The participation of the Ottoman Greeks was significant, since they thereby confirmed their loyalty to the Ottoman Empire. Although the members of different communities attended the meetings during the 1910–11 boycotts, meetings started to become much more anti-Christian as the fraternal atmosphere of the 1908 Revolution evaporated.

As argued in the earlier chapters, these public meetings and the mass mobilization of different segments of society were not a secret undertaking or a CUP conspiracy, as is widely accepted in Turkish political thought. Instead, like other political and social actors, the Ottoman government and the CUP tried to make use of these meetings. As the political and social power of the committee increased, its hegemony in these public demonstrations grew. However, the power of the CUP and the Ottoman government over the mobilization of the masses was not absolute. On the contrary, in the course of the boycott movement, the Ottoman political elite found itself trying to limit the mobilization of the people at the grassroots level. During the protest meetings, the crowds did not disperse quickly. Initiatives arose to form volunteer battalions to support the Ottoman army: public meeting waves gave rise to volunteer-enlisting initiatives, particular organizations for forming battalions and a network of these organizations. These volunteer societies effectively communicated with each other in Asia Minor, from Trabzon to Erzurum, from Konya to İzmir, and from Salonica to Edirne.

The government considered these initiatives an interference of the common people in the affairs of the imperial state, so it ordered the governors to prevent such mobilization activities and wanted them to convince the Ottoman citizens that the government was in charge. In some towns, the convened crowds refused to disperse and demanded guarantees that the government was doing its best to solve the national problems. The Ottoman government ordered the governors to use military force to disperse the crowds if they insisted on continuing their actions. The newspapers used various arguments to limit public meetings to formal and conventional forms. Furthermore, the elites expressed the view that the boycott should go no further than the customers' refusal to buy certain goods; picketing stores or assaulting merchants were banned and condemned, particularly in the 1908 and 1910–11 boycotts.

The network between the boycotters in different parts of the empire facilitated the emergence of an empire-wide social movement. The modern communication technology and networks that emerged in the nineteenth century—such as telegraph services, the daily press and civil organizations—contributed to the construction of such a network and the mobilization of people dwelling in various parts of the Ottoman Empire. The mobilization of Ottoman society after the 1908 Revolution provided a social base for the emergence of the 1908 Ottoman boycott. One of the most active elements of the boycott movement, the port workers, were on strike for almost two months before the emergence of the boycott. The sharp rise in the number of newspapers and civil organizations as a result of the revolution allowed the boycott movement to make use of the revolutionary atmosphere to construct its own network. Boycott organizations such as the Harb-i İktisadi Cemiyeti (Society for Economic Warfare), the Boykotaj Sendikası (Boycott Union) and the boycott journal *Gâve* appeared in the initial days of the boycott. Ottoman newspapers and journals in Turkish, Greek, Armenian and other languages zealously supported the boycott against Austria and Bulgaria, contributing to the popularization of the movement.

Until the Balkan Wars, the boycott organization depended to a great extent on the network of the port workers. In turn, the boycott organizations and the movement also reinforced the network and the social power of the port workers in the Ottoman Empire. The port workers and the boycott organizations generally used telegraph services to communicate with each other, while local boycott organizations proclaimed their announcements in the daily press. The Muslim merchants who were involved in the movement were organized in boycott unions. They were to a great extent co-opted into the movement due to the boycott certificates that they received from the boycott organizations. These certificates were to ratify the legitimacy and power of the boycott movement and also expanded the scope of the boycott network. (In spite of this growing legitimacy, the Boycott Society did not legalize itself in 1909 when it became officially mandatory to register civil organizations.) Kürt Ali Ağa in 1908 and Kerim Ağa in 1910–11 rose as the most prominent figures of the movement in Istanbul and Salonica. The boycott network reinforced its operation between different towns of the empire and strengthened its power over the local bureaucrats and notables.

After the Balkan Wars, the configuration of the boycott network and organizations evolved into a much more nationalist form. From this point on, the organization was made up of local nationalist cadres and local nationalist notables who worked for the elimination of the non-Muslims in the Ottoman Empire. Boycott organizations began to work like nationalist gangs, particularly in the provinces. This is why, during the 1913–14 boycott, the names of political figures such as Eşref Kuşçubaşı (a well-known member of the Teşkilat-ı Mahsusa) were mentioned in the documents. The evolution of the boycott organizations and network, comprising people from all walks of life, contributed a great deal to the construction of a Turkish nationalist network. Therefore, the movement as a whole indicates that Turkish nationalism, together with its political organizations such as the CUP, was not only an intellectual current, but also had deep social origins. This social base was fed from different sources. The immigrants from Crete and Macedonia constituted both a street force in terms of grassroots politics, and a significant number of entrepreneurs within the framework of *Milli Itkisat* policies. The urban notables who owned lands and modest capital in the provinces were at least mobilized by the policies of the CUP, if not actual members of the organization itself. Social movements such as the boycott movement and its social network played a crucial role in the popularization of ideas and political thoughts. The corporations and guilds that survived at the beginning of the twentieth century, such as that of the port workers, were a crucial social base in the political life of the Ottoman Empire. Besides the military bureaucrats (who are those most often represented as the main social base of Turkish nationalism) and civil bureaucracy and professional classes (such as lawyers, doctors and teachers), the workers' guilds established one of the main components of the nationalist movement.

Other types of public gatherings and conventions happened apart from the mass public meetings against foreign states, such as public conferences that took place in theater halls and coffee-houses. The audiences of these conferences and lectures were informed about the goals of the boycott movement and learned how and why to boycott. The audience found an opportunity to express their thoughts and feelings and well-known intellectuals, journalists and political figures addressed people in these public places during each boycott wave. Such public meetings in the neighborhood context reinforced the place of the boycott within people's daily life.

The most conspicuous aspects of the boycotts in the Ottoman Empire were concrete actions. A classical concrete action in the context of a boycott is the picketing of a store. Ostracism of a personal, social or national target is the main goal of a boycott movement. Yet ostracism and picketing require different vehicles of enforcement. Demonstrations began in front of famous Austrian stores, such as Stein, in 1908. These demonstrations were not just protest meetings, but also constituted *de facto* picket lines. Some Austrian shops had to put up French and British flags in order to appease the crowds gathered around their shops. The boycotted stores were closely watched both by the boycotters and the Ottoman public. After 1910, watchmen were stationed around boycotted shops to keep away prospective customers; those who continued to frequent these establishments were pulled out of the shops by force. Such incidents worried the Ottoman government, since they were undermining the public order. After the Balkan Wars, the intensity, persistence and frequency of picketing increased and the different patterns of direct action now included violence. This worsened over the course of the boycott movement, eventually becoming the organized gang violence of 1913 and 1914, which was a precursor to the ethnic clashes that would occur during WWI.

In its most basic definition, the boycott was the consumers' refusal to buy certain products. The boycotters tried to convince the public and the merchants to act in accord with the rules of the boycott movement. However, it was not easy to obtain the consent of the Ottoman public, particularly of those interest groups who benefitted from breaching boycott regulations, so these official regulations were accompanied by acts of violence against those who did not comply. Those merchants who insisted on conducting business with boycotted countries and businessmen were in many cases stopped by force. Boycotted merchandise such as sugar, flour, glass and fezzes were all destroyed or publicly burned, if their owners tried to get them.

The most spectacular direct action during the 1908 Ottoman boycott was the "Fez-Tearing Feast" (*fes yırtma bayramı*), when fezzes were taken from people's heads and torn. The newspapers described and defined these actions as "carnival." These actions created an extraordinary atmosphere that contributed to the construction of an empire-wide social movement. The violent character of the boycott movement increased after 1908 in both extent and scope. Inspection teams were established to control whether merchants stocked boycotted items in their stores. Assaults on shops, merchandise, caravans, gardens, individuals and groves became quite widespread after 1910, and the means of production, goods and agricultural produce were often destroyed. The ultimate goal of these inspections and assaults was to intimidate the owners and compel them to leave the town or the region. Many Greek shops were marked to identify them as a target. Their front walls were inscribed with slogans in chalk, or their windows were covered with boycotting signs. These boycotting marks terrified the owners of the shops and stores, and many of them had already shut down their business as early as 1910. It was common for Muslim customers entering non-Muslim stores to receive a verbal warning after 1913, and instances of physical force toward those customers were no longer the exception. Violence and clashes between different communities compelled both the minister of the interior, Talat Bey, and an International Inquiry Commission to conduct a tour of western Asia Minor in 1914. The boycott movement and the violence it entailed forced thousands to leave their homeland, while thousands of Muslim immigrants arrived from elsewhere in the Ottoman Empire. The boycotting started to resemble banditry and became entirely different from the "Fez-Tearing Feasts."

The boycott movement that appeared during the Second Constitutional Period represented the economic aspect of the process of elimination of non-Muslims from the Ottoman Empire. It formed part of the *Milli İktisat* (National Economy) policies that gradually established themselves throughout the period. In Turkish historiography, the *Milli İktisat* is largely regarded as an intellectual current alone, a branch of rising Turkish nationalism. As an economic and social phenomenon, however, boycotts played as influential a role after the 1908 Revolution as political factors such as diplomacy, wars, high politics and political ideas did. The boycott movement is responsible for generating the social force that underpinned *Milli İktisat* thought and politics. It mobilized and organized Muslims within the framework of rising Turkish nationalism, turning it from an abstract idea into a social reality.

Ideas of constructing the national economy became popular immediately after the 1908 Revolution. Thoughts on the development of a native industry, the abolition of the capitulations, and the social and economic revolution that should follow the political one were some of the issues related to the *Milli İktisat* that were discussed publicly. It was not a coincidence that the national economy debates and the invention of native products arose immediately after the 1908 Revolution. The *Milli İktisat* constituted the economic dimension of the rising Turkish nationalism, and the theory started to gain popularity during this particular period.[39] It was claimed that the classical liberal theory and its policies that prevailed after the Tanzimat reforms in the nineteenth century had destroyed small Muslim producers. The *Milli İktisat* thesis gave the nation and the state a new mission to rescue the empire's main group (Muslims/Turks) from economic and social decline. This is why theorists of Turkish nationalism and national economy advocates were mostly the same. Political figures and nationalist intellectuals—such as Ziya Gökalp, Tekin Alp, Yusuf Akçura and Ahmet Muhiddin—developed theories of the national economy by using the works of German economists, such as List, Wagner and Schmoller. For them, the Muslim and Turkish component of the empire should be dominant in the economic sphere. They argued that the concrete interests of the nation should remain at the center, and not the abstract concepts of the Manchester School. The German example taught them that a strong and powerful state might achieve this goal, by intervening in the economy.[40]

Thoughts on the development of a national industry and economy were not entirely new in the Second Constitutional Period. These goals and projects had existed in Ottoman economic thought even before the revolution in 1908. However, economic policies and thoughts on economic theories had not been topics of widespread discussion before. Several preliminary attempts at industrialization had already taken place in the course of the nineteenth century.[41] Yet these did not happen within the framework of a critique of classical liberalism: *laissez faire, laissez passer* was dominant in all economic policies and thought. Nevertheless, as the CUP started to gain influence during the Second Constitutional Period, *étatism* and protectionism gradually began to dominate Muslim/Turkish thought. The organization and discourse of the boycott movement from 1908 to 1914 marks this very transition.

At first, it was generally argued that the state should not intervene in commercial and economic life. Demands for protectionism by means of high tariffs were exceptional. It was the citizens who should work hard for the development of a native economy, by changing their economic preferences as consumers. It was inevitable that the empire had to compete with the European economic powers, and the Ottoman public should be mobilized to buy primarily Ottoman products. The 1908 Ottoman boycott contributed to this process and popularized the demands for a native economy. Economic debates, such as protectionism versus liberalism, which had been confined to scholarly works and textbooks, became widespread in the public sphere after 1908, through journals and newspapers.[42]

Historians working on Turkey have argued that *Milli İktisat* gained prominence particularly after the Balkan Wars. Yet, as argued above, significant aspects of National Economy can also be detected on different levels during the 1908 boycott. It was one of the first instances of a popular nationalist economic awakening. The concepts of encouraging native industry, creating an Ottoman economy, and protecting the Ottoman economy and welfare entered the Ottoman public's consciousness. Nationalist economic symbols, such as national headgear and meetings in favor of a native economy, became popular during the boycott movement. To use and buy Ottoman products became a fashion, and this was a significant cultural factor in the rise of *Milli İktisat*.

Muslim merchants and working classes, the social groups that supported the boycotts, organized themselves and moved into the public eye for their own interest within a social movement. The Muslim merchant class, particularly in Asia Minor, became active after the 1908 Revolution, as did the boycott movement, with the support of the CUP. For instance, Muslim merchants and local notables created a national bank, Konya Bankası (Bank of Konya) in 1909.[43] In addition to establishing banks and other economic institutions, Muslim merchants and notables in the provinces also published journals and organized voluntary associations that supported the national economy. For instance, *Ticaret-i Umumiyye Mecmuası* (Journal of Public Trade) was published by prominent merchants.[44]

Epilogue

Muslim merchants not only published journals, but also established civil organizations, such as Cemiyet-i Müteşebbise (Society of Entrepreneurs), Ticaret ve Ziraat ve Sanayii Cemiyet-i Milliyesi (National Society for Trade, Agriculture and Industry), Osmanlı Sanatkaran Cemiyeti (Ottoman Artisan Society) and Milli Fabrikacılar Cemiyeti (Nationalist Industrialist Society).[45] Journalists in the provinces encouraged wealthy Muslims to contribute to these organizations. Alonside these interest groups and organizations, other civil organizations also appeared. The clubs of the CUP, the Cemiyet-i İlmiye-i İslamiye (Society of Islamic Science) and Türk Ocağı (Turkish Hearth) were organizations that worked hard for the national economy and the development of a Muslim/Turkish industry. These organizations and nationalist newspapers like *Tanin* organized evening courses for the Muslim and Turkish population, in order to improve their skills for the market.[46] As a result, they were able to replace foreigners and non-Muslims. Young Turks and Muslim notables consolidated the power of the national merchant class by making the Turkish language mandatory in business transactions.[47]

The 1908 boycott to a great extent propagated an Ottomanist discourse and included and defined the non-Muslim communities within the domains of the native economy. However, after 1910, the so-called dominance of non-Muslims in the economy began to be harshly criticized; it was openly declared that they were no longer loyal to the ideals of Ottomanism. The CUP attempted to enhance the status of Muslims and Turks in the economy by mobilizing public opinion. The economic boycott emerged as a weapon to which the Muslim and Turkish elite resorted when they sought to eliminate non-Muslims from the economy. The enterprises of several prominent Muslims in the provinces were regarded as a part of the boycott movement, even by foreign companies and consuls. Concepts such as *İktisadi Cihad* (Economic Holy War) or *İktisadi Harb* (Economic Warfare) were widely used in the daily press, in intellectual debates and popular slogans. This was a social and economic complement to a political nationalist project. One of the main slogans of Turkish nationalism appeared during this period: it told non-Muslims "to leave the country if they did not love it."

Many Muslim entrepreneurs took advantage of these circumstances and expanded their investments. The boycotts embraced different sections of society, such as merchants and the working class, and gave them increased agency. In this way, the influence of the boycott movement vastly surpassed the original designs of the Unionists and protesters themselves. Different social actors became active in this process, causing foreign observers—such as the British, French and Greek consuls—to refer to the social forces behind the boycott movement. The Jewish community and the *dönme* in Salonica, Muslim notables in the provinces, and the leaders of the port workers in port cities were blamed for being the ultimate instigators of the movement, in addition to the Ottoman bureaucracy, which was said to have nationalist and anti-non-Muslim tendencies.

Popular Ideology, Islam and the Mobilization of the Masses

The mobilization of people constitutes one of the essential ingredients of a social movement. Social scientists have analyzed the mobilization process by focusing on its different aspects. Ideologies and discourses are directly related with culture, which constitutes one of the main ingredients of the concept of social class. Therefore, ideology matters, since it is related to the mobilization of the population and the idea of political legitimacy, and since it deeply influenced the social actions of different segments of Ottoman society. Ideology has different meanings; the concept of "popular ideology" refers here to an amalgam of discourses that does not pursue coherence and comprises different competing ideologies as well as the dominant ideology of the ruling elite.

The ideology and discourse of a social movement play a crucial role in the mobilization of the masses. In bold terms, the employment of an ideology in a social movement appeals to the common people and attracts the attention of public opinion. Popular ideologies that address the masses and their discourse are directly related to the emergence of mass movements. Mass movements and the mobilization of people emerge not only because of concrete material interests and the organizational skills of the participants, but also as a result of a legitimizing discourse. The ideology of a social movement is also related to culture. The ideology created by the organizers of a movement generally attempts to refer to popular thoughts, belief systems, myths, conventions, traditions, symbols, and the like.

Modern ideologies are also a component of mass society and mass politics. It is not only social movements, but also states, governments and political parties that utilize popular ideologies in order to convince ordinary people of their cause and to consolidate their hegemony over society. The expansion of the public sphere, the flourishing of civil organizations, and the introduction of communication facilities, general suffrage and parliamentary politics—these all brought competing ideologies onto the agenda. This is why the emergence of mass movements coincided with the transformation of political thought into political programs and popular ideologies, such as socialism, nationalism, feminism, populism and so on.

Ottoman intellectuals gave birth to a number of modern political ideologies, including Ottomanism, Islamism and Turkism in the course of the nineteenth century, particularly after the emergence of a modern education system and a modern daily press. Ottomanism was the idea that all people living in the domains of the Ottoman Empire—irrespective of their creed, language, religion and ethnic origin—would be equal citizens of the empire. Ottomanism as an ideology and discourse emerged in different clothes in the discourse of different actors.[48] Similarly, Islamism as a political project and ideology appeared in various guises, aiming at the union of the empire on the basis of Islamic identity. It represented the politicization of Islam and was an attempt to reconcile religion and modernity. Turkism was a latecomer among these three main currents, and brought to the fore the argument that the Turkish element should be the dominant nation in the empire.

Since the intellectual history of the Ottoman Empire is one of the better-studied fields, political thought and the debates among Ottoman intellectuals form a significant part of the historiography.[49] The history of the Young Ottomans and the Young Turks in particular depends to a great extent on intellectual history. Although constituting a significant contribution to the literature, this aspect of

Ottoman historiography also has a number of pitfalls. The intellectual history narratives that depict the period are based only on political thought and to a great extent ignore the social context.

First of all, the classifications made by these studies have given rise to the belief or certainty that distinct ideological camps existed amongst the Ottoman intellectuals.[50] The idea of Ottomanism, the politicization of Islam, and Turkist thought are all seen as representing distinct schools of thought. Although as a means of understanding the intellectual currents in the Ottoman Empire such a classification may have some merits, the literature appears to be based on the idea that these currents actually existed as discourses isolated from each other. This clear-cut perception of intellectual history started with Yusuf Akçura's well-known article, "*Üç Tarz-ı Siyaset*" (Three Genres of Politics), that was published in 1904.[51] However, as new studies on the social and political history of Turkey indicate, Ottoman intellectual thought was much more complex and had different affiliations, relations and complex identities.

The political programs, journals or schools of thought often embraced various elements from the above-mentioned intellectual currents. Intellectuals, political organizations and journals that pursued a political project did not propagate a pure ideology such as Ottomanism, Islamism or Turkism; different elements of these ideologies can be found within the works of intellectuals.[52] Early Turkish nationalism also consisted of different paths with different political agendas. Turkish nationalists who immigrated into the Ottoman Empire from Russia had different political projections regarding a prospective nationalist program than did the native Turkish nationalists, who did not want to forget entirely an Ottomanist discourse.[53] This is why studies that focus on the relationship between social and political developments and ideologies, and the impact of one on the other, usually refer to interconnections. For instance, Zürcher has argued that many Young Turks supported the idea of Ottomanism, while being emotionally attached to Turkism and living as devout Muslims.[54] Hanioğlu, an expert on the Young Turks, has delineated the main characteristic of the politics of the CUP as "political opportunism." He asserts that Young Turks recruited Turkism, Ottomanism and Islamism interchangeably, although they were in favor of a dominance of the Turkish element over the other communities of the empire.⁵⁵ Zürcher has claimed that not even Mustafa Kemal used the word *milli* (nation) in its modern sense in order to refer to Turks before 1923: he referred instead to Ottoman Muslims. Muslim identity was still the dominant ingredient in the early nationalist movement. The definition of "us" was very much defined in opposition to the non-Muslims, and this is why it is better to talk about a "Muslim nationalism."⁵⁶

The ideologies and discourses of social movements are much more complex, eclectic and populist when compared to those of intellectuals. Social movements address people who embrace various interests, sensitivities, conventions and affiliations. This made intellectuals employ a broad political discourse in facilitating the mobilization of the people: their ultimate concern was not consistency or coherence, but convincing the people to take action. This is also true for emerging mass politics in general. One may trace this emergence in the writings of contemporary journalists and columnists, who were amongst the most popular personalities of their age. They did not write about sophisticated and analytical issues in the way of theoreticians, philosophers or scholars, but took advantage of various ideas in an eclectic and superficial manner in order to convince the public on a particular subject or policy.⁵⁷ These popular political figures, such as famous columnists, utilized various elements of different political agendas in their narratives, and their usage of popular ideas, symbols and references enhanced their influence on society.

Similarly, social movements also made use of various ideas. An amalgam of popular discourse and symbols constituted the popular ideologies.⁵⁸ Popular movements created their own popular ideologies and discourses, in order to facilitate the mobilization of ordinary people and legitimize their demands and slogans. Different fragments of popular ideology may be over-emphasized in particular cases, and this selection may change from one case to another, or can alter according to changing times and circumstances. For instance, the popular ideology that emerged during the 1908 Ottoman boycott was to a great extent made up of Ottomanist discourses and symbols. However, it also employed the symbols of ancient Turkish culture, pre-Ottoman Anatolian Islamic cultures, and the ideals of modern citizenship and the new regime promoted during the Second Constitutional Period.

This popular ideology was efficient in mobilizing port workers, merchants and ordinary consumers from different communities all over the empire to participate in the boycott movement.

The boycotts after 1910 were organized against the Greek presence within the Ottoman Empire and aimed to mobilize the Muslim population, and for this reason Islam and Islamic discourse constituted a major part of their ideology and discourse. However, the targeted population tried to employ an Ottomanist argument in defending their economic and communal interests. The Greek merchants and notables in the provinces consulted the Ottomanist discourse in an attempt to prevent anti-Greek boycotting activities, by arguing that their loss was the loss of everyone in the empire. By this time, however, the elites no longer included non-Muslims within the definition of Ottomanism. Other ingredients formed the amalgam of a popular ideology whose different fragments were articulated in various ways by different actors.[59] Being made up of different political and social actors, the boycott movement therefore used a changing popular ideology between 1908 and 1914. Boycotters not only made recourse to a popular discourse, but also consciously propagated a popular ideology. Different classes that took action within the boycott movement also had various discourses and ideologies; these popular ideologies were related to their respective cultural backgrounds. The different discourses reflected their proponents' cultural world, which played a significant role in the formation of social classes and in their social behavior. Religious identity and the cultural baggage of different sections of society started to play a more significant role in the making of the social classes and their relationships with each other. This is why the Muslim merchant and working classes in the Ottoman Empire at the beginning of the Second Constitutional Period were entirely different from those of 1914. During the nineteenth century, the middle classes of the different ethnic communities had very distinct cultures, tastes and identities, which prevented their collaboration. Economic and commercial collaborations that could erode these differences rarely existed. This facilitated the tensions between the different communities, and the above-mentioned changes constituted one of the main pillars of their class structure and class identity.

NOTES

Introduction

1. As Monroe Friedman has argued, a boycott is "an attempt by one or more parties to achieve certain objectives by urging individual consumers to refrain from making selected purchases in the marketplace." Monroe Friedman, 1999, p. 4. Monroe has also referred to another version of boycott by the name of "buycott," which promotes what to buy rather than dictating what not to buy. This particular action usually appears in the context of national economy movements which advise the public to buy national merchandise in particular. The boycott movement in the Ottoman Empire started with the boycott of foreign and non-national merchandise and then turned into a buycott of Muslim/Turkish products. For the concept, see: Friedman, 1999, p. 201.
2. Minda, 1999, pp. 27–28.
3. For the tobacco protest in Iran, see: Keddie, 1966; Foran, 1993; Moaddel, 1994. For the boycotts in China, see: Wang, 2001; Kiong, 2002; Remer, 1979; Jordan, 1994.

Chapter 1 Class and the Problem of Agency in the Ottoman Empire

1. One should also underline the fact that in the last decades a number of seminal studies on the social history of the Ottoman Empire and Turkey have appeared in which different social actors have entered the stage. However, although the quantity of these studies continues to increase, they are still marginal within the literature, and their impact on social and political thinking in contemporary Turkey is rather weak. I would like to mention

Donald Quataert's work as one of these seminal studies that deeply influenced young scholars in Turkey: Quataert, 1983. See also Quataert's article on new developments in historiography that intend to go beyond the narratives mainly focused on the political and military elite in Turkey's history: Donald Quataert, 2003, pp. 15–30. This does not mean, however, that there are no earlier studies that mention social resistance practices in the Ottoman Empire and Turkey. See the following works as very limited early examples: Uluçay, 1955 and İnalcık, 1964, pp. 623–649. Studies on gender have also contributed to this new trend in historiography, although the quantity of monographs is still very limited. Many of the works are on prominent women or women's movements, but not on patriarchy and gender relationships.

2. Keyder, 1995, pp. 30–32.
3. Keyder, 1999, p. 3.
4. Pamuk, 1987, pp. 53 and 150.
5. For the general structures of the agrarian economy and the dominance of small peasant producers see: Keyder and Tabak (eds), 1991.
6. For an example of a scholarly defense of this view see the work of Vryonis: Vryonis, 1969–1970, p. 286.
7. Augustinos, 1997, p. 174.
8. Kurmuş, 1982, pp. 18–20; Göçek, 1999, p. 211–213.
9. For the attempts of the Ottoman state to redress the balance see: Bağış, 1998, pp. 57–77 and 107–113.
10. Frangakis-Syrett, 1999, pp. 18–20.
11. Exertzoglou, 1999, pp. 90–91.
12. Kasaba, 1993, p. 70.
13. Ibid., p. 74; For similar claims see: Kurmuş, 1982, p. 158.
14. Exertzoglou, 1999, p. 98.
15. Kasaba, 1988.
16. Keyder, 2003, p. 61.
17. The most extreme position in this regard is the one defended by Metin Heper. See Heper, 1985a; or Heper, 1985b.
18. İnsel, 1996, p. 79.
19. Keyder, 1995, p. 54.
20. Ibid., p. 69.
21. Göçek, 1999, p. 9.
22. Ibid., pp. 178–180.
23. Eldem, 1999, p. 295.
24. Göçek, 1999, p. 104. For Göçek, the resources from which they derived their power in the last instance were under the control of the sultan.
25. Ibid., p. 241.

NOTES 233

26. For these effective instances of resistance see: Quataert, 1983.
27. Sussnitzki, 1966 (originally published in German in 1917 as "Zur Gliederung wirtschaftlicher Arbeit nach Nationalitäten in der Türkei"). This is one of the main, most extensively quoted texts to claim that Muslims were absent in trade. However, although Sussnitzki has asserted that "trade is characterized by a very significant absence of the largest of the Turkish ethnic groups," he does not ignore the Muslim/Turkish element in different economic sectors, such as industry.
28. Kaiser, 1997.
29. Ibid., p. 31.
30. Ökçün, 1970.
31. It is important to note, however, that this evaluation and calculation was made by the journal *Sanayi*, the representative of Muslim/Turkish entrepeneurs. Toprak, 1982, p. 191.
32. Niyazi Berkes does not mention the state of the Muslim merhant class after the Ottoman classical system of the fifteenth and sixteenth centuries started to disintegrate. He mentions the rise of non-Muslim merchants and their relationship with the Great Powers, but claims that there is not enough information about their Muslim counterparts. He does not claim that the Ottoman merchant class disappeared, but rather underlines the decline of the guild system and the artisans. Yet, it is apparent for him that the main agents in the social and economic history of the Ottoman Empire were the state elite and the Great Powers, apart from the structural changes. Berkes, 1970, pp. 273–279.
33. Even Huri İslamoğlu–İnan, who aims for a total history of the Ottoman Empire, mentions the Muslim merchant class only to claim their disappearance: "merchant capital was increasingly integrated into the economic division of labour of the European market; internal trade and market networks declined relative to foreign trade and trade shifted from inland centers to coastal towns; the indigenous and predominantly Muslim merchant classes were dealt a blow as foreign merchants or their agents—the Christian minorities—gained precedence." İslamoğlu-İnan, 1987, p. 11.
34. Kafadar, 1986, pp. 191–218.
35. For a typical example see: Ahmad, 1996, pp. 25–26.
36. Boratav, 1995, p. 15. Similar to the hegemonic view, he has claimed that it was only during WWI and the Kemalist takeover that this Muslim bourgeoisie started to grow, as a result of political circumstances (p. 27).
37. Keyder, 2003, p. 142.
38. For instance, Kasaba has mentioned them within this context. See Kasaba, 1993, p. 88.

39. Buğra, 2003, pp. 67–72. Buğra has also claimed that the landowners and the merchants, who were among the founders of the banks established between 1908 and 1918, cannot be considered to constitute the original Turkish entrepreneurial class. Although she does not explain why, their relationship with the Unionists is likely to be the reason.
40. Issawi, 1982; see also: Buğra, 2003, pp. 73–74; Keyder, 1995, p. 93–95; İnsel, 1996, p. 138.
41. For a summary see: Keyder, 2003a, p. 69.
42. Keyder, 2003b, p. 156.
43. Keyder, 1995, p. 51.
44. Ahmad, 1996, pp. 25–60.
45. Turgay, 1982.
46. Kasaba, 1993, p. 94.
47. Quataert, 2000b, p. 124.
48. Quataert, 2000a, p. 824.
49. Ibid., pp. 834–841.
50. Quataert, 1993a. Quataert reveals how the patterns of industrial production in the Ottoman Empire changed after the Industrial Revolution.
51. Karpat, 2001, p. 91.
52. Ibid., p. 94.
53. Somel, 2010, p. 153.
54. Tanatar-Baruh, 1993.
55. Tanatar-Baruh, 1997, p. 39.
56. Ibid., pp. 41–44.
57. Edhem Eldem, 1997, p. 61.
58. Frangakis-Syrett, 2008, pp. 47, 48, 50, 54, 55. A chapter in this edited volume was dedicated to the Muslim community in Smyrna, in the form of an interview with Fikret Yılmaz who defined it as an "unknown" community. Chistoph Neumann and Işık Tamdoğan asked him about different aspects of the Muslim presence in Smyrna in the course of the town's history. One of the main subjects of the interview was the economic activity of the Muslim social classes. Although he repeated the traditional discourse on Muslims in the economy to a certain extent, his narrative depicted well the active involvement of the Muslim classes in the economic and social life of Smyrna. "Bilinmeyen Bir Cemaatin Portresi: Müslümanlar, Firket Yılmaz'la Söyleşi," 2008, pp. 71.
59. Gilbar, 2003, p. 9.
60. Ibid., p. 21.
61. Ibid., pp. 27, 31.

62. Aktar, 2006a, p. 170.
63. Ibid., p. 175, 193, 196–197. Aktar focuses not only on Istanbul, but also makes comparisons with other cities, such as İzmir and Bursa. See also Aktar, 2006b, p. 224. Yediyıldız focuses on the silk industry in Bursa and asserts that Muslims preserved their place in the economy. Yediyıldız, 1992, pp. 273–280.
64. Mataracı, 2005, p. 8.
65. Karpat, 2001, p. 97.
66. Ibid., p. 103.
67. Akkaya, 2001/2002, pp. 285–294; Akın, 2005, p. 75.
68. Quataert, 1988, p. 14.
69. Avni [Şanda], 1935.
70. Erişçi, 1951.
71. Sülker, 1955.
72. Sülker, 1968.
73. Sencer [Baydar], 1969.
74. Şnurov and Y. Rozaliyev, 1970; Şnurov, 1973; Rozaliev, 1974; Rozaliyev, 1978; Şişmanov, 1978.
75. Two studies can be regarded as an outcome of this accumulation: Tüm İktisatçılar Birliği (Union of Economists), *Türkiye İşçi Sınıfı ve Mücadeleleri Tarihi*, 1976; and the popular illustrated three-volume history of the Turkish working class: *Resimli Türkiye İşçi Sınıfı Tarihi*, 1975.
76. Hakkı Onur [Zafer Toprak], 1977, p. 277–295.
77. For a classification of different trends in the historiography on the working class see: van der Linden, 2007, p. 169,
78. Sayılgan, 1972 , p. 70–72; Darendelioğlu, 1973, p. 16–17, 34; Sencer, 1974, p. 55–58; Ahmad, 1995, p. 16–17; Ülken, 1992, p. 206–207; Tunçay, 1991, p. 22.
79. Van der Linden, 2003, pp. 235–43. In a similar vein, Hanagan and van der Linden have asserted that a definition of labor should include "the vast world of unfree labor, including apprentices, bonded laborers, soldiers, serfs, indentured labor, prison labor, and slaves, as well as the world of the underemployed and the part-time worker." Hanagan and Van der Linden, 2004, p. 1.
80. Hobsbawm, 1984.
81. Thompson, 1963.
82. Eley, 1990, p. 24.
83. Some critiques also accuse Thompson of concentrating on the activities of artisans, rather than the struggles of the working class. See, for instance, Calhoun, 1982. For Calhoun, the people that Thompson discussed were not

even the workers, only dissolving artisans. Therefore, his critique was very different from that of Eley and had more in common with the approach of Turkish historiography.
84. This claim is not unique to the historiography of Turkey. These types of claims are generally based on the comparison of a particular country with an ideal model that has experienced a "proper" modernization process. This country is generally Great Britain. For instance, a similar tendency also appeared in German historiography regarding the place of the bourgeoisie in national history. It has widely been claimed that Germany had its own way of development (*Sonderweg*, or special path). Roughly speaking, the German bourgeoisie was weak and shy before the landed aristocracy (*Junkers*) and, therefore, failed in its supposed struggle against it. For a critique of this point of view see: Blackbourn and Eley, 1984. This approach presupposes a conflict between the rising bourgeoisie and the landed aristocracy in England during the emergence of capitalism. Yet, many studies have refuted this theory and shown how capitalist relationships emerged in rural areas and in agriculture. Brenner, 1995, pp. 213–327; Wood, 1991.
85. Sewell, Jr., 1986, pp. 50–51.
86. Johnson, 1979, p. 67.
87. Aminzade, 1979, p. 102.
88. "Introduction," *The Workplace before the Factory: Artisans and Proletarians 1500–1800*, 1993, pp. 6–10.
89. Samuel, 1977, p. 8, 39. According to him, "capitalism in the nineteenth century grew in various ways. Mechanization in one department of production was often complemented by an increase of sweating in others; the growth of large firms by a proliferation of small producing units; the concentration of production in factories by the spread of out-work in the home" p. 17.
90. Vatter, 1998, pp. 55–9; Vatter, 1994, pp. 1–20.
91. Quataert, 1993a.
92. For a good review of the literature mentioned, see: Comninel, 1987.
93. Eley, 1993.
94. Maza, 2003.
95. Anderson, 1964, pp. 26–53.
96. Quataert, 1983.
97. For a theoretical discussion on both Thompson's work and the literature on class formation see: Sewell, Jr., 1990, pp. 68–71.
98. Sewell, Jr., 1979, pp. 52–57.
99. Therefore, Mustafa Oral was not correct in claiming that porters had no class consciousness during the boycott movement. Oral, 2005, pp. 64.

Chapter 2   The Emergence of the Economic Boycott as a Political Weapon, 1908

1. Beard and Hayes, 1908, p. 746.
2. Ünal, 1998, p. 135
3. There are numerous documents in the Ottoman archives regarding the aspiration of Austria-Hungary to annex Bosnia-Herzegovina. See: *Bosna Hersek ile İlgili Arşiv Belgeleri*, (Ankara: T. C. Başbakanlık Devlet Arşivleri Genel Müdürlüğü, 1992), pp. 72–78; 131–134; 237–240; 265–267. There are also countless news items and articles in the Ottoman periodicals regarding the political goals of Austria and Bulgaria: "Bosna Meselesi," *İkdam*, 1 October 1908, p. 2; "Bulgaristan'ın İdaresi," *Tanin*, 23 September 1908, pp. 6–7; "Berlin Muahedesinin Tekrar Tedkiki," *Sabah*, 3 October 1908, p. 3; "Bosna'nın İlhakı," *Sabah*, 2 October 1908, p. 3; "Bulgaristan'ın İstiklali," *Tanin*, 1 October 1908, p. 2–3; "Devlet-i Aliye – Bulgaristan," *İkdam*, 1 October 1908, p. 1.
4. In this chapter I will mainly concentrate on the mobilization patterns that emerged during the boycott movement and in different sections of Ottoman society, as well as their agency. For more detailed information see: Çetinkaya, 2004; Elmacı, 1996; Elmacı, 1997; Yavuz, 1978; Davison, 1983.
5. "Hariciye Nazırı ile Mülakat," *İkdam*, 7 October 1908, p. 2.
6. The owner of the newspaper *Servet-i Fünun*, Ahmet İhsan Tokgöz, mentioned in his memoirs, published in several newspapers that Horasani was Ubeydullah Efendi. Ömer Hakan Özalp referred to these memoirs in his introduction to the memoirs of Ubeydullah Efendi; Özalp, 2002, pp. 49–50; for the original copies of Ahmet İhsan see: "Merhum Ubeydullah," *Uyanış (Servet-i Fünun)*, Vol. 18–82, 26 August 1937, p. 211; and *Akşam*, 25 August 1937. Since this information appeared in the Republican period, scholars such as Roderic H. Davison had different guesses regarding the identity of Horasani. Davison thought that Horasani was Rıza Tevfik, who was very active after the promulgation of the constitution and in the boycott movement in Istanbul. This was a logical guess, but turned out not to be correct. Davison, 1983, p. 5.
7. İrtem, 1999, p. 300. Süleyman Kani İrtem and the Balcı brothers were probably friends from the Feyziye Mektebi. İrtem graduated in 1890, Kazım Balcı in 1891, and Ziya Balcı in 1892.
8. Quataert, 1987, p. 105.
9. "Nemse Vapuru," *İttihat ve Terakki*, 11 October 1908, p. 4.
10. "Dün Geceki Nümayişler," *Tanin*, 7 October 1908, p. 7; "Nümayişler," *İkdam*, 7 October 1908, p. 2; "Evvelki Akşamki Nümayişler," *Millet*,

8 October 1908, p. 3; "Devlet-i Osmaniye – Bulgaristan," *İttihat ve Terakki*, 8 October 1908, p. 1; İbnü'z-Ziya, "İcmal-i Dahiliye," *İstişare*, Vol. 1, p. 236.
11. "Nümayişler," *Sabah*, 8 October 1908, p. 3; "Dünkü Nümayiş," *İkdam*, 8 October 1908, p. 4; "Vatanı Sevenlere," *İkdam*, 8 October 1908, p. 4; "Evvelki Geceki Nümayişler," *Tanin*, 8 October 1908, pp. 6–7; "Gece İçtimaları," *Sabah*, 8 October 1908, p. 3; "Ne Yapmalıyız?" *Tanin*, 10 October 1908, pp. 4–5; "Payitaht'ta Nümayişler," *İttihad*, 11 October 1908, p. 4.
12. Selanik Ahalisi, "Mukarrerat," *İttihat ve Terakki*, 9 October 1908, p. 4; "Dünkü İctima-i Umumi," *İttihat ve Terakki*, 9 October 1908, pp. 3–4; "Ajans Telgrafları- Selanik," *Musavver Geveze*, 13 October 1908, p. 8; "Bulgaristan İstiklali ve Bosna Hersek İlhakının Vilayete Tesiratı, Osmanlı Milletinin Avrupa'ya Protestosu," *İkdam*, 12 October 1908, pp. 3–4.
13. O Sintagmatikos, "Enas Polemos," *Ergatis*, 18 October 1908, p. 1.
14. "Şuun-ı Dahiliye – Avusturya ve Bulgaristan'ı Protesto Etmek Üzere Vilayatda Akd Edilen Umumi İçtimaat," *İttihat ve Terakki*, 11 October 1908, p. 4.
15. BOA. DH. MKT, 2672/55, 07.Za.1326.
16. Fehmi, 1993, p. 22.
17. "Miting," *Anadolu*, 11 October 1908, pp. 1–2.
18. "Dünkü Nümayiş," *İttihad*, 11 October 1908, p. 1.
19. "Bugünkü Miting," *İkdam*, 13 October 1908, p. 3; "Dünkü Cesim İctima," *Tanin*, 14 October 1908, p. 8; "Dünkü İctima-i Umumi," *Sabah*, 14 October 1908, pp. 3–4; "Sultan Ahmet İctima-i Umumiyesi," *İkdam*, 14 October 1908, p. 4; "Dünkü İctima-i Umumi," *Millet*, 14 October 1908, p. 4; "İstanbul'da Miting," *İttihat ve Terakki*, 15 October 1908, p. 4; "Tanin Refikimizden," *İttihad*, 18 October 1908, p. 1.
20. "Avusturya Malları," *Tanin*, 16 October 1908, p. 8; "Nümayişler," *İkdam*, 15 October 1908, p. 2; "Ahiren Dedeağaç'ta Avusturyalılar…" *Sabah*, 17 October 1908, p. 4; "Konya'da," *Tanin*, 19 October 1908, p. 7; "Boykotaj," *Sabah*, 20 October 1908, p. 4; "Musevilerin Mitingi," *İkdam*, 20 October 1908, p. 4; "Mısır'da Boykotaj," *Sabah*, 22 October 1908, p. 4.
21. "To En Aidinio Syllalitirion," *Amaltheia*, 16 October 1908, p. 3.
22. "Boykotaj Hakkında," *Şura-yı Ümmet*, 4 December 1908, p. 6; "Miting," *İkdam*, 22 November 1908, p. 4.
23. "İzmir'de Nümayiş," *Tanin*, 2 November 1908, p. 4; "İzmir'de Nümayişler," *Sabah*, 2 November 1908, p. 3; "Beyrut Muhabirimizden Aldığımız Bir Mektub," *Sabah*, 2 November 1908, p. 4; "Avusturya Emtiasına Boykotaj," *Tanin*, 31 October 1908, p. 4; "Harb-i İktisadi," *Millet*, 23 October 1908, p. 3; "Nümayiş," *İttihad*, 31 October 1908, p. 4; "İstanbul'da Bulunan Sırblılar," *Anadolu*," 18 Ekim 1908, p. 2.
24. "Samsun Osmanlı İttihad-ı Milli Klubü," *Aks-ı Sada*, 29 December 1908, p. 3.

NOTES 239

25. "Saray-ı Hümayun Civarında," *Sabah*, 8 October 1908, p. 3.
26. For a typical example see: Akşin, 1998.
27. BOA, İradeler, İrade-i Hususi, Genel No. 908, Hususi No. 23, 1 November 1908.
28. "Karamanlı Koçu Namında Birisi," *İkdam*, 9 October 1908, p. 4; "Nümayişçiler," *Tanin*, 10 October 1908, p. 5.
29. "Bir Muhavere-i Siyasiye," *Musavver Geveze*, 8 October 1908, pp. 2–4; for a similar argument see also: İmza Mahfuzdur, "[Boykot] Yahud Ticaret Aforozu," *İkdam*, 14 October 1908, p. 4.
30. M. Ragıb, "Avusturya ve Bulgaristan Emtiası," *Millet*, 20 October 1908, p. 4.
31. "Ticaret Aforozu," *İkdam*, 18 October 1908, p. 3; "Bir Mağaza İdarehanesinin Hareketi," *Sabah*, 21 October 1908, p. 4; "Boykotaj," *Sabah*, 2 January 1909, p. 3; "Avusturya Vapurlarıyla Haydarpaşa'ya," *Şura-yı Ümmet*, 26 December 1908, p. 5; "Beyrut'ta Harb-i İktisadi," *Millet*, 18 October 1908, p. 4; "Nemse Bulgar Emtiası," *İttihat ve Terakki*, 15 October 1908, p. 4.
32. "Kavala'da," *Sabah*, 22 November 1908, p. 3; "Kavala Hadisesi," *Sabah*, 24 November 1908, p. 3.
33. "Dünkü Şayia," *Sabah*, 7 January 1909, p. 3; "Avusturya Emtiasına Boykotaj," *Sabah*, 28 December 1908.
34. Emiroğlu, 1994, p. 18.
35. "Avusturya Emtiası Yakılıyor," *İttihad*, 20 December 1908, p. 4.
36. "Boykotaj," *İttihat ve Terakki*, 23 December 1908, p. 2; "Tercüman-ı Hakikat'den," *Anadolu*, 18 October 1908, p. 1.
37. "Avusturya Malları," *Musavver Geveze*, 11 October 1908, p. 1.
38. Friedman, 1999, p. 72; Jordan, 1991.
39. Toprak, 1994, p. 297.
40. For detailed information on the boycott organizations and the journal of boycott society *Gâve*, published in Smyrna, see my previous study Çetinkaya, 2004.
41. "İzmir'de Çıkan İttihad Gazetesi," *İttihat ve Terakki*, 12 December 1908, p. 3.
42. "Fesler ve Kalpaklar," *İttihat ve Terakki*, 15 December 1908, p. 3.
43. Ferruh, "Fes mi Kalpak mı?" *İttihad*, 22 December 1908, pp. 2–3; "Serpuş Meselesi," *İttihad*, 1 November 1908, pp. 1–2.
44. Boykotaj Cemiyeti Namına İmza Mahfuzdur, "Aydın Tahrirat Müdürü Ebu-el Ahir Efendiye," *Gâve*, 18 Kanunuevvel 1324 (31 December 1908), p. 4.
45. Yalman, Istanbul (1970), p. 84.
46. Yücel, 1990, p. 181. Hasan Ali Yücel also remembers that the Chinese boycott against the United States was mentioned as an example of boycotting in those days.
47. Uran, 1956, p. 30.

48. Amca, 1989, p. 54; Moralı, 1976, p. 50; Tokgöz, 1993, p. 173; Nur, 1967, p. 278; Emre, 1960, p. 115.
49. "Smirnaiki İho," *Amaltheia*, 21 December 1908, p. 3; "Ta Fesia," *Amaltheia*, 23 December 1908, p. 2.
50. "Fes-Kalpak Meselesi," *İttihat ve Terakki*, 16 December 1908, p. 1.
51. "Avusturya Emtiası," *İkdam*, 11 October 1908, p. 3; "Avusturya Emtiasına Karşı," *Tanin*, 11 October 1908, pp. 3–4; "Ticaret Aforozu," *İkdam*, 15 October 1908, p. 3; "Bir Muhavere-i Siyasiye," *Musavver Geveze*, 8 October 1908, pp. 2–4; "Efkar-ı Umumiye," *İttihad*, 18 October 1908, p. 1.
52. "Dün Bazı Kimseler..." *Sabah*, 16 October 1908, p. 2; "Ticaret Aforozu," *İkdam*, 20 October 1908, p. 3; "Avusturya Aleyhinde Nümayişat-ı Hasmane," *İttihad*, 17 October 1908, p. 4; İbnü'z-Ziya, "İcmal-i Dahiliye," *İstişare*, Vol. I, p. 283.
53. "Şehrimizde Avusturya Menafini..." *Sabah*, 11 October 1908, pp. 3–4.
54. Karilerinizden Edib, "Avusturya Malları," *Tanin*, 10 October 1908, p. 5; "Tanin," *Tanin*, 10 October 1908, p. 5.
55. İmza Mahfuzdur, "Boykot yahud Ticaret Aforozu," *Millet*, 14 October 1908, p. 4.
56. "Avusturya Mallarını Almayınız," *Tanin*, 15 October 1908, p. 7.
57. Mühendis Nevres, "Boykotaj," *Sabah*, 23 October 1908, p. 3.
58. "Boykotaj," *İkdam*, 12 November 1908, p. 2.
59. "Boykotaj Hakkında," *İttihat ve Terakki*, 12 November 1908, p. 3.
60. "Bu Kere Şehrimizde..." *İttihad*, 11 November 1908, p. 2.
61. "Boykotaj," *İttihat ve Terakki*, 23 December 1908, p. 2.
62. "Avusturya Emtiasının Adem-i..." *Serbesti*, 3 December 1908, p. 3; "Avusturya Aleyhinde Boykotlama," *Şura-yı Ümmet*, 5 January 1909, p. 5; "Yanya'da Boykotaj," *İttihad*, 4 December 1908, p. 3; "Boykotaj," *İkdam*, 13 November 1908, p. 4.
63. İzmir Boykotaj Cemiyeti, "Aynen Tezkeredir," *İttihad*, 8 December 1908, pp. 2–3; "İttihad Gazetesi İdarehanesine," *İttihad*, 1 January 1909, p. 4.
64. Boykotaj Cemiyeti Namına, "Boykotaj Cemiyeti Tarafından Verilen İlannamedir," *İttihad*, 11 November 1908, p. 2; "Vilayat- Boykotaj Cemiyeti," *İttihat ve Terakki*, 17 November 1908, p. 4.
65. Çetinkaya, 2001, pp. 261–274. Cerrahoğlu [Kerim Sadi], 1970a, p. 83; Cerrahoğlu [Kerim Sadi], 1970b, pp. 83–84.
66. "Kısm-ı Muhavere," *Gâve*, 17 December 1909, pp. 2–3.
67. "Belediye ile Kahraman Arabacılar Beyninde Tahdis Edub Yıllardan Beri Süren İhtilafı Gave Hal Etdi," *Gâve*, 31 December 1908, p. 2.
68. Karakışla, 1998, p. 30.
69. Quataert, 1983.

NOTES 241

70. Keyder, Özveren and Quataert, 1994, pp. 121–155; Keyder, 2003, pp. 47–70.
71. "Avusturya Vapurları," *İkdam*, 13 October 1908, p. 3; "Mavnacılar ve Salapuryacılar…" *İkdam*, 14 October 1908, p. 4; "Sevahil-i Osmaniye'de Avusturya Lloyd Vapurları," *Sabah*, 16 Ekim 1908, pp. 2–3.
72. "Nemse Vapuru," *İttihat ve Terakki*, 11 October 1908, p. 4; "Selanik'te İntişar Eden Yeni Asır Gazetesinden:" *İkdam*, 12 October 1908, p. 3; "7000 Çuval Dakik…" *İkdam*, 12 October 1908, p. 3; "Sevahil-i Osmaniye'de Avusturya Lloyd Vapurları," *Sabah*, 16 October 1908, pp. 2–3; "Suriye'de Boykotaj," *İttihat ve Terakki*, 11 November 1908, pp. 2–3; "Telgraflar," *Sabah*, 17 October 1908, p. 4; "Evvelki Gün Beyrut Limanında…" *İkdam*, 18 October 1908, p. 3; "Suriye Sevahilinde Boykotaj," *İttihat ve Terakki*, 22 November 1908, p. 2; "İzmir, Selanik, Kavala," *İkdam*, 20 October 1908, p. 3; "Nemse Vapurları," *İttihad*, 20 October 1908, pp. 3–4.
73. "Boykotaj," *İkdam*, 31 October 1908, p. 3.
74. "Boykotaj," *Sabah*, 17 October 1908, p. 4; "Ticarete Aforozu," *İkdam*, 18 October 1908, p. 3; "Mavnacılar ve Boykotaj," *İkdam*, 21 October 1908, p. 4.
75. "Boykotaj," *İkdam*, 15 November 1908, p. 2; "Ticaret Aforozu," *İkdam*, 18 October 1908, p. 3; "Hamallar," *Sabah*, 22 November 1908, p. 3; "Boykotaj," *Şura-yı Ümmet*, 23 November 1908, p. 7; "Avusturya Şikayetler," *İkdam*, 24 November 1908, p. 3; "Boykotajı İhlale Tasaddi," *Sabah*, 29 January 1909, p. 3; "Boykotaj," *Volkan*, 11 December 1908, p. 4.
76. "Boykotaj," *Şura-yı Ümmet*, 29 November 1908, p. 4; "Boykotaj," *İkdam*, 26 November 1908, p. 3; "Boykotaj," *Sabah*, 28 November 1908, p. 3; "Gümrük Hamalları," *Sabah*, 12 December 1908, pp. 3–4; "Avusturya Emtiasına Boykotaj," *Şura-yı Ümmet*, 13 December 1908, p. 8.
77. "Boykotaj Kahramanları," *Aks-ı Sada*, 24 January 1909, pp. 5–6. *Aks-ı Sada* published articles in support of the boycotting actions of the port workers in Samsun. For instance see: "Yaşasın Kayıkçılarımız," *Aks-ı Sada*, 9 March 1909, p. 4; "Arz-ı İhtiram," *Aks-ı Sada*, 12 December 1908, p. 3.
78. Trabzon İskelesi Umum Mavnacıları, "Boykotaj," *Tanin*, 15 December 1908, p. 3; Trabzon İskelesi Umum Mavnacıları, "Trabzon'dan Alınan Telgrafnamedir:" *İkdam*, 15 December 1908, p. 3.
79. "Boykotaj," *Tanin*, 26 December 1908, p. 3; "Boykotaj," *İkdam*, 28 December 1908, p. 3.
80. Esnaf Lonca Odası Usta Başısı Mehmed Ömer bin Hasan, Mehmed bin Hasan, Mustafa, "Avusturya Emtiasına Karşı…" *Sabah*, 21 January 1909, p. 4.
81. Hamallar Kethüdası Raşid Sami Kapudan – Kayıkçılar Kethüdası Mustafata Kapudan, "Boykotaj," *Sabah*, 7 December 1908, p. 3.
82. "Dünkü Miting," *Serbesti*, 10 January 1909, p. 4. Fights occurred among the port workers, but the Ottoman press was careful not to harm their popularity,

while still critizing their fights. "Evvelce Hamalların Müteaddid..." *Volkan*, 25 January 1909, p. 4.
83. "Boykotaj Devam Etmeli," *Serbesti*, 6 December 1908, p. 2; "Boykotaj," *Tanin*, 29 November 1908, p. 4.
84. "Boykotaj," *İttihat ve Terakki*, 10 December 1908, p. 2; "Boykotaj," *İttihad*, 8 December 1908, p. 2; "İstanbul, Köylü, Gave," *Gâve*, 17 December 1908, p. 4.
85. Rıhtım Hamallar Kolbaşısı Ali, "Avusturya Emtiasına Karşı Boykotaj," *Sabah*, 21 January 1909, p. 4; Rıhtım Hamallar Kolbaşısı Ali, "Boykotaj," *İkdam*, 21 January 1909, p. 2.
86. Karakışla, 1998, p. 46; Gülmez, 1985, p. 798; Güzel, 1985, p. 803.
87. "Boykotaj ve Freie Presse Gazetesinin Meyuseti," *İttihat ve Terakki*, 12 December 1908, pp. 2–3; "Boykot Cevlanı," *İkdam*, 12 December 1908, p. 3.
88. "Boykotajın Hadim-i Hakikileri," *Serbesti*, 2 December 1908, p. 3; "207 Mühr ve İmza ile Varid Olan Varakadır," *İkdam*, 2 December 1908, p. 2; "Boykotaj–Hamallara Teşekkür," *Sabah*, 2 December 1908, pp. 2–3; "Boykotaj," *Şura-yı Ümmet*, 26 January 1909, p. 2.
89. "Fatih Ders-i Amm Efendiler Tarafından Varid Olmuşdur," *İkdam*, 5 December 1908, p. 2.
90. "Boykotaj," *Serbesti*, 26 November 1908, p. 4; "Boykotaj," *Tanin*, 9 December 1908, p. 3.
91. İzmir Boykotaj Cemiyeti, "Kayıkçıların Cemiyeti ve Boykotaja Riayeti," *İttihad*, 24 December 1908, pp. 2–3.
92. "Amelenin Boykotaj Hususundaki Nümayişi," *İttihad*, 8 December 1908, p. 1; "To Austriakon Atmoploion," *Ameltheia*, 18 December 1908, p. 2.
93. "Boykotaj," *Serbesti*, 6 December 1908, p. 4; "Hamallara ve Mavnacılara Teşekkür," *Sabah*, 5 December 1908, p. 3; "Gümrük Hamalları," *İkdam*, 5 December 1908, p. 2.
94. "Boykotaj," *Şura-yı Ümmet*, 21 January 1909, p. 8; "Boykotaj," *İkdam*, 31 January 1909; "Boykotaj," *İkdam*, 5 February 1909, p. 3; "Boykotaj Kalktı mı?" *Sabah*, 5 February 1909, p. 4.
95. "Boykotun Hitamı," *İkdam*, 6 February 1909, p. 3; "Boykotaj," *Sabah*, 6 February 1909, p. 3; "Boykotaj," *İkdam*, 12 February 1909, p. 3; "Boykotaj," *Sabah*, 24 February 1909, p. 3.
96. "Osmanlı Boykotaj Sendikası İstanbul Merkezinden:" *İkdam*, 27 February 1909, p. 1; "Boykotajın Refi," *İkdam*, 27 February 1909, p. 1; "Boykotajın Hitamı," *Sabah*, 27 February 1909, p. 2; "Dün Boykotaj Sendikası Tarafından Matbuamıza Tebliğ Olunmuştur:" *Sabah*, 27 February 1909, p. 2.
97. "Boykotajdan Sonra," *Şura-yı Ümmet*, 28 February 1909, p. 5.
98. "Mavnacılar ve Tüccar," *İkdam*, 13 October 1908, p. 4; "Salapuryacı ve Mavnacı..." *Şura-yı Ümmet*, 7 January 1909, p. 6; "Boykotaj," *Sabah*, 28 January 1909, p. 4.

NOTES 243

99. Quataert, 1998, pp. 113-114.
100. "Yağ Kapanı Mavnacıları," *Şura-yı Ümmet*, 10 February 1909, p. 8; "Liman Dairesinin Nazar-ı Dikkatine," *Serbesti*, 31 December 1908, p. 4; "Sirkeci Hamalları Kahyası," *Sabah*, 14 January 1909, p. 4; "Dersaadet Gümrüğü Hamallarından Alınan Varaka," *Serbesti*, 21 February 1909, p. 3.
101. Quataert, 1993b, p. 59-69.
102. "Gümrük Hamalları," *İkdam*, 10 November 1908, p. 3; "Boykotaj," *Sabah*, 9 February 1909, p. 4; "Ermeni Hamallarının Avdeti," *İkdam*, 10 November 1908, p. 3.
103. Karakışla, 1998, p. 196.
104. Ferit Bey, who would take the surname "Hamal" (porter) in the Republican Era, was a *kethüda* of porters and a *katib-i mesul* (responsible scribe) in the CUP. He was also sent into exile (1919-20) on Malta after the Armistice of Moudros and Istanbul's occupation by the Allied Forces. On Malta, he was among many other prominent political figures of the CUP. In 1942, he became a member of the Varlık Vergisi Tespit Komisyonu (Wealth Tax Estimation Commission).
105. İrtem, 1999, p. 303.
106. "Mavnacıların Grevi," *Sabah*, 5 March 1909, p. 3; "Hamalların Gavgası," *Sabah*, 6 March 1909, p. 3; "İstanbul Limanı," *Şura-yı Ümmet*, 8 March 1909, pp. 3-4; "Boykotaja Karşı Boykotaj," *Sabah*, 9 March 1909, s. 3; "Mavnacılar," *Serbesti*, 12 March 1909, p. 2.
107. "Hamalların Boykotajı," *Serbesti*, 20 March 1909, p. 3.
108. "Tüccarımıza," *Bağçe*, 27 October 1908, back cover.
109. "Selanik Tüccarlarının Teşebbüsü," *İttihat ve Terakki*, 11 October 1908, p. 4.
110. "İslam ve Ermeni Muteberanından Yirmi Yedi Zatın İmza ve Mühürlerini Havidir, "Karahisar-ı Sahib'den Aldığımız Mektubdur," *İttihad*, 14 November 1908, p. 3.
111. "Bir Numune-i Hamiyet," *Anadolu*, 7 December 1908, p. 2.
112. "Avusturya Emtiası," *İkdam*, 8 October 1908, p. 4; "Avusturya Emtiasını Almayınız," *Tanin*, 9 October 1908, p. 7; Karilerinizden Edib, "Avusturya Malları," *Tanin*, 10 October 1908, p. 5; "Tanin," *Tanin*, 10 October 1908, p. 5; "Şeker Siparişleri," *İttihat ve Terakki*, 15 October 1908, p. 4; "Rica-i Mahsus," *Anadolu*, 11 October 1908, p. 1.
113. "Avusturya Emtiasına Karşı," *İkdam*, 10 October 1908, p. 4; "Selanik'de Avusturya Emtiasının...," *İkdam*, 16 October 1908, p. 4; "Kastamonu Tacirlerinin İstanbul'daki...," *İkdam*, 16 October 1908, p. 4; Beyrut Heyet-i Ticariye-i Osmaniyesi, "Avusturya Malları," *Tanin*, 22 October 1908, p. 7; "Avusturya Emtiasına Karşı-Derne'den Telgraf," *Tanin*, 28 October 1908, p. 8; "İşkodra Tacirlerinin Hamiyeti," *İttihat ve Terakki*, 6 December 1908, p. 2; "Anadolu," *Anadolu*, 14 October 1908, p. 1.

114. "Trabzon Vilayeti Muhabbet-i Milliye Ticaret Komisyonunun Şayan-ı Takdir Bir Kararı," İttihad, 14 October 1908, p. 4; Bodrum Ahali-i Osmaniyesi Namına Hayim Galante, Mihail Trandafios, Edhem, "İzmir İttihad Gazetesi İdarehanesine," İttihad, 20 October 1908, p. 4.
115. "Boykotaj," İttihat ve Terakki, 29 November 1908, pp. 2–3.
116. Corci Petro Papasoğlu, "Varaka," İttihad, 19 October 1908, p. 4.
117. "(İstanbul) Gazetesinden Boykotajdan," Sabah, 23 October 1908, p. 3; "Yerli Elbiseciler," Sabah, 25 October 1908, p. 3; "Avusturya Malı Almamağa..." İttihad, 22 October 1908, p. 4; "Boykotaj Münasebetsizlikleri," İttihat ve Terakki, 10 November 1908, p. 3.
118. "Nemse ve Bulgarya Malları Bir Tehlike," Aks-ı Sada, 24 November 1908, p. 4.
119. Şayak Tüccarlarından Kefelizade Asım, "Aynen Varaka," Aks-ı Sada, 26 December 1908, p. 3.
120. "Hala Avusturya Şekeri Gelecek mi?" İttihad, 4 November 1908, pp. 1–2; "Şeker Meselesi," İttihad, 5 November 1908, p. 3; İmza Mahfuzdur, "İttihat ve Terakki Gazetesi İdarehanesine," İttihad, 5 December 1908, p. 3.
121. İzmir Boykotaj Cemiyeti, "Şahadetname," İttihad, 9 December 1908, pp. 3–4; "İzmir Boykotaj Cemiyeti'nden," İttihad, 15 December 1908, p. 3; Hayim Franko, "İttihad Ceridesi İdarehanesine," İttihad, 16 December 1908, pp. 3–4; "Aydın'dan Yirmi İki Muteber..." İttihad, 27 December 1908, p. 2.
122. Osmanlı Tüccarından İsrail ve Salomon, "Avusturya Hukuk-ı Meşruhe-i Milliyemize..." İttihat ve Terakki, 1 December 1908, p. 4.
123. "Şayan-ı Takdir Bir Eser-i Hamiyet," İttihat ve Terakki, 23 November 1908, p. 3; "Boykotaj ve Fraye Press," İttihat ve Terakki, 27 November 1908, p. 2.
124. Bosna Hersek Cemiyet-i Hayriye-i Osmaniyesi, "Bursa'daki Bosnalılardan Alınan Telgrafnamenin Suretidir," İkdam, 12 November 1908, p. 2.
125. "Avusturya Eşyası," Serbesti, 17 November 1908, p. 2; "Boykotaj," İkdam, 19 November 1908, p. 3; "Boykotaj," İkdam, 20 November 1908, p. 3; "Boykotaj," Tanin, 16 December 1908, p. 3.
126. "Karahisar'da Boykotaj," Sabah, 13 November 1908, p. 4; "Boykotaj," İkdam, 13 November 1908, p. 4; "Boykotaj," Tanin, 22 November 1908, p. 3; "Boykotaj," İkdam, 22 November 1908, p. 3; "Boykotaj," Serbesti, 23 November 1908, p. 3; "Boykotaj," Şura-yı Ümmet, 22 November 1908, p. 6; "Harb-i İktisadinin Bir..." İkdam, 13 December 1908, pp. 4–5; "Avusturya'da Bir Milyon Lira Zarar!" Sabah, 14 November 1908, p. 3; "Avusturya Aleyhinde Boykotlama," Şura-yı Ümmet, 5 January 1909, p. 5.
127. Rüsumat Memurlarından Hakkı, "Hamiyet Namı Tahtında İhtikar-ı Denaetkarane," Musavver Geveze, 16 October 1908, p. 2; "Boykotaj," İkdam, 3 December 1908, p. 2; "Selanik Tüccarından ve..." İkdam, 11 December 1908, p. 3; "Beyrut'da Boykotaj," Şura-yı Ümmet, 8 January 1909, p. 5;

NOTES 245

"Sen Petersburg 24 Kanunisani 1909," *Sabah*, 27 January 1909, p. 4; "Boykotaj," *İkdam*, 21 February 1909, p. 3.
128. Sp. Th. Foros, "Boykotaz," *Amaltheia*, 23 December 1908, p. 1; "Boykotaj ve Serpuş-i Milli," *Serbesti*, 1 December 1908, p. 1; "Boykotaj Hakkında," *İkdam*, 23 October 1908, p. 3; Mehmed Cavid, "Fes Fabrikaları," *İkdam*, 26 October 1908, p. 2; Seniha Nezahet, "Avusturya ve Bulgar Mallarını Almayalım," *Millet*, 11 October 1908, p. 3; "Anadolu," *Anadolu*, 14 October 1908, p. 1; "Avusturya, Bulgar, Alman Malı Kullanmayalım!" *Millet*, 9 October 1908, p. 3.
129. "Patriotikai Ekdiloseis," *Amaltheia*, 13 October 1908, p. 3.
130. "Ticaret Aforozu," *İkdam*, 15 October 1908, p. 3; "Avusturya Malı Almayınız," *Tanin*, 18 October 1908, p. 5; "Mühendis Nevres, Boykotaj," *Sabah*, 24 October 1908, p. 3; "Avusturya Şekerleri," *Sabah*, 5 November 1908, p. 4; "Bazı Vatandaşlarımızın..." *İttihat ve Terakki*, 15 October 1908, p. 4; "İki Kişi Arasında," *Musavver Geveze*, 10 October 1908, p. 6; "Rus Emtiası," *İttihat ve Terakki*, 10 November 1908, p. 3; "Haftalık Notlar, Siyasi," *Bağçe*, 30 November 1908, p. 2; "Yine Avusturya ve Bulgar Malları," *İttihad*, 19 October 1908, p. 3.
131. Toprak, 1985, pp. 1345–1347.
132. For instance see: Ahmed Rasim, "Fes-Aforoz," *Sabah*, 17 October 1908, p. 3; "Avusturya Emtiası," *İkdam*, 11 October 1908, p. 3; "Enzar-ı Dikkate," *Anadolu*, 11 November 1908, p. 3; "Avusturya Mallarını Almayınız," *Tanin*, 18 October 1908, p. 5; "Boykotaj ve Serpuş-ı Milli," *Serbesti*, 1 December 1908, p. 1; "Avusturya Şekerleri," *Sabah*, 5 November 1908, p. 4; "Avusturya Mallarını Almayınız," *Tanin*, 20 October 1908, p. 7; "Boykotaj Hakkında," *İkdam*, 23 October 1908, p. 3; "Boykotaj," *İkdam*, 1 November 1908, p. 3.
133. Panayotopoulos, 1983, p. 117.
134. Faruki Ömer, "Fırsattan İstifade," *Volkan*, 27 December 1908, p. 2.
135. Two scholars have also mentioned the boycott as an incentive for Ottoman entrepreneurs to invest in their own country. Birinci, 1990, p. 20; Kayalı, 1998, p. 72.
136. "Avusturya Ticaretine Karşı-Anadolu," *Anadolu*, 14 October 1908, p. 1.
137. "Harb-i İktisadi, Avusturya Macaristan Emtiası," *Anadolu*, 18 October 1908, p. 1; "Seyyar Muhabirimizden," *Anadolu*, 16 November 1908, pp. 2–3; "Konya Bankalarımız," *Anadolu*, 19 November 1908, pp. 2–3.
138. "Muhavere-i İktisadiye," *Musavver Geveze*, 12 October 1908, pp. 7–8; see also: M. Ragıb, "Avusturya ve Bulgaristan Emtiası," *Millet*, 20 October 1908, p. 4.
139. Selanikli Tevfik, "Memalik-i Osmaniyenin İstikbal-i İktisadiyesi," *Sabah*, 23 December 1908, p. 1; "Avusturya Emtiası," *İkdam*, 11 October 1908,

p. 3; İbrahim Fatin, "Harb-ı İktisadiye- Muvaffakiyetler," *Serbesti*, 7 December 1908, p. 3; "Mühendis Nevres, "Boykotaj," *Sabah*, 24 October 1908, p. 3; "Avusturya Emtiasını Almayalım," *Millet*, 10 October 1908, p. 4; "Ticaret Afarozu," *İkdam*, 17 October 1908, p. 3; "Hakiki Boykot," *İkdam*, 6 December 1908, p. 2; "Hakiki Boykot," *İkdam*, 9 December 1908, p. 3; "Boykotaj Yapanlara Müjde," *İkdam*, 1 December 1908, p. 3; "Yine Avusturya ve Bulgar Malları," *İttihad*, 19 October 1908, p. 3; İzmir Osmanlı Kibrit Şirketi Namına Kirkor Köleyan, "İttihad Gazetesi Müdüriyetine," *İttihad*, 26 November 1908, p. 4.
140. "Şehrimizde Avusturya Emtiası Almamak..." *İttihad*, 24 October 1908, p. 4.
141. Menfaat-i Millet Cemiyeti, "Dün (Avusturya Mallarını Almayalım) Sürnamesiyle..." *Sabah*, 11 October 1908, pp. 3–4; "Rica-i Mahsus," *Anadolu*, 11 October 1908, p. 1.
142. *Boşboğaz* published a poem which used this terminology; "Fes-Kalpak," *Boşboğaz*, 14 December 1908, pp. 2–3.
143. "Kato i Avstria," *Ergatis*, 18 October 1908, p. 2.
144. BOA. DH. İ-UM. 19–3/1–60.
145. "Fes-Kalpak," *Şura-yı Ümmet*, 13 December 1908, pp. 3–4; "Kalpak İktisası," *Gâve*, 17 December 1908, p. 4; "Rüsumat Emaneti Evrak..." *İkdam*, 8 December 1908, p. 3; "Dün Bazı Devair-i..." *Sabah*, 13 December 1908, p. 3; "Kalpak," *İkdam*, 14 December 1908, p. 3; "Kalpak Giymek Mecburi Değildir," *İkdam*, 16 December 1908, p. 3; "Kaypak İksası," *Şura-yı Ümmet*, 16 December 1908, p. 4; "Kalpak," *Şura-yı Ümmet*, 21 December 1908, p. 4; "Polis Kalpakları," *İkdam*, 12 November 1908, p. 3; "Polis Kalpakları," *İkdam*, 13 November 1908, p. 4; "Serpuş Meselesi," *Şura-yı Ümmet*, 5 January 1909, pp. 5–6; "Polis Kalpakları," *İkdam*, 26 November 1908, p. 2; "Polislerin Kalpakları," *Sabah*, 20 February 1909, p. 3.
146. "Smirnaiki İho," *Amaltheia*, 21 December 1908, p. 3.
147. "Yeni Fesler," *Tanin*, 12 October 1908, p. 7.
148. "Gerçi Memleketimizde Fes..." *Sabah*, 12 October 1908, p. 3; "Kırşehir'den Matbuamıza Keşide Edilen Telgrafnamenin Suretidir," *İkdam*, 16 October 1908, p. 4; "Gümülcine Ahalisi Avusturya," *İkdam*, 16 October 1908, p. 4; "Akhisar'dan Aldığımız Mektubda Yazılıyor," *Tanin*, 16 October 1908, p. 8; "Beyaz Fesler," *İkdam*, 14 October 1908, p. 4; "Fesler Hakkında, İzmir'de Nümayiş," *Sabah*, 11 December 1908, p. 2; "Beyrut Muhabirimizden Aldığımız Bir Mektub," *Sabah*, 2 November 1908, p. 4; "Harb-i İktisadi," *Millet*, 23 October 1908, p. 3; "Mısır'da Boykotaj ve Beyaz Fesler," *İttihat ve Terakki*, 3 November 1908, pp. 2–3; "Anadolu," *Anadolu*, 14 October 1908, p. 1.
149. A. Mazhar, "Ramazan Mektubu," *Musavver Geveze*, 14 October 1908, pp. 5–6.

150. Edhem Nejat, "Fes ve Kalpak," *Sabah*, 7 November 1908, pp. 3–4; Ahmed Rasim, "Fes-Aforoz," *Sabah*, 17 October 1908, p. 3; Ahmed Rasim, "İstişare Mecmua-i muhteremesine Takdime-i Nacizanemdir: Fes Hakkında," *İstişare*, Vol. 1, pp. 273–277; Ahmed Rasim, "Fes Hakkında," *İstişare*, Vol. 1, pp. 316–320; Mühendis Nevres, "Boykotaj," *Sabah*, 24 October 1908, p. 3.
151. Deringil, 1991, pp. 47–65.
152. Hobsbawm, 1997, p. 5.
153. "Boykotaj ve Kılınclar," *Sabah*, 30 November 1908, p 1; Plevne Tarih-i Harbi Müellifi Miralay Mahmud Talat, "Kılınclarımız," *İttihat ve Terakki*, 22 December 1908, p. 4; "Bir İhtar-ı Sıhhat-ı Vatanperverane," *Millet*, 20 October 1908, p. 4; "Fesler-Arakıyyeler," *İkdam*, 12 October 1908, p. 3; "Fes Fabrikası," *İttihat ve Terakki*, 11 October 1908, p. 4; "Fes Fabrikası," *Sabah*, 16 October 1908, p. 4; "Tebrik," *Anadolu*, 31 January 1909, p. 3; "Konya Makaronya Fabrikası," *Anadolu*, 16 November 1908, p. 3; "Manisa Mensucat-ı Dahiliye Şirket," *İttihat ve Terakki*, 24 November 1908, p. 4; "Manisa'da [Boykotaj] Ehemmiyet..." *İttihat ve Terakki*, 24 November 1908, p. 4; "Hereke Fabrikası Müdür-i Mesulüne," *İttihad*, 24 October 1908, p. 4.
154. "Mamulat-ı Dahiliye Teavün Cemiyeti," *İttihad*, 2 January 1909, p. 4.
155. İzmir Osmanlı Kibrit Şirketi Namına Kirkor Köleyan, "İttihad Gazetesi Müdüriyetine," *İttihad*, 26 November 1908, p. 4.
156. "Olimpos Palas Müsteciri," *Bağçe*, 17 November 1908, back cover; "İlan: Hereke Fabrika-i Hümayunu Fesleri," *Sabah*, 12 October 1908, p. 4; "İlan-Osmanlı Vatandaşlarına Müjde," *Tanin*, 19 October 1908, p. 8; "Karlman Mağazası Hakkında Bir İki Söz," *Tanin*, 21 October 1908, p. 8; "Mustafa Şamlı ve Mahdumları, "İlanlar- Mağazamızda İtalyan Fabrikasının..." *Tanin*, 22 October 1908, p. 8; "Bayram Hediyeliği İçin Halis Yerli," *Tanin*, 24 October 1908, p. 8; "Vatan Malları," *Tanin*, 12 December 1908, p. 4; "İlan-ı Mühim: Hereke Fabrikası Fesleri," *Serbesti*, 16 March 1909, p. 4; "İlan," *Millet*, 25 October 1908, p. 4; "Harb-i İktisadi," *Millet*, 22 October 1908, p. 4; "Hamiyyetli Vatandaşlarımızdan Ricamız," *Musavver Geveze*, 11 October 1908, p. 2; "Avusturya Mağazaları," *Musavver Geveze*, 11 October 1908, p. 6; "İlan: Hereke Fabrika-i Hümayunu Fesleri," *Sabah*, 12 October 1908, p. 4; "Patriotikai Ekdiloseis," *Amaltheia*, 13 October 1908, p. 3.
157. "Emborikos Apokleismos," *Amaltheia*, 17 December 1908, p. 3.
158. "Halkın Avusturya Postahanelerine..." *Şura-yı Ümmet*, 25 November 1908, p. 7; "Avusturya Postahanesi," *İkdam*, 29 November 1908, p. 2; "Ecnebi Postahaneleri," *İttihad ve Terakki*, 3 December 1908, p. 1; Mercan Mahallesi Sakinlerinden Telgraf Nezaretine Mensub: Hamdi, "Ceride-i Feridelerinin İlk..." *Sabah*, 11 October 1908, pp. 3–4; Mülga Meclis-i Maliye Azasından Bedri, "Avusturya Postaları ve Vazife-i Hamiyet," *Millet*, 14 October 1908,

p. 4; "Avusturya Postaları," *Tanin*, 15 October 1908, p. 7; "Ecnebi Postahaneler," *İttihat ve Terakki*, 14 December 1908, p. 2; Ahmed Reşid, "Memleketimizde Ecnebi Postahaneleri," *İstişare*, 14 January 1909, pp. 721–728; İbnü-z-Ziya, "Memleketimizde Ecnebi Postahaneleri," *İstişare*, 20 January 1909, pp. 769–774; "Posta Nezaretine, Samsun Postahanesi Memurini Gayri Kafidir," *Aks-ı Sada*, 6 February 1909, p. 4.

Chapter 3 The Shift from Foreign to "Internal" Enemies, 1910–11

1. Çetinkaya, 2001, pp. 15–24; Kerimoğlu, 2008, pp. 33–54.
2. Katsiadakis, 1992, p. 370.
3. Çetinkaya, 2004.
4. Ahladi, 2008, pp. 188–190; Kerimoğlu, 2008, pp. 192–198.
5. Adıyeke, 1993, pp. 235–246.
6. Adıyeke, 2000, pp. 244–250.
7. Katsiadakis, 1995, p. 32.
8. FO, 294/50, No. 23, 14 May 1910, p. 29; FO, 195/2357, No. 23, 14 May 1910, p. 448.
9. MMZC, Vol. V, 1910, pp. 163–164.
10. FO, 195/2358, No. 29, 19 May 1910, p. 7.
11. FO, 195/2357, No. 56, 15 May 1910, p. 450.
12. FO, 195/2335, No. 25, 13 May 1910, p. 93.
13. "Girit için Miting ve Gönüllü Taburları," *İttihad*, 12 June 1910.
14. FO, 195/2364, No. 36, 29 May 1911, p. 172.
15. FO, 195/2342, No. 25, 26 May 1910, p. 234.
16. FO, 195/2342, No. 18, 10 June 1910, p. 297.
17. CPC, Turquie 1897–1914, 306, Document No. 172, Paris, 5 August 1910. The correspondence of French diplomatic circles indicated that the boycott campaign had an anarchic character that undermined the compliance of Ottoman people with their government's laws. Therefore, the French ambassador wanted to warn the Ottoman government about this fact in a friendly manner.
18. "O Apokleismos stin Konstantinupoli," (Boycott in İstanbul), *Embros* (Athens), 6 June 1910.
19. BOA, DH. MUİ. 103–1/23, Documents No. 1-2-3, 11–12 June 1910.
20. BOA, DH. MUİ. 104–1/21, Documents No. 1–2, 14 June 1910.
21. BOA, DH. MUİ. 102–1/38, Document No. 3, 6 June 1910.
22. BOA, DH. MUİ 110/23, Document No. 1, 26.C.1328.
23. BOA, DH. MUİ. 109/54, Document No. 1, 21 June 1910.

NOTES 249

24. BOA, DH. MUİ. 99/43, Document No. 1, 30 May 1910.
25. FO, 195/2358, No. 85, 8 July 1910, p. 157. There were officers in a similar position to the commander in Limni in other places. Although the local ranks of the Ottoman bureaucracy to a great extent supported the boycott in advance, some, like Nureddin Efendi, the director of the Customs House in Salabora, were against the movement. Nureddin Efendi was considered an enemy of Ottomanism by the Boycott Committee of Preveze and removed from his position. It is possible that he did not allow the boycotters to work freely in the Customs House, a vital place for the boycott movement. The Preveze Boycott Committee even published an announcement criticizing him in *Rumeli*, a newspaper published in Salonica; FO, 195/2358, No. 85, 8 July 1910, p. 157.
26. BOA, DH. MUİ. 100–1/35, Documents No. 3, 7–8, 2–4 June 1910.
27. BOA, DH. MUİ. 102–2/17, Document No. 11, 15 June 1910.
28. BOA, DH. MUİ. 100–2/8, Documents no. 2/1–3, 14–17 June 1910.
29. BOA, DH. MUİ. 100–2/8, Documents No. 1, 1 June 1910.
30. FO, 195/2360, No. 39, 6 June 1910, pp. 196–199.
31. Manisa Milli Taburlar Kumandanı Süleyman Sırrı, "Manisa'dan Çekilen Telgraf Sureti," *İttihad*, 12 June 1910.
32. Urla'da Gönüllü Cemiyeti Reisi Tevfik, "Urla'dan Çekilen Telgraf Sureti," *İttihad*, 12 June 1910.
33. Nazilli'de Milli Alay Kumandanı Sadettin, "Nazilli'den Çekilen Telgraf Sureti," *İttihad*, 12 June 1910.
34. "Foça-i Atik'ten çekilen Telgraf Sureti," *İttihad*, 12 June 1910; "Menemen'den Çekilen Telgraf Sureti," *İttihad*, 12 June 1910; "Girit İçin Miting ve Gönüllü Taburları," *İttihad*, 12 June 1910.
35. FO, 195/2347, No. 18, 7 June 1910, p. 279.
36. FO, 195/2335, No. 30, 13 June 1910, p. 120.
37. BOA, DH. MUİ. 102–2/17, Document No. 17–18, 11 June 1910.
38. BOA, DH. MUİ. 102–1/4, Documents No. 1–2, 7 June 1910.
39. CPC, Turquie 1897–1914, 306, Document No. 46, Manastır, 22 June 1910.
40. FO, 195/2360, No. 41, 15 June 1910, p. 206.
41. BOA, DH. MUİ. 110/38, Document No. 2, 25 June 1910.
42. FO, 195/2347, No. 35, 2 June 1910, pp. 251–253.
43. BOA, DH. MUİ. 106/9, Documents No. 2–3, 19 June 1910.
44. CPC, Turquie 1897–1914, 307, Document No. 41–43, Smyrna, 11 April 1911.
45. Kechriotis, 2011, p. 80.
46. AYE, A-21, 1910–1911, No. 87, 1911.
47. FO, 195/2360, No. 41, 15 June 1910, p. 204.

48. BOA, DH. MUİ. 108–1/9, Document No. 2, 25 June 1910.
49. FO, 195/2345, No. 55, 17 June 1910, p. 115. Similar rumors regarding the Cretan immigrants' actions against Greeks had appeared in İzmir already in 1909. A boycott against the Greeks was provoked in late August of 1909, but was halted by the elites, particularly the CUP. The Cretans of Smyrna were very active in this early attempt at a boycott. Stories of such picketing efforts by the Cretans were published in Greek newspapers, such as *Patris*. However, the governor of Aydın, Kazım Bey, repudiated such stories and assured the government that there were no blockades of shops. Yet, afterwards he still wanted the Boycott Society to publish a statement in order to condemn any assaults on individuals. Even this early example from 1909 indicates that boycotting activities were going hand in hand with these kinds of offenses. BOA, DH. MUİ. 5–2/15, Documents No. 1, 3; 23–4 August 1909.
50. FO, 195/2342, No. 32, 23 June 1910, p. 326.
51. FO, 195/2360, No. 85, 6 October 1910, p. 378.
52. BOA, DH. SYS. 22/1–28, Document No. 1/1, 13 September 1910.
53. BOA, DH. SYS. 22/1–30, Document No. 2, 11 October 1910.
54. BOA, DH. SYS. 22/1–12, Document No. 5, 22 March 1911. The shop was closed down in May 1910.
55. "To Mpoikataz eis Thessalonikin," (The Boycott in Salonica), *Embros* (Athens), 22 August 1910.
56. BOA, DH. MUİ. 102–2/17, Document No. 67, 6 July 1910.
57. BOA, DH. MUİ. 102–2/17, Document No. 41, 27 June 1910.
58. AYE, A-21, 1910–1911, Antalya, 26 March 1911.
59. "Ai Tarachodeis Skinai tis Smirnis," (Scenes of Chaos in Smyrna), *Embros* (Athens), 31 May 1910. The article quoted a report of Muslim crowds attacking Greek shops in the bazaar of Smyrna. Most of the shops were closed because of the chaotic atmosphere, and those who refused to close their stores were threatened with knives. Many scuffles occurred during the day. *Embros* claimed that the Greeks also bravely fought against the Muslims, although it argued that the Muslims injured the Greeks. "To Mpoikotaz stin Thessalonikin," (Boycott in Salonica), *Embros* (Athens), 9 June 1910. According to *Embros*, one of the Greek restaurants was attacked by a group of Muslims and its furniture was destroyed.
60. BOA, DH. SYS. 22/2–2, Document No. 2, 21 February 1911.
61. CPC, Turquie 1897–1914, 307, Document No. 41–43, Smyrna, 11 April 1911.
62. FO, 195/2360, No. 72, 16 August 1910, p. 331.
63. AYE, A-21, 1910–1911, Smyrna, No. 919, 19 March 1911.
64. CPC, Turquie 1897–1914, 307, Document No. 105, Smyrna, 8 June 1911; CPC, Turquie 1897–1914, 307, Document No. 57–62, Paris, 23 April 1911.

Notes

65. FO, 195/2360, No. 75, 30 August 1910, p. 348.
66. BOA, DH. SYS. 22/1–6, Document No. 2, 5 November 1910.
67. FO, 195/2383, No. 22, 30 April 1911, p. 85. Pantaleon was one of the first companies in the port of Smyrna to be boycotted, at the very beginning of the boycott movement. See "Ai Tarachodeis Skinai tis Smirnis," (Scenes of Chaos in Smyrna), *Embros* (Athens), 31 May 1910.
68. FO, 195/2383, No. 71, 23 September 1911, p. 290.
69. Köse, 2004, pp. 461–482.
70. BOA, DH. SYS 22/1–24, Document No. 4, 30 November 1910.
71. FO, 195/2383, No. 12, 22 February 1911, p. 40. When the British consul visited the governor-general in Smyrna regarding a compensation application he seized the opportunity to reiterate new position of the government.
72. BOA, DH. SYS. 22/2–4, Document No. 2, 27 September 1911.
73. FO, 195/2383, No. 65, 6 September 1911, p. 268; FO, 195/2383, No. 68, 20 September 1911, p. 277; FO, 195/2383, No. 69, 23 September 1911, p. 280.
74. BOA, DH. SYS. 22/2–4, Document No. 6/1, 10 October 1911.
75. BOA, DH. SYS. 22/2–4, Document No. 10/1, 5 November 1911; FO, 195/2383, No. 80, 31 October 1911, p. 329; FO, 195/2383, No. 82, 8 November 1911, p. 335.
76. BOA, DH. SYS. 22/1–18, Document No. 14, 31 July 1910.
77. FO, 195/2358, No. 82, 28 June 1910, p. 127.
78. BOA, DH. SYS. 22/1–28, Document No. 28, 7 May 1911.
79. BOA, DH. SYS. 22/1–28, Documents No. 31–32, 10 May 1911.
80. "Episodia," (Incidents), *Proodos*, 5 June 1910.
81. AYE, A-21, 1910–1911, Smyrna, No. 1023, 27 March 1911.
82. FO, 195/2383, No. 24, 31 March 1911, p. 94. After 15 days, following the requests and diplomatic pressure that the British Embassy in Istanbul put on the Ottoman government, the case of Fritz Vadova was solved. The British consul in Smyrna believed that the governor-general and chief of police, Cemal Bey, had difficulties in controlling the boycott organizations. FO, 195/2383, No. 33, 15 April 1911, p. 140.
83. BOA, DH. SYS. 22/1–25, Document No. 3, 26 July 1911.
84. FO, 195/2360, No. 75, 30 August 1910, p. 347.
85. Ahladi, 2008, p. 196.
86. BOA, DH. MUİ. 109/16, Document No. 2, 28 June 1910.
87. Kerim Ağa was the head of the porters in Salonica and the leader of the boycott movement. Detailed information about him and his activities will follow below.
88. FO, 195/2358, No. 82, 28 June 1910, p. 126. After these instances of violence, three Muslims (one of whom was a Cretan boatman) were arrested. The Ottoman press condemned these actions and considered them illegal.

However, those who managed to remove the boycott marks from their storefronts were still few and far between in July 1910; FO, 195/2358, No. 85, 8 July 1910, p. 157.
89. "Boykot," *Rumeli*, 28 June 1910.
90. FO, 195/2358, No. 83, 29 June 1910, p. 135.
91. "İzmir Harb-i İkitsadi Heyetinin Beyannamesidir:" *İttihad*, 11 September 1910. The expression in article seven of the declaration was: "7. Memleket dahilinde işaretli olan Yunanlı mağazalarından ahz ü itada bulunmamak ve yanlışlığa meydan kalmamak üzere her mağazadan şehadetname sual etmek."
92. FO, 195/2358, No. 79, 18 June 1910, pp. 106–107.
93. "O Emporikos Polemos," (The Economical War), Proodos, 5 June 1910.
94. Naziktir Muzaffer, *Girid Kurbanları* (Victims of Crete), (Dersaadet, Edib Matbaası, 1326).
95. "Hakaretler İslamlara Mahsurdur," *İttihad*, 1 September 1910.
96. Naziktir Muzaffer, *Girid Kurbanları*, pp. 12–13.
97. *Girid* (Crete), (Bab-ı Ali: Matbaacılık Osmanlı Anonim Şirketi, 1325–1326).
98. *Girid: Mazisi, Hali, İstikbali* (Crete: Its Past, Present, Future), (Kostantiniye: Matbaa-i Ebuziya, 1328), p. 76.
99. Ibid., p. 79.
100. The Boycott Society also made use of this kind of discourse. See Boykotaj Teshilat Komisyonu, "Beyanname," *İttihad*, 20 June 1910; Halit Tevfik, "Boykotaj Kalkabilir mi?" *İttihad*, 29 August 1910.
101. AYE, A-21, 1910–1911, Smyrna, 24 February 1911. This source quotes a declaration of the Boycott Society that appeared in the newspaper *Köylü*, issuing a warning to the employees of postal services, the Administration of Public Debt and the Customs, who regularly ate in a Greek restaurant. *Köylü* announced that if the officials continued to eat there, their names would be publicized in the newspaper.
102. BOA, DH. SYS. 22/1–27, Document No. 3, 15 March 1911.
103. CPC, Turquie 1897–1914, 306, Document No. 46, Manastır, 22 June 1910.
104. CPC, Turquie 1897–1914, 307, Document No. 50, Pera, 22 April 1911.
105. The Boycott Society started to publish lists after 15 June 1910. "İzmir Boykotaj Cemiyeti'nden," *İttihad*, 2 Haziran 1326 (15 June 1910). The lists published by boycott societies, particularly the Boycott Society of Smyrna, were very detailed. "Harb-i İktisadi Heyetinin Beyannamesidir," *İttihad*, 18 September 1910.
106. BOA, DH. SYS. 22/1–26, Document No. 6, 10 May 1911; BOA, DH. SYS. 22/1–6, Document No. 11, 23 June 1911.

NOTES 253

107. BOA, DH. SYS. 22/1–26, Document No. 7, 8 May 1911.
108. BOA, DH. SYS. 22/1–10, Document No. 4, 5 November 1910.
109. BOA, DH. İD. 130/1, Document No. 59, 26 February 1911.
110. CPC, Turquie 1897–1914, 307, Document No. 108–109, Mersin, 22 June 1911. For an early warning of the Boycott Society in a declaration for the same reason, see "İzmir Boykotaj Cemiyeti'nden," İttihad, 15 July 1326 (28 July 1910).
111. BOA, DH. SYS. 22/1–6, Document No. 7, 30 October 1910.
112. AYE, A-21, 1910–1911, Antalya, 26 March 1911.
113. FO, 195/2347, No. 23, 29 June 1910, p. 327.
114. BOA, DH. MUİ. 115/18, Document No. 2, 24 July 1910; BOA, DH. MUİ 102–2/17, Document No. 45, 2 July 1910.
115. BOA, DH. MUİ 102–2/9, Document No. 1, 9 June 1910.
116. CPC, Turquie 1897–1914, 306, Document No. 136, Athens, 24 July 1910.
117. BOA, DH. MUİ. 102–2/17, Document No. 46, 6 July 1910.
118. BOA, DH. MUİ. 111/38, Documents No. 1–2, 3–9 July 1910.
119. CPC, Turquie 1897–1914, 307, Document No. 82, Athens, 29 April 1911; CPC. Turquie 1897–1914, 307, Document No. 92, Smyrna, 2 May 1911.
120. The government forced the Boycott Society in Istanbul to send an order also to Yanya, because the boycott there was still continuing and foreign merchants' interest were significantly damaged. BOA, DH. MUİ. 113/49, Document No. 1, 14 July 1326 (27 July 1910).
121. FO, 195/2342, No. 32, 23 June 1910, p. 324.
122. BOA, DH. MUİ. 109/54, Document No. 1, 21 June 1910.
123. BOA, DH. SYS. 22/1–24, Documents No. 2–3, 14–17 November 1910.
124. This declaration, submitted to the foreign consuls, appeared even in Greek newspapers; "Perierga Pramata en Smyrni: Mpoikotatzides Grafontes pros tous Proksenous," (Strange Incidents in Smyrna: Boycotters address the Consuls), Embros (Athens), 16 July 1910.
125. Boykotaj Heyeti, "Beyanname: Osmanlı Vatandaşlarımıza," İttihad, 27 June 1910.
126. "İzmir Boykotaj Cemiyeti'nden," İttihad, 25 September 1910.
127. Kerimoğlu, 2008, pp. 201–202.
128. Ahladi, 2008, p. 198. Not even a single copy of this newspaper has survived in the libraries or archives of Turkey.
129. FO, 195/2360, No. 75, 30 August 1910, pp. 347–348.
130. FO, 195/2345, No. 15, 20 June 1910, p. 116.
131. FO, 195/2335, No. 33, 29 June 1910, pp. 129–131.
132. BOA, DH. MUİ 110/40, Documents No. 1, 3/1, 2–7 July 1910; BOA, DH. MUİ. 109/48, Documents No. 1–3, 2–11 July 1910; BOA, DH. MUİ 111/8,

Documents No. 1–2, 7–8 July 1910. The boycotters not only made use of the telegraph to communicate with each other, but they also demanded assistance from the Ottoman government. For instance, the leader of the Boycott Society in Kuşadası, Mustafa Ahmed, wrote to the Ministry of War to request help with communications; BOA, DH. MUİ 110/23, Document No. 1.
133. FO, 195/2383, No. 20, 25 March 1911, p. 77.
134. CPC, Turquie 1897–1914, 307, Document No. 41–43, Smyrna, 11 April 1911.
135. AYE, A-21, 1910–1911, No. 102, Smyrna, 2 April 1911.
136. "İzmir Boykotaj Cemiyeti'nden," İttihad, 25 September 1910.
137. BOA, DH. MUİ. 125/24, Documents No. 2–3, 26–28 August 1910. The telegrams of the Boycott Society forwarded to the Administration of Public Security by the Ministry of the Interior stated that this organization had not even submitted a letter of application for a legal foundation.
138. FO, 195/2360, No. 85, 6 October 1910, p. 377–381.
139. See BOA, DH. MUİ. 102-2/9, Document No. 18, 12 June 1910, for the declaration of the Boycott Commission for Facilities (*Aydın Vilayeti Boykotaj Teshilat Komisyonu*).
140. FO, 195/2358, No. 79, 18 June 1910, p. 103. The *Proodos* claimed that these certificates appeared both in Istanbul and Salonica. These certificates reminded Greek newspaper of the 1908 Austrian Boycott during which these certificates were first issued. "O Apokleismos," (The Boycott), *Proodos*, 7 June 1910.
141. "İzmir Boykotaj Cemiyeti'nden," İttihad, 13 June 1910.
142. "İzmir Boykotaj Cemiyeti, "Beyanname," İttihad, 27 July 1910.
143. BOA, DH. SYS. 22/1–28, Document No. 34, 31 July 1911.
144. FO, 195/2383, No. 20, 25 March 1911, p. 78.
145. BOA, DH. MUİ. 2-7/29, Documents No. 6, 7–9, 3–5; 4–8 September 1910.
146. FO, 195/2362, No. 21, 24 July 1910, p. 72.
147. "İzmir Harb-i İktisadi Heyetinin Beyannamesidir," İttihad, 11 September 1910.
148. One of the first declarations of the boycott societies was the one by the Eyüp Sultan Boycott Society, published in *Tanin*. In the fourth article, the declaration asked the Ottoman public to discern *Rums* from *Yunanis*. "Boykotaj," *Tanin*, 25 June 1910.
149. FO, 195/2358, No. 79, 18 June 1910, p. 103; the declaration regarding Ottoman Greeks is in article 2.
150. "Boykotaj Hakkında," *Tanin*, 18 June 1910.
151. For instance, see: "Sholia tis [Tanin]," (The Comment of [Tanin]), *Proodos*, 6 June 1910. In this comment, *Tanin* stated that Ottoman citizens were able

to distinguish an Ottoman Greek from a Hellene and that their patriotism would prevent them from boycotting their own citizens.
152. "Alli Opsis tou Apokleismou," (The Other Facet of the Boycott), *Proodos*, 11 June 1910.
153. Kechriotis, 2009, p. 26.
154. FO, 195/2335, No. 54, 20 October 1910, p. 240; FO, 195/2335, No. 58, 12 November 1910, p. 257. The arguments between Mr Gallia, the British consul, and the governor-general of the province of Edirne continued until September 1911. FO, 195/2364, No. 8, 16 February 1911, p. 37; FO, 195/2364, No. 14, 6 March 1911, p. 60; FO, 195/2364, No. 36, 29 May 1911, p. 172; FO, 195/2364, No. 40, 29 September 1911, p. 191.
155. FO, 195/2358, No. 83, 29 June 1910, p. 135.
156. FO, 195/2383, No. 35, 22 April 1911, p. 146.
157. AYE, A-21, 1910–1911, Antalya, 24 March 1911.
158. BOA, DH. MUİ. 102–2/17, Document No. 67, 6 July 1910.
159. "İzmir Boykotaj Cemiyeti'nden," *İttıhad*, 23 Haziran 1326 (6 July 1910). The original expression in Turkish is "Yunaniler ve Yunan Kafalılar."
160. "O Apokleismos," (The Boycott), *Proodos*, 7 June 1910.
161. "İzmir Harb-i İktisadi Heyetinin Beyannamesidir," *İttıhad*, 11 September 1910.
162. Harisios Vamvakas, "O Emporikos Apokleismos," (The Economic War), *İsopolitia*, 20 June 1910.
163. Vangelis Kechriotis has demonstrated how different kinds of tension appeared between Christians and Muslims during the Second Constitutional Period in daily life in Smyrna, by focusing on various social and cultural issues. Kechriotis, 2009, pp. 18–27.
164. FO, 195/2342, No. 32, 23 June 1910, p. 325.
165. AYE, A-21, 1910–1911, Smyrna, No. 919, 19 March 1911.
166. CPC, Turquie 1897–1914, 307, Document No. 41–43, Smyrna, 11 April 1911.
167. CPC, Turquie 1897–1914, 306, Document No. 21, Rodos, 11 June 1910.
168. Mihail Sofroniadis, "Gkiavour!" (Infidel), *Ap'Ola*, 19 September 1910, in Sofroniadis, 2005.
169. FO, 195/2347, No. 23, 29 June 1910, p. 327.
170. "Emborikos Apokleismos Boulgaron kai Tourkon," (Bulgarian and Turkish Economic War), *Embros* (Athens), 24 November 1910.
171. BOA, DH. MUİ. 102–2/17, Document No. 1, 11 June 1910.
172. BOA, DH. MUİ. 102–2/17, Document No. 3, 9 June 1910; BOA, DH. MUİ. 102–2/17, Document No. 36, 30 June 1910.
173. FO, 195/2335, No. 30, 13 June 1910, p. 120.
174. BOA, DH. MUİ. 102–2/17, Document No. 67, 6 July 1910.

175. BOA, DH MUİ 105/12, Document No. 1, 16 June 1910.
176. BOA, DH. MUİ. 106/9, Document No. 2–3, 19 July 1910.
177. FO, 195/2358, No. 84, 1 July 1910, p. 145.
178. FO, 195/2345, No. 2, 21 May 1910, p. 90.
179. BOA, DH. SYS. 22/1–24, Document No. 5, 1 December 1910.
180. BOA, DH. MUİ. 102–2/9, Document No. 8, 14 June 1910.
181. BOA, DH. MUİ. 108–1/46, Document No. 3, 2 July 1910.
182. "Bu Nasıl Osmanlı?" *Tanin*, 20 June 1910; "Bu Nasıl Osmanlı? Tanin Refikimizden:" *İttihad*, 23 June 1910.
183. "Kostaki İnceoğlu," *Tanin*, 25 June 1910; "Harb-i İktisadi Cemiyeti'nden Varid Olan Cevab Şudur," *Tanin*, 25 June 1910.
184. Kechriotis, 2009, p. 25.
185. "Boykotajın Tesiri- İslamiyet'e Tecavüz," *İttihad*, 16 September 1910.
186. BOA, DH. MUİ. 102–2/17, Documents No. 70–71–72, 5 July 1910.
187. FO, 195/2343, No. 48, 10 October 1910, p. 117.
188. G.A. Bousios [Yorgos Boşo Efendi], "I Ektelestiki Eksousia kai epi tou Boykotaj Epitropi," (The Executive Power and the Boycott Society), *İsopolitia*, 27 June 1910.
189. "To Mpoikotaz stin Thessalonikin," (Boycott in Salonica), *Embros* (Athens), 9 June 1910.
190. "I Katastasis Epideinoutai," (The Situation is Getting Worse), *Embros* (Athens), 15 June 1910.
191. BOA, DH. MUİ. 110/38, Documents No. 1–2–3, 25 June 1910.
192. BOA, DH. MUİ. 107/39, Documents No. 7–8, 24 June 1910.
193. FO, 195/2360, No. 39, 6 June 1910, p. 198.
194. CPC, Turquie 1897–1914, 306, Document No. 251–252, Cidde (Jeddah), 15 October 1910.
195. "Rum Cemaati ve Yunaniler," *İttihad*, 26 May 1910.
196. "Yine Rumlar ve Yunaniler," *İttihad*, 30 May 1910.
197. BOA, DH. MUİ. 117/56, Documents No. 1–2, 6 August 1910.
198. FO, 195/2360, No. 54, 6 July 1910, p. 265.
199. BOA, DH. SYS. 22/1–24, Documents No. 23–24, 24 April 1911.
200. BOA, DH. MUİ. 104–1/46, Documents No. 1–8, 14–25 June 1910.
201. "İzmir Boykotaj Cemiyetinden," *İttihad*, 15 June 1910.
202. BOA, DH. SYS 22/1–22, Document No. 2, 5 August 1911.
203. BOA, DH. SYS 22/1–22, Document No. 3, 6 September 1911.
204. BOA, DH. MUİ. 107/19, Document No. 2, 23 June 1910.
205. BOA, DH. SYS. 22/1–26, Documents No. 2–3, 1 November 1910.
206. BOA, DH. SYS. 22/1–26, Document No. 1, 8 October 1910.
207. FO, 195/2358, No. 115, 10 September 1910, p. 348.

NOTES 257

208. BOA, DH. MUİ. 109/46, Document No. 3, 29 June 1910.
209. BOA, DH. MUİ. 102-2/9, Documents No. 2-3, 9 June 1910.
210. BOA, DH. MUİ. 99/43, Document No. 1, 30 May 1910.
211. BOA, DH. SYS. 22/1-24, Document No. 35, 13 June 1911.
212. BOA, DH. SYS. 22/1-24, Document No. 38, 7 June 1911.
213. AYE, A-21, 1910-1911, Midilli, No. 235, 30 March 1911.
214. BOA, DH. MUİ. 22/1-10, Document No. 11, 4 April 1911 and BOA, DH. MUİ. 22/1-10, Document No. 4, 5 November 1910.
215. AYE, A-21, 1910-1911, Midilli, No. 235, 30 March 1911.
216. BOA, DH. SYS. 22/1-15, Document No. 2, 22 April 1911.
217. BOA, DH. SYS. 22/1-15, Document No. 6, 9 May 1911.
218. BOA, DH. SYS. 22/1-10, Document No. 13, 28 May 1911 and BOA, DH. SYS 22/1-15, Document No. 13, 6 June 1911.
219. İzmir'de Çiviciler İçinde Yorgi İstradi, "Tebaa-i Osmaniyeden Çivici ve Demirci Yorgaki İstradi," *İttihad*, 19 August 1910.
220. Fahri, "Boykotaj Niçin Kalkmaz," *İttihad*, 4 July 1910.
221. M. Sai, "Boykotaj Münasebetiyle, Umum Hamiyetli Osmanlılara," *İttihad*, 4 July 1910.
222. FO, 195/2360, No. 11, 7 February 1910.
223. BOA, DH. MUİ. 66.2/1, Document No. 22, 10 March 1909.
224. "Bir İslam Bakkaliye Ticarethanesi," *İttihad*, 26 October 1910.
225. "Autocheiriasmoi," (Suicides), *Proodos*, 6 June 1910.
226. CPC, Turquie 1897-1914, 307, Document No. 51-53, Rodos, 22 April 1911.
227. CPC, Turquie 1897-1914, 307, Document No. 106, Smyrna, 27 May 1911.
228. "O Apokleismos," (The Boycott), *Proodos*, 7 June 1910.
229. CPC, Turquie 1897-1914, 306, Document No. 180, Tarabya, 6 August 1910.
230. CPC, Turquie 1897-1914, 307, Document No. 36, Pera, 28 March 1911.
231. FO, 881/9802, Greece Annual Report 1910, p. 3.
232. FO, 881/10003, Greece Annual Report 1911, p. 4.
233. BOA, DH. HMŞ. 9/14, Document No. 1, 4 October 1911; BOA, DH. HMŞ. 22/2, Document No. 1, 4 October 1911.
234. "Şehr-i Cari-i Ruminin..." *İttihad*, 16 September 1910.
235. AYE, A-21, 1910-1911, Dardanelles, 21 March 1911. The Greek ambassador and the local consuls also claimed that the boycott was a weapon used by the local merchants and notables to serve their personal interests; BOA, DH. SYS. 22/1-31, Document No. 3, 29 October 1911. The British merchants brought a similar claim onto the agenda in an earlier example. See BOA, DH. SYS. 22/1-24, Document No. 6, 30 November 1910.
236. CPC, Turquie 1897-1914, 307, Document No. 131, Salonica, 3 September 1911.

237. CPC, Turquie 1897–1914, 307, Document No. 68, Vienna, 28 April 1911. It was not necessarily a native interest, but according to the French consul, Austria and Germany were the Greeks' biggest competitors for trade in the Ottoman Empire. CPC, Turquie 1897–1914, 307, Document No. 75–76, Athens, 26 April 1911.
238. "O Emporikos Apokleismos İrhısen," (The Commercial Boycott Has Started), *Proodos*, 5 June 1910.
239. "Eskişehir Boykotaj Cemiyetinden:" *İttihad*, 4 July 1910.
240. "To Kritikon Zitima," (The Cretan Question), *Proodos*, 6 June 1910.
241. "O Emborikos Apokleismos," (The Economic War), *Embros* (Athens), 26 June 1910.
242. "Autocheiriasmoi," (Suicides), *Proodos*, 6 June 1910.
243. For a typical illustration see: Mihail Sofroniadis, "Hronografima: Sic Transit Gloria Mundi!.." (Column: Thus the Fame on Earth is Fleeting), *Proodos*, 18 January 1911, in Sofroniadis, 2005.
244. Oral, 2005, pp. 60–68.
245. CPC, Turquie 1897–1914, 307, Document No. 174–175, Trabzon, 14 November 1911. The Article "Boykot" was published in *Meşveret* on 11 November 1911.
246. AYE, A-21, 1910–1911, No. 9047, Salonica, 13 August 1911.
247. FO, 195/2342, No. 21, 18 April 1910, p. 137. The two boatmen were condemned to five weeks imprisonment and costs under section 179 of the Ottoman Criminal Code on 25 June 1910; FO, 195/2342, No. 33, 28 June 1910, p. 329.
248. BOA, DH. MUİ. 102–2/7, Documents No. 37–38, 21 June 1910.
249. FO, 195/2360, No. 41, 15 June 1910, p. 206.
250. FO, 195/2360, No. 54, 6 July 1910, p. 266.
251. BOA, DH. MUİ. 102–2/7, Documents No. 34, 35, 48, 55–59, 27 June–3 July 1910.
252. BOA, DH. MUİ. 113/49, Document No. 2, 16 July 1910.
253. BOA, DH. MUİ 107/54, Document No. 2, 7 July 1910.
254. BOA, DH. MUİ. 109/50, Document No. 10, 4 July 1910.
255. "İzmir Boykotaj Cemiyeti'nden: Hamiyetli Hamal ve Arabacılarımıza," *İttihad*, 11 July 1910.
256. FO, 195/2358, No. 82, 28 June 1910, p. 126.
257. "O Monos Ostis Meta..." *Embros* (İstanbul), 12 June 1910. (Article Lacks a Headline).
258. "Afteresie ton Hamalidon," (Malpratice of Porters), *Proodos*, 6 June 1910.
259. "O Apokleismos," (The Boycott), *Proodos*, 7 June 1910.
260. CPC, Turquie 1897–1914, 306, Document No. 180, Tarabya, 6 August 1910.

NOTES 259

261. "Biaion yfos tou M Vezirou Apenanti tou Presbeuti mas," (The Fierce Wording of the Grand Vizier against our Ambassador), *Embros* (Athens), 27 May 1910.
262. "Ai Scheseis Elladas kai Tourkias," (Turkish-Greek Relations), *Embros* (Athens), 30 May 1910.
263. FO, 195/2360, No. 39, 6 June 1910, p. 198.
264. "Havadis-i Mahalliye [Boykota Dair]," *İttihad*, 28 June 1910. The governor also argued that boycott was a weapon of weak states against stronger ones. According to him, one should not expect the Ottoman nation to boycott a weak and small Greece. However, Greece was backed by the Great Powers, and this was why it was legitimate for the Ottomans to utilize the weapon of boycott. This argumentation was also a defense for the boycott, even though he harbored fears.
265. "Harb-i İktisadi Dolayısıyla..." *İttihad*, 30 Haziran 1326 (13 July 1910).
266. "Anti-Greek Boycott to Be Ended: Turkish Ministerial Circular," *The Manchester Guardian*, 2 July 1910. Foreign newspapers were paying attention to every little sign regarding the cessation of the boycott. "The Greek Boycott in Turkey," *The Manchester Guardian*, 27 October 1910.
267. For instance, see: İzmir Boykotaj Cemiyeti, "Beyanname," *İttihad*, 27 July 1910.
268. BOA, DH. MUİ. 98–1/56, Document No. 2, 29 May 1910.
269. İzmir Boykotaj Cemiyeti, "Beyanname. Hamiyetli Osmanlılara!" *İttihad*, 4 July 1910.
270. İzmir Boykotaj Cemiyeti, "Beyanname: Muhterem Osmanlılara!" *İttihad*, 10 July 1910.
271. FO, 195/2360, No. 54, 6 July 1910, p. 266.
272. FO, 195/2358, No. 83, 29 June 1910, p. 135.
273. BOA, DH. 102–2/17, Document No. 61, 21 June 1910. There are several telegrams to the provinces but this is the first one.
274. FO, 195/2362, No. 21, 24 July 1910, p. 72.
275. For instance, a typical definition of the concept of boycott was sent to Yanya. BOA, DH. MUİ. 113/49, Document No. 1, 27 July 1910.
276. BOA, DH. MUİ 105/12, Document No. 1, 16 June 1910.
277. FO, 195/2360, No. 58, 15 July 1910, p. 276. A meeting was held as result of the remonstrance of the Italian merchants. In this meeting, the British consul stated that the boycott in Smyrna had been ordered by the Boycott Committee, as had happened in Constantinople. Therefore, he claimed, they should not trouble their ambassadors with these complaints since they knew about the boycott in Istanbul.
278. BOA, DH. SYS. 22/1–1, Document No. 2, 20 September 1910.

279. BOA, DH. SYS. 22/1–2, Document No. 1, 20 September 1910.
280. FO, 195/2358, No. 107, 1 September 1910, p. 301.
281. FO, 195/2358, No. 115, 10 September 1910, p. 347.
282. FO, 195/2360, No. 91, 3 November 1910, pp. 398–403.
283. A similar telegram was sent to Edirne province; BOA, DH. SYS. 22/1–4, Document No. 1, 29 September 1910. Or again to Salonica BOA, DH. SYS 22/1–27, Document No. 1, 15 September 1910.
284. CPC, Turquie 1897–1914, 306, Document No. 126, London, 22 July 1910.
285. BOA, DH. SYS. 22/2–1, Document No. 2, 19 February 1911.
286. FO, 195/2360, No. 99, 30 November 1910, p. 428; FO, 195/2360, No. 103, 20 December 1910, p. 445.
287. BOA, DH. SYS. 22/1–28, 3 November 1911.
288. For a similar claim see: "İ Katastasis Epideinoutai," (The Situation is Getting Worse), *Embros* (Athens), 15 June 1910.
289. CPC, Turquie 1897–1914, 306, Document No. 38, Tarabya, 19 June 1910; CPC, Turquie 1897–1914, 307, Document No. 50, Pera, 22 April 1911.
290. AYE, A-21, 1910–1911, No. 87, 1911. The report wanted Greek diplomats to highlight the fact that the Greeks did not oppose the free will of the Ottoman nation, but their excessive actions.
291. BOA, DH. MUİ. 112–2/17, Document No. 40, 20 June 1910.
292. BOA, DH. SYS. 22/1–31, Document No. 6, 4 November 1911; BOA, DH. SYS. 22/1–30, Document No. 2, 11 October 1910; for a similar telegram from the governor of Karesi see BOA, DH. SYS. 22/1–10, Documents No. 5–6, 9 November 1910.
293. CPC, Turquie 1897–1914, 307, Document No. 51–53, Rodos, 22 April 1911. The consul replied by reminding him that some characteristics of the West produced disease. Therefore, one should also make sure to include the cure together with the imitation that would bring disease.
294. FO, 195/2364, No. 14, 6 March 1911, p. 61; FO, 195/2364, No. 27, 26 April 1911, p. 123.
295. FO, 195/2360, No. 41, 15 June 1910, p. 204.
296. BOA, DH. MUİ. 117/64, Document No. 3, 26 July 1910.
297. BOA, DH. MUİ. 112–2/7, Document No. 35, 29 June 1910.
298. BOA, DH. MUİ. 108–2/3, Document 1, 5 July 1910.
299. FO, 195/2342, No. 32, 23 June 1910, p. 326.
300. BOA, DH. MUİ. 112–2/7, Document No. 45, 2 July 1910.
301. BOA, DH. MUİ. 110/26, Document No. 2, 4 July 1910.
302. CPC, Turquie 1897–1914, 306, Document No. 79–80–81, Trabzon, 7 July 1910.
303. BOA, DH. SYS. 22/1–17, Documents No. 3, 5/2, 1 January–10 April 1911.

NOTES   261

304. BOA, DH. HMŞ. 9/14, Document No. 1, 4 October 1911.
305. CPC, Turquie 1897–1914, 307, Document No. 57–62, Paris, 23 April 1911.
306. BOA, DH. MUİ. 112–2/7, Document No. 41, 26 June 1910.
307. AYE, A-21, 1910–1911, Antalya, 24 March 1911.
308. AYE, A-21, 1910–1911, Dardanelles, 21 March 1911.
309. BOA, DH. MUİ 113/49, Document No. 3, 13 July 1910.
310. BOA, DH. MUİ 109/46, Document No. 2, 9 July 1910.
311. BOA, DH. SYS. 22/2–3, Document No. 2, 29 July 1911.
312. FO, 195/2360, No. 95, 17 November 1910, p. 419.
313. BOA, DH. SYS. 22/1–24, Document 21, 26 April 1911.
314. BOA, DH. MUİ 108–1/48, Documents No. 2 and 3, 28–30 June 1910.
315. BOA, DH. MUİ. 112–2/7, Documents No. 56, 57, 30 June-1 July 1910.
316. BOA, DH. MTV. 46/3, Document No. 1, 8 January 1911.
317. BOA, DH. MTV. 46/3, Document No. 3, 25 March 1911.
318. BOA, DH. MUİ 112–2/7, Document No. 58, 12 June 1910.
319. BOA, DH. SYS. 22/1–26, Document No. 5, 19 November 1910.
320. BOA, DH. SYS. 22/1–3, Document No. 1, 22 September 1910. The government sent a reminder of its neutrality to Aydın province three months before, requesting the governor to cease the participation of local bureaucrats in the boycott movement; BOA, DH. MUİ 102–2/9, Document No. 9/1, 16 June 1910.
321. BOA, DH. SYS. 22/1–7, Documents No. 1–3, 28 October – 10 November 1910.
322. BOA, DH. MUİ. 115/18, Documents No. 1–2, 24–25 June 1910, The date of the meeting was 8 June 1910.
323. BOA, DH. SYS 22/1–28, Document No. 37–39, 4 November 1911.
324. CPC, Turquie 1897–1914, 307, Document No. 174–175, Trabzon, 14 November 1911. He also summarized his views to the French consul of Trabzon in one of their meetings.
325. BOA, DH. SYS 22/1–28, Document No. 37–39, 4 November 1911.
326. M. Fahrettin, "Boykotaj Etrafında Enzar-ı Millete," *İttihad*, 27 October 1910.
327. "Tire Boykotaj Komisyonundan İzmir Boykotaj Komisyonuna," *İttihad*, 27 October 1910; "İzmir Boykotaj Komisyonundan Tire Boykotaj Komisyonuna," *İttihad*, 27 October 1910.
328. "İzmir Boykotaj Cemiyeti'nin Beyannamesi," *İttihad*, 28 October 1910.

Chapter 4 The Muslim Protest: the Economic Boycott as a Weapon in Peacetime, 1913–14

1. Zürcher, 2006, p. 11.
2. For instance, see: "Adalar Meselesi," *İkdam*, 8 February 1914, p. 2; "Adalar Meselesi," *İkdam*, 10 February 1914, p. 2; "Adalar Meselesi," *İkdam*,

11 February 1914, p. 1. Similar news items were continuously published every day.
3. Akşin, 1998, p. 383.
4. Adanır, 2006, p. 22.
5. For examples of such news items from *İkdam*, see: "Varna'da Miting, Yunan Mezalimi," *İkdam*, 5 June 1914, p. 3; "Yunan Mezalimi," *İkdam*, 11 June 1914, p. 3; "Yunan Mezalimi, Selanik Cemaat-i İslamiyesinin Muhtırası," *İkdam*, 12 June 1914, p. 3; "Yunan Mezalimi," *İkdam*, 13 June 1914, p. 4.
6. Dündar, 2008, p. 193.
7. FO. 195/2458, File of "Anti-Christian Boycott," (former reference 306/3080), Enclosure No. 2, Memorandum, pp. 537–538.
8. "Rum Mekteblerinde neler okutuluyor," *İkdam*, 8 June 1914, p. 2; "Sakız'da Müslümanlar Tehlikededir," *İkdam*, 10 June 1914, p. 2; "İzmir'de Küstahlıklar," *İkdam*, 8 March 1914, p. 1. For instance, a gendarme and a guard of the Regie were killed in an assault on a police station in Karareis/ Smyrna. *İkdam* claimed that this assault had not been executed by Greek bands or Greek soldiers, but by the native Greeks. The newspaper expressed "grief" over this incident. "İzmir Vaka," *İkdam*, 17 June 1914, p. 2.
9. This idea was expressed in the reports of the British consuls. For instance, see: FO. 195/2458, No. 308, 6 May 1914, p. 326.
10. Ahmad, 1995a, pp. 177–178.
11. Bilgi (Ed.), 1997, pp. 66–71.
12. *Müslümanlara Mahsus*, ([n. p.], 1329). This is a short version and does not involve a list of Muslim merchants. *Müslümanlara Mahsus*, ([n. p.], 1329) is the longest version, with a red cover page, and includes a long list of Muslim merchants. This is probably the last version and published at the very beginning of 1914. *Müslümanlara Mahsus Kurtulmak Yolu*, ([n. p.], 1329). *Müslüman ve Türklere*, ([n. p.], 1329) is the shortest version, but does include a list of Muslim merchants. This short list indicates that it was published particularly for the Asian part of Istanbul, since the addresses of these merchants belong to this region.
13. Zafer Toprak has introduced *Müslümanlara Mahsus* to the historiography on Turkey. His transliteration of the pamphlet also reveals that there are significant differences between different existing leaflets. Toprak, 1985, pp. 179–199.
14. Tör, 2000. Nevhiz received many presents from her relatives at her birth. As a result, her father decided to leave her a *rüzname-i hayat* (diary) as a present in order to leave her with memories of her childhood. In this diary, he mentioned crucial political and social developments in the Ottoman Empire, in addition to family affairs. Thanks to this diary we also have information about Ahmet Nedim's propaganda activities.

Notes 263

15. His son and the brother of Nevhiz was Vedat Nedim Tör. Vedat Nedim was educated in Berlin and participated in the communist movement in Turkey until the Turkish Communist Party was put on trial in 1927. Thereafter he turned to Kemalism and continued to be an influential figure in Turkey's cultural life.
16. Tunaya, 2000, p. 38.
17. I will refer only to the longer and most developed version of this pamphlet in this chapter.
18. Tör, 2000, pp. 122–123. The pamphlets were free for the people, but on sale for merchants in order to collect money for their reprint.
19. Ibid., p. 124.
20. AYE, A21a, 1914, Ayvalık, No. 6251, 23 February 1914.
21. "Anthellinikos Diogmon eis tin Mikran Asian," *Embros*, 14 March 1914.
22. *Kavm-i Cedid* (The New Nation) was written by Ubeydullah Afgani and published in 1913.
23. "Ta Pathimata ton Omogenon," (Atrocities incurred by the Nation), *Ekklisiastiki Alitheia*, 8 March 1914.
24. *Müslümanlara Mahsus*, pp. 3–4; *Müslümanlara Mahsus Kurtulmak Yolu*, p. 4.
25. *Müslüman ve Türklere*, p. 2–4.
26. *İzmir Tüccaran ve Esnefan-ı İslamiyyesine Mahsus Rehber*, ([n. p.], 1330). The pamphlet mentions the marriage ceremony of Enver Paşa and Naciye Sultan, which took place on 5 March 1914. Therefore, the pamphlet must have been published after this date. This pamphlet has been transcribed and published by Engin Berber. *İzmir 1876 ve 1908 (Yunanca Rehberlere Göre Meşrutiyette İzmir)*, 2008, pp. 115–135.
27. Ibid., p. 6; Mehmet Rasim [Dokur] contributed to the War of Independence by sending cloth to the army. Therefore, on his first visit to Tarsus, Mustafa Kemal (with Latife Hanım) visited him and had dinner at his house.
28. Ibid., p. 7.
29. FO, 195/2458, No. 84, 11 July 1914, p. 470.
30. *Müslüman ve Türklere*, p. 2–4.
31. Toprak, 2003, pp. 10–20.
32. *Müslümanlara Mahsus*, p. 5; *Müslümanlara Mahsus Kurtulmak Yolu*, p. 7; *Müslüman ve Türklere*, p. 5.
33. *Müslümanlara Mahsus*, p. 7; *Müslümanlara Mahsus Kurtulmak Yolu*, p. 9.
34. *Müslümanlara Mahsus*, p. 8–9; *Müslümanlara Mahsus Kurtulmak Yolu*, pp. 10–11.
35. *Müslümanlara Mahsus*, p. 14; *Müslümanlara Mahsus Kurtulmak Yolu*, p. 16.
36. *Müslümanlara Mahsus*, p. 15; *Müslümanlara Mahsus Kurtulmak Yolu*, p. 17.
37. *Müslüman ve Türklere*, pp. 5–6.
38. *Müslüman ve Türklere*, p. 9.

39. *Müslümanlara Mahsus*, pp. 16–18.
40. *Müslümanlara Mahsus Kurtulmak Yolu*, pp. 36–48.
41. *Müslümanlara Mahsus*, pp. 35–37. *Müslüman ve Türklere* offered a particular address at the Kadıköy post office where readers could register new names of Muslim merchants and craftsmen who were absent from the short list in the pamphlet. *Müslüman ve Türklere*, back cover.
42. Tör, 2000, p. 127.
43. Hüseyin Kazım (Kadri), *Rum Patriğine Açık Mektup: Boykot Müslümanların Hakkı Değil midir?* (İstanbul: Yeni Turan Matbaası, 1330).
44. Ibid., p. 5.
45. Ibid., p. 8.
46. Ibid., p. 10.
47. Ibid., pp. 11–12.
48. Ibid., pp. 12–13.
49. "Boykot Değil, Hemcinsine Muavenet," *İkdam*, 10 March 1914, p. 1.
50. Ibid.
51. FO, 195/2458, No. 81, 7 July 1914, (The date of the report is 25 June 1914), pp. 513–514.
52. "To Zitima kai i Katastasis," (The Situation and the Problem), *Ekklisiastiki Alithia*, 15 March 1914.
53. "İ Ekthesis kai ta Porizmata Aftis," (The Report and Its Attachments), *Ekklisiastiki Alithia*, 29 March 1914.
54. "İslam Şirket-i Ticariyesi," *İkdam*, 10 June 1914, p. 4; "Müslüman Tüccar Heyeti," *İkdam*, 9 June 1914, p. 2; "İdaresi ve Sermayesi Müslüman Bir Şirket," *İkdam*, 22 February 1914, p. 1.
55. "Türk ve Müslüman Tüccara, Esnafa, Türk Ocağından," *İkdam*, 8 June 1914, p. 5.
56. FO. 195/2458, No. 20, 18 February 1914, p. 211.
57. FO. 195/2458, No. 20, 18 February 1914, pp. 211–214.
58. "Ta Pathimata ton Omogenon," (Atrocities incurred by the Nation), *Ekklisiastiki Alitheia*, 8 March 1914; and BOA, DH. KMS. 63/58, 1 April 1914.
59. BOA, DH. KMS. 63/58, 1 April 1914.
60. BOA, DH. KMS. 63/58, 1 April 1914. The articles of 25 and 27 February.
61. "Ta Pathimata ton Omogenon," (Atrocities incurred by the Nation), *Ekklisiastiki Alitheia*, 8 March 1914.
62. BOA, DH. KMS. 63/58, 1 April 1914. "İzmir Mıntıkasında."
63. "O Pros tin Kyvernisin Mazvatas," (The Report to the Government), *Ekklisiastiki Alitheia*, 1 March 1914.
64. The Balkan Wars and the treaties between the Ottoman Empire and Bulgaria facilitated the ethnic cleansing of Bulgarians in Eastern Thrace. Dündar, 2008, pp. 182–191.

NOTES 265

65. FO, 195/2456, No. 17, 31 March 1914, pp. 5–6.
66. FO, 195/2458, No. 23, 26 February 1914, pp. 236–239. In one of the sessions of the International Commission in Valona (Avlonya, Vlore), the Albanian delegate Müfid Bey argued that the persecution of Albanians in the province of Aydın had increased after the arrival of Rahmi Bey as governor and requested the intervention of the Great Powers. FO, 195/2458, No. 65, 3 February 1914, p. 242. (The original dispatch of the British delegate Harry H. Lamb was sent from Valona to London on 5 December 1913).
67. BOA, DH. KMS. 20/4, 1332.Ca.12.
68. "Ta Pathimata ton Omogenon," (Atrocities incurred by the Nation), *Ekklisiastiki Alitheia*, 8 March 1914.
69. Prokopiou, 1928, pp. 37–41.
70. BOA, DH. İD. 108–2/30, 14 March 1914.
71. BOA, DH. H., 70/2, 3 April 1914.
72. BOA, DH. HMŞ., 14/77, 16 Mart 1914. The patriarchate sent this note to the government only two days after the Armenian merchants of Bandirma had sent their telegram.
73. BOA, DH. ŞFR. 40/86, 25 April 1914.
74. BOA, DH. KMS. 23/46, 3 June 1914.
75. BOA, DH. KMS. 23/46, 15 June 1914.
76. BOA, KMS. 23/53, 14 June 1914.
77. BOA, DH. ŞFR. 42/8, 15 June 1914; BOA. DH. ŞFR. 42/30, 17 June 1914.
78. BOA, DH. ŞFR. 42/34, 17 June 1914; BOA. DH. ŞFR. 42/35, 17 June 1914; BOA. DH. ŞFR. 42/33, 17 June 1914; BOA, DH. ŞFR. 42/38, 17 June 1914; BOA, DH. ŞFR. 47/7, 15 June 1914); BOA, DH. ŞFR. 42/36, 17 June 1914; BOA, DH. ŞFR. 42/37, 17 June 1914; BOA, DH. ŞFR. 42/32, 17 June 1914.
79. For these answers from the governors, see: BOA, KMS., 23/53, 1332.Ş.4. They were received between 17 and 27 June 1914.
80. BOA, KMS, 23/53, 1332.Ş.4.
81. AYE, A21a, 1914, Istanbul, 13 March 1914.
82. FO, 195/2458, File of "Anti-Christian Boycott," (former reference 306/3080), Enclosure No. 1, (report on the tour in the districts of Brusa and Smyrna), pp. 513–514.
83. Ibid., p. 516.
84. Ibid., p. 521.
85. FO, 195/2458, No. 6, 6 June 1914, p. 383.
86. FO, 195/2458, File of "Anti-Christian Boycott," (former reference 306/3080), Enclosure No. 1, (report on the tour in the districts of Brusa and Smyrna), pp. 518–519.
87. Ibid., p. 520.

88. Ibid., pp. 523–524.
89. FO, 195/2458, No. 84, 11 July 1914, p. 484 (report from 6 July 1914).
90. AYE, A21a, 1914, No. 15479, Midilli, 22 May 1914.
91. FO, 195/2458, File of "Anti-Christian Boycott," (former reference 306/3080), Enclosure No. 1, (report on the tour in the districts of Brusa and Smyrna), p. 521.
92. FO. 195/2458, No. 3, 2 July 1914, p. 380 (a brief note attached to this file). The date on Karabinazade's note is 28 Mayıs 330 (10 June 1914).
93. AYE, A21a, 1914, Urla, No. 15685, 23 May 1914.
94. FO, 195/2458, No. 81, 7 July 1914, pp. 436–451.
95. AYE, A21a, 1914, 4 May 1914.
96. AYE, A21a, 1914, 5 May 1914.
97. FO. 195/2458, File of "Anti-Christian Boycott," (former reference 306/3080), Enclosure No. 1 (report on the tour in the district of Brusa and Smyrna), p. 515.
98. Ibid., pp. 520–521.
99. FO, 195/2458, No. 81, 7 July 1914 (the date of the report is 27 June 1914), p. 442.
100. FO, 195/2458, File of "Anti-Christian Boycott," (former reference 306/3080), Enclosure No. 1 (report on the tour in the districts of Brusa and Smyrna), p. 525.
101. AYE, A21a, 1914, Pera, No. 16153, 27 May 1914.
102. AYE, A21a, 1914, Ayvalık, No. 8443, 16 March 1914.
103. FO, 195/2458, File of "Anti-Christian Boycott," (former reference 306/3080), Enclosure No. 1 (report on the tour in the districts of Brusa and Smyrna), p. 526.
104. Ibid., p. 527.
105. Ibid., p. 529.
106. FO, 195/2458, No. 81, 7 July 1914 (date of the report is 25 June 1914), p. 438.
107. AYE, A21a, 1914, No. 5667, 27 February 1914 (article on Kula).
108. Prokopiou, 1928, pp. 40–41.
109. FO, 195/2458, File of "Anti-Christian Boycott," (former reference 306/3080), Enclosure No. 1 (report on the tour in the districts of Brusa and Smyrna), p. 530. In another report, both Fahri Bey and Sarıköylü Hasan were once again mentioned because of their activities in Ödemiş: FO, 195/2458, No. 84, 11 July 1914, p. 471.
110. FO, 195/2458, No. 81, 7 July 1914 (date of the report is 25 June 1914), p. 439.
111. AYE, A21a, 1914, Kastelorizo, No. 2955, 1 February 1914.
112. For instance, see: FO, 195/2458, No. 84, 11 July 1914, p. 471.

Notes

113. FO, 195/2458, No. 84, 11 July 1914, p. 480.
114. Taçalan, 1971, pp. 69–71.
115. Ibid., pp. 72–73.
116. FO, 195/2458, File of "Anti-Christian Boycott," (former reference 306/3080), Enclosure No. 2, Memorandum, p. 538.
117. FO, 195/2458, No. 402, 2 June 1914, p. 371.
118. "Epi to Neo Takririo," (On the New Memorandum), *Ekklisiastiki Alitheia*, 30 June 1914.
119. "To Zitima kai i Katastasis," *Ekklisiastiki Alitheia*, 15 March 1914.
120. FO, 195/2458, No. 24, 4 May 1914, p. 323.
121. FO, 195/2456, No. 17, 31 March 1914, pp. 515, 517.
122. "Cavit Bey'in Beyanatı," *İkdam*, 17 June 1914, p. 2.
123. "Muhaceret Meselesi, Talat Bey'in Seyahati," *İkdam*, 16 June 1914, p. 2.
124. BOA, DH. ŞFR. 40/11, 14 April 1914. Taner Akçam also quotes the document: Akçam, '2008, pp. 88–89.
125. BOA, DH. EUM.VRK. 13/22, 1 August 1914.
126. "Muhaceret Meselesi, Talat Bey'in Seyahati," *İkdam*, 17 June 1914, p. 1.
127. For an example of news about the Greeks who emigrated first from Babaeski to Istanbul and then to Salonica, see: "Rum Muhacirleri," *İkdam*, 8 February 1914, p. 4.
128. "İ Thesis tou Omogenous Sticheiou," (The State the Nation), *Ekklisiastiki Alitheia*, 1 March 1914.
129. "Apofaseis kai Energiai ton Patriarchion," (The Decisions and Activities of the Patriarchate), *Ekklisiastiki Alitheia*, 1 March 1914.
130. "İ Partiarchiki Epitropi," (The Committee of Patriarchate), *Ekklisiastiki Alitheia*, 29 March 1914.
131. "Ayvalık Kaymakamının Azli," *İkdam*, 17 June 1914, p. 2.
132. "Muhaceret Meselesi," *İkdam*, 18 June 1914, p. 3.
133. "Yunan Mezalimi, Bab-ı Alinin Muhtırası," *İkdam*, 18 June 1914, p. 1.
134. "Muhaceret Meselesi, Talat Bey'in Seyahati," *İkdam*, 20 June 1914, p. 3.
135. BOA, DH. ŞFR. 42/166, 1 July 1914.
136. BOA, DH. ŞFR. 43/18, 3 July 1914.
137. BOA, ŞFR. 42/173, 2 July 1914.
138. BOA, DH. ŞFR. 42/198, 5 July 1914.
139. BOA, DH. ŞFR. 42/208, 6 July 1914.
140. BOA, DH. ŞFR. 42/199, 5 July 1914.
141. BOA, DH. ŞFR. 43/12, 14 July 1914.
142. The deportation of Greeks and Bulgarians occurred because the flow of Muslim immigrants after 1912 brought about a land shortage in 1914. Dündar, 2001, p. 184.
143. *Osmanlı Mebusan Meclisi Reisi Halil Menteşe'nin Anıları*, 1986, pp. 165–166.

144. Kerimoğlu, 2008, pp. 209–210; Kerimoğlu, 2006 (Publishing date is September 2008), p. 101.
145. Akçam, 2008, pp. 82–107.
146. Akçam, 2006, pp. 169–170.
147. Oral Tradition Archive LD 28, Center for Asia Minor Studies, Region: Sydia-Salihli, Village: Tatarti, Interview with Dimosthenis Stamatios.
148. Prokopiou, 1928, p. 41.
149. "Kiriakos Miçopulos'un Tanıklığı," Oral Tradition Archive of the Center for Asia Minor Studies, in *Göç: Rumlar'ın Anadolu'dan Mecburi Ayrılışı (1919–1923)*, 2002, pp. 140–143. This account of Miçopulos is valid for different reasons. First, it indicates that his father had a Turkish shareholder at the beginning. Therefore, Muslim merchants did invest in industry, even with non-Muslim partners. Second, the argument that the immigrants were employed in anti-non-Muslim agitation is similar to the discourse mentioned above. Fanatics claimed that Turkish women were killed and nailed to bridges in the lost territories. They advised Muslims not to give a single penny to those who killed their co-religionists. Furthermore, he depicted immigrants as clever people who established new enterprises and started to compete with Christians.
150. BOA, DH. KMS., 25/29, 18 June 1914.
151. BOA, DH. EUM. EMN. 85/7, 6 July 1914.
152. FO, 195/2458, File of "Anti-Christian Boycott," (former reference 306/3080), Enclosure No. 2, Memorandum, pp. 538–539.
153. AYE, A21a, 1914, Ayvalık, No. 8443, 16 March 1914.
154. AYE, A21a, 1914, No. 3390, 31 January 1914.
155. "Grammata Mitoropoliton," (Letters of Metropolitan Bishops), *Ekklisiastiki Alitheia*, 15 March 1914.
156. FO, 195/2458, File of "Anti-Christian Boycott," (former reference 306/3080), Enclosure No. 6 (account of the conversation between Rahmi Bey, governor of Smyrna, and Dr Nazim Bey), p. 553.
157. FO, 195/2458, No. 96, 27 July 1914, p. 585. He also reported that Turkish officers did not hesitate to publicly show their feelings against the Greeks and quoted a talk of Hacim Bey, the chief of police in Smyrna, who said: "Our duty is to hate the Greeks, whether Hellene or raya, and further our duty is to make them feel we hate them. They are our enemies; until we have swept them out, we can have no peace." FO, 195/2458, No. 96, 27 July 1914, pp. 584–585.
158. AYE, A21a, 1914, Ayvalık, No. 9345, 23 March 1914.
159. Mehmed Reşid visited the town on 1 August 1913. Bilgi (Ed.), 1997, p. 68.
160. The boycott movement gained its power in a very short time. The British consul Matthews reported that, with the exception of a few localities, the

movement prevailed throughout the region. FO, 195/2458, No. 92, 21 July 1914, p. 504.
161. FO, 195/2458, No. 82, 8 July 1914, pp. 453–461.
162. FO, 195/2458, No. 96, 27 July 1914, p. 587.
163. FO, 195/2458, No. 92, 21 July 1914, p. 509.

Epilogue: The Boycott Movement and Mass Politics in the Second Constitutional Period

1. For a more detailed debate on the concepts of public sphere and mass politics and their transformation in the Ottoman context after the 1908 Revolution, see: Çetinkaya, 2008, pp. 125–140.
2. Habermas, 1989, p. 5. Joan B. Landes has also made a similar distinction between the "iconic spectacularity of the Old Regime" and the "textual order of the bourgeois public sphere." Landes, 1993, p. 67.
3. Habermas, 1989, p. 30.
4. Calhoun, 1992, p. 4.
5. Habermas, 1999, p. 231.
6. Negt and Kluge, 1993, p. 10.
7. Ryan, 1992; and Landes, 1993.
8. Negt and Kluge, 1993, pp. 179, 189, 195–198.
9. Fraser, 1992, p. 123. Geof Eley has also mentioned that the public sphere is made up of a variety of publics, such as the peasantry, the working class, and nationalist movements, which have "cultural and ideological contest and negotiation" between them. Eley, 1992, p. 306.
10. Habermas, 1999, p. 235.
11. Hill and Montag, 2000, p. 5; Montag, 2000, p. 133.
12. Mardin, 1995. For similar claims see also his, Mardin, 1969.
13. İslamoğlu, 2002, pp. 12–13; Abbot, 2000, p. 228.
14. Hann, 1995, p. 165; Hann, 1996.
15. Trentmann, 2000, p. 4.
16. Hobsbawm, 1992, pp. 263–265.
17. Kırlı, 2004.
18. Kırlı, forthcoming.
19. Deringil, 1998.
20. Özbek, 2005; Özbek, 2002.
21. Köker (Ed.), 2008; *İkinci Meşrutiyet'in İlanının 100'üncü Yılı*, 2008; Kutlu, 2004.
22. Özbek, 2007.
23. For a debate on different patterns of social mobilization in the Ottoman Empire after the 1908 Revolution, see: Çetinkaya, 2010.

24. I am grateful to Mehmet Ö. Alkan who shared the preliminary findings of his detailed research on civil organizations in the Ottoman Empire with me. This detailed index of civil organizations is forthcoming in two volumes.
25. Tunaya, 1996 [1959], p. 28.
26. For an evaluation of the chaotic atmosphere of the post-July days, see: Toprak, 1997; Dağlar, 2008.
27. Zürcher, 1998; Akşin, 1998; Ahmad, 1995.
28. Çetinkaya, 2001.
29. Sencer [Baydar], 1969; Karakışla, 1998.
30. Karakışla, 1998, p. 198.
31. For the most significant group of feminists and their journal *Kadınlar Dünyası* in the Ottoman Empire, see: Çakır, 1994.
32. Van Os, 1997.
33. Van Os, 2001, pp. 335–347.
34. For the place of women and feminists in the nationalist movements and state policies regarding the destitute Muslim women in the Ottoman Empire, see: Karakışla, 2005.
35. Alkan, 2003, pp. 4–12. I am grateful to Alkan for allowing me to read his forthcoming book, which is an index of civil organizations of Ottoman communities and will be published in two volumes. See also: Alkan, 1998.
36. Quataert, 2000, pp. 172–191.
37. For an evaluation of Gustave Le Bon's theory, see: Çetinkaya, 2008, pp. 18–20. The significance and place of Le Bon in Turkish political thought is also mentioned in: Hanioğlu, 2006, pp. 93–97.
38. By simple language I mean inscriptions that are received as pictures or signs by illiterate people. One does not need to be able to read to understand symbolic words such as "toilet," "telephone," "police," and the like. The boycott movement also popularized words such as *boykotaj*, *harb-i iktsadi*, *milli*, *yunani*, *rum*, and so on. They were no longer merely words, but also signs.
39. See Zarevand for a description of how nationalists recruited an Islamic discourse and popularized the concepts of the national economy. Zarevand's narrative not only underlined the activities of nationalist cliques, but also mentioned different aspects of rising nationalism at an early date. Zarevand [Zaven Nalbandian and Vartouhie Nalbandian], 1971, [first published in 1926 in Boston].
40. Toprak, 1995, pp. 10–22.
41. Toprak, 1985, pp. 1345–1347.
42. Toprak, 1982, p. 107.
43. Ibid., p. 153.
44. Ibid., p. 113.
45. Ibid., pp. 205–209.

46. Ibid., p. 82.
47. Ibid., p. 216.
48. For different versions of Ottomanism during the nineteenth and early twentieth centuries, see: Somel, 2002.
49. Bernard Lewis's narrative, for example, is to a great extent a history of culture and political thought: Lewis, 1968. Niyazi Berkes's study also takes into account secularism as an intellectual current; Berkes, 1964. Both writers have conceived of the history of the late Ottoman Empire as a struggle between good and evil, modernists (Westernizers) and reactionaries.
50. An encyclopedia of well-known scholars in Turkey makes use of such a classification; this work has become very influential in studies on Turkey. *Tanzimat'tan Cumhuriyet'e Türkiye Ansiklopedisi*, 1986.
51. This long article first appeared in 1904 in *Türk*, published in Cairo, and classified alternative policies for the Ottoman Empire in three different paths: Ottomanism, Islamism and Turkism. The first two, according to Yusuf Akçura, were out of date for the Ottoman Empire; his view was that it was better to follow the policy of Turkism. His article was published many times as a pamphlet. Akçura, 1993.
52. A new edition of a major work on Turkish political thought classifies Turkish intellectual history in a much more sophisticated way. The common inclination in the articles is to reveal how different currents of thought were interrelated with each other. *Modern Türkiye'de Siyasi Düşünce*, Vol. I–IX, 2001–2009.
53. For two different paths in early Turkish nationalism, see: Arai, 1994.
54. Zürcher, 1994, p. 133.
55. Hanioğlu, 2001, p. 296.
56. Zürcher, 2005.
57. Therefore, figures such as journalists can be classified somewhere between philosophers and grassroots politicians, or as an intelligentsia distinct from the intellectuals, as they might be classified in East European societies. The intelligentsia plays a crucial role in popularizing ideologies. Çetinkaya, 2002, pp. 91–102.
58. Neither the social movements of the nineteenth century (such as workers' and nationalist movements) nor the so-called new social movements of the twentieth century (such as feminism and the green and the gay movements) restrict themselves to a particularistic interest or discourse of a distinct class or social group, but refer to various elements of common culture. For an evaluation and comparison between new social movements and mass movements of the nineteenth century, see: Calhoun, 1995.
59. For cultural elements such as rituals, symbols and *Weltanschauung*, and their employment in discourses and social movements, see: Fine, 1995, pp. 128–129.

BIBLIOGRAPHY

I Archives

i. BOA   (Prime Ministry Ottoman Archives, Istanbul)
   DH.   (Ministry of Internal Affairs)
   MKT.   (Mektubi Kalemi)
   İ-UM.   (İdare-i Umumiye)
   MUİ.   (Muhaberat-ı Umumiye İdaresi Kalemi)
   SYS.   (Siyasi Kısım)
   İD.   (İdari Kısım)
   HMŞ.   (Hukuk Müşavirliği)
   MTV.   (Mütenevvia Kısmı)
   KMS.   (Kalem-i Mahsus Müdüriyeti)
   H.   (Hukuk Kalemi)
   ŞFR.   (Şifre Kalemi)
   EUM.VRK.   (Emniyet-i Umumiye Müdürlüğü, Evrak Odası Kalemi
   EUM. EMN. (Emniyet Kalemi)
   İradeler, İrade-i Hususi,
ii. AYE (Greek Foreign Ministry Archives, Athens)
    A-21 (Files on economic war against Greeks 1910–11)
    A21a (Files on anti-Greek movements 1914)
iii. NA-PRO (British National Archives, Public Record Office, London-Kew)
     FO. (Foreign Office)
     195 Embassy and Consulates, Turkey (formerly Ottoman Empire): General Correspondence (Constantinople, Sublime Porte, Smyrna, Beirut, Salonica, Trabzon, Erzurum, Jerusalem, Aleppo, Edirne (and vice-consuls in these provinces), 1908–14).
     294 Consulates, Salonica, Ottoman Empire, General Correspondence.
     881 Confidential Print (Annual Reports of Turkey and Greece 1908–14).
iv. AMAE (French Foreign Ministry Archives, Paris)

CPC (Correspondance Politique et Commerciale / Nouvelle Série Turquie / 1897–1914 / Politique Étrangère)
305: Relations avec la Grèce, 1908–09
306: Relations avec la Grèce. Boycottage du commerce grec, 1910
307: Relations avec la Grèce, 1912–14
308: Relations avec la Grèce. Protection des Hellènes par la France etc. Mars. 1912–14.
v. CAMS (Center for Asia Minor Studies, Athens) Oral Tradition Archive, LD 28.

II Printed Official Documents

i. *Ekklisiastiki Alitheia* (Official Journal of Greek Orthodox Patriarchate)
ii. MMZC (Meclis-i Mebusan Zabıt Cerideleri – Records of the Ottoman Parliament)
iii. *Bosna Hersek ile İlgili Arşiv Belgeleri.* Ankara: T.C. Başbakanlık Devlet Arşivleri Genel Müdürlüğü, 1992.

III Periodicals

Tanin
İkdam
Rumeli
Sabah
İttihad
Gâve
Aks-ı Sada
İttihat ve Terakki
Millet
Musavver Geveze
Anadolu
Şura-yı Ümmet
Serbesti
Volkan
İstişare
Bağçe
Boşboğaz
Proodos
Ergatis
Amaltheia
Embros (Athens)
Embros (Istanbul)
Isopolitia
The Manchester Guardian

IV Pamphlets

Girid (Crete), (Bab-ı Ali: Matbaacılık Osmanlı Anonim Şirketi, 1325–26).

Girid Mazisi, Hali, İstikbali (Crete: Its Past, Present, Future), (Kostantiniye: Matbaa-i Ebuziya, 1328).

Hüseyin Kazım [Kadri], *Rum Patriğine Açık Mektup: Boykot Müslümanların Hakkı Değil midir?* (İstanbul: Yeni Turan Matbaası, 1330).

İzmir Tüccaran ve Esnefan-ı İslamiyyesine Mahsus Rehber, (Publishing Place and Publishing House does not exist, 1330), in Engin Berber (Translator), *İzmir 1876 ve 1908 (Yunanca Rehberlere Göre Meşrutiyette İzmir)*, (İzmir: İBB Kent Kitaplığı, 2008).

Müslümanlara Mahsus, (Publishing Place and Publishing House does not exist, 1329), (The Long Version).

Müslümanlara Mahsus, (Publishing Place and Publishing House does not exist, 1329), (The Short Version).

Müslümanlara Mahsus Kurtulmak Yolu, (Publishing Place and Publishing House does not exist, 1329).

Müslüman ve Türklere, (Publishing Place and Publishing House does not exist, 1329).

Naziktir Muzaffer, *Girid Kurbanları* (Victims of Crete), (Dersaadet. Edib Matbaası, 1326).

V Secondary Sources

Abbot, John. "The Village Goes Public: Peasants and Press in Nineteenth-Century Altbayern." *Paradoxes of Civil Society, New Perspectives on Modern German and British History*. Frank Trentmann (Ed.). New York: Berghahn Books, 2000.

Adanır, Fikret. "Bulgaristan, Yunanistan ve Türkiye Üçgeninde Ulus İnşası ve Nüfus Değişimi." *İmparatorluktan Cumhuriyete Türkiye'de Etnik Çatışma*. Erik Jan Zürcher (Ed.). İstanbul: İletişim Yayınları, 2006.

Adıyeke, Ayşe Nükhet. *Osmanlı İmparatorluğu ve Girit Bunalımı (1896–1908)*. Ankara: Türk Tarih Kurumu, 2000.

Adıyeke, Nükhet. "Osmanlı Kaynaklarına Göre Türk-Yunan İlişkilerinde Girit Sorunu (1896)," *Çağdaş Türkiye Tarihi Araştırmaları Dergisi*, Vol. I, No. 3, 1993, pp. 235–246.

Ahladi, Evangelia. "İzmir'de İttihatçılar ve Rumlar: Yunan-Rum Boykotu (1908–1911)," *Kebikeç*, No. 26, 2008.

Ahmad, Feroz. *İttihat ve Terakki 1908–1914*. İstanbul: Kaynak Yayınları, 1995a.

Ahmad, Feroz. "Osmanlı İmparatorluğu'nun Son Dönemlerinde Milliyetçilik ve Sosyalizm Üzerine Bazı Düşünceler." *Osmanlı İmparatorluğu'nda Sosyalizm ve Milliyetçilik (1876–1923)*. Erik J. Zürcher and Mete Tunçay (Eds). İstanbul: İletişim Yayınları, 1995b.

BIBLIOGRAPHY

Ahmad, Feroz. "Doğmakta Olan Bir Burjuvazinin Öncüsü: Genç Türklerin Sosyal ve Ekonomik Politikası 1908–1918." *İttihatçılıktan Kemalizme*. İstanbul: Kaynak Yayınları, 1996.
Akçam, Taner. *A Shameful Act: The Armenian Genocide and the Question of Turkish Responsibility*. New York: 2006.
Akçam, Taner. *'Ermeni Meselesi Hallolunmuştur' Osmanlı Belgelerine Göre Savaş Yıllarında Ermenilere Yönelik Politikalar*. İstanbul: İletişim Yayınları, 2008.
Akçura, Yusuf. *Üç Tarz-ı Siyaset*. Ankara: Türk Tarih Kurumu, 1993.
Akın, Yiğit. "Erken Cumhuriyet Dönemi Emek Tarihçiliğine Katkı: Yeni Yaklaşımlar, Yeni Kaynaklar," *Tarih ve Toplum Yeni Yaklaşımlar*, No. 2, Autumn 2005.
Akkaya, Yüksel. "Türkiye'de Emek Tarihinin Sefaleti Üzerine Bazı Notlar," *Toplum ve Bilim*, No. 91, Kış 2001/2002.
Akşin, Sina. *Jön Türkler ve İttihat ve Terakki*. Ankara: İmge Yayınevi, 1998.
Aktar, Ayhan. "Şark Ticaret Yıllıkları'nda 'Sarı Sayfalar:' İstanbul'da Meslekler ve İktisadi Faaliyetler Hakkında Bazı Gözlemler, 1868–1938." *Türk Milliyetçiliği, Gayrımüslimler ve Ekonomik Dönüşüm*. İstanbul: İletişim Yayınları, 2006a.
Aktar, Ayhan. "Bursa'da Devlet ve Ekonomi," *Türk Milliyetçiliği, Gayrımüslimler ve Ekonomik Dönüşüm*. İstanbul: İletişim Yayınları, 2006b.
Alkan, Mehmet Ö. "1856–1945 İstanbul'da Sivil Toplum Kuruluşları." In A.N. Yücekök, İ. Turan, M.Ö. Alkan. *Tanzimattan Günümüze İstanbul'da STK'lar*. İstanbul: Tarih Vakfı, 1998.
Alkan, Mehmet Ö. "Osmanlı'da Cemiyetler Çağı," *Tarih ve Toplum*, No. 288, October 2003, pp. 4–12.
Amca, Hasan. *Doğmayan Hürriyet*. İstanbul: 1989.
Aminzade, Ronald. "The Transformation of Social Solidarities in Nineteenth-Century Toulouse." *Consciousness and Class Experience in Nineteenth-Century Europe*. John M. Merriman (Ed.). London: Holmes and Meier, 1979.
Anderson, Perry. "Origins of the Present Crisis," *New Left Review*, No. 23, January–February 1964, pp. 26–53.
Arai, Masami. *Jön Türk Dönemi Türk Milliyetçiliği*. İstanbul: İletişim Yayınları, 1994.
Augustinos, Gerasimos. *Küçük Asya Rumları Ondokuzuncu Yüzyılda İnanç, Cemaat ve Etnisite*. Ankara: Ayraç, 1997.
Avni [Şanda], Hüseyin. *1908'de Ecnebi Sermayesine Karşı İlk Kalkınmalar*. İstanbul: Akşam Matbaası, 1935.
Bağış, Ali İhsan. *Osmanlı Ticaretinde Gayri Müslimler*. Ankara: Turhan Kitabevi, 1998.
Beard, C.A. and C.H. Hayes. "Record of Political Events," *Political Science Qaurterly*, Vol. XXIII, No. 4, December 1908.
Berkes, Niyazi. *100 Soruda Türkiye İktisat Tarihi*. Vol. II. İstanbul: Gerçek Yayınevi, 1970.

Berkes, Niyazi. *The Development of Secularism in Turkey.* Montreal: McGill University Press, 1964.
Bilgi, Nejdet (Ed.). *Dr. Mehmed Reşid Şahingiray Hayatı ve Hatıraları.* İzmir: Akademi Kitabevi, 1997.
Birinci, Ali. *Hürriyet ve İtilaf Fırkası.* İstanbul. Dergah, 1990.
Blackbourn, David and Geoff Eley. *The Peculiarities of German History: Bourgeois Society and Politics in Nineteenth-Century Germany.* Oxford: Oxford University Press, 1984.
Boratav, Korkut. *Türkiye İktisat Tarihi 1908–1985.* İstanbul: Gerçek Yayınevi, 1995.
Brenner, Robert. "The Agrarian Roots of European Capitalism." *The Brenner Debate: Agrarian Class Structure and Economic Development in Pre-Industrial Europe.* H. Aston and C.H.E. Philpin (Eds). Cambridge: Cambridge University Press, 1995.
Buğra, Ayşe. *Devlet ve İşadamları.* İstanbul: İletişim Yayınları, 2003.
Çakır, Serpil. *Osmanlı Kadın Hareketi.* İstanbul: Metis Yayınları, 1994.
Calhoun, Craig. *The Question of Class Struggle: Social Foundations of Popular Radicalism during the Industrial Revolution.* Chicago: University of Chicago Press, 1982.
Calhoun, Craig. "Introduction: Habermas and the Public Sphere." *Habermas and the Public Sphere.* Craig Calhoun (Ed.). Cambridge: MIT, 1992.
Calhoun, Craig. "New Social Movements of the Early Nineteenth Century." In *Repertoires and Cycles of Collective Action.* Mark Traugott (Ed.). Durham, NC: Duke University Press, 1995.
Cerrahoğlu [Kerim Sadi], A. "Osmanlı Döneminde İlk Sosyalist Yayınlar," *ANT Sosyalist Teori ve Eylem Dergisi*, No. 4, Ağustos 1970a.
Cerrahoğlu [Kerim Sadi], A. "Gave'ye Karşı Baha Tevfik," *ANT Sosyalist Teori ve Eylem Dergisi*, No. 5, Eylül 1970b.
Çetinkaya, Y. Doğan. "İstanbul'da 1908 Seçimleri," *Toplumsal Tarih*, Vol. XV, No. 89, May 2001, pp. 15–24.
Çetinkaya, Y. Doğan. "Liberal, Sosyalist, İttihatçı Boykot Gazetesi: *Gave*," *Müteferrika*, No. 20, Autumn 2001, pp. 261–274.
Çetinkaya, Y. Doğan. "Orta Katman Aydınlar ve Türk Milliyetçiliğinin Kitleselleşmesi." *Modern Türkiye'de Siyasi Düşünce, Milliyetçilik*, Vol. V. Tanıl Bora (Ed.). İstanbul: İletişim Yayınları, 2002, pp. 91–102.
Çetinkaya, Y. Doğan. *1908 Osmanlı Boykotu: Bir Toplumsal Hareketin Analizi.* İstanbul: İletişim Yayınları, 2004.
Çetinkaya, Y. Doğan. "Tarih ve Kuram Arasında Toplumsal Hareketler," *Toplumsal Hareketler: Tarih, Teori ve Deneyim.* Y. Doğan Çetinkaya (Ed.). İstanbul: İletişim Yayınları, 2008.
Çetinkaya, Y. Doğan. "1908 Devrimi'nde Kamusal Alan ve Kitle Siyasetinde Dönüşüm," *İ.Ü. Siyasal Bilgiler Fakültesi Dergisi*, No. 38, March 2008, pp. 125–140.

BIBLIOGRAPHY 277

Çetinkaya, Y. Doğan. "1908 Devrimi ve Toplumsal Seferberlik." İstanbul: Tarih Vakfı Yurt Yayınları, 2010.
Comninel, George C. *Rethinking the French Revolution: Marxism and the Revisionist Challenge.* London: Verso, 1987.
Dağlar, Oya. "II. Meşrutiyet'in İlanının İstanbul Basını'ndaki Yansımaları (1908)," *İ.Ü. Siyasal Bilgiler Fakültesi Dergisi,* No. 38, March 2008.
Darendelioğlu, İlhan. *Türkiye'de Komünist Hareketler.* İstanbul: 1973.
Davison, Roderic H. "The Ottoman Boycott of Austrian Goods." *3. International Congress of the Social and Economic History of Turkey.* Princeton: 1983.
Deringil, Selim. "Osmanlı İmparatorluğu'nda 'Geleneğin İcadı,' 'Muhayyel Cemaat,' Panislamizm," *Toplum ve Bilim,* No. 54–55, Summer/Autumn, 1991, pp. 47–65.
Deringil, Selim. *Well-Protected Domains.* London: I.B.Tauris, 1998.
Dündar, Fuat. *Modern Türkiye'nin Şifresi: İttihat ve Terakki'nin Etnisite Mühendisliği (1913–1918).* İstanbul: İletişim Yayınları, 2008.
Eldem, Edhem. "Istanbul 1903–1918: A Quantitative Analysis of a Bourgeoisie," *Boğaziçi Journal Review of Social, Economic and Administrative Studies,* Vol. XI, No. 1–2, 1997.
Eldem, Edhem. *Osmanlı Bankası Tarihi.* İstanbul: Türkiye Ekonomik ve Toplumsal Tarih Vakfı ve Osmanlı Bankası Tarihi Araştırma Merkezi, 1999.
Eley, Geoff. "Edward Thompson, Social History and Political Culture: The Making of a Working-class Public, 1780–1850." *E.P. Thompson Critical Perspectives.* Harvey J. Kaye and Keith McClelland (Eds). Philadelphia: Temple, 1990.
Eley, Geoff. "Nations, Publics, and Political Cultures: Placing Habermas in the Nineteenth Century." *Habermas and the Public Sphere.* Craig Calhoun (Ed.). Cambridge: MIT, 1992.
Eley, Geoff. "Liberalism, Europe and the Bourgeoisie 1860–1914." *The German Bourgeoisie.* London: Routledge, 1993.
Elmacı, Mehmet Emin. "Bosna Hersek'in Avusturya Tarafından İlhakı ve Doğurduğu Tepkiler (1908–1912)." Unpublished MA Thesis, Ege University, 1996.
Elmacı, Mehmet Emin. "İzmir'de Avusturya Boykotajı," *Tarih ve Toplum,* Vol. XXVII, No. 161, May 1997.
Emre, Ahmet Cevat. *İki Neslin Tarihi.* İstanbul: 1960.
Erişçi, Lütfü. *Türkiye'de İşçi Sınıfının Tarihi (özet olarak).* İstanbul: Kutulmuş Basımevi. 1951.
Exertzoglou, Haris. "The Development of a Greek Ottoman Bourgeoisie: Investment Patterns in the Ottoman Empire, 1850–1914." In *Ottoman Greeks in the Age of Nationalism.* Dimitri Gondicas and Charles Issawi (Eds). Princeton: The Darwin Press, 1999.
Fehmi, Abdülmecid. *Manastır'ın Unutulmaz Günleri.* İzmir: 1993.

Fine, Gary Alan. "Public Narration and Group Culture: Discerning Discourse in Social Movements." In *Social Movements and Culture*. Hank Johnston and Bert Klandermans (Eds). Minneapolis: University of Minnesota Press, 1995.

Foran, John. *Fragile Resistance: Social Transformation in Iran from 1500 to the Revolution.* Boulder: Westview Press, 1993.

Frangakis-Syrett, Elena. "The Economic Activities of the Greek Community of İzmir in the Second Half of the Nineteenth and Early Twentieth Centuries." In *Ottoman Greeks in the Age of Nationalism*. Dimitri Gondicas and Charles Issawi (Eds). Princeton: The Darwin Press, 1999.

Frangakis-Syrett, Elena. "Uluslararası Önem Taşıyan Bir Akdeniz Limanının Gelişimi: Smyrna (1700–1914)." *İzmir 1830–1930 Unutulmuş Bir Kent Mi? Bir Osmanlı Limanından Hatıralar*. Marie-Carmen Smyanelis (Ed.). İstanbul: İletişim Yayınları, 2008.

Fraser, Nancy. "Rethinking the Public Sphere: A Contribution to the Critique of Actually Existing Democracy." *Habermas and the Public Sphere*. Craig Calhoun (Ed.). Cambridge: MIT, 1992.

Friedman, Monroe. *Consumer Boycotts*. London: Routledge, 1999.

Gilbar, Gad G. "The Muslim Big Merchant-Entrepreneurs of the Middle East, 1860–1914," *Die Welt des Islams*, Vol XVIII/1, 2003.

Göç: Rumlar'ın Anadolu'dan Mecburi Ayrılışı (1919–1923). (For Turkish translation ed. Herkül Milas). İstanbul: İletişim Yayınları, 2002.

Göçek, Fatma Müge. *Burjuvazinin Yükselişi İmparatorluğun Çöküşü*. Ankara: Ayraç Yayınevi, 1999.

Gülmez, Mesut. "Tanzimat'tan Sonra İşçi Örgütlenmesi ve Çalışma Koşulları (1839–1919)." *Tanzimat'tan Cumhuriyet'e Türkiey Ansiklopedisi*, Vol. III. İstanbul: İletişim Yayınları, 1985.

Güzel, Şehmuz. "Tanzimat'tan Cumhuriyet'e İşçi Hareketi ve Grevler." *Tanzimat'tan Cumhuriyet'e Türkiye Ansiklopedisi*, Vol. III. İstanbul: İletişim Yayınları, 1985.

Habermas, Jürgen. *The Structural Transformation of the Public Sphere: An Inquiry into a Category of Bourgeois Society*. Cambridge: MIT, 1989.

Habermas, Jürgen. "The Public Sphere." *Jürgen Habermas on Society and Politics: A Reader*. Steven Seidman (Ed.). Boston: Beacon Press, 1999.

Hanagan, Michael and Marcel van der Linden. "New Approaches to Global Labor History," *International Labor and Working-Class History*, No. 66, Fall 2004.

Hanioğlu, Şükrü. *Preparation for a Revolution, The Young Turks 1902–1908*. Oxford: Oxford University Press, 2001.

Hanioğlu, Şükrü. "Osmanlı-Türk Seçkinciliğinin Unutulan Kuramcısı." *Osmanlı'dan Cumhuriyet'e Zihniyet, Siyaset ve Tarih*. İstanbul: Bağlam Yayıncılık, 2006.

Hann, Chris. "Philosophers' Models on the Carpathian Lowlands." *Civil Society, Theory, History, Comparison*. John A. Hall (Ed.). (Cambridge: 1995).

Hann, Chris. "Introduction: Political Society and Cvil Anthropology." *Civil Society: Challenging Western Models*. Chris Hann and Elizabeth Dunn (Eds). London: 1996.
Heper, Metin. *The State Tradition in Turkey*. Walkington: The Eathen Pres, 1985a.
Heper, Metin. "The Strong State and Democracy: The Turksih Case in Comparative and Historical Perspective." In *Democracy and Modernity*. S.N. Eisenstadt (Ed.). Leiden: Brill, 1985b.
Hill, Mike and Warren Montag. "Introduction: What Was, What Is, the Public Sphere? Post-Cold War Reflections." *Masses, Classes and the Public Sphere*. Mike Hill and Warren Montag (Eds). London: Verso, 2000.
Hobsbawm, Eric J. "The Making of the Working Class 1870–1914." *Worlds of Labour*. London: 1984.
Hobsbawm, Eric. "Mass Producing Traditions: Europe 1870–1914." *The Invention of Tradition*. Eric Hobsbawm and Terence Ranger (Eds). Cambridge: Cambridge University Press, 1992.
Hobsbawm, Eric. "Introduction: Inventing Traditions." *The Invention of Tradition*. Eric Hobsbawm and Terence Ranger (Eds), Cambridge: Cambridge University Press, 1997.
İkinci Meşrutiyet'in İlanının 100'üncü Yılı. İstanbul: Sadberk Hanım Müzesi, 2008.
İnalcık, Halil. "Application of the Tanzimat and its Social Effects." *Belleten*, No. 28, 1964, pp. 623–649.
İnsel, Ahmet. *Düzen ve Kalkınma Kıskacında Türkiye*. İstanbul: Ayrıntı Yayınları, 1996.
İrtem, Süleyman Kani. *Meşrutiyet Doğarken 1908 Jön Türk İhtilali*. İstanbul: Temel, 1999.
İslamoğlu, Huri. "Property as a Contested Domain: A Reevaluation of the Ottoman Land Code of 1858." *New Perspectives on Property and Land in the Middle East*. Roger Owen (Ed.). Cambridge: Harvard University Press, 2002.
İslamoğlu-İnan, Huri. "Introduction: 'Oriental Despotism in World-System Perspective." *The Ottoman Empire and the World Economy*. Huri İslamoğlu-İnan (Ed.). Cambridge: Cambridge University Press, 1987.
Issawi, Charles. "The Transformation of the Economic Position of the Millets in the Nineteenth Century." *Christians and Jews in the Ottoman Empire*, Benjamin Braude and Bernard Lewis (Eds). New York: Holmes and Meier Inc, 1982.
Johnson, Christopher H. "Patterns of Proletarianization: Parisian Tailors and Lodéve Woolens Workers." *Consciousness and Class Experience in Nineteenth-Century Europe*. John M. Merriman (Ed.). London: Holmes and Meier, 1979.
Jordan, Donald A. *Chinese Boycotts versus Japanese Bombs, The Failure of China's Revolutionary Diplomacy 1931–32*. Michigan: University of Michigan Press, 1991.
Kafadar, Cemal. "A Death in Venice (1575): Anatolian Muslim Merchants Trading in the Serenissima." *Journal of Turkish Studies*, Vol. 10, 1986, pp. 191–218.

Kaiser, Hilmar. *Imperialism, Racism and Development Theories: The Construction of a Dominant Paradigm on Ottoman Armenians*. Ann Arbor: Gomidas Institute, 1997.

Karakışla, Yavuz Selim. "Osmanlı İmparatorluğu'nda 1908 Grevleri," *Toplum ve Bilim*, No. 78, Autumn 1998.

Karakışla, Yavuz Selim. "Osmanlı Sanayi İşçi Sınıfının Doğuşu 1839–1923." Donald Quataert and Erik Jan Zürcher (Eds). *Osmanlı'dan Cumhuriyet Türkiye'sine İşçiler 1839–1950*. İstanbul. İletişim Yayınları, 1998.

Karakışla, Yavuz Selim. *Women, War and Work in the Ottoman Empire: Society for the Employment of Ottoman Muslim Women 1916–1923*. İstanbul: Ottoman Bank Archives and Research Center, 2005.

Karpat, Kemal. *The Politicization of Islam Reconstructing Identity, State, Faith and Community in the Late Ottoman State*. Oxford: Oxford University Press, 2001.

Kasaba, Reşat. "Was There a Comprador Bourgeoisie in Mid-Nineteenth Century Western Anatolia?" *Review*, Vol. IX, No. 2, Spring 1988.

Kasaba, Reşat. *Osmanlı İmparatorluğu ve Dünya Ekonomisi*. İstanbul: Belge Yayınları, 1993.

Katsiadakis, Helen Gardikas. "I Elliniki Kivermisi kai to Kritiko Zitima: 1908." (The Greek Government and the Cretan Question. 1908). *Afieroma ston Panepistimiako Daskalo Vas. VI. Sifiroera*. Athens: 1992.

Katsiadakis, Helen Gardikas. *Greece and the Balkan Imbroglio: Greek Foreign Policy 1911–1913*. Athens: 1995.

Kayalı, Hasan. *Jön Türkler ve Araplar*. İstanbul: Tarih Vakfı Yurt Yayınları, 1998.

Kechriotis, Vangelis. "II. Meşrutiyet Dönemi İzmir'de Hıristiyanlar ve Müslümanlar Arasında Günlük İlişkier," *Toplumsal Tarih*, No. 184, April 2009.

Kechriotis, Vangelis. "Experience and Performance in a Shifting Political Landscape: The Greek-Orthodox Community of Izmir/Smyrna at the turn of the 20th Century," *Deltio Kentrou Mikrasiatikon Spoudon*, No. 17, Athens: 2011.

Keddie, Nikkie R. *Religion and Rebellion in Iran: The Tobacco Protest of 1891–1892*. London: Frank Cass, 1966.

Kerimoğlu, Hasan Taner. "İttihat ve Terakki Cemiyeti'nin Rum Politikası 1908–1914." Unpublished PhD Thesis. Dokuz Eylül University, İzmir, 2008.

Keyder, Çağlar and Faruk Tabak (Eds). *Landholding and Commercial Agriculture in the Middle East*. Albany: Suny Press, 1991.

Keyder, Çağlar, Y. Eyüp Özveren and Donald Quataert. "Osmanlı İmparatorluğu'nda Liman Kentleri: Bazı Kurumsal ve Tarihsel Perspektifler." Çağlar Keyder, Y. Eyüp Özveren and Donald Quataert. *Doğu Akdeniz'de Liman Kentleri (1800–1914)*. İstanbul: Tarih Vakfı Yurt Yayınları, 1994.

Keyder, Çağlar. "Europe and the Ottoman Empire in mid-nineteenth Century: Development of a Bourgeoisie in the European Mirror." Paper Presented to the Colloquim of the European Assocaition for Banking History V. East Meats West: Baking, Commerce and Investment, İstanbul 15–16 October 1999.

BIBLIOGRAPHY 281

Keyder, Çağlar. *Türkiye'de Devlet ve Sınıflar.* İstanbul: İletişim Yayınları, 1995.
Keyder, Çağlar."Birinci Dünya Savaşı Arifesinde Liman Şehirleri ve Politika." *Memalik-i Osmaniye'den Avrupa Birliği'ne.* İstanbul: İletişim Yayınları, 2003a.
Keyder, Çağlar. "Mısır Deneyimi Işığında Türk Burjuvazisinin Kökeni." *Memalik-i Osmaniye'den Avrupa Birliği'ne.* İstanbul: İletişim Yayınları, 2003b.
Kırlı, Cengiz. "Coffeehouses: Public Opinion in the Nineteenth-century Ottoman Empire." *Public Islam and the Common Good.* Armando Salvatore and Dale F. Eickelman (Eds). Leiden: Brill, 2004.
Kırlı, Cengiz. "Surveillance and Constituting the Public in the Ottoman Empire." *Publics, Politics and Participation: Locating the Public Sphere in the Middle East and North Africa.* Seteney Shami (Ed.). New York: SSRC, forthcoming.
Kiong, Wong Sin. *China's Anti-American Boycott Movement in 1905: A Study in Urban Protest.* New York: Peter Lang, 2002.
Köker (Ed.), Osman. *Yadigar-ı Hürriyet.* İstanbul: Birzamanlar Yayıncılık, 2008.
Köse, Osman. "Osmanlı-Amerikan İlişkilerinde Bir Kriz: Hacı David Vapur Kumpanyası Boykotu (1911)," *Belleten,* Vol. LXVIII, No. 252, August 2004.
Kurmuş, Orhan. *Emperyalizmin Türkiye'ye Girişi.* Ankara: Savaş Yayınları, 1982.
Kutlu, Sacit. *Didar-ı Hürriyet Kartpostallarda İkinci Meşrutiyet 1908-1913.* İstanbul: Bilgi Üniversitesi Yayınları, 2004.
Landes, Joan B. *Women and the Public Sphere in the Age of the French Revolution,* Ithaca: Cornell University Press, 1993.
Lewis, Bernard. *The Emergence of Modern Turkey.* Oxford: Oxford University Press, 1968.
Mardin, Şerif. "Power, Civil Society and Culture in the Ottoman Empire." *Comparative Studies in Society and History.* No. 11, 1969.
Mardin, Şerif. "Civil Society and Islam." *Civil Society, Theory, History, Comparison.* John A. Hall (Ed.). Cambridge: Polity Press, 1995.
Matarachi, Aliye F. *Trade Letters as Instances of Economy, Ideology and Subjectivity.* Istanbul: Ottoman Bank Archives and Research Center, 2005.
Maza, Sarah. *The Myth of the French Bourgeoisie.* Cambridge: Harvard University Press, 2003.
Minda, Gary. *Boycott in America: How Imagination and Ideology Shape the Legal Mind.* Illinois: Southern Illinois University Press, 1999.
Moaddel, Mansoor. "Shi'i Political Discourse and Class Mobilization in the Tobacco Movement of 1890-92." *A Century of Revolution: Social Movements in Iran.* John Foran (Ed.). Minneapolis: University of Minnesota Press, 1994.
Modern Türkiye'de Siyasi Düşünce, Vol. I-IX. İstanbul: İletişim Yayınları, 2001-2009).
Montag, Warren. "The Pressure of the Street: Habermas' Fear of the Masses." *Masses, Classes and the Public Sphere.* Mike Hill and Warren Montag (Eds). London: Verso, 2000.
Moralı, Nail. *Mütarekede İzmir Önceleri ve Sonraları.* İstanbul: 1976.

Negt, Oskar and Alexander Kluge. *Public Sphere and Experience: Toward an Analysis of the Bourgeois and Proletarian Public Sphere*. Minneapolis: University of Minnesota Press, 1993.

Nur, Rıza. *Hayat ve Hatıratım*. İstanbul: 1967.

Onur, Hakkı [Zafer Toprak]. "1908 İşçi Hareketleri ve Jön Türkler," *Yurt ve Dünya*, No. 2, March 1977, pp. 277–295.

Oral, Mustafa. "Meşrutiyet'ten Cumhuriyet'e Antalya'da Yunan Karşıtı Sosyal Hareketler: Giritli Göçmenler ve Kemalist Hamallar," *Toplumsal Tarih*, No. 138, Haziran 2005.

Osmanlı Mebusan Meclisi Reisi Halil Menteşe'nin Anıları. İstanbul: Hürriyet Vakfı Yayınları, 1986.

Osmanlı Sanayii 1913, 1915 Yılları Sanayi İstatistiki. A. Gündüz Ökçün (Ed.). Ankara: Siyasal Bilgiler Fakültesi Yayını, 1970.

Özalp, Ömer Hakan. "Giriş: Mehmed Ubeydullah Efendi'ninHayatı ve Eserleri." *Mehmed Ubeydullah Efendi'nin Malta Afganistan ve İran Hatıraları*. İstanbul: 2002.

Özbek, Nadir. *Osmanlı İmparatorluğu'nda Sosyal Devlet, Siyaset, İktidar ve Meşruiyet 1876–1914*. İstanbul: İletişim Yayınları, 2002.

Özbek, Nadir. "Philanthropic Activity, Ottoman Patriotism and the Hamidian Regime 1876–1909," *International Journal of Middle East Studies*, Vol. XXXVII, No. 1, 2005.

Pamuk, Şevket. *The Ottoman Empire and World Capitalism*. Cambridge: Cambridge University Press, 1987.

Panayotopoulos, Alkis J. "On the Economic Activities on the Anatolian Greeks mid 19th Century to Early 20th," *Deltio Kentrou Mikrasiatikon Spoudon*, No. 4, Athens, 1983.

Prokopiou, Sokratis. *San Psemmata kai San Alitheia*. Athens: 1928.

Remer, C.F. *A Study of Chinese Boycotts*. New York: John Hopkins University Press Reprints, 1979.

Quataert, Donald. *Social Disintegration and Popular Resistance in the Ottoman Empire, 1881–1908: Reactions to European Economic Penetration*. New York: New York University Press, 1983.

Quataert, Donald. "Giriş." *Osmanlı'dan Cumhuriyet Türkiye'sine İşçiler (1839–1950)*. Donald Quataert and Erik J. Zürcher (Eds). İstanbul: İletişim Yayınları, 1988.

Quataert, Donald. *Ottoman Manufacturing in the Age of the Industrial Revolution*. Cambridge: Cambridge University Press, 1993a.

Quataert, Donald. "Labor Policies and Politics in the Ottoman Empire: Porters and the Sublime Porte, 1826–1896." *Humanist and Scholar, Essays in Honor of Andreas Tietze*. Heath W. Lowry and Donald Quataert (Eds). İstanbul: Isis Press, 1993b.

Quataert, Donald. "Selanik'teki İşçiler 1850–1912." *Osmanlı'dan Cumhuriyet Türkiye'sine İşçiler 1839–1950*. Donald Quataert and Erik Jan Zürcher (Eds). İstanbul: İletişim Yayınları, 1998.

BIBLIOGRAPHY 283

Quataert, Donald. "The Age of Reforms 1812–1914." In *An Economic and Social History of the Ottoman Empire*. Halil İnalcık and Donald Quataert (Eds). Cambridge: Cambridge University Press, 2000a.

Quataert, Donald. *The Ottoman Empire 1700–1922*. Cambridge: Cambridge University Press, 2000b.

Quataert, Donald. "Ottoman History Writing at Crossroads." *Turkish Studies in the United States*, (Eds) Donald Quataert and Sabri Sayarı. Bloomington: Indiana University Press, 2003.

Resimli Türkiye İşçi Sınıfı Tarihi, Vol I-II-III. Süleyman Üstün and Yücel Yaman (Eds). Illustrated by Tan Oral. İstanbul: Vardiya Yayınları, 1975.

Rozaliev, Y.N. *Türkiye Sanayi Proleteryası*. İstanbul: Yar Yayınları, 1974.

Rozaliyev, Y.N. *Türkiye'de Kapitalizmin Gelişme Özellikleri*. İstanbul: Onur Yayınları, 1978.

Ryan, Mary P. "Gender and Public Access: Women's Politics in Nineteenth-Century America." *Habermas and the Public Sphere*. Craig Calhoun (Ed.). Cambridge: MIT, 1992.

Safley, Thomas Max and Leonard N. Rosenband. "Introduction." *The Workplace before the Factory: Artisans and Proletarians 1500–1800*. Ithaca: Cornell University Press, 1993.

Samuel, Raphael. "Workshop of the World: Steam Power and Hand Technology in mid-Victorian Britain," *History Workshop*, No. 3, Spring 1977.

Sayılgan, Aclan. *Türkiye'de Sol Hareketler*. İstanbul: 1972.

Sencer [Baydar], Oya. *Türkiye'de İşçi Sınıfı –Doğuşu ve Yapısı*. İstanbul: Hobora Kitabevi, 1969.

Sencer, Muzaffer. *Türkiye'de Siyasi Partilerin Sosyal Temelleri*. İstanbul: 1974.

Sewell, Jr., William H. "Property, Labor, and the Emergence of Socialism in France, 1789–1848." *Consciousness and Class Experience in Nineteenth-Century Europe*. John M. Merriman (Ed.). London: Holmes and Meier, 1979.

Sewell, Jr., William H. "Artisans and Factory Workers, and the Formation of the French Working Class, 1789–1848." *Working-Class Formation: Nineteenth-Century Patterns in Western Europe and the United States*, Ira Katznelson and Aristide R. Zolberg (Eds). Princeton: Princeton University Press, 1986.

Sewell, Jr., William H. "How Classes are Made: Critical Reflections on E. P. Thompson's Theory of Working-class Formation." *E. P. Thompson: Critical Perspectives*, Harvey J. Kaye and Keith McClelland (Eds). Philadelphia: Temple University Press, 1990.

Şişmanov, Dimitır. *Türkiye İşçi ve Sosyalist Hareketi Kısa Tarih (1908–1965)*. İstanbul: Belge Yayınları, 1978.

Smyanelis, Marie-Carmen. "Bilinmeyen Bir Cemaatin Portresi: Müslümanlar, Firket Yılmaz'la Söyleşi." *İzmir 1830–1930 Unutulmuş Bir Kent Mi? Bir Osmanlı Limanından Hatıralar*. İstanbul: İletişim Yayınları, 2008.

Şnurov, A. and Y. Rozaliyev. *Türkiye'de Kapitalistleşme ve Sınıf Kavgaları*. İstanbul: Ant Yayınları, 1970.

Şnurov, A. *Türkiye Proleteryası.* İstanbul: Yar Yayınları, 1973.

Sofroniadis, Mihail. "Gkiavour!" (Infidel), *Ap'Ola,* 19 Eylül 1910. In Mihail Sofroniadis. *Apo tin Apolitarhia ston Kemalismo: Artra apo ton Elliniko tipo tis Konstantinoupolis 1905–1921.* Atina: 2005.

Sofroniadis, Mihail. "Hronografima: Sic Transit Gloria Mundi!.." (Column: Thus the Fame on Earth is Fleeting), *Proodos,* 18 January 1911. In Mihail Sofroniadis. *Apo tin Apolitarhia ston Kemalismo: Artra apo ton Elliniko tipo tis Konstantinoupolis 1905–1921.* Atina: 2005.

Sofroniadis, Mihail. *Apo tin Apolitarhia ston Kemalismo: Artra apo ton Elliniko tipo tis Konstantinoupolis 1905–1921.* Atina: 2005.

Somel, Selçuk Akşin. "Osmanlı Reform Çağında Osmanlıcılık Düşüncesi (1839–1913)." *Modern Türkiye'de Siyasi Düşünce.* Mehmet Ö. Alkan (Ed.). İstanbul: İletişim Yayınları, 2002.

Somel, Selçuk Akşin. *Osmanlı'da Eğitimin Modernleşmesi (1839–1908),* İstanbul: İletişim Yayınları, 2010.

Sülker, Kemal. *Türkiye'de Sendikacılık.* İstanbul: 1955.

Sülker, Kemal. *100 Soruda Türkiye'de İşçi Hareketleri.* İstanbul: Gerçek Yayınevi, 1968.

Sussnitzki, A. J. "Ethnic Division of Labor" (originally published in German in 1917 as "Zur Gliederung Wirtschaftslicher Arbeit nach Nationalitaten in der Turkei,"). *The Economic History of the Middle East 1800–1914,* Charles Issawi (Ed.). Chicago: The University of Chicago Press, 1966.

Taçalan, Nurdoğan. *Ege'de Kurtuluş Savaşı Başlarken.* İstanbul: Milliyet Yayınları, 1971.

Tanatar-Baruh, Lorans. "A Study in Commercial Life and Practices in Istanbul at the Turn of the Century: The Textile Market." Unpublished MA Thesis, Boğaziçi University, 1993.

Tanatar-Baruh, Lorans. "At the Turn of the Century, Textile Dealers in an International Port City, Istanbul," *Boğaziçi Journal Review of Social, Economic and Administrative Studies,* Vol. XI, No. 1–2, 1997.

Tanzimat'tan Cumhuriyet'e Türkiye Ansiklopedisi. Murat Belge (Ed.). İstanbul: İletişim Yayınları, 1986.

Thompson, E.P. *The Making of the English Working-Class.* London: 1963.

Tokgöz, Ahmet İhsan. *Matbuat Hatıralarım.* İstanbul: 1993.

Toprak, Zafer [Hakkı Onur]. "1908 İşçi Hareketleri ve Jön Türkler," *Yurt ve Dünya,* No. 2, March 1977, pp. 277–295.

Toprak, Zafer. *Türkiye'de Milli İktisat (1908–1918).* Ankara: Yurt Yayınları, 1982.

Toprak, Zafer. "1913–1914 Müslüman Boykotajı," *Toplum ve Bilim,* No. 29/30, Spring-Summer 1985, 179–199.

Toprak, Zafer. "Tanzimat'ta Osmanlı Sanayii." *Tanzimat'tan Cumhuriyet'e Türkiye Ansiklopedisi,* Vol. V. İstanbul: İletişim Yayınları, 1985.

Toprak, Zafer. "Fes Boykotu." *Dünden Bugüne İstanbul Ansiklopedisi,* Vol. III. İstanbul: 1994.

Toprak, Zafer. *Milli İktisat-Milli Burjuvazi.* İstanbul: Tarih Vakfı Yurt Yayınları, 1995.
Toprak, Zafer. "Hürriyet-Müsavat-Uhuvvet 'Her Yerde Bir Politika Tufanı Var.'" *Manastır'da İlanı-ı Hürriyet 1908–1909 Fotoğrafçı Manakis Biraderler.* Roni Margulies (Ed.). İstanbul: YKY, 1997.
Toprak, Zafer. "Osmanlı Donanması, Averof Zırhlısı ve Ulusal Kimlik," *Toplumsal Tarih,* No. 113, May 2003, pp. 10–20.
Tör, Ahmet Nedim Servet. *Nevhiz'in Günlüğü "Defter-i Hatıra."* İstanbul: Yapı Kredi Yayınları, 2000.
Trentmann, Frank. "Introduction: Paradoxes of Civil Society," *Paradoxes of Civil Society, New Perspectives on Modern German and British History.* Frank Trentmann (Ed.). New York: Berghahn Books, 2000.
Türkiye İşçi Sınıfı ve Mücadeleleri Tarihi. Ankara: TİB, 1976.
Tunaya, Tarık Zafer. *Hürriyet'in İlanı.* İstanbul: Arba, 1996[1959].
Tunaya, Tarık Zafer. *Türkiye'de Siyasal Partiler, İttihat ve Terakki, Bir Çağın, Bir Kuşağın, Bir Partinin Tarihi.* İstanbul: İletişim Yayınları, 2000.
Tunçay, Mete. *Türkiye'de Sol Akımlar-I (1908–1925).* İstanbul: BDS Yayınları, 1991.
Turgay, A. Üner. "Trade and Merchants in Nineteenth-Century Trabzon: Elements of Ethnic Conflict." *Christians and Jews in the Ottoman Empire,* Benjamin Braude and Bernard Lewis (Eds). New York: Holmes and Meier Inc, 1982.
Ülken, Hilmi Ziya. *Türkiye'de Çağdaş Düşünce Tarihi.* İstanbul: 1992.
Uluçay, Çağatay. *XVIII ve XIX. Yüzyıllarda Saruhan'da Eşkiyalık ve Halk Hareketleri.* İstanbul: Berksoy Basımevi, 1955.
Ünal, Hasan. "Ottoman Policy during the Bulgarian Independence Crisis 1908–9: Ottoman Empire and Bulgaria at the Outset of the Young Turk Revolution," *Middle Eastern Studies,* Vol. 34, No. 4, October 1998.
Uran, Hilmi. *Hatıralarım.* Ankara: 1956.
Van der Linden, Marcel and Michael Hanagan. "New Approaches to Global Labor History," *International Labor and Working-Class History,* No. 66, Fall 2004.
Van der Linden, Marcel. "Labour History as the History of Multitudes," *Labour/ Le Travail,* No. 53, Fall 2003.
Van der Linden, Marcel. "Labour History: The Old, the New and the Global," *African Studies,* Vol. LXVI, No. 2–3, August-December 2007.
Van Os, Nicole. "Bursa'da Kadın İşçilerin 1910 Grevi," *Toplumsal Tarih,* No. 39, March 1997.
Van Os, Nicole. "Osmanlı Müslümanlarında Feminizm." *Modern Türkiye'de Siyasi Düşünce: Tanzimat ve Meşrutiyet'in Birikimi,* Vol. I. Mehmet Ö. Alkan (Ed.) İstanbul: İletişim Yayınları, 2001.
Vatter, Sherry. "Millitant Journeymen in Nineteenth-Century Damascus: Implications for the Middle Eastern Labor History Agenda." *Workers and Working Classes in the Middle East: Struggles, Histories, Historiographies.* Albany: State University of New York Press, 1994.

Vatter, Sherry. "Şam'ın Militan Tekstil İşçileri: Ücretli Zanaatkârlar ve Osmanlı İşçi Hareketi, 1850-1914." *Osmanlı'dan Cumhuriyet Türkiye'sine İşçiler 1839-1950*. İstanbul: İletişim Yayınları, 1998.

Vryonis, Speros. "The Byzantine Legacy and Ottoman Forms." *Dumbarton Oaks Papers*, No. 23-24, 1969-1970.

Wang, Guanhua. *In Search of Justice: The 1905-1906 Chinese Anti-American Boycott*. Cambridge: Harvard University Press, 2001.

Wood, Ellen Meiksins. *The Pristine Culture of Capitalism: A Historical Essay on Old Regimes and Modern States*. London: Verso, 1991.

Yalman, Ahmet Emin. *Yakın Tarihte Gördüklerim ve Geçirdiklerim*, Vol. I. (?).

Yavuz, Erdal. "1908 Boykotu," *ODTÜ Gelişme Dergisi*, 1978 Özel Sayısı.

Yediyıldız, M. Asım. "XIX. Yüzyılda Bursa İpek Sanayi ve Ticaretinde Gayrimüslimlerin Yeri," *Uludağ Üniversitesi İlahiyat Fakültesi Dergisi*, Vol. IV, No. 4, 1992.

Yücel, Hasan Ali. *Geçtiğim Günlerden*. İstanbul: 1990.

Zarevand [Zaven Nalbandian and Vartouhie Nalbandian]. *United and Independent Turania: Aims and Designs of the Turks*. Leiden: E.J. Brill, 1971 [First published in1926 in Boston].

Zürcher, Erik J. "İslam Milliyetçiliğinin Dili." *Savaş, Devrim ve Uluslaşma: Türkiye Tarihinde Geçiş Dönemi (1908-1924)*. İstanbul: İstanbul Bilgi Üniversitesi Yayınları, 2005.

Zürcher, Erik J. *Turkey: A Modern History*. London: I.B.Tauris, 1994.

Zürcher, Erik Jan. "Giriş: Demografi Mühendisliği ve Modern Türkiye'nin Doğuşu." *İmparatorluktan Cumhuriyete Türkiye'de Etnik Çatışma*. Erik Jan Zürcher (Ed.). İstanbul: İletişim Yayınları, 2006.

INDEX

1905 Therrisso Uprising, 90
1908 Revolution, 1, 3, 9, 21, 25, 26, 40,
    54, 55, 79, 81, 89, 90, 111, 119,
    123, 209, 210, 211, 213, 214, 217,
    218, 222–224, 269 n. 1

Abdülhamid II, 47, 90, 209, 211
Adalar Meselesi (Islands Question), 162, 163
Administration of Customs, 64, 65,
    143, 144,
Ahmet Ağa, 142
Ahmet Nedim Servet Tör, 165
Ahmet Rasim, 85
Alsancak, 115
Annuaire Oriental, 26, 28
Arabacı, 141, 144, 149, 240 n. 67, 258
    n. 255
Armenians, 9, 10, 16, 21–23, 42, 45,
    46, 59, 69, 73, 93, 129, 136, 137,
    161, 163, 174, 175, 176, 180–182,
    211, 219, 265 n. 72
Austria-Hungary, 1, 7, 13, 39–42,
    44–66, 70–81, 83–87, 148,
    150, 215, 219, 237 n.3,
    258 n. 237,
Averof, 168

Bahattin (Şakir) Bey, 42, 43
Balkan Wars, 8, 31,40, 91, 160, 161,
    165–168, 173, 174, 176, 179, 186,
    197–199, 210, 217, 219, 221, 224,
    264 n. 64
Bandits, 190–203
Bannes, 13, 65, 94, 123, 124, 216, 217
Banque de Mettelin, 132
Blockades, 51, 60, 74, 91, 95, 105, 133,
    134, 149, 154, 250 n. 49
Boatmen, 58, 59, 61, 62, 67, 100, 114,
    118, 139, 140, 142, 143, 145, 153,
    154, 157, 158, 258 n. 247
Bosna Hersek Cemiyet-i Hayriye-i
    Osmaniyesi, 78
Bosnia-Herzegovina, 1, 2, 39–42, 217,
    237 n. 3, Bosnian, 48, 78, 126, 215
Boşo Efendi, see Georgios Bousios
Bousios, Georgios, 128, 256 n. 188
Boycott Heroes, 33, 61, 141
Boycott Society (*Boykotaj Cemiyeti*), 52,
    53, 55–58, 63–66, 70, 77, 99, 102,
    105–123, 127, 129,131, 132, 134,
    135, 140, 141, 144, 146–148, 151,
    154, 156–159, 219, 239 n. 40, 250
    n. 49, 252 n. 100 n. 101, 253 n.
    120, 254 n. 132 n. 137
Boycott Union (*Boykot Sendikası*), 57, 61,
    72, 74, 76, 87, 146, 219
Boykot Heyeti, Dersaadet, 117
Boykot Sendikası, see Boycott Union
Boykot, Hakiki (Genuine Boycott), 72,
    78, 82, 139, 242 n. 88, 246 n. 139

288 THE YOUNG TURKS AND THE BOYCOTT MOVEMENT

Boykotaj Cemiyeti, see Boycott Society
Boykotaj Teshilat Komisyonu, 56, 117, 118, 252 n. 100, 254 n. 139
Bulgaria, 1, 2, 7, 13 39–46, 55–60, 72–75, 93, 125, 133, 161, 182, 183, 197, 211, 215, 217, 219, 237 n. 3, 264 n. 64, 267 n. 142

Carters, see *Arabacı*
Cemiyet-i Müteşebbise, 137
Chamber of Commerce, 67, 71, 131, 134, 135
Civil Society, 2, 9, 12, 13, 30, 40, 55, 57, 205–208
Class, social, 2, 4, 5, 6, 9, 10, 12–38, 47, 56, 58, 66, 72, 73, 76, 79, 81, 93, 94, 114, 115, 120, 124, 135, 139, 164, 192, 202, 204–206, 208, 210–213, 220, 223–226, 228, 230
Coercion, 99, 101, 106, 110, 114, 115, 145, 146, 153, 155, 205, 217
Committee of Union and Progress (CUP), 4, 5, 7, 12, 13, 21, 23, 24, 30, 31, 39, 40–43, 45, 46, 48, 54–56, 59, 61, 62, 63, 66, 67, 70, 72, 79, 81, 86, 89, 92–94, 107, 111, 121, 138–141, 146, 152, 161–163, 165, 170, 176, 187, 188, 190, 191, 197, 198, 200–202, 209, 211–218, 220, 23–335, 228, 243 n. 104, 250 n. 49
Comprador bourgeoisie, 17
Consciousness, class, 19, 20, 33, 35, 37, 38, 224, 236 n. 99
Constitutional Revolutions, 3
Crete, 108, 109, 112, 126, 145, 146, 153, 220, annexation to Greece, 62, Cretan Question, 87, 89–97, 128, 145, 146, Cretan Assembly, 90
Crowds, 42–51, 62, 92–96, 105, 114, 123, 126, 127, 133, 146, 153, 174, 193, 209, 210, 215, 216, 218, 221, 250 n. 59

Ders-i amm efendileri, 64
Direct Actions, 4, 48–55, 72, 91, 96–107, 123, 133, 134, 139, 211
Donanma Cemiyeti, 111, 112, 124, 139, 140, 167, 169, 174, 214
Dönme, 139, 226

Edhem Eldem, 27
Edhem Nejat, 85
Emtia-i Ecnebiye Gümrüğü, 64
Enosis, 1, 91
Enver Paşa, 202, 263 n. 26
Essentialism, 3
Exceptionalism, 3

Fehim Ağa, 141
Fezzes, 44, 47, 51, 52, 65, 75, 80, 84–86, 128, 129, "Fez-tearing feast," 52–54, 73, 221, 222

Gavur (infidel), 124, 168
Georges, 169
Gönüllü Cemiyeti, see Volunteer Society
Guruci Company, 132

Hacı David Company, 103
Hamal, see Porter
Hamiyet, 49, 50, 52, 64, 80, 125
Harb-i İktisadi Cemiyeti, see Society of Economic Warfare
Hellenes, 7, 9, 45, 115, 118–121, 130, 131, 136, 137, 159, 163, 180, 184, 255 n. 151, 268 n. 157, philhellenism, 155
Heybeliada School of Theology, 134
Historiography, on Turkey, 2, 3, 5, 6, 13, 18, 19, 40, 68, 82, 119, 160, 202, 205, 222, 227, 228, 232, 235, 236, on social class, 14, nationalist, 10, 47, traditional, 92, 68, on non-Muslims, 10, 22, on World-system Theory, 14, 21, 37, on Modernization School, 14, 21, 37, on Muslim working-class, 30–33, 35, 207, Muslim merchants, 22, 23, 36
Hobsbawm, E.J., 33

INDEX 289

Hüseyin Kazım, 173, 174, 198
Hüseyin Reis, 142

İkinci Meşrutiyet, see Second
 Constitutional Period
İktisadiyun Fırkası, 83
Immigrants, 8, 126, 161, 162, 178, 201,
 217, 220, 222, 250 n. 49, 267 n.
 142, 268 n. 149, muhacir, 186, 190,
 201, 267 n. 127
İnkilab-ı İktisadi ve Ticariye, 166
Islam, 5, 29, 35, 47, 91, 108, 109, 119,
 120, 123–125, 128, 136, 139,
 146, 200, 225–230, 270 n. 39,
 271 n. 51
İttihad-ı anasır, 212
İzmir Tüccaran ve Esnefan-ı İslamiyyesine
 Mahsus Rehber, 166, 167

Kalpak, 47, 51, 52, 61, 84–86
Kavm-i Cedid, 166
Kerim Ağa, 107, 114, 117–120, 133,
 140–145, 149, 189, 219, 251 n. 87
Khodja, 124, 146, 149
Komitadjis, 5, 202
Kramer beerhouse, 76, 77
Kürt Ali Ağa, 60–64, 219
Kuşçubaşı Eşref, 179, 191, 202, 220

Lightermen, 58–62, 64, 66, 68, 70, 71,
 120, 129, 133, 139, 140, 144, 148, 149
Lloyd Maritime Company, 59, 65, 83, 106

M.H. Clonarides & Co. LTD, 149
Macedonia, Question, 162, 163
Mahmut Muhtar Paşa, 121
Mamulat-ı Dahiliye Teavün Cemiyeti, 86
Manisa Mensucat-ı Dahiliye Şirketi, 86
Mass politics, 2, 6, 9, 12, 204–227, 229,
 269 n. 1
Mavnacı, see Lightermen
Medrese, 146
Meeting, Public, 2, 9, 41, 43–47, 49,
 52, 56, 57, 62, 64, 71, 74, 78, 83,

84, 91–99, 111, 113, 125–127, 149,
 158, 159, 210, 211, 215–218, 220,
 221, 224
Menfaat-i Millet Cemiyeti, 84
Milli İktisat, see National Economy
Mobilization, social, 2, 4, 5, 10, 38,
 40, 42, 44, 48, 55, 62, 70, 73, 81,
 91–98, 110, 111, 123, 124, 136,
 143, 144, 146, 151, 153, 161–163,
 165, 174, 188, 198, 203–205,
 207–211, 215–218, 226, 229, 237,
 269 n. 23, patterns of, 9, 210
Mosques, 48, 64, 93, 109, 123, 124,
 170, 178, 187, 189
Müdafaa-i Milliye Cemiyeti, 111
Muhabbet-i Milliye Ticaret Komisyonu, 74
Muhacir, see Immigrants
Muslim merchants, 6, 15, 17, 20–25,
 28–30, 35, 36, 37, 71–79, 181,
 224, 230, 233 n. 33
Muslim working-class, 6, 12, 20,
 30–35, 38, 120, 135, 212, 213,
 224, 226, 230, port workers, 5,
 33, 35, 41, 47, 52, 58–72, 74, 75,
 78, 79, 87, 103, 105, 112, 114, 115,
 118–120, 127, 131, 138–145, 149,
 151–154, 156, 158, 203, 213, 219,
 220, 226, 230, 241
Muslim/Turkish nationalism, 2, 5, 8,
 38, 161, 167, 210, 214, 217
Muslims, in lost territories, 2, 29, 161,
 162, 166, 170, 190, 217
Müslüman ve Türklere, 164–176
Müslümanlara Mahsus Kurtulmak Yolu,
 164–176
Müslümanlara Mahsus, 164–176
Müstemin, 123

National commodity, invention of, 14,
 51, 80, 85, 208, 223
National Economy, 8, 14, 22, 78–82, 84,
 87, 119, 135, 136, 138, 160, 164,
 169, 171, 173–175, 201, 214, 215,
 220, 222–225, 231 n. 1, 270 n. 39

Nationalism, as a social phenomenon, 5, 38, 222
Nazım Bey, Dr., 189, 201
Nazım Paşa, 106
New Turks, 85
Niyazi Bey, 98
Non-Muslims, 4, 8, 10, 15, 21, 93, 96, 110, 144, 146, 158, 211, 212, elimination of, 5, 9, 10, 13, 24, 88, 119–136, 160, 161, 163, 164, 167–179, 182,184, 187, 190, 191, 198, 214, 219, 222, 225, 229, 230, bourgeoisie, 13–19, 21, 25–29

Ordinary people, 2, 6, 7, 93, 166, 199, 208–211, 214, 216, 227, 229, 230
Osmanlı Kibrit Şirketi, 86
Ottoman Bank (*Osmanlı Bankası*), 20, 27, 69, 83, 126, 127
Ottomanism, 7, 29, 77, 87, 88, 128, 134, 136, 155, 212, 225, 227, 228, 230, 249 n. 25, 271 n. 48 and n. 51

Pamphlets, 4, 8, 11, 108, 109, 160, 163–173, 186, 194, 198, 200, 217
Pantaleon Oriental Navigation Company, 103, 127, 251 n. 67
Patriarchate, Greek Orthodox, 99, 129, 161, 173, 175, 178, 180, 192–195, 201, 265 n. 265, 267 n. 129, n. 130, Armenian, 69, 161, 181
Picketing, 49–51, 55, 91, 99, 101, 103, 104, 106, 122, 126, 133, 134, 156, 159, 179, 186, 187, 190, 196, 218, 221, 250 n. 49
Placards, 4, 57, 107–110, 112, 217
Place de la liberté (hürriyet meydanı), 92
Place du Dix Juillet (10 Temmuz Meydanı), 93
Plunders, 184, 185, loot, 177, 184–186, 188, 190
Popular Ideology, 226–230
Port administration, 59, 67–71, 113, 154

Porters (*Hamal*), 50, 56, 58–71, 82, 94, 99, 100, 105, 114, 117, 127, 129, 140–145, 148–150, 152, 158, 202, 236 n. 99, 243 n. 104, 251 n. 87, 258 n. 258
Posters, 49, 52, 54, 57, 106–110, 112, 124, 154, 188, 216
Protest, 2, 7, 13, 23, 25, 40–50, 53, 55, 57, 58, 68, 71, 91–93, 100, 103, 105, 109, 125, 126, 133, 148, 159, 178, 192, 195, 210, 214, 218, 221, 226
Public demonstration, 1, 4, 9, 40, 42–50, 52, 54, 55, 64, 65, 71, 93, 113, 124, 126, 178, 210, 211, 213, 215, 216, 218, 221
Public sphere, 2, 9, 12, 50, 79, 81, 84, 204–209, 212, 213, 216, 224, 227

Quataert, Donald, 25, 29, 36, 41, 232 n. 1

Rahmi Bey, 179, 182, 189, 193, 195, 196, 197, 201, 202, 265 n. 66, 268 n. 156
Regie, 114, 157, 196, 262 n. 8
Rıza Tevfik, 64, 66, 87, 237 n. 6
Rum, 7, 109, 120, 121, 146, 166, 169, 180, 191, 198, 254 n. 148, 270 n. 38

Samsun Osmanlı İttihad-ı Milli Kulübü, 47
Samuel, Raphael, 34
Second Constitutional Period, 10, 14, 24, 43, 48, 54, 70, 82, 89, 90, 112, 119, 135, 173, 175, 204, 209–211, 213–215, 222, 223, 230, 255 n. 163, 269
Sheikh Abdurrahman Selam, 123
Sheikh Mustafa Galayani, 94
Singer Sewing Machines, 103
Social movement, 7, 12, 14, 30, 35, 38, 41, 55, 62, 79, 123, 136, 205, 218, 221, 224, 226, 227
Society of Economic Warfare (*Harb-i İktisadi Cemiyeti*), 4, 56–58, 111, 113, 219

INDEX 291

Strike, 1, 31, 32, 40, 58, 63, 66, 67, 70, 71, 87, 142, 143, 152, 153, 208, 211–213, 219
Süleyman Nazif, 158
Süllü Ağa, 141
Talat Bey (Paşa), 41, 146, 183, 185, 192, 193, 195–197, 222
Tanzimat, 208, 223
Tatil-i Eşgal, 63
Tellal, 99, 106, 129, 216
Thompson, E.P., 33, 235 n. 83, 236 n. 97
Türk Ocağı, 175, 176
Turkish nationalism (see Muslim/ Turkish nationalism)

Ubeydullah Efendi, 41, 237 n. 6, 263 n. 22

Venizelos, Eleftherios, 90, 91, 145, 184
Violence, 8, 52, 99, 101, 104, 105, 107, 145, 152, 154, 161, 173, 176–178, 187, 188, 190–192, 194, 202, 214, 221, 222
Volunteers, 53, 54, enlisting, 91, 95–98, 218
Volunteer Society (*Gönüllü Cemiyeti*), 97

Workers, see Muslim working-class, Boatmen, Lightermen, Porters, Historiography on Muslim working-class
World War I, 8, 10, 21–23, 82, 162, 197, 198, 210, 221, 233 n. 36

Yunan, 107, 109, 120–122, 146, 252 n. 91, 254 n. 148, 255 n. 159

www.ingramcontent.com/pod-product-compliance
Lightning Source LLC
Chambersburg PA
CBHW070018010526
44117CB00011B/1624